Child Abuse, Family Rights, and the Child Protective System

A Critical Analysis from Law, Ethics, and Catholic Social Teaching

Edited by
Stephen M. Krason

THE SCARECROW PRESS, INC.
Lanham • Toronto • Plymouth, UK
2013

Published by Scarecrow Press, Inc.
A wholly owned subsidary of The Rowman & Littlefield Publishing Group, Inc.
4501 Forbes Boulevard, Suite 200, Lanham, Maryland 20706
www.rowman.com

10 Thornbury Road, Plymouth PL6 7PP, United Kingdom

British Library Cataloguing in Publication Information Available

Library of Congress Cataloging-in-Publication Data

Child abuse, family rights, and the child protective system : a critical analysis from law,
ethics, and Catholic social teaching / [edited by] Stephen M. Krason.
    pages cm. -- (Catholic social thought ; No. 7)
    Includes index.
    ISBN 978-0-8108-8669-8 (cloth : alk. paper) -- ISBN 978-0-8108-8670-4 (electronic)
    1. Children--Legal status, laws, etc.--United States. 2. Church and social problems--
Catholic Church I. Krason, Stephen M., editor of compilation. II. Society of Catholic
Social Scientists.
    KF3735.C45 2013
    344.7303'276--dc23
                                    2013011094

♾™ The paper used in this publication meets the minimum requirements of American
National Standard for Information Sciences—Permanence of Paper for Printed Library
Materials, ANSI/NISO Z39.48-1992.

Printed in the United States of America

Catholic Social Thought

This series focuses on Catholic social thought and its application to current social, political, economic, and cultural issues. The titles in this series are written and edited by members of the Society of Catholic Social Scientists. They survey and analyze Catholic approaches to politics, sociology, law, economics, history, and other disciplines. Within these broad themes, authors explore the Church's role and influence in contemporary society.

The Society of Catholic Social Scientists was formed in 1992 to rejuvenate a distinctively Catholic scholarship in the social sciences.

This book is dedicated to the members of the Society of Catholic Social Scientists and of the Catholic Social Workers National Association

Table of Contents

viii

Foreword

By Ronald J. Rychlak
Mississippi Defense Lawyers Association Professor of Law
University of Mississippi School of Law

Catholic social teaching is a treasure trove of wisdom regarding the proper structure of a just society and the way to live a holy life. The Catholic Church proclaims that human life is sacred and that the dignity of the human person is the foundation of a just and moral vision for society. Marriage and the family are the central social institutions and they must be supported. *The Catechism of the Catholic Church* says that the family is the original cell of social life.

Any just society cares for its children. Under the doctrine of subsidiarity, the first right and responsibility falls to the parents and the family. Unfortunately, there are times when society feels the need to intervene. No one can doubt that there are times when this is necessary. The problem is the difficulty of assessing the needs of a family unit from the outside.

My first professional interaction with the child protective system (CPS) came years ago when, as a fairly new law professor, I was asked to work on the appeal of the Kelly Michaels case. Kelly was a daycare worker at a nursery school in New Jersey. She had been convicted of sexual abuse of thirty-three children, and she was sentenced to forty-seven years imprisonment.

Some of the allegations made by the children were bizarre, and the physical evidence was essentially non-existent, but as the father of a couple of young children at the time, my initial sympathies were with the prosecution. I had my doubts about the appeal.

Then we discovered that these same bizarre allegations had been made by other children at other locations. The only commonalty was that in each case, the children were questioned by the same team of investigators. I was eventually persuaded, and so was the New Jersey Supreme Court. It overturned Kelly's conviction, declaring that "the interviews of the children were highly improper and utilized coercive and unduly suggestive methods." Unfortunately, Kelly Michaels is not the only person to have been victimized by over-zealous governmental officials trying to protect children.

On April 27, 2012, prominent social scientists gathered at The Catholic University of America in Washington, D.C. to apply their expertise to the problems of the CPS. The six papers presented at that conference are at the heart of this book, and they apply Catholic social teachings and related ethical and legal principles in an effort to protect families and children.

In his piece, Stephen M. Krason examines the legislation that transformed American thinking about child abuse and family relations, the Mondale Act. He argues persuasively that this Act helped create a runaway, abusive system in which 66-80 percent of reports made to the CPS are totally unfounded and many others involve very minor matters. These false and exaggerated charges have involved millions of families, causing untold devastation.

William L. Saunders shows us that things are not getting better. In fact, "human rights law" based on international agreements is now serving further to undermine the family.

Michael E. Rosman examines the constitutional implications of when the CPS and related police authorities interfere with family relations, and he calls for procedural rules to minimize the impact on the family.

James R. Mason III looks at the procedures related to CPS inspections and the Fourth Amendment, in what he has dubbed "the battle for the front door." He shows that in almost three out of four cases, incursions are unnecessary and cause more harm than good.

Patrick F. Fagan, in a paper co-authored by Anna Dorminey and Emily Hering, continues his excellent work of laying out the evidence related to safe and dangerous places for children.

In the context of these papers, one has to conclude that the CPS far too often moves children from safety to danger.

Ruth A. White employs the concept of CPS workers (and others) as "street-level bureaucrats" who are forced to negotiate ethical dilemmas borne out of poorly designed public policy and insufficient federal funding. The volume concludes with two *amicus curiae* briefs, filed by the Society of Catholic Social Scientists, which put theory into practice.

At the end of the day, one is left with concern for children who encounter actual abuse, but also with a new concern for adults who are falsely accused and for families that are torn apart by a system that encourages false accusations. Since the investigations and prosecutions are made "in the name of protecting children," that system also tempts authorities to circumvent the rights of the accused.

The papal encyclical *Rerum Novarum* forbids the state to "exercise intimate control over the family," and says that the state may intervene only when the family is in "exceeding distress" or if within it there are "grave disturbances of mutual rights." Relying on teachings such as these, the authors of the articles in this book set forth an ethic grounded in Catholic social teaching. Procedures derived from that ethic must make their way into public policy. The alternative is continuation of a system that too often hurts what it is intended to help.

Oxford, Mississippi
July 6, 2012

Preface and Acknowledgements

By Stephen M. Krason

I have written about the problem of false reporting of child abuse and neglect directed against parents for over a quarter of a century. Even though it is clear, by any amount of careful study, that the problem is a massive one, it has seemed persistently to be "below the radar screen." While perhaps more people have a sense of it today than when I first wrote about it—maybe because so many parents across the United States have been victimized by the child protective system (CPS)—most seem to be unaware of it. Those who are ardently and actively "pro-family" seldom seem to place it on their list of the many threats posed to the family by today's secular, relativistic culture. This is so even though it means that the state can reach right into the sacred precincts of the household and undertake actions that can grievously disrupt the life of a family, wreak havoc on parent-child relationships, and even destroy families. Even public officials—the ones who made the decisions to bring the CPS into existence and now sustain it and keep it funded or oversee it—seem hardly attuned to or interested in looking into the realities. The CPS, even though it largely took shape only forty years ago, is now part of the framework. The people who man it and their legislative and organizational allies have convinced many of its utter necessity to combat the on-going epidemic of child abuse. Their routine practices escape careful scrutiny, and it is only when an outrageous event occurs (e.g., when a child whose likely maltreatment they were aware of, but did not act decisively about, dies) that they face searing public criticism—at least for awhile. The reactions to such events seldom get to the heart of the problems with the CPS, and often just add to the existing threatening, troublesome, and counterproductive arrangements—and just put more pressure on innocent parents. As one commentator put it, elected officials do not want to put clamps on the CPS because they fear being seen as coddling child abusers. Even though it is supposed to be subject to judicial oversight, especially by juvenile courts, typically such judges allow the CPS a substantially free hand, as they do not want to interfere with their attempts to end what they are sure is a national scourge. In fact, as this book shows, the evidence is overwhelming that most of what the CPS does is not address true child abuse or neglect, but rather chase after false reports (many made anonymously) or those that concern trivial or minor matters that most people would say in no way rise to the level of child abuse or neglect. Their apologists, leaders, and operatives are driven by often-fallacious notions about the family, such as that spanking is a form of brutality, all parents are potential abusers, and children can be as effectively reared by those outside the family as by parents. The CPS is a system that in its conception forty years ago had a utopian type of vision: it must be aimed at preventing all *possible* abuse or neglect. So legislators around the country put in place utterly vague laws, so that no one could tell for sure all that fit into the categories of "abuse" and "neglect," and the meanings could be infinitely expanded. The CPS would be given sweeping authority and discretion. This arrangement of things became the basis, in theory at least, for a universal monitoring of all American families. All utopias become dystopias, however. Thus, we have the nightmare of so many innocent parents accused and families intruded upon, frightened, separated, and their rights trampled upon. The CPS is a touch of the totalitarian.

The evidence has never shown that child abuse and neglect are truly a crisis in America, much less something that could be just around the corner in every American family. The cultural decay of the last several decades in America, with the serious decline of marriage and the family, widespread moral relativism, the pervasiveness of illicit drugs, and a range of other social pathologies intuitively—and the articles in this book provide support for this—makes one think that there is more of it (i.e., what commonsensically one would understand to be abuse, not some concocted notion of it) than there was earlier in American history. Still, it has been difficult to get reliable statistics to back this up. In spite of the spectacular cases which the media grabs onto—and seldom involve intact families or often even parents—there is not as much talk about a "child abuse epidemic" as there was, say, in the 1980s. Indeed, even major studies are now conceding that there is less child abuse than there used to be—even with the prevailing loose definition of it. There is much reason to seriously doubt that we ever had an epidemic or crisis of child abuse. The response to this "crisis" may rightfully be called destructive because of the following: the ordeals inflicted upon and serious damage done to so many innocent families by the CPS, the ballooning of the state's role to allow it to monitor families and intervene into them often at the drop of a pin, the counterproductive effects of a system that spends so much time chasing after trivia that it cannot protect children from true threats, the undercutting of legitimate and essential parental authority and childrearing efforts because parents always have to look over their shoulders, and the CPS's seeming imperviousness to the psychological, emotional, and even physical harm children are exposed to when it improperly removes them from their homes. It is not an exaggeration, then, to speak of a "false crisis" and a "destructive response" when examining American law and public policy on child abuse/neglect and the CPS. The articles in this book give further specifics and details that explain why this is so.

The articles in this collection were all presented as papers at a conference co-sponsored by the Society of Catholic Social Scientists (SCSS) and the Catholic Social Workers National Association (CSWNA) at The Catholic University of America in Washington, D.C. on April 27, 2012. They represent an assessment of different aspects of this question by scholars and professionals in law, social work, political science, sociology, and psychology. Together, they present a good up-to-date, overall look at the problems of the child abuse laws and the CPS. There have been writings about this subject over the years—including a few book-length studies—although most have not been done by scholars or often been sufficiently in-depth. A major aim of both the conference and the book was indeed to do a scholarly, up-to-date, reasonably comprehensive, book-length examination that could be a valuable resource for people seeking to better understand the problems of the current law and public policy on child abuse/neglect and the CPS and to work for change. The book also to some degree, in certain articles, looks at different aspects of this question from the standpoint of Catholic social teaching, as was appropriate for a conference sponsored by the above two groups and is part of the Catholic Social Thought Series.

My article leads off the book. It provides an overarching look at the origins of our current child abuse/neglect policy with the 1974 Mondale Act (the Child Abuse Prevention and Treatment Act, or CAPTA). Like most important social, political, legal, and cultural developments, however, it did not just appear. The prior history and background of "child-saving" in the United States is also surveyed. The extent of the problem of false abuse and neglect allegations against parents is discussed, as are striking examples of the kinds of innocent parental actions or inactions that trigger CPS interventions. The vague nature of the abuse/neglect laws and the troublesome attitudes and perspective of CPS operatives, mentioned above, is examined. Also discussed is the nature of the arrangements for the reporting of alleged abuse, the "one-sided liability" of the laws that helps motivate abuse investigations even for trivial matters, and the secretiveness and unaccountability of the CPS. The absence of Bill of Rights protections for parents when faced by a CPS investigation is discussed, as is the recent international threat to parental rights and the family that has emerged from the UN Convention on the Rights of the Child. It discusses specific reasons why, as noted above, the current system is counterproductive. It also advocates what can only be called sweeping change in how we deal with child abuse and neglect in the United States.

William L. Saunders' article focuses on how American policy on child abuse/neglect and the CPS, as it functions, might be evaluated in light of both prevailing international human rights principles and Catholic social teaching. Both traditionally have emphasized respect for parental rights and the importance of the family. He also examines in some detail the UN Convention on the Rights of the Child.

The article by Michael E. Rosman is one of two in this collection that exclusively focus on the actions of the CPS—and police in support of them—in intruding into families from a legal and constitutional perspective. The first and second parts of his article consider how the basic American constitutional principle of due process has been held by courts to apply in family and parental rights questions generally and in CPS removals of children from their homes specifically. The third part addresses specifically temporary removals—probably the most frequent type—and the kinds of evidence courts have held to be necessary to do this. He also proposes the alternative, which other commentators have also sometimes suggested, of removing the alleged perpetrator from the home instead of the child. The fourth part of his article concerns the Fourth Amendment implications of forced CPS medical examinations of children, mandates for medical treatment irrespective of parental preference, and the CPS pressuring parents to consent to monitoring of their family relations. The fifth part discusses how parental due process rights are violated when juvenile courts give ready rubber-stamps to CPS actions in intervening into families. He emphasizes the need for such courts to pay closer attention to constitutional due process requirements.

The other article addressing constitutional and legal questions, concerning additional aspects of the question of applying the Fourth Amendment to CPS contacts with families, is by James R. Mason, III. He brings to bear his experience in litigating many of these cases for the Home School Legal Defense Association (HSLDA). He points out how, after CAPTA's passage, states generally viewed CPS investigations as not subject to Fourth Amendment restraints. This assumption is something that HSLDA, with considerable success, has battled in the courts and he recounts some of the leading cases. He also mentions some of the major litigation approaches and strategies HSLDA has used.

The article by Patrick F. Fagan, Anna Dorminey, and Emily Hering presents a massive amount of social science research data that disputes one of the central principles that drives the CPS and the entire structure of American public policy on child abuse: that all parents are potential abusers, that child abuse and neglect can lurk in all families. Their article shows conclusively something that I introduce in my article: that it is in broken, "blended," and "untraditional" families and situations of cohabitation, single-parentage and the like that child abuse and neglect are by far most prevalent. Their data makes clear that it is intact families (i.e., with biological parents who are married) that provide the most reliable protection against child abuse and neglect—as well as intimate partner violence, generally.

Finally, Ruth A. White's article argues that current policy on child abuse/neglect—and the thinking behind the child welfare system, generally—operates from the beginning from a flawed and misconceived premise. Echoing something that Fagan, Dorminey, and Hering say in their article, she argues that the root of much child maltreatment is conditions of poverty and unemployment. Elaborating in detail on something I mention in my article, she says that current federal government funding arrangements have only aggravated this problem by funneling money disproportionately to placing children outside of their homes instead of assisting family preservation. She also develops further the criticisms of foster care that I mention. Writing from the standpoint of a social worker, she says that the current approach to child welfare creates clear ethical dilemmas for people in her profession—the "frontline workers"—who are expected to deal with child abuse/neglect, but not permitted to address the real nature of the problem or given the proper kinds of resources to do so.

Also included in this volume as appendices are the *amicus curiae* briefs the SCSS submitted in three of the leading U.S. Supreme Court cases (two were companion cases) in the last two decades where parental rights, the CPS, and state control over the family were in question. Incidentally, the Index encompasses only the articles and does not include material from the appendices.

It was decided to permit the authors to utilize the citation methods distinctive for their own disciplines (i.e., political science, law, social work, sociology, and psychology), so the reader will notice a difference in these in the various articles.

I want to thank all of the following: The Catholic University of America for permitting the SCSS and the CSWNA to hold on-site the conference this book was based on; the CSWNA and its President Kathleen Neher for assisting in the publicity for the conference and securing the authorization for continuing education credit for the social workers who attended; the SCSS and Franciscan University of Steubenville for financial assistance, and the SCSS for permission to use portions of my article which appeared in parts of two earlier articles, from *The Catholic Social Science Review* and the SCSS's anthology, *Defending the Family: A Sourcebook* (1998), of which I was also co-editor; Fr. D. Paul Sullins, Ph.D. of the Department of Sociology at The Catholic University of America for his help in organizing the conference and in handling the many on-site preparations; Professor Ronald J. Rychlak of the University of Mississippi School of Law for helping to secure, through his law school, the authorization for continuing legal education credit for the lawyers who attended the conference and for his Foreword; Karen Homol for secretarial and computer assistance in the preparation of the manuscript for publication; C.J. Norris for computer and editorial assistance; Eric Mammolenti for computer assistance; Mary Barrar for editorial advice and assistance; Maria Montagnini for preparing the Index and for proofreading assistance; and Bennett Graff of Scarecrow Press for his usual considerable and indispensable assistance in working the book through the various stages of approval and production to insure that it was added as the latest title in the Scarecrow Press/SCSS Catholic Social Thought Book Series.

The Mondale Act and Its Aftermath: An Overview of Forty Years of American Law, Public Policy, and Governmental Response to Child Abuse and Neglect

By Stephen M. Krason

The Background of Current Law on Child Abuse and Neglect and the Child Protection System

Public policy in the United States on child abuse and neglect and the formation of what we now call the child protective system (CPS)—which this article argues has been deeply troublesome—was shaped by a landmark piece of legislation passed by Congress and signed into law by President Richard M. Nixon in 1974 called the Child Abuse Prevention and Treatment Act (CAPTA), or the "Mondale Act" (after its prime sponsor, Senator and later Vice President Walter F. Mondale). The Act made federal funds available to the states for child abuse prevention and research programs on the condition that they passed laws which mandated the following: reporting by certain professionals (such as physicians) of even *suspected* cases of child abuse and neglect; the setting up of specialized child protective agencies, usually housed within state and corresponding county public social service or child welfare agencies, to deal with abuse and neglect; the granting of complete immunity from criminal prosecution or civil liability for the mandated reporters and CPS investigators regardless of their actions and even if the allegations are grossly erroneous; the insuring of confidentiality of records and proceedings in each case; and the providing for appointment of a guardian *ad litem* in judicial proceedings for children alleged to have been abused or neglected.[1] Effectively, CAPTA transformed public policy with respect to child abuse and neglect by means of a new federal grant-in-aid program to the states, the way in which public policy in so many different areas from the early twentieth century onward has been reshaped.[2] CAPTA's mandates encompassed all kinds of known and suspected child maltreatment, including physical abuse, sexual abuse, physical neglect, and psychological and emotional maltreatment. CAPTA never defined these terms, however, and there has not been and is not today any widely accepted definition of them even among professionals working in the field.[3] (As we shall also see, the problem of definition has been a major reason for an ongoing explosion of false abuse/neglect reports.) CAPTA further required the U.S. Secretary of Health, Education, and Welfare (later Health and Human Services) to establish a National Center on Child Abuse and Neglect to act as "a clearinghouse for the development of information and dissemination of information about child protective research and programs." The center, initially headed by noted child abuse expert Douglas J. Besharov (later, as we shall see, he became a major critic of current child abuse/neglect policies), used most of its funding for research and training grants to individuals and for special grants to the states. Although the latter comprised only about 20% of the available funds, it emerged as the most important part of the statute for the future of child abuse/neglect enforcement in the United States.[4]

As is stated below, the states had adopted some of the above sorts of changes even before being stimulated to do so by CAPTA. These were the ideas that were being pushed by professionals in the child protective and social welfare communities and their legislative allies throughout the country, and whenever a particularly gruesome child abuse case was picked up by the media it tended to stimulate a legislative response (which is something we have continued to see with the aftermath of the Casey Anthony trial in 2011 and ex-Penn State coach Jerry Sandusky sex abuse cases). Some states even went beyond what the federal statute required by, for example, mandating *every citizen* to report known or suspected abuse/neglect and providing both criminal and civil immunity for false reporting even if willful (actually, the establishment of hotlines and the practice of accepting anonymous reports have meant that the reporter's name may never be known in many cases anyhow). The Sandusky case prompted Senators Robert Casey and Barbara Boxer to propose amending CAPTA to require the states receiving federal funds under the Act to mandate that every adult report suspected child abuse or neglect.[5] This almost certainly would mean that, as with the mandated professional reporters currently, any person could face civil or criminal liability if he failed to report.

The Earlier History of Child Protection in America

The effort that culminated in the Mondale Act and the formation of the current CPS emerged from a long history in the U.S. of efforts to utilize law and government to combat actual or perceived family and youth problems. The common law recognized that parents had to have discretion in disciplining their children in the home, and held a presumption in favor of the reasonableness of any such parental action. If there was severe abuse the criminal law could intervene, but a parent could not be held civilly liable for excessive punishment.[6] In spite of this, the law in both England and early America permitted courts, on a local level, to intervene in families and even to take away children if they found parents unfit or children not being raised in such a way as to further the good of the community.[7]

What some have called the "child-saving movement" began in earnest in the 1820s with the opening of the New York House of Refuge. This institution sought to "save" children from what was believed to be a sure life of crime stimulated by their being abused, neglected, poor, or delinquent. A pattern was set in state laws for the next hundred years of viewing any of these categories as being a valid rationale for state intervention and removal from the family home.[8]

Later in the nineteenth century came the reform school movement. Laws influenced by this movement sought to remove delinquent or "ill-treated" children from their families and put them into reform schools in the countryside, away from what was viewed as the corrupting atmosphere of the cities. Typically, an "ill-treated" child would be one whose parents were alcoholics, criminals, or guilty of scandalous behavior. The children targeted by these efforts were usually from poor and immigrant families. The behavioral standards that society sought to shape in the children were those of an upright, productive Christian. The perspective of the relationship of the family and the state was one that continued the pattern set down by the early Puritans, and the state was viewed as an appropriate tool to regiment family life for the social good.[9]

Celebrated cases like the "Mary Ellen" case of 1875, in which a young girl was physically abused when apprenticed to her illegitimate father, led to the forming of numerous Societies for the Prevention of Cruelty to Children. These societies began as sort of quasi-governmental bodies, and the law gave them broad police powers of investigation and arrest.[10]

Dr. Allan C. Carlson, President of the Howard Center (a think tank devoting much attention to family questions), writes that the "child-savers" of the nineteenth century were "a well-funded and highly educated elite, enjoying the economic backing of private philanthropists."[11] Most of the funding and effort in the child welfare area today comes from government, although such philanthropic involvement continues.[12] Reflecting the perspective about the role of government and the private-public relationship then in place, the nineteenth-century effort was carried out by local government (primarily through the courts) and by private organizations like the Societies for the Prevention of Cruelty to Children. In the latter part of that century a shift seems to have taken place in how the private effort was carried out. Whereas previously it had been done informally, with people in communities simply helping maltreated children by "taking them in" and in other ways—as seen perhaps in Mark Twain's *Huckleberry Finn* where the widow lady and others protect Huck from his abusive, alcoholic father—it began, especially in urban areas, to be dealt with formally and institutionally, and to a greater degree with the involvement of the law.

The private and local "child-saving" efforts of the nineteenth century were strongly buttressed by the shaping of a new doctrine called *parens patriae,* which was taken from English equity where it had been used to justify the state's acting as a sort of parent to protect the estates of orphaned minors. The doctrine was recast, starting with the important Pennsylvania Supreme Court decision of *Ex parte Crouse* (1838),[13] to justify removing children from the custody of their parents "when [the parents were] unequal to the task of education or unworthy of it" and committing them to the "common guardianship of the community."[14] Almost as significantly, the court also ruled that such removal to reformatories did not require any kind of due process proceeding.[15]

According to Carlson, the doctrine of *parens patriae* has been the underlying legal basis for state intervention into the family in the name of promoting child welfare, fighting child abuse and neglect, and so on, until the present day. He argues that the absence of any *specific* constitutional protection for the family in the U.S.—in spite of the fact that the older common law tradition underlying the Constitution[16] did provide such protection, as we saw above—made the triumph of *parens patriae* possible.[17]

In the late nineteenth century the juvenile justice movement began, providing what Carlson calls "the first overt linkage of social science and social work to the law." This movement was responsible for stimulating the organization of the juvenile courts in the states. This movement also spurred on the practice of seeking to identify "probable delinquents" who would be removed from their families and their supposedly unfit parents—mostly in the immigrant, poor, and various minority communities. With this new movement came some measure of a shift from the practice of simply separating children from their "unfit" parents; now, natural parents and their children were both "to be treated as clients and given therapeutic services, with 'the best interests of the child' at heart."[18] Nevertheless, it was a coercive system, which sought to reshape the lives of these "clients" along the lines of the modern American vision of ideal family life held by the social workers and juvenile court judges who were its main enforcers.[19]

In the early twentieth century, some child welfare experts began to move their thinking away from a focus on the problems of poor, fringe, and immigrant groups toward an increasing suspicion of parents in general. The deficiencies they pointed to in parents no longer concerned traditional morality or Christian conduct and demeanor, but behavior which was seen as an obstacle to a child's psychological well-being. Even while child-saving from early on in American history was often footloose with the natural rights of parents,[20] it typically had been done in the name of religious and moral reasons. In the twentieth century it increasingly came to be done for non-religious humanistic ends. Carlson quotes one prominent book of the 1920s—and this was not an atypical position among professionals in the family field at the time—as saying that parents could no longer "shield themselves behind natural rights" and that it was "only a question of time before the parent's psychological handling of the child" would be subjected to the scrutiny of the state.[21] Quotations such as these make it clear that the outrageous ideas that have been circulated by some experts and activists of recent years, such as licensing parents, are nothing novel.[22]

Even though we have seen the soft spots historically in American law's protection of the family, such a radical undercutting of family rights as was advocated by some early twentieth-century experts was not readily embraced by courts. For example, in the famous parental educational rights case of 1925, *Pierce v. Society of Sisters,* the U.S. Supreme Court said that, "The child is not the mere creature of the State;

those who nurture him and direct his destiny have the right, coupled with the high duty, to recognize and prepare him for additional obligations."[23]

The juvenile justice movement continued as the twentieth century wore on, and succeeded in transforming the way the law dealt with troubled minors state by state. Juvenile courts and the practices of the juvenile justice system became deeply implanted. A certain idealism about the system's reparative and reforming capabilities remained, but the reality was often very different. Conditions in juvenile facilities were often harsh. Carlson says, "the system became known for its procedural nightmares, arbitrariness, and cruelty."[24] The juvenile justice movement seemed to grind to a screeching halt in the throes of the "due process revolution" of the 1960s.[25] In its 1966 *Kent v. U.S.* decision,[26] the U.S. Supreme Court took note of the problems of the juvenile courts. Then, in 1967, the Court's *In re Gault* decision[27] held that juveniles had the same due process rights as adults, including the right to a notice of charges against them, the right to a public hearing, the right to counsel, the right to confront witnesses against them, and protection against self-incrimination. Additionally, the Court's majority attacked the doctrine of *parens patriae*, which it spoke of as having a vague meaning and a doubtful basis in common law history.[28]

Interestingly, however, even as the long-running juvenile justice movement was running out of steam, child-saving was finding a new purpose for its efforts: the "newly discovered" child abuse and neglect problem. The 1960s were a period of considerable attention to this matter both in scholarly and professional journals and in popular publications. There was a general willingness to pay attention to such articles because the decade was a time in which, as Carlson puts it, there "was a general attack on the American middle-class family model."[29] Literature in the fields of sociology and social work was particularly noted for its critical stance toward traditional family life and celebrating of various "alternative lifestyles."[30]

This new attention on child abuse and neglect naturally created the impression of the existence of a serious problem, and fueled the movement for legal change. In the early 1960s, a small group of physicians, led by Dr. C. Henry Kempe, developed the conviction that the only way to deal with child abuse/neglect was to pass laws requiring certain categories of professionals to report suspected cases. In 1963, they convinced the U.S. Children's Bureau to draft a model statute that required physicians to file reports to designated authorities about children with serious physical injuries that had been inflicted by other than accidental means. Within only four years all the states passed such laws. These were what Besharov called the "first generation" of reporting laws. They were directed solely at physicians and required the reporting only of "serious physical injuries" or "non-accidental injuries." A number of states then expanded their reporting laws to make it mandatory to report other types of child maltreatment and to add other categories of professionals besides physicians to the list of required reporters.[31]

The Explosion of Reports (Mostly False) of Child Abuse and Neglect since CAPTA's Passage

In 1963, at the time that the first generation of (limited) reporting laws were being put into place, there were 150,000 reports of abuse and neglect nationwide. By 1972, just prior to the passage of CAPTA, there were 610,000. In 1982, there were 1.3 million.[32] In 1984, ten years after passage, the number had climbed to 1.5 million.[33] By 1991, the number was 2.7 million reports annually,[34] by 1993 it was 2,936,000,[35] and by 1997 it rose to three million.[36] The trend continued in the first decade of the twenty-first century. In 2009 it was 3.3 million.[37] This meant that there was an astounding increase in reports of *2438%* in the over forty-five years since the first reporting laws! It must be kept in mind that these figures merely tell us about the increase in reports; they do *not* verify that an expanding epidemic of actual child abuse and neglect occurred over this time, as they are often cited to supposedly prove.

Most states have central registries on which they enter names of people who supposedly have been child abusers or neglecters.[38] In 2006, the federal Adam Walsh Child Protection and Safety Act became law, which established a centralized database—i.e., a national registry—of persons who (supposedly) have been "substantiated" as child abusers.[39] While the experience with this national registry is so far limited, if the state registries are any indication it is entirely unclear that the only names appearing on it will be of genuine child abusers or neglecters, or even that most names will not be of people only accused but never proven to have done anything. What is not usually realized is that people's names can be entered into such registries—and frequently are—if they have not been convicted, or even accused, of any crime–or even if it has never been shown that they have abused or neglected any children. In Ohio in 1994, the state Department of Human Services, under pressure from the American Civil Liberties Union and other organizations, purged 471,000 names—mostly of parents—from its Central Registry on Child Abuse primarily because the allegations were unsubstantiated.[40] This was an astonishing 78.5% of the names in the registry! Things were not much different twenty years later. A federal court in Illinois noted early in the last decade that upon neutral review 74.5% of indicated findings of abuse or neglect in that state were reversed. In the same decade in Pennsylvania the substantiation rate kept steadily dropping, from 18% in 2006, to 17% in 2007, to 16% in 2008, to 15.5% in 2009, to 14.8% in 2010.[41] Such figures do not appear to be substantially out of line with the national situation. We are able to put the statistical picture in focus by considering federal government data, studies, and the assessments of noted authorities over the past three decades or so. One study in the late 1970s, by which time our current policies were in high gear, showed that nationally 65% of allegations—which involved 750,000 children—were "unfounded."[42] Another in the mid-1980s concluded the same: about 80% of child sexual abuse complaints,[43] and yet another at that time showed that 60% of abuse complaints in general were unfounded.[44] Besharov, who played an important role in shaping our current national policy, wrote in the mid-1980s that 65% of abuse/neglect reports nationwide "prove[d] to be unfounded" and that "over 500,000 families [annually] are put through investigations of unfounded reports."[45] By 2000, he wrote that the percentage of false reports was still in the 65-66% range and the number of innocent families investigated annually had increased to about 700,000.[46] He said that in one representative year (1997), unfounded reports involved 2,046,000 children.[47] Even among substantiated cases, the number of cases of *serious* maltreatment of children (e.g., involving death, life-threatening situations, or serious injury) is small;[48] actually, most "substantiated" cases of abuse or neglect involve "minor situations," such as slapping and poor housekeeping.[49] As far as sexual abuse cases are concerned, only a small percentage (6%) "were considered serious";[50] the rest presumably involved something on the order of inappropriate touching, fondling, etc.[51] He concludes that "the high level of unwarranted [state] intervention" has led to a condition in which the child-protective "system is overburdened with cases of insubstantial or unproven risk."[52] In 1986, even employing very loose standards of what abuse and neglect are (see below), child protective agencies (cpa's) themselves concluded that only around 40% of reports were valid.[53] In 1994, the U.S. Department of Health and Human Services published a study that said that in 1992 alone there were 1,227,223 false reports of child abuse.[54] The Second U.S. Circuit Court of Appeals in 1994 overturned New York State's procedures for entering people's names in their registry because the "standard of evidence used...posed an unacceptably high risk of error." The Court said that in spite of "'the grave seriousness of the problems of child abuse and neglect...we find the current system unacceptable.'"[55] A 1993 *Reader's Digest* article on the subject quotes New York University law professor Martin Guggenheim as saying that "'[h]undreds of children each week are needlessly removed from families'" due to false abuse and neglect allegations.[56] When discussing the rise of child abuse in his periodical *The Index of Leading Cultural Indicators,* former U.S. Education Secretary William J. Bennett noted the view of certain authorities that a "child abuse establishment" of professionals "actually encourages false charges of child abuse."[57] Abigail Van Buren ("Dear Abby"), who was long one of the leaders in the charge against child abuse, admitted in the 1990s after running a letter about a parent facing a false abuse report that she was startled at how many other parents wrote to say they had had the same experience.[58] According to Department of Health and Human Services data (NCANDS - the National Child Abuse and Neglect Data System), of the 3.3 million reports in 2009 only 14.4% were substantiated.[59] This means that while for more than three decades the number of unfounded reports apparently was between three-fifths and two-thirds, now it has shot up to well over 80%.

By the way, the term "substantiated" in the CPS lexicon generally means that it is established that child maltreatment occurred—though, as mentioned and further discussed below, it is questionable that many of the parental behaviors that fit the CPS categories of "abuse" or "neglect" really constitute that in the minds of the average person—whereas the term "indicated" means that there is no proof that maltreatment occurred, but "there is reason to suspect" that it did, or even that it "could happen." This seems like a bit of a verbal slight-of-hand and it is not clear what it means. Sometimes an "indicated" determination of abuse is simply treated as if it occurred and, in fact, some states really do not distinguish between the terms. This can easily, of course, have the effect of inflating the supposed number of cases of actual abuse.[60]

What the above means is that throughout almost the entire time that the Mondale Act has been in existence, much more than a majority of child maltreatment reports around the country have been unfounded, and recently there is no question that the percentage has spiked upward even further. We now have a situation where a massive state bureaucracy with sweeping coercive power is having millions upon millions of dollars being poured into it each year even though perhaps 85% of its actions are completely unnecessary.

A question might be asked about why in recent years we have seen the apparent jump of three-fifths or two-thirds to four-fifths or higher of false reports. The answer to this is unclear. Perhaps the limited demands regarding respecting parental rights put on the CPS by the 2003 CAPTA amendments and court decisions upholding the Fourth Amendment rights of parents in CPS investigations—both discussed below—have motivated at least some cpa's to screen reports better. Maybe the criticism the CPS has received from some authorities about how chasing so many trivial or non-existent problems has caused it to miss the true cases of abuse and also the celebrated cases of children who died from maltreatment even after the CPS knew about a problem—these topics are also discussed below—have also motivated more screening and a concern by some cpa's to investigate more selectively. Or maybe, alternatively, the CPS is becoming even more aggressive in investigating everything that is reported, and thus they find that more and more of the complaints are false. Also, in an era where people are hearing on daytime television and the like about the ever expanding number of behaviors that supposedly constitute child abuse and Homeland Security is telling everyone to keep a sharp eye out for suspicious activity, it would not be surprising that there would be an even further increase in the number of false reports. Or, possibly, the three-fifths or two-thirds figure for some time was too low. The bottom line, however, is that the "epidemic" of child abuse—*real* child abuse—that the American public heard so much about in the 1960s, 1970s, and 1980s is just not there, and probably never was.

The experience of facing false charges—perhaps it is better to call it an ordeal—can happen to any parent merely by a stranger picking up the telephone and anonymously calling a well-publicized hotline number or the local children's services or child-welfare agency to say, without any evidence, that a parent maltreated his or her child. (It is clear from the above statistics that this involves a massive number of children and families each year.) The result of this can be a disruption of family life, legal troubles and financial difficulties growing out of parents having to defend themselves, and the forced separation of children from their parents that can go on for months or years. While parents can do things to protect their children and families from many of the threats the current culture poses to them (e.g., controlling their associations with bad playmates or peers, limiting television use or putting screening software on computers to stop the invasion of immoral influences, homeschooling them to circumvent the negative influences of public or other institutional schools), it is almost impossible to fully insulate one's family from the threat of a system that on very little pretense can simply reach into the home and take away one's offspring. The massive incidence of false abuse/neglect allegations shows that current law and public policy on child abuse and neglect and the routine actions of the CPS are a major threat to the American family today.

Examples of Outrageous Applications of the Child Abuse and Neglect Laws

Sometimes—although all too seldom—CPS officials will acknowledge that a family has been falsely accused of abuse or neglect. They typically say that such episodes are exceptions and unfortunate, uncommon events (and often attribute them to insufficient training for their personnel due to inadequate funding). The statistics cited indicate, on the contrary, that they are *clearly the rule and not the exception.* An article on the problem of false reporting in *Reader's Digest* in 1993 spoke about "systemic abuse."[61]

The cases we now recount would most likely be so responded to by CPS spokesmen, or else they would say that despite what seems to have happened there really may have been abuse or neglect but it just was not found. There is probably no better place to start than the Jordan, Minnesota, case in 1983-84, which gained significant national attention and late in 1994 was the subject of an extensive ten-year retrospective report on National Public Radio. This ugly story in the annals of American "child-saving" began when a previously convicted child molester, James Rud, who had been charged with molesting two children he babysat, falsely told police in the small town that he was part of a child sex ring which included mostly parents. Eventually, twenty-four adults, mostly parents, faced criminal charges and their children were all taken from them. What followed was a series of despicable prosecutorial tactics and intimidation of both parents and children by state social welfare agencies and hired psychologists. There was no physical evidence that showed any physical or sexual abuse had taken place, except by Rud. Under extraordinary pressure and by means of suggestive techniques in therapy and promises of reunion with their families if they cooperated, many of the children began to claim their parents had abused them. With skimpy cases, the politically ambitious prosecutor tried to plea-bargain with the accused parents to get them to confess to something in exchange for the return of their children. Some parents were asked to make perjured testimony against others, and even offered money. One couple refused and demanded a trial. The entire case against all the parents unraveled when at the trial Rud, who had struck a plea bargain to testify against the other parties who were his supposed co-conspirators, was unable to identify the couple in the courtroom. He later confessed in a jailhouse radio interview that he had made the whole thing up, and the children later recanted.[62]

Even after the whole case collapsed, the children were not returned to their parents for months. In the years following, many of the children suffered psychological and drug problems. There were cases of attempted suicide among the children and divorce among the parents. A civil suit by the parents against Scott County, Minnesota, was dismissed because the Minnesota courts held that state agencies were absolutely immune from liability. Even though the attorney general of Minnesota had to intervene in the case, the prosecutor, in spite of tactics involving both doubtful ethicality and legality, only received a minor reprimand and continued to practice law.[63]

In many, many cases that we have gathered information about, the same situation comes up as in the Jordan case: a) that authorities seem to work from the premise that the parents are guilty and they have to prove themselves innocent; b) that when it becomes apparent that authorities realize that no abuse or neglect has occurred they still persist to try to find something; c) that in spite of legal strictures they keep cases and investigations open, and efforts are made by authorities to coerce false confessions of guilt or (if a criminal investigation) to plea-bargain with the threat that children will not be returned otherwise;[64] d) that parents have long struggles getting their children back even after they are exonerated; and e) that after their sometimes nightmarish battles with the agencies are over they find they have no legal recourse because of the state's immunity.

The statistics showing the multitude of false child abuse and neglect allegations in the U.S. suggest that there are repetitions, in varying degrees, of the Jordan Case all across the country. Only a few, of course, find their way into the media and popular or professional publications. Some of these which have come to our attention illustrate how child protective agencies and even regular law enforcement agencies treat almost anything as abuse or neglect, how parents are viewed with much suspicion and those who come to the agencies' attention regarded almost automatically as guilty, and how the system is—to use the title of a book on the subject—"out of control."[65]

For several years, San Diego County, California, got some bad press attention for the antics of its cpa. In a case that began in 1989, a Navy man stationed there was accused of sexually abusing his eight-year-old daughter, even though a roving stranger had assaulted five other little girls, some in the same neighborhood, using the same apparent *modus operandi*. Nevertheless, the father was arrested for the act and his daughter taken by the agency. After over a year under the control of the agency and in enforced separation from her family—and, it was later learned, after repeated agency attempts to get her to implicate her father—the daughter accused him. The case was later dismissed and the father's arrest record expunged when DNA evidence indicated he could not have been the assailant. This, however, was only after endless interrogations, forced therapy, resulting psychological problems of the mother (which led to a suicide attempt), and well over $100,000 in legal fees. When the girl was finally returned to the family, her behavior had markedly changed as a result of the episode.[66]

Another celebrated San Diego case dragged on for over five years. It involved a physically deformed man who was alleged to have committed all sorts of bizarre acts when watching children with his wife at a local church. The man was kept in jail awaiting trial for over two years, charged with an assortment of acts of physical, sexual, and ritual abuse. There was absolutely no physical evidence in the case and no sign of the children having been assaulted. The three- and four-year-old children denied being abused until undergoing therapy. When some later testified, they contended that among other things the man had stabbed a giraffe and an elephant, had taken them to a house and placed them on a bed coated with black oil, and had drowned rabbits in a church baptismal font. The prosecutors thought all this was credible.[67]

In light of episodes such as these, a grand jury charged that San Diego County's child protective agencies and their network of contracted therapists were out of control and were operating without checks and balances. The California Juvenile Justice Commission suggested a possible criminal conspiracy among the county's child protection workers.[68] Still, I know of no indictments or other legal action subsequently taken against them.

Two books on the subject, Mary Pride's *The Child Abuse Industry* and Brenda Scott's *Out of Control,* detail many, many outrageous cases of false abuse and neglect allegations. Some examples are the following. Two children were summarily taken from their parents after the one, a boy, went to school with a mark on his nose and eye after being hit by a tennis ball while playing catch. Both children were returned to their parents only after months in state custody, during which time they were abused and neglected. The parents were financially drained by the legal bills from the case.[69] A father was reported, apparently by a neighbor, after the latter watched his two-year-old daughter sitting in his lap trying to undo his shirt buttons. Presumably, the neighbor saw this as a sign of likely sexual abuse or some such thing. The police initially investigated and dismissed the matter, but then came back at the behest of child protective workers who seized the child. She remained in foster care for weeks. The family got her back only after a legal fight whose costs resulted in their losing their home.[70] Another family was repeatedly investigated and monitored for four years and at one point lost their infant daughter for nine months because an agency alleged that her small size indicated she was "failing to thrive." This notion has been taken uncritically from medical literature by psychologists—and then picked up by child protective workers—and applied to the physical and mental development of children. Promoters of this notion often claim that such insufficient development is a sign of "psychological abuse," a term that, in turn, is never clearly defined. In the case in question, the agency never seemed interested in the fact that both the girl's mother and maternal grandmother were below five feet tall, and so genetics was probably the reason. The child protective workers were convinced it *had* to be abuse.[71] Another mother was "substantiated" in an agency's files as a sexual abuser because she washed her seven-year-old son's foreskin in the bathtub due to the fact that he was so sloppy about doing it—as probably many boys at that age are.[72] A little girl was removed from her parents' custody after she slightly fractured her leg when stepping on a pencil. The agency "bargained" with the parents, as in the Jordan case: they would get their daughter back if they admitted guilt and told them they then would only have to attend a few parenting classes.[73] Another set of parents brought their baby to the emergency room of St. Louis's Cardinal Glennon Hospital upon the recommendation of their physician to find out why the infant was spitting up so much. After the hospital found no physical problem, they accused the parents of emotional neglect (which the hospital personnel admitted they could not define). Child protective authorities regularly monitored the family as suspected abusers after that. The late, famous investigative reporter Jack Anderson brought this case to light on his radio program.[74]

Medical matters and hospital emergency rooms like the latter are a fruitful source of false abuse complaints. Often, for example, parents bring a child to an emergency room with a certain type of rash and attending medical personnel, not usually specialists in dermatology, conclude it is a burn that *must* have been inflicted by the parents. In Dayton, Ohio, parents took their baby daughter to their long-time pediatrician when she developed a rash. Usually, parents are likely to be treated more reasonably and with more respect by their own physicians than emergency room doctors, but in this case the pediatrician thought that the problem was caused by the child being repeatedly shaken. Further tests showed that the child had fractured three ribs and maybe a leg. A specialist later discovered that other physical signs showed the presence of a rare bone disease called osteogenesis imperfecta. This and not abuse was the cause of the symptoms. The pediatrician, however, had reported the parents to the county Children's Services Bureau, which despite the final medical findings was sure the child was abused and took custody of her. The agency requested a police investigation, but that turned up nothing. After a year and a half of repeated agency investigations and medical examinations of the child, great financial drain on the family, and increasing evidence of the disease, the agency dropped the case.[75]

In Jefferson County, Ohio, three solid Christian couples connected with Franciscan University of Steubenville (where I am on the faculty) got in trouble with the Children's Services agency after home births, which are legal in the state. In one of the cases, the couple were "indicated" as neglecters and apparently entered into the state child abuse registry because at the midwife's direction they provided the initial treatment for a common condition babies get after birth before bringing him to a hospital emergency room. The agency said there was neglect because the parents had failed to seek medical treatment within a ten-hour period, even though such a specific requirement does not exist anywhere in the pertinent state statute or regulations of the state's Division of Social Services and it is doubtful that either of these gave the county cpa the authority to fashion it on its own. Further, the couple was left to believe that their name would be permanently kept in the registry, even though the state regulations expressly stated that "indicated" parties shall have their names removed within five years of the disposition of the case.[76]

Another of these cases involved a couple whose baby was only in the "low normal" category in weight gain several weeks after birth, as it turned out because he had trouble learning to nurse properly. Their pediatrician, who they had chosen mostly because their HMO left them few choices, reported them after they resisted giving feeding supplements. He said that the baby risked brain damage otherwise—even though other physicians and a lactation specialist who were consulted were satisfied with the baby's progress. Carlson indicates that legal complications from home birthing, which is enjoying a resurgence of popularity in the U.S. but is strongly disliked by the medical profession, are not unknown elsewhere.[77] This case shows that parents are sometimes investigated as abusers or neglecters because they are caught up in disputes between physicians about the type of medical care for their children.

In Michigan in 2011, there was an egregious example of the extreme to which the CPS and prosecutorial authorities will go to back medical practitioners against parents in making health care judgments for their

children. Physicians at DeVos Children's Hospital in Grand Rapids
began an aggressive chemotherapy regimen on a young boy with
Ewing's sarcoma, a serious form of bone cancer, which as time went on
caused him to become gravely ill because of side-effects. Certain of the
drugs used had not been approved by the Food and Drug Administration
for use in children, and it was known that they could cause them serious
side-effects. Even though a PET scan had revealed that the boy was now
cancer-free, the attending physicians refused to discontinue the
aggressive treatment, saying that there could still be cancer cells in his
body. The parents took their son from the hospital, began a nutrition
regimen for him at home, and arranged to have their family physician do
regular PET scans to check about any recurrence of the cancer. Without
the intensive chemotherapy, he quickly got better. The physicians at the
hospital, pursuant to their stated understanding of the requirements of
state law, reported the parents to the CPS for medical neglect. The local
CPS and prosecutor concluded no neglect had occurred, but the
hospital's physicians were not satisfied. They prodded state CPS officials
to go after the parents until the former appointed a special prosecutor
who charged the parents with medical neglect. The prosecutor lined up
physicians who were supposed experts in child abuse to testify, even
though they had never seen the boy. The lead physician from the hospital
insisted in her testimony that it should always be medical professionals
and never parents who should balance the risks and make the decision
about continued treatment for a child. Ultimately, the judge dismissed the
charges, but the case is continuing because the special prosecutor
appealed the decision.[78]

Pride lists a number of other things that agencies in various cases she
has record of have threatened to remove children from their parents for:
scolding and spanking, or on the other hand permissiveness; withholding
TV-watching privileges, or on the other hand supposedly neglecting
children by using the TV as a babysitter; parents raising their voices in
anger, or on the other hand failing to show proper emotion toward their
children; and parents failing to exercise 24-hour supervision over their
children, or on the other hand "repressing" their children by exercising
24-hour supervision.[79] *As this makes clear, the child protective system
often puts parents in a "catch-22" situation; they are literally "damned
if they do and damned if they don't."*

Scott tells how in Arizona children have been taken away from their
parents because of "sexual abuse" for such reasons as the children
accidentally have seen their parents unclothed; the parents have bathed a
four-year-old; and fathers were seen kissing their young daughters on the
mouth.[80] Without specifying the state, Scott additionally says that

caseworkers have found child "maltreatment" when a parent has been late picking up his or her children from school or placed too high an expectation on a child. They further have found what they have called "passive abuse" for such things as the parents not having a testamentary will and their working too much.[81]

The media gave much attention to a Georgia story in 1994 when a woman was reported to police for slapping her unruly nine-year-old son in a supermarket. She wound up in jail, and her husband had to cash in his IRA to bail her out. It was only after a fusillade of negative public reaction to the arrest and also after intrusive investigations into the family by child protective authorities that the local prosecutor decided not to press charges. Actually, there are many cases of parents being accused of child abuse for simple spanking, even though this is not forbidden by any state's law and, in fact, many state statutes, such as Ohio's (my state), expressly say this is *not* child abuse.

In Aurora, Colorado, a father was criminally charged for a mild act of corporal punishment toward his rebellious seventeen-year-old son. A nationally syndicated columnist described James Kelley as "exasperated" with the son who had left home to cohabit with his girlfriend and "was neglecting his health and education." When the son denied stealing a stereo from his father's car, Kelley slapped him. For this act of "non-sparing of the rod," Kelley was arrested and charged by local authorities with battery. The jury hearing the case acquitted him.[82]

A mother in Virginia was found guilty of neglect by a county social service agency for the following: she did not want to rouse her sleeping three-year-old in her car parked in front of her house while she ran a ten-minute errand next door and the child awoke in the meantime and wandered into a neighbor's house, and she also allowed her nine-year-old son to watch his younger sisters for 25 minutes as a way of developing responsibility. The agency established age limits for babysitting even though state law was silent about it. A neighborhood busybody apparently reported the mother, even though she and her husband were upright and well-respected parents. That reports for such flimsy reasons are not uncommon in Virginia was illustrated by the mother's telling the press, "Every time I tell this story, someone says, 'Well you should hear what happened to so-and-so.'"[83]

Scott recounts a similar "neglect" case against a single mother, a category of persons especially vulnerable to agency assault. She left her eleven-year-old daughter—note that she was eleven, not, say, two—home to watch TV while she ran to the store. In the meantime, a neighbor turned her in and when she got home the child was gone, taken into the custody of the authorities. The girl was placed in foster care for three months until her twelfth birthday when, in the estimation of the agency, she magically became mature enough to be left home alone.[84] In a similar case, a Christian couple took an early morning newspaper route so they could raise the money to send their children to a Christian school. They figured there would be no problem leaving the children at home asleep while they delivered the papers, since the oldest was almost twelve. They got home one day to find out that, after an anonymous tip, the children had been taken by the police due to "lack of supervision." The oldest was incarcerated in a juvenile detention center for two days and the younger two children put in foster homes for those days until the parents agreed that one would always stay at home with them until the oldest turned twelve. That was *two weeks* later.[85] A case such as this makes people especially realize the inanity of the "child protective" system.

We have mentioned Christian families being targeted. Although those cases probably did not develop because of the parents' religious preference, there are other occasions when this seemingly has been the reason. Pride speaks about a Missouri family doing homeschooling in connection with a satellite evangelical Christian school program. Even though the school district raised little question about the academic quality of the program, the child welfare bureaucracy—upon the urging of local public school officials—accused the parents of educational neglect because the program was too "'religiously centered'" and so their child's "'behavior or associations...were injurious to his welfare.'"[86] The New York State Council of Family and Child Caring Agencies, a professional group comprised of child welfare agencies, says that parents who display an "over involvement in religion" are to be suspected as possible abusers.[87] Scott writes about the case of a Christian mother who the local cpa ordered to undergo psychiatric evaluation after her daughter was removed by the agency from school and put into a foster home because the mother had allegedly spanked her. The psychiatrist told her that certain religious beliefs "prejudiced" a person against being a good parent and insisted she was unfit if she believed the Bible taught that God wanted children to grow up with loving discipline.[88]

Perhaps more outrageous than any of the above cases, even the Jordan one, was the case in Wenatchee, Washington, in 1994-1996. The local police department, spearheaded by its Chief Sex Crimes Investigator, Detective Robert Perez, and the county cpa claimed that a child sex abuse ring had been operating in the city of 24,000 in which somewhere around one hundred people were singled out as supposed child abusers. Over forty were arrested, nearly thirty sent to prison (on the basis of confessions secured from the accused and their allegedly abused children under pressure), and around fifty children taken away from their parents by the cpa. The case witnessed threats and pressure tactics against people, including those in the media, who threatened to expose the abuses of the authorities or to provide exonerating evidence about the accused to an extent almost unimaginable for the United States of America.[89]

The case began after the local cpa was told by state officials to clean up apparent corruption, which seems to have involved payments to at least one of its employees from a local adoption agency for supplying the agency with children.[90] Most of the charges in the case stemmed from allegations by Detective Perez's foster daughter, a disturbed eleven-year-old who Perez later had committed to a psychiatric facility in another state after she went on a rampage in his house. In unrecorded conversations with Perez and on a driving tour of the town, she accused much of the population of abuse and identified twenty-three places where incidents supposedly took place. An astounding 3,200 charges of child abuse were filed against one woman. *Time* magazine reported that "Perez...recruited several other children to corroborate...[the girl's] charges."[91] *Time* also said that "[i]t is a wonder Perez got the investigator's job in the first place, since he has a history of petty crimes and domestic strife, and a dismal 1989 police-department evaluation described him as having a 'pompous, arrogant approach' and said he appeared 'to pick out people and target them.'"[92]

In any event, after the foster daughter's initial allegations—which her older sister, who also came to live in the Perez home, later added to—the case proceeded to the round up and happenings indicated above. One woman said she confessed only after hours of interrogation, enforced sleeplessness, and threats. A ten-year-old girl hauled out of her school classes signed a statement accusing her mother and other adults of sex orgies after four hours of interrogation, the threat that her mother would be arrested if she did not sign, and the promise that she could go home if she did. Mormon parents who had unwisely gone to the cpa for help when they feared their troubled eldest son had molested their youngest daughter found themselves caught up in the investigation, accused of abuse, and sent to prison for eleven years. Their five children were subjected to "repressed memory" therapy (see below) to supposedly "recover" their knowledge of sexual abuse. All later recanted their accusations against their parents, which were made in the wake of this therapy. The eldest daughter, age sixteen, objected and was taken away forcibly to a secured facility in Idaho to help her overcome her "denial" of her parents' behavior and her "psychological loyalty" to her family. She later ran away and went into hiding. A businessman who ran a group

foster home, and was commended by the cpa for his efforts, was accused
by Perez's foster daughter—who he had had removed from his home for
unruly behavior. The man later found most of the charges dropped when
he hired a private lawyer—as opposed to the public defenders who
represented most of the accused, who were low-income people—but
legal bills cost him his house and put him deeply in debt. Perhaps most
outrageous were the charges brought against several people connected
with the Pentecostal Church of God House of Prayer. Perez's daughter,
and later other children, made outrageous claims of orgies in the church.
The claim was made that if any child was too exhausted after these
Sunday episodes to go to school on Monday, he or she could get a note
from the pastor. After one Sunday school teacher was acquitted—again,
after hiring private counsel—a juror told the local press that there was no
evidence but just a seeming witch-hunt. After the church pastor,
Reverend Bob Roberson, objected to the attacks on the church, he and
his wife were arrested for abuse and had their young daughter taken from
them. They were jailed for over four months with bail set at $1 million,
allegedly to keep them from continuing their public opposition. They
were later acquitted. One defense investigator was refused the
opportunity to interview some of the children because the cpa suddenly
alleged there were reports that he was wanted for abuse. The authorities
claimed they were going to investigate the reporter for the Spokane
television station who carried out what *The Wall Street Journal* called a
"relenting, generally remarkable exposé of the Wenatchee prosecutions."
One CPS caseworker who tried to intervene in one of the cases after one
of the children told him she had lied was criminally charged with
witness-tampering and fired. He later fled with his family to Canada to
avoid false child abuse charges. An extensive report on the investigation
by public defender Kathryn Lyon detailed the miscarriage of justice and
charged that Perez "abused the children in order to persecute the
adults."[93]

The town's civilian and police officials strongly supported Perez's
investigation and actions and initially state officials did too. In the fall of
1995, however, Washington Governor Mike Lowry and the state's House
Speaker wrote to the federal Justice Department requesting a civil rights
investigation of the authorities. Early in 1996, Attorney General Janet
Reno—whose prosecutorial reputation had been enhanced by child abuse
cases, certain of which had involved highly questionable tactics and
obliviousness to false charges[94]—turned them down, claiming that
federal law did not apply.[95]

Issue after issue of *The Home School Court Report*, the publication
of the Home School Legal Defense Association (HSLDA), recounts

cases from around the country of the CPS going after homeschooling families—even though homeschooling is legal in every state, with a varying range of notification and reporting requirements for parents to meet—for everything from "educational neglect," to failing to fill out the proper forms or missing filing deadlines, to failure to meet requirements not mandated by law, to withdrawing their "special needs" children from public schools to teach them at home, to bogus claims of neglect following anonymous hotline complaints by someone who does not like the fact that they are homeschooling, to medical neglect allegations following a "botched" diagnosis of a child in an emergency room. One of the most outrageous cases in recent years happened in upstate New York in 2009, where a farm family (the Cressys) found themselves running afoul of both the local CPS and law enforcement because of confusion about what the homeschool notification requirements were. After this got straightened out and the local school superintendent commended them on how good their curriculum looked, the CPS still came after them with the assistance of the county sheriff. On different occasions, a CPS operative and a sheriff's investigator demanded numerous documents and entered the family's home—all this was done without a warrant or court order—and threatened the parents and harangued them about how their homeschooling would damage their children. They were "invited" to a meeting at the sheriff's office where they were unexpectedly arrested for child endangerment—"all for failing to file homeschool paperwork with the local school district." This was a novel interpretation of the child endangerment law, to say the least, and was even more irregular since New York does not even have a criminal truancy statute and the matter had already been cleared up by the school district. The sheriff's department in league with the CPS arbitrarily decided to go after the parents, and the local prosecutor readily went along. The CPS piled on with a parallel action in family court, which state law permits in the case of criminal abuse or neglect charges (which there never should have been in this case). The case garnered much publicity (even nationally) and the local media demanded that the charges be dropped. The prosecutor persisted, however, until finally with HSDLA spearheading the defense the case was entirely shifted to family court, the charge dropped, and the family's ordeal spanning several months was over. It was clear that the earlier days of arresting parents for homeschooling, which with the expansion of the practice around the country had become very infrequent, were not over.[96]

Then there was the case in February 2012 where a North Carolina father, responding to his teenage daughter's Facebook rant against him for expecting normal obedience and respect and the carrying out of usual age-appropriate household chores and after his successive efforts to "ground" her failed, made a You-Tube video of himself shooting apart the laptop computer he had bought her and upgraded, and arguably since she was a minor he has full control over (he previously had tried to deny her its use for a time). While this was supposed to teach her a lesson about abusing her computer and the local police commended him for it, the local cpa nevertheless investigated him after some people watching the video—or the daughter's friends?—contacted it. One wonders two things: Is the CPS in the business of undercutting the norms of parental obedience and respect, and of insuring that unruly teens will be restrained? By springing into action upon getting calls about this, does the CPS respond to the mob—or to justice? Indeed, the latter does not seem out-of-line with how the CPS has worked for some time. I remember the former head of the cpa in Jefferson County, Ohio, where I live—who went on to a job with the child welfare bureaucracy at the state level—saying how his agency would respond differently to some parental action in a more rural part of the County than in its largest city, Steubenville. What he meant was that it would respond as the popular sentiment indicated.

When we see cases such as the above—duplicated (except for every part of the most outrageous ones) many thousands of times each year in the United States—we can understand Professor Guggenheim's statement that those in the system "separate children [from their parents] for petty reasons and for no reason all the time."[97] The San Diego County grand jury mentioned above alleged that possibly the majority of the children removed from their homes by the county's cpa and put in foster homes should have been left alone.[98] We can also understand Richard Wexler's analysis of the breakdown of child abuse/neglect reports. Wexler is a journalist who has written and produced numerous reports about the false reporting problem and authored the book *Wounded Innocents* about it. He is now the Executive Director of the National Coalition for Child Protection Reform. He estimates that for every 100 reports of abuse or neglect, "'at least 58 are false [outright]; 21 are mostly poverty cases (deprivation of necessities); 6 are sexual abuse; 4 are minor physical abuse; 3 are emotional maltreatment; 3 are 'other maltreatment'; 1 is major physical abuse.'"[99] Gary B. Melton, who was the lead author of the 1993 report of the U.S. Advisory Board on Child Abuse and Neglect and has written extensively on the subject, says that in his consultations with physicians on child protection teams at major medical centers around the U.S. "all have said that they very rarely encounter [cases of] severe battering."[100] The latter and sexual abuse along the lines of rape, incest, and intense sexual touching or groping, is probably what most people have in mind when they think of abuse. As we have seen and note further below, what constitutes "sexual abuse" and "minor physical abuse" is often a subject of controversy and many of these cases probably involve actions that most people would not tend to think of as abuse.[101] Pride writes that only 2 to 5% of the reports of abuse and neglect each year actually involve what under the law would be crimes against children.[102] Analyzing NCANDS and NIS-4 data—NIS-4 is the most recent of the periodic Congressional-mandated studies of child abuse data around the country—David Finkelhor, Lisa Jones, and Anne Shattuck of the Crimes Against Children Center at the University of New Hampshire assert—even in the context of the prevailing loose definition of terms, both in law and in CPS understanding (as discussed below)—that in the period 1992-2009 sexual abuse against children declined by 61% and physical abuse declined 55%.[103]

Why Are So Many Innocent Parents Being Accused Under the Current Child Protective Apparatus?

The Problem of Definition: The Child Abuse/Neglect Statutes

The first serious problem about the current abuse and neglect statutes is that they in no way provide a precise definition of what constitutes the offense. This is summed up by an oft-quoted passage from Jeanne M. Giovannoni and Rosina M. Becerra's book, *Defining Child Abuse*: "Many assume that since child abuse and neglect are against the law, somewhere there are statutes that make clear distinctions between what is and what is not child abuse and neglect, but this is not the case. Nowhere are there clear-cut definitions of what is encompassed by the terms."[104] This has not changed much since they wrote in the late 1970s. Writing in 2000, Besharov states, "[c]onfusion about reporting is largely caused by the vagueness of reporting laws." Such laws are "often vague and overbroad."[105] Along these lines, Trevor Armbrister's 1993 *Readers' Digest* article especially singled out "the broad category of 'neglect,'" which accounts for almost half of reports, as causing agency abuse.[106] As indicated above, this problem of lack of clarity of definition traces itself back to the second generation of reporting laws and the Mondale Act. Lawyers and legislators are well aware of the need for statutes to meet the basic, traditional constitutional tests of vagueness and overbreadth. The former holds that a statute or regulation cannot impose penalties without giving a clear idea of the sort of conduct that is prohibited; the latter says that activity cannot be proscribed or restricted which is beyond the legitimate reach of government, and that government cannot forbid or inhibit conduct which is constitutionally protected, and it cannot reach beyond conduct that is illegal to restrain conduct that is legal.[107] In fact, it is an ancient principle of the Anglo-American legal tradition that a law has to make clear what it demands. One is prompted to think that if this were any other area of law than child abuse/neglect, many of the statutes long since would have been struck down, in whole or in part, as unconstitutionally vague or overbroad. Efforts to declare state statutes in the child abuse/neglect area unconstitutional on these grounds have achieved little success, and we know of no federal court that has intervened on these grounds.[108]

The definitional problems of typical child abuse/neglect statutes is illustrated by the one in my state of Ohio. Under the Ohio statute, an "abused child" is one who "[i]s the victim of sexual activity" as defined under the criminal code of Ohio, or "[i]s endangered" as defined by Ohio law, or "[e]xhibits evidence of any physical or mental injury or death, inflicted other than by accidental means, or an injury or death which is at variance with the history given of it." A child who has received corporal punishment "or other physical disciplinary measure" by a parent, guardian, et al., however, "is not an abused child."[109] In some respects, the definition of "abuse" here may be less vague than the statute's definition of a "neglected" and "dependent" child below (all three of these can result in the removal of a child from his home). Also the fact that the provision regarding sexual abuse refers to the provisions of the Ohio criminal code means that a substantial amount of case law is available which has clarified what actions are encompassed. Still, there can be problems even with the latter. Some of the definitions given under the "Sex Offenses" section of the Ohio Criminal Code (Section 2907.01) could be construed to apply to innocent acts.[110]

The term "endangered child" above in the Ohio statute is similarly troublesome. The Ohio Code elsewhere defines—or *attempts* to define— child endangerment (Chapter 2919.22); it is a term, however, which is possibly inherently undefinable. The following provision illustrates this. "No person, who is the parent [et al.]...of a child under eighteen years of age or a mentally or physically handicapped child under twenty-one years of age, shall create a substantial risk to the health or safety of the child, by violating a duty of care, protection, or support."[111] It is clear that this definition could be construed—and often will be, in light of the very critical view held of parents by the child protective system—to regard the parents as responsible for many normal situations a child might get into (e.g., mishaps occurring while doing reasonable household chores, accidents he might have).

The term "injury" in the above statutory definition of child abuse is fraught with danger because it is actually never defined. The term draws no distinction between injuries of any degree, so that a temporary red mark left from a slap is treated the same as a broken bone or a crushed skull (and, in fact, parents have been held to be abusers and lost their children because of the former). Further, what is a "mental injury"? This is a subject that is, to say the least, highly imprecise. How does one "exhibit evidence" of a mental injury? Children may exhibit all kinds of psychological or psychiatric symptoms that, true, could be the result of maltreatment by parents, but could also be the result of many other factors (some of which are not or are only dimly understood, since man knows surprisingly little about the human mind). Indeed, there are too many cases in which medical authorities, social workers, counselors, and others conclude that certain odd behavior or psychological tendencies just *had* to have been the result of child abuse, even though they are unable to say how and have no clear evidence to support such a conclusion. Nor is it altogether reasonable to conclude that a child is abused just because of an injury "which is at variance with the history given of it." As some of the above case studies demonstrate, medical authorities make mistakes or sometimes simply do not know enough about certain particular areas of medicine to make correct judgments. Also, consider that parents who might be aware of the problem of false abuse allegations and so are wary of saying something that could result in their facing unmerited charges, might inadvertently make inconsistent statements, etc. simply because they are being overly careful. For example, in the current anti-parent climate, they might fear that a hospital emergency room, etc. will not believe how an unusual accidental injury or something on that order occurred.

Even though the Ohio child abuse statute specifically states that "a child exhibiting evidence of corporal or other physical disciplinary measure by a parent, guardian, custodian, [et al.]...is not an abused child,"[112] the child endangerment provision in Chapter 2919.22, casts such parental immunity in doubt. That provision does not permit parents, guardians, et al. to "Administer corporal punishment or other physical disciplinary measure, or physically restrain the child in a cruel manner or for a prolonged period, which punishment, discipline, or restraint is excessive under the circumstances and creates a substantial risk of physical harm to the child;" [or] "[r]epeatedly administer unwarranted disciplinary measures to the child, when there is a substantial risk that such conduct, if continued, will seriously impair or retard the child's mental health or development."[113]

As the above discussion of case histories makes apparent, and the following section on social worker and professional attitudes reinforces, almost any parental physical disciplinary measure can—and often will— be interpreted to fall within the prohibitions of this provision. There is no set or necessarily reasonable standard that will be used to determine if a punishment is "excessive under the circumstances and creates a substantial risk." What constitutes "physical harm"? The statute does not say. With the general animus toward any kind of corporal punishment on the part of psychologists and other child welfare "experts,"[114] one can expect that for some even the slightest pain or a very temporary red mark caused by a mild spanking will be viewed as serious. What is a "cruel manner"? In these days of the relativization of terminology, unreasonable sensitivities, extreme political opportunism, and the zealous promotion of ideological agendas, many things are called "cruel" or "mean-spirited" that are not. What are "unwarranted disciplinary measures," and what does "repeatedly" mean? The statute is silent about this. Who decides what is "unwarranted"? Can strangers in a government agency make a better judgment about what is needed discipline for a child than his parents who are with him day in and day out? How does one judge whether chosen disciplinary measures will "seriously impair" "mental health" or "development"? The latter are nebulous notions, with no fixed or clear definition. Psychiatrists and psychologists would have serious conflicting opinions about these things and, as the view of these disciplines about the matter of homosexuality indicates, their thinking often is shaped by political pressures and the desire to conform to mainstream thinking for professional advancement.[115] Moreover, general rules about the development of children are hard to come by. Individuals are very different, and it is those who are closest to them—and have a unique parental affection for them and naturally desire the best for them[116]—who will generally have the best insight into this.

Under the Ohio statute, a "neglected child" is defined, *inter alia*, as one "[w]ho lacks proper care because of the faults or habits of his parents, guardian, or custodian," or "[w]hose parents [et al.] neglect or refuse to provide him with proper or necessary subsistence, education, medical or surgical care, or other care necessary for the child's health, morals or well-being" or "[w]hose parents [et al.] neglect or refuse to provide the special care made necessary by the child's mental condition."[117] There are two other sections of the Ohio child abuse/neglect statute that deal with a "dependent child" and a "child without proper parental care" (these are additional dimensions of the matter of neglect). A dependent child is defined, *inter alia*, as one who is "homeless or destitute," or one "[w]ho lacks adequate parental care by reason of the mental or physical condition of the child's parents [et al.]," or one "[w]hose condition or environment is such as to warrant the state, in the interests of the child, in assuming the child's guardianship."[118] A "child without proper parental care" is defined as one "whose home is filthy and unsanitary; whose parents, stepparents, guardian, or custodian permit him to become dependent, neglected, abused, or delinquent; whose parents [et al.], when able, refuse or neglect to provide him with necessary care, support, medical attention, and educational facilities; or...fail to subject such child to necessary discipline."[119]

These provisions present many questions. What is "proper" parental care? What is meant by "faults or habits" of the parents, et al.? Could these include behavior that while traditionally thought virtuous might now in the minds of some be viewed as unacceptable? Are parents' faults or habits, in any event, enough to deprive them of their offspring? What is "proper or necessary subsistence"? Too much sugar in the child's diet? Too little? Would designer jeans have to be bought for the child? We saw above the problem with trying to say what is appropriate medical care. It often becomes the subject of one physician's opinion, or viewpoint, about what may be harmful to a child. Often this involves mere speculative harm, or else may be a point that physicians or other medical authorities may disagree about.[120] What is "proper or necessary education"? Does it exclude homeschooling, since this is outside the academic norm and disliked by educational professionals even while homeschooled pupils are on average excelling academically and even outstripping many pupils in institutionalized schools?[121] What is included under neglecting to provide a child special care necessitated because of his mental condition? One problem is that there is much, much disagreement about what constitutes a "mental condition." For example, the eagerness to push children into some kind of medical or psychological treatment for hyperactivity, attention deficit disorder, and the like is very controversial. Are parents who balk at this neglectful? Would taking a "special needs" child out of a public school to teach him at home because he didn't make progress and the school failed to protect him from bullies—as happened in a case in Virginia—constitute neglect under the Ohio statute, as Virginia authorities intimated it was in that state?[122]

Under the "dependent child" provision, what is meant by "proper care or support"? Nice clothes (designer jeans, again)? Does a view about childrearing that an agency does not approve of constitute improper care? There is plenty of evidence to indicate that agencies around the country intervene frequently into families for that very reason, as in the cases in which parents choose spanking as a means of discipline. Agencies and juvenile court judges would probably hold that "proper support" includes emotional support. What is emotional support? What is an unsatisfactory physical or mental condition of a parent? The statute never says. Who is to determine it? What is included under the terms "condition or environment"? There is no definition given of this extremely broad phrase. What is a "filthy and unsanitary" home? Obviously, this is substantially a matter of opinion. For some, it would be utter squalor, for others a little dust on the coffee table. Social workers have held children to be abused or neglected because they have found clothes and papers laying around, sometimes even when the clothes have been neatly folded.[123] What is "necessary discipline"? Will not agencies be the determiners of it? Will it even be possible for parents to attempt to administer discipline if agencies are to say, essentially out of the blue and without warning, that a particular childrearing practice is unacceptable?

The above analysis of Ohio's statute, which is typical of child abuse and neglect statutes around the country, shows well the great definitional problems with the current statutes. It also suggests how difficult it is to draft a statute on the subject that even spells out clearly what the forbidden behavior is.

The Problem of Definition: Agencies, Social Workers, and Experts; Attitudes of the Child Protective System

If the statutes are vague as to what child abuse and neglect are, the agencies charged with enforcing them are no better. As Besharov states, "Existing standards set no limits on intervention and provide no guidelines for decision-making."[124] It is up to the social workers to decide what is meant by "abuse" and "neglect." Exactly how relative is their understanding of these terms is illustrated by the above case studies. It is also seen in statements and standards set out by the CPS itself. Pride, for example, cites two publications put out by the State of Missouri— viewed as one of the leaders in the fight against child abuse/neglect—one of which was partially funded by the U.S. Department of Health and Human Services. They speak of the following as reasons for state intervention into the family and/or reasons why parents have been deprived of their children: a child's neglected appearance and, on the other hand, over-neatness; disruptive behavior and, on the other hand, passive or withdrawn behavior; parents' being critical of their child; isolated families who don't take part in community or school activities; inadequate parenting skills; emotional neglect; unspecified neglect (which evidently is something other than non-provision of shelter, nutrition, medical care, or education); lack of supervision; and emotional abuse or neglect.[125] We have already spoken about the indefiniteness and lack of agreement about the meaning of many of these terms. It is clear that some are so broad that almost any behavior or action can fit into them, no matter how innocent. No doubt there *have* been genuine cases of abuse or neglect where conditions or phenomena such as these have existed, but they are obviously present in normal situations (e.g., some parents just want their children to be very, very neat; all kinds of children can be disruptive for an array of reasons or no clear reason at all; some children are by nature withdrawn, etc.).

In a very similar vein, Scott lists the following expanded list that the National Committee for the Prevention of Child Abuse specifies as signs of abuse: the child has a chronically unkempt appearance; the child is overly neat or a girl is dressed in an overly feminine way; the child is too loud or too talkative; the child exhibits shyness; low-self esteem is apparent from the child's actions or words; the child uses aggressive or passive behavior; there is a reluctance to participate in sports; there are noticeable signs of fractures, burns, bruises, cuts, welts, or bite marks; the child has sexual knowledge inappropriate for his/her age or acts out above maturity level; the child complains of pain or itching, or there is unusual bleeding or bruises are noticed in or around the genital area; the child seems constantly hungry or fatigued; there is a noticeable lack of supervision; there is delayed physical, emotional, or intellectual behavior; the parent is chronically late for meetings, picking up the child, etc.; the child exhibits chronic health problems; the parent fails to promptly repair the child's broken eyeglasses; there is a noticeable need for dental work; the loss of a parent due to death or illness (the remaining parent may become physically or sexually abusive as a result of the stress); the presence in the home of a stepfather; the child lives in an untidy home; the child is pulled out of school to be taught at home; the parent appears to suffer depression, apathy, or hopelessness; and there are reports from the child about occasionally sleeping in a parent's bed.[126]

In fact, Pride and Besharov both cite studies that show that social workers and others employed in child protective agencies do not agree among themselves about what is or is not child abuse or neglect.[127]

In spite of the uncertainty of agency personnel themselves about what is abuse and neglect, the above case studies and many other examples that one could cite give a rather clear impression that agencies interpret these vague and unclear laws decisively against parents, that parents are often not given the least benefit of the doubt.

The above case studies, the very fact of the existence of such vague and unclear laws (which have been so substantially shaped by childrearing "experts" and those working in the child protection field), and the application of these laws in such an anti-parent fashion in so many cases betrays in the CPS an attitude of hostility to the family—or at least one showing a complete lack of awareness of what it really means to be a parent or what family life really involves. Pride speaks about how so many social workers are either older, Caucasian females who have had a poor personal home life (divorced, etc.) and carry with them all the related emotional "baggage," or are young, Caucasian, middle- or upper-middle-class females, never married, and fresh out of college, with no experience or significant training in dealing with children.[128] Scott, writing a half decade later, concurs with this, and indicates that one additional group, which has not been known lately for its affection for the family, is now increasingly represented among agency social workers: homosexuals.[129] She points out further that a number of states do not even require caseworkers to possess college degrees in social work or a related field (in a certain sense that may actually not be bad since, as noted above, sociology and social work programs are notorious for their critical stance toward the family) and that the training, workshops, etc. that most caseworkers have to get on the job are sharply slanted against the family and parents (seeing all as actual or potential abusers, etc., as noted below).[130]

Apart from the question of hostility to the family, just how ignorant agencies often are to the complexities and dynamics of family life and the nature of children—indeed, the naiveté with which they often approach these matters—is seen in the very generalizations they are so well known for making. To be sure, this was observed above in the whole, unrealistic range of supposed conditions and "symptoms" that they believe indicate maltreatment—which, as we have said, are more typically seen in perfectly normal situations. It also is seen in their use of such "tools of the trade" as risk assessment forms, in which caseworkers give numerical rankings to how well parents measure up in various categories on the forms and then add up the total to supposedly determine how great a risk a child faces in the home.[131] Besides being completely subjective (Scott relates that while some agencies have guidelines of what conditions render a child "at risk," the assessments basically are left to the discretion of the individual caseworker[132]), it should not have to be pointed out that family life, with its uncertainties, difficulties, and burdens, is not something that can be easily and instantaneously reduced to a number on a sheet. Such an attempt to quantify a difficult problem that is not so intrinsically subject to quantification is a typical bureaucratic-type procedure. It is probably supposed to act as a kind of check on agency discretion or a means of helping to insure competent judgment and accountability by the bureaucracy. In fact, it creates surrealism about the entire subject of abuse/neglect and easily leads to false and unjust conclusions.

The agencies' naiveté in their understanding of children is further seen in some of the leading "doctrines" that they shape their policies and actions around. These include what Pride calls "the doctrine of the immaculate confession." This holds that children simply do not lie, especially when relating incidents of child abuse.[133] Anyone who has been around children much knows that they indeed do lie and they often relate things that never happened. Young children, especially, are well known for the stories and fantasies they relate. On the subject of children not lying specifically about abuse, the Institute for Psychological Therapies says bluntly, "There is no empirical evidence to support this claim. There have been no controlled studies to test it."[134]

An interesting, seemingly contradictory, corollary to this doctrine of the immaculate confession is that if a child, in spite of suggestions from interrogators, denies he was ever abused, or if he makes an accusation and later recants it, his denials and recantations are supposed to be rejected. This corollary has even sometimes been enshrined into the law.[135]

Another corollary of the immaculate confession doctrine, which also seems to contradict it, is the "Child Sexual Abuse Accommodation Syndrome." This syndrome holds the following: 1) sexually abused children tend to contradict themselves; 2) sexually abused children cover up the incident; 3) sexually abused children often show no emotion after the event; and 4) sexually abused children often wait a long time before making their accusations. As Pride puts it, according to this syndrome "all the evidence typically used to show no sexual abuse occurred...has now been captured to prove the very opposite."[136]

Another doctrine is what Pride calls "the doctrine of total depravity," which holds that all parents are actual or potential abusers, and that all home environments are abusive. Thus, all state interventions are justifiable. This doctrine corresponds with the changes that Carlson says (above) have occurred in the thinking of child savers over the past century. In actuality, it is not *all* parents who are the likely abusers. Abuse—*genuine* abuse—is uncommon in intact families, especially in the absence of such factors as alcohol or drug abuse. Abuse disproportionately occurs in cases of single parentage, foster parentage, "live-in" boyfriends, and the like.[137] It is also much more likely to occur in poor families than those that are better off economically.[138]

One can understand, when considering such guiding beliefs of the child protective system, why the especially outrageous cases mentioned above were taken so seriously by it.

The same confusion about what abuse and neglect are that we have said characterizes social workers in the agencies is shared by physicians—as perhaps some of the above case histories indicate—and judges. The same study involving social workers cited by Besharov above showed that an even higher percentage of physicians than the former were unclear about what constituted "child maltreatment."[139] Besharov also notes that the same survey, as well as a review of various court opinions, leads to the same conclusion about judges. They seem to decide cases of abuse and neglect that come before them on the basis of the context of the circumstances. Besharov says that they "are saying that, although they cannot define child maltreatment, they know it when they see it."[140]

The Ease of Reporting, the Mandatory Reporting Requirements, the Veil of Secrecy, and the Immunity Problem

Three other factors that contribute substantially to the great number of false abuse/neglect allegations and the ensuing agency intrusion into families are the ease of making reports to agencies; the legal pressures placed on various professionals and other occupational groups that encourage them to report in doubtful cases to protect themselves; and the blanket legal immunity given to the agencies and their personnel.

Regarding the ease of making reports, hotlines have been set up in many communities to take reports. These are well publicized in the local and national media, with the phone numbers frequently given. People are encouraged to report any suspected cases of abuse (without, of course, being provided a definition provided of what it is). If there is no hotline in a particular area, the local cps's number is readily available, and reports are encouraged. Reports can be made anonymously, and on hotlines generally are. All that is usually needed to trigger an agency investigation is an anonymous report. Hotline calls may or may not be screened and no attempt necessarily needs to be made to determine if there is any validity to a report, nor is any threshold of probable cause clearly required by law before an investigation is undertaken or even (generally) additional action taken, including removal of children. The result is that, in effect, anonymous reporters—not even cpa's themselves—are often deciding what the vague laws on child abuse/neglect actually mean. If their reports automatically give rise to investigations and cpa interventions into families, they essentially become the arbiters of child protection policy.[141] Most state statutes or the regulations issued pursuant to them mandate the investigation of all reports of even *suspected* abuse or neglect (though there may be some screening). Children in schools are taught about child abuse and the child protective system, and through different programs or types of courses, indirectly encouraged to be aware of anyone possibly abusing them, even family members, and to report them. Various community, professional, senior citizen, and other groups are specifically encouraged to be attuned to the possibility of child abuse and neglect, and to report their suspicions. For example, New York State mandated special child abuse training for physicians, nurses, and an entire range of medical professionals and other occupational groups some years ago as a condition for retaining their licenses. This writer was told that some training programs were strikingly anti-family. Speakers go around to different groups to talk about the subject, usually presenting the skewed and even bizarre perspectives of the child protective establishment discussed in this paper. One senior citizen group in Illinois, for example, was told to keep their eyes open for parents who *hugged and kissed* their children because they might be practitioners of incest.[142] Since the passage of the Mondale Act, there have been large-scale media and outreach campaigns, carried on by the CPS, law enforcement agencies, and different organizations, to "educate" the public about child abuse. These campaigns have sought to convince people of the "epidemic" of abuse and about the need to look out for and report it, but have done little to *truly* educate the public about what it is (which, as we have said, the CPS, judges, professionals, and lawmakers are not sure of themselves).

The laws respecting mandated reporters (we discussed above the legislative background to mandated reporting) encourage false allegations because they typically state that if such reporters fail to report even suspected abuse/neglect, they can be criminally prosecuted. In Ohio, for example, failure to make such a report is a fourth-degree misdemeanor.[143] The laws, then, have created a system driven to a certain extent by fear, much as we see in totalitarian regimes. Physicians, teachers, day care center workers and other mandated reporters make reports—often on the slightest pretext—because they figure that it is better to speak up than not speak up for the sake of self-protection. Some, it is true, probably do so because they share the suspicious stance vis-à-vis the family that permeates much of the child protective apparatus, but many do so simply to cover themselves. Probably as long as there are penalties for non-reporting, or at least penalties for non-reporting of something less than there is substantial certainty about, or the lack of a corresponding possibility of a penalty for making a false report (the mandatory reporters generally are given a statutory blanket immunity from suit for making false or even malicious reports), the problem of substantial numbers of baseless reports will continue.[144]

It should be noted that in addition to motivating untrue reports to official agencies against parents—which can have the effect of destroying their families—the legal pressure to report that is imposed on physicians, dentists, psychiatrists, psychologists, and other health care professionals has the obvious tendency to disrupt the relationship between practitioner and patient or client. This is a relationship that must be based on trust, and the legal mandates, arguably, sow suspicion. Moreover, this may discourage parents who need help in dealing with a difficult family situation from seeking help for fear that they will be accused. It may also discourage parents from seeking help, say, from psychologists or psychiatrists for their troubled children who they believe may need it for fear that the latter's problems will be blamed on them and they will be reported. The latter seems to be a reasonable fear in a time when abuse has become the ready explanation for so many things.[145]

Another factor that contributes mightily, in my judgment, to the abuses spawned by the statutes is the fact that all investigations and proceedings are kept confidential—even the names of the children and parents (except in the uncommon situation of criminal charges). Proceedings generally are closed to the public and reports of cases are not issued. This is because the area of law in question is mostly treated in the manner of American juvenile law generally. The view of recent decades in American juvenile law has been that matters should be kept out of the public view because then the children involved (i.e., juvenile offenders) will not be stigmatized, and so it will be easier for them to reform and go on to be upright and productive citizens. Numerous commentators on the problems of the child protective system have argued that this confidentiality—this veil of secrecy—encourages outrageous and even illegal conduct on the part of the agencies because they are protected from public scrutiny and accountability.[146] Along with the agencies and (usually) the juvenile courts not releasing information about non-criminal abuse/neglect cases, the parents involved similarly will seldom take their plight to the public. This in most cases either will be because of lack of access to journalistic organs or, more typically, fear that such action will spark a reaction from the authorities that will result in their losing their children. As Armbrister writes in *Reader's Digest*, "Confidentiality laws are supposed to protect kids; instead they shield bureaucrats."[147] We might add that they were supposed to protect families, too; instead, they provide a basis for assaulting them.

If the secrecy of the child protective system has helped prompt its abusive practices, the immunity its institutions and agents possess from either criminal prosecution or civil liability has made it ever more likely (this is in addition to the immunity which mandated reporters possess). This is typically a blanket statutory immunity, even when the agents have acted in bad faith or maliciously. Again, we note Armbrister's comment: "Police can be charged with crimes and hauled into court. Child-protective agencies should not be treated differently."[148]

Another incentive for the CPS to intrude upon parental rights is what Mary Pride calls the "one-sided liability" of the child abuse laws. Social workers and/or state agencies can be sued or even criminally prosecuted for *not* removing a child from his home who afterwards is harmed or killed, but generally are immune from suit when they wrongly remove a child, even without grounds and regardless of how much damage is done to the child or the parent-child relationship. So, they err on the side of excessive caution to protect themselves.

Regarding the juvenile courts, they are not a significant check upon the CPS. First, most CPS contacts with a family do not end up in juvenile court.[149] Second, as Professor Paul Chill of the University of Connecticut Law School has written, there are substantial obstacles faced by parents when confronting the CPS in juvenile court. He writes that in legal proceedings after a removal (generally in juvenile court) the CPS has tilted the legal "playing field" decisively against the parents as the burden is shifted entirely to them to show that they are fit instead of on the CPS to justify its continued control of the child.[150] Like the CPS operatives covering themselves, juvenile court judges often engage in a kind of "defensive judging." For example, they will issue an order to permit a child to be removed from a home or will uphold an "emergency" removal on the basis of weak evidence with the thought that it is better to err in the direction of excessive intervention because to do otherwise is more likely "to come back to haunt them."[151] As judicial officers, they are not subject to legal liability for a bad decision, but may face media attacks and defeat at the polls when they seek reelection. Chill tells us that the passage of the federal Adoption and Safe Families Act of 1997, while supposedly aimed at the good purpose of giving children who have been in the unstable and even dangerous (see below) foster care system for extended periods the chance for the permanency of adoption, has in practice made it easier for the CPS and juvenile courts to terminate the rights of the natural parents—even if unjustifiable. The Act created an incentive to do that because to qualify for federal funds the states are generally required to seek a termination of parental rights for any child who remains in foster care for 15 out of 22 consecutive months.[152] Thus, there is now a financial incentive for the child welfare system to secure adoptions for children in foster care—even if wrongfully there—just as there has been a financial incentive to put them in foster care in the first place, since programs to keep families intact generally cannot qualify for the same amount of federal funding as foster-care programs do.[153]

The Inattention to the Rights of Accused Parents Under the Current Laws, Dangerous Recent Legal Developments, and the New International Threat

Throughout our discussion, we have dealt with the implicit theme of parental rights. Numerous U.S. Supreme Court decisions in our history have acknowledged such rights[154] and, as we noted, they are rooted in our common law background—which in turn was shaped by the Western natural law tradition and Christianity. We here ask about another dimension of rights that obviously presents itself when considering false reports: the legal rights of the accused. In a lengthy article published in 1988, relying upon data cited in Pride's book,[155] I related the following about how few constitutional rights of the accused apply in child abuse/neglect cases handled exclusively by agencies or by juvenile courts. We summarize that information here. Pride compiled data about the civil rights of those accused of child abuse in each of the fifty states. She considered which states guarantee five basic due process rights generally given in criminal cases: the right to be informed of the charge while under investigation, the right to trial by jury, the right to access to records being kept about a person, the right to have an unsubstantiated record removed or not to have a record kept on file until after a hearing, and the right to challenge information kept on file about a person. Persons accused of non-criminal child abuse or neglect—most of whom are parents—had none of these rights in thirty-one states. Some states guaranteed one or more of these rights; none protected all of them. None of the fifty states required that the accused be told of the charges. Only one permitted a person to request a jury trial. Sixteen permitted access to records under at least some conditions, while fourteen protected against unsubstantiated records being kept in the file at least as a general rule, and fourteen permitted challenges to the record.[156] Another aspect of due process that also is not found in child abuse proceedings is the right to appeal, provided in state statues for both criminal and civil matters.[157] As Pride writes, even if on paper one has a right to appeal civil matters such as decisions in child abuse proceedings, he may not be able to effectively pursue that appeal. Appellate courts seldom make their own findings of fact; normally they accept the facts as determined at a trial court or hearing (in child abuse/neglect matters, it is usually a civil hearing) and will just consider questions of law. The rub here is that in child abuse/neglect proceedings one has no right to review the record in most states, as has been noted, and in fact, no evidence upon which to base an appeal may even have been presented at the hearing. Recall that state agencies really do not need evidence to conclude that abuse or neglect has occurred or to take away children or impose other sanctions, and hearing judges are generally not required to solicit it.[158]

A further fact about the constitutional rights of those accused of non-criminal child abuse or neglect was the view of the CPS and even law enforcement officials that the guarantee of the Fourth Amendment against unreasonable searches and seizures did not necessarily apply. We have already seen the wide latitude social workers have in removing children from their homes even without evidence of abuse or neglect; this in itself is a "search and seizure." In some states, when accompanied by a police officer, social workers have been able to force entry into a private dwelling. Often, however, social workers secure entry even when not entitled to by threats or deception (i.e., saying they have a right to enter without a warrant when they do not) or simply because parents do not know that they have a right to refuse. Also, once let into a home, a social worker has virtually *carte blanche* to look around for anything to build a case against parents. They can even do a strip search of a child to find evidence of sexual abuse.[159] The statutes do not require a warrant for any of this. They also usually permit authorities to circumvent judicial approval for their actions or for taking custody of a child if they believe the child to be imminently in danger (generally, without defining what this means)—and Chill says that this seldom happens except when such a situation supposedly exists.[160] We see below that, after not being willing to do so previously, courts in recent years have begun to respond positively to Fourth Amendment challenges to warrantless CPS entries into the homes of families.[161]

A new study of all fifty state statutes and pertinent agency regulations, of course, would be a major, extended undertaking and could not have been attempted in the course of preparing the present article. Still, I am not aware of any significant trend within state legislatures to extend such procedural guarantees and there has been only limited federal action in this area. I am also unaware of any judicial trend requiring greater protections, except (to some degree) in the area of search and seizure. Works after Pride's, such as Scott's, indicate that the above constitutional deficiencies still exist, by and large. She even discusses these other basic procedural rights, not included in Pride's above analysis but indicated by the case studies that she cites (some noted above), which are denied to accused parents: the right to confront accusers and to cross-examine the complainants, the right to use case law as a defense, the protection against double jeopardy, the right to be regarded as innocent until proven guilty, and the right to examine the evidence.[162] I might add that one is not protected against the use of hearsay evidence in these proceedings, statute of limitations protections have been eroded, and there is absolutely no sense that, in an era in which the constitutional right of privacy has been so strongly promoted (especially in other intimate matters), courts view it as having any application to what happens within the confines of the family.

While some of these protections that Scott contends are denied to parents accused by the CPS are self-explanatory or have been previously discussed, it is necessary to comment here on other ones. The right to confront is denied, first of all, by the fact that so many complaints are made anonymously, so the identity of the complainants is not even known. If the complainant is, say, a child's physician and the parents thus know his identity, they are still not generally afforded the right to confront him in a legal proceeding. Indeed, even in criminal child abuse cases, the law has been changed in some states to remove the right of the accused to confront a child witness in court for fear of the child being traumatized. The U.S. Supreme Court, after some initial hesitancy, has held that this is not in violation of the Sixth Amendment. Other legal innovations, which have changed traditional criminal law practices, have involved the abolition of both minimum age provisions in the law below which children are presumed incompetent to testify and the need for corroboration for a child's testimony to stand, and the greater willingness to allow hearsay testimony to be introduced in court. The latter includes not just out-of-courtroom testimony (i.e., videotaped testimony by children-victims), but also by third parties to whom children supposedly confided tales of their abuse.[163]

Scott speaks about double jeopardy because even if parents are exonerated by a criminal court, agency actions and proceedings against them in juvenile and civil courts may often still go ahead. Also, as noted above, criminal exoneration is no guarantee they will get their children back if the children have been taken away. It is true that American law has traditionally permitted this, and not considered it double jeopardy. Still, it gives one pause to wonder if this legal interpretation does not promote injustice, and so such a traditional approach to double jeopardy should perhaps be reevaluated. On the question of being innocent until guilt is proven, the above case histories have demonstrated that regarding the parents as guilty as soon as an accusation is made, even without any evidence, and then expecting them to bear the (sometimes overwhelming) burden of proving themselves innocent, is one of the major injustices in the operation of the child protective system.[164] It is true, again, that American law has provided the means for this to occur because it does not seek to apply the standards of criminal courts to juvenile matters. Nevertheless, once again, the injustice of this is evident from the many cases of false accusation like those above. The elimination of statute of limitations protection—wherein if one is to be charged, it must be done within a stated period of time, usually a few years, after the alleged offense occurred—has resulted in people being threatened with both criminal and non-criminal charges indefinitely. A cpa, for example, can commence an investigation and take action against parents, in many cases, for alleged acts happening years ago. Civil suits and criminal charges can be filed against parents or others for alleged abuse occurring decades before. Recent attention to the latter fact has come about as a result of the so-called "repressed memory syndrome," in which putative acts of abuse committed years ago and repressed by the person because of their dreadful nature are supposedly brought back into a person's consciousness with the help of therapy, hypnosis, and so on. The validity of the entire matter of repressed memory syndrome has come under considerable criticism from within the discipline of psychology itself.[165]

As indicated, there has been progress since Pride's 1986 book in establishing clear legal precedents that Fourth Amendment search and seizure requirements apply, and slight movement regarding other rights. HSLDA and such figures as constitutional lawyer Dr. Edwin Vieira, Jr. played a crucial role in securing these Fourth Amendment precedents. In the 1990s, HSLDA won major cases in Alabama and New York, while Vieira did so in Maryland. These cases have essentially held that agency social workers cannot enter a home without permission unless they have been issued a warrant by a judge, and that an anonymous abuse/neglect report is not sufficient grounds to justify issuing the warrant.[166] A watershed case was *Calabretta v. Floyd* in the Ninth U.S. Circuit of Appeals (West Coast) in 1999, where HSLDA successfully sued for damages on behalf of one of their member families for a Fourth Amendment violation by social workers. Since then, HSLDA reports that federal courts have increasingly upheld Fourth Amendment restraints on cpa's.[167] James R. Mason, III's paper in this volume discusses many of these cases.

There has been slight movement in the courts even on the related, but broader, probable cause question that anonymous complaints are insufficient justification to begin an investigation. One of the most notable examples is the 2003 *Cleveland County v. Stumbo* case in North Carolina, even though it happened also in the context of a search and seizure question.[168] Another case, melding together aspects of probable cause and search-and-seizure questions, occurred in 2009. Brooklyn Family Court in New York City held that an anonymous complaint was insufficient to establish probable cause to grant a court order to require a family to admit a CPS operative into their home as part of an investigation. The court did not apply a probable cause standard to the question of whether the cpa could commence the investigation in the first place.[169] In 2004, HSLDA stated that only sixteen states specified any standard in their child welfare laws that "comes even close to the constitutional requirement for 'probable cause.'"[170]

Also, the CAPTA amendments of 2003 require social workers to tell parents of the nature of the accusations against them on first contact.[171] These amendments also require that CPS operatives be trained about the constitutional and other legal rights of families.[172] States have not necessarily moved quickly in implementing these CAPTA amendments. By 2007, only 22 states had implemented these changes in some form.[173] Even some of these may not have completely or adequately implemented them.

Another area—not exactly on point, but related—where we have witnessed some measure of judicial vindication of parental rights has been in the aftermath of unwarranted removals of children from their family homes and placement in foster care. In 2007, the U.S. Circuit Court of Appeals for the Ninth Circuit held that parents may sustain a federal civil rights action for damages against a cpa for such a removal in the absence of a court order. In that same year, the U.S. Supreme Court refused to reverse a similar damage judgment in another case.[174]

The question is, why have we had this denial of basic constitutional guarantees? The answer is substantially found in the fact that child abuse/neglect matters usually do not find their way into the criminal justice system (this would most likely happen with sexual abuse cases, but then, if parents or other permanent caretakers are involved, it would be carried out simultaneously with non-criminal proceedings). As mentioned, they are treated under a state's juvenile law, or in a manner closely connected with it. In other words, they are civil matters but civil matters of a special type. As indicated above, juvenile court procedures have been set up to be less formal than normal court proceedings and the usual legal rules and guarantees do not always apply.[175] We have previously mentioned how courts are not usually responsive to overbreadth and vagueness challenges to child abuse/neglect statutes;

here we see the disregarding of an assortment of Bill of Rights protections. Why have American legislators, judges, and citizens permitted this to happen? The simple answer is that the child abuse issue—the entire matter of child maltreatment—has been one which in recent decades has whipped the country into a frenzy, that has caused people to throw reasonableness, good judgment, and basic fairness to the wind. Children are being harmed, so the response has been that we must *do something.* What has been done has occurred without careful reflection and without a judicious concern for the likely consequences—or even a willingness to take another look at the nature of the supposed solution once the consequences have occurred. In my 1988 article, I mentioned the following reasons as to why I thought this frenzy has occurred: social workers and state bureaucrats were trained in a university and professional context that is morally relativistic, anti-family, pro-statist, and pro-permissive parenting; the numbers of social workers with the background of divorce and poor personal home life and all the emotional "baggage" that goes with it (mentioned above) is at an all-time high; it followed on the momentum of the sexual revolution, which had helped to undermine the family in different ways and parental authority in particular by promoting permissive sexual practices and reproductive choices among minors without parental approval, and from that the step to more sweepingly undermining parental authority was not so great; the widespread practices of contraception and abortion, which were also part of this revolution, gave rise to anti-child and then resulting anti-family attitudes; readily available and resorted-to abortion and even sometimes infanticide—the ultimate violence against children—was bound to have be a kind of perverse example for some who were already "on the edge" (maybe due to alcohol or drugs) to stimulate them to engage in child abuse or neglect, even more so with the explosion of cohabitation and "blended family" arrangements when they are living with someone else's children who they have no personal attachment to—with the result that more actual child maltreatment occurred and led people to believe there was a veritable explosion of it; the subliminal guilt that many felt about having or taking part in abortion led some to look for an excuse and a cause (i.e., having an abortion is not as bad as hurting an actually born child, atoning for what one had done by aggressively protecting others' children); the same was seen with some who had allowed their own families to be fractured by divorce—which was now abundantly resorted-to—and their children to suffer for it (they reasoned that they at least had not *abused* them); the anti-natalist ethic that had taken hold meant that many fewer people had experience raising children or had only raised one or two long ago so they easily developed misconceptions that perfectly innocently parental behaviors were abusive or neglectful; and the anti-family influence of contemporary feminism, which emerged at roughly the same time as the movement for the current child abuse laws.[176] One must quickly add that, by the very nature of things, whenever someone hears about a child being hurt or not adequately taken care of, emotions overcome reason. Often people do not even take the time to determine if what they hear is true; they just want action taken. We, of course, live in a time of instantaneous electronic media and sound-bite reporting, which spreads such accounts far and wide to many millions, without bothering even to look a little further into the story.

American law has adopted what criminal justice professor Philip Jenkins of Penn State University calls "therapeutic values."[177] Such values have their roots in the thinking of the social work, counseling, and other "helping" professions, and of sociologists, psychologists, and other social scientists (social scientists have been increasingly influential in shaping public policy); their assumptions and understanding about human nature and society, however, are very problematic.[178] Jenkins says that therapeutic values, as respects the law, hold "that courts are in the business of enforcing social hygiene rather than imposing punishment." The current laws about child abuse and neglect were substantially shaped by categories of people who abide by such therapeutic values: "academics [in the fields mentioned], feminist theorists, therapists, pediatricians, children's rights advocates, and lawyers [who are working especially in this area]." He explains how those holding therapeutic values approach the role of law. Their views are contrary to the assumptions of the adversarial system of justice, which permit the accused to probe and try to disprove the testimony of an accuser in a public setting and hold that witnesses are to be believed only about specifics if they impress a judge and a jury with their credibility. These upholders of therapeutic values believe that the courts really "have no business regulating the actions of objective professionals such as social workers or medical authorities seeking to protect children." They think that they can correctly judge, from their professional understanding of the subject, that when a child or someone else has alleged that abuse occurred that it in fact did. To put obstacles—such as legal restraints—in the path of acting quickly to protect the child is to fail in their task to help him, to alleviate his suffering. One would not demand constitutional rights when visiting his physician, who can only have his interests at heart. How, then, should rights matter in something like child abuse, where the only concern must be therapeutic—to heal the situation, treat the victim, and separate him from the perpetrator until therapy can correct the problems of each?[179]

When we realize the nature of therapeutic values, we can understand why proposals have been made for such things as licensing parents, coercive "child abuse prevention" programs from a child's birth (in which "potentially abusive parents" are identified at that point and placed in "parenting programs"), and the creation of a national corps of "health visitors" to regularly go to each child's home until he starts school to check up on his parents.[180] It goes without saying that the devoted advocate of therapeutic values has little or no sense of the natural rights of parents.

While all of these legal problems are caused by the nature of both our federal and state laws, a new threat to the family has loomed on the international horizon which, if not approached properly by the U.S. Government, may render fruitless any efforts to correct our own laws— and may have the effect of extending the threat to families throughout the world. This is the United Nations Convention on the Rights of the Child, which was motivated by the thinking of, and drafted by, Western and Western-oriented "child-savers" and has now been widely ratified by nations around the world, some with reservations, although the U.S. Senate has not yet done so. A detailed discussion of the convention is not possible here. I will merely quote from a letter the Society of Catholic Social Scientists sent to all the members of the Senate in 1995, urging a vote not to ratify. The letter was primarily drafted by political scientist and journalist Dr. Thomas A. Droleskey and contributed to by this writer.

> It is clear that the Convention on the Rights of the Child seeks to subject parents to close bureaucratic supervision. Parents who do not educate or raise their children according to the dictates of the prevailing cultural trends will be subject to all kinds of civil and criminal penalties, if not the seizure of their children. This is a form of ideological totalitarianism.
>
> Article 12 of the Convention states that children have the "right" to express their own views freely in all matters. All matters? Child-rearing? Discipline? The fact there are some self-appointed child advocates, such as Hillary Clinton, who believe that children as young as *seven* years of age can assert legal rights indicates that it would be possible under the Convention for grammar school students to sue their parents in order to express their views. This is absurd. Children are children. They need to *learn* about life. They need to *respect* their parents. They need to understand the virtues of humility and obedience, of submission to lawful authority. Also, of course, they will not be able to sue or otherwise oppose their parents on their own. The state will do it for them, with "child advocates" supplanting parents and deciding what is best for children.

Article 13 asserts that children have the right to receive all kinds of information through the "media of the child's choice." Parents concerned about protecting the purity and innocence of their children would be legally barred from censoring the television watched in the home, the movies their children choose to watch, and the books they choose to read. And those parents who do not have a television in their homes might be forced to secure one in order to respect their children's "right" to receive information. Is it overkill to point out that child pornography laws would be invalidated by this article of the Convention? Article 17 extends this "right" to national and international sources in the media.

Article 14 discusses the right of each child to freedom of religion. This appears, at first glance, to be praiseworthy. The article, however, contains an implicit threat to the rights of parents to raise their children. Can a child who does not want to receive religious education sue his parents for abuse because the parents refuse to honor the child's wishes? Can parents who tell their children to engage in family prayers be judged guilty of not respecting a child's freedom *from* religion? This is an attempt on the part of the secularists to free children from the influence of parents who desire to pass along transcendent truths to their children.

Article 16 immunizes children from any degree of parental censorship insofar as correspondence is concerned. While confidentiality is an important part of correspondence, parents nevertheless have to monitor the activities of their children, particularly those in the adolescent years. Can one seriously suggest that a parent has no right to determine if his child is being solicited by a pornographer or child molester? Does a parent have no right to determine if his child is receiving contraband drugs through the mail? This is absurd.

Article 18 seems likely to encourage the displacement of parents in raising their children by the state as it calls for the expansion in the state role in providing facilities to care for children.

Article 19 provides the basis for the establishment of dangerous, coercive state structures to track and pressure parents who violate the Convention's notion of their children's "rights." In fact, Article 43 establishes perhaps the ultimate in distant, arrogant bureaucratic structures–an international committee of ten "experts" to oversee the progress of the Convention's implementation. In other words, ten individuals will dictate to the hundreds of millions of parents in the world how to raise their children.

It appears as though Article 30, which guarantees a child the right to use his own language, might sanction the use of profanity. A parent would be powerless to tell his child to speak clearly and nobly, never using any vile language. And Article 31, giving children the "right to rest and leisure," would make it difficult for parents to command

their children to do anything. All a child would have to do to avoid
chores or assignments is to say that he is entitled to rest and
leisure.[181]

The U.S. is one of a few counties that still has not adopted the
Convention. If it does, this is a serious matter because under the U.S.
Constitution (Article VI) a treaty (which is what the Convention is)
becomes the "supreme Law of the Land." The constitutions and laws of
every American state have to conform to and/or give way to a treaty.[182]
The laws of each state on child welfare matters would have to be
reshaped according to the Convention. As the above makes clear, the
powers of the state to intervene into the family and matters of
childrearing would be even more sweeping than they currently are. Since
international law now is seen as concerning individuals directly—and not
just a means of ordering relations among nations—the "rights" specified
by the Convention could be effectuated by children directly against their
parents. Children would seem to be guaranteed a right to sue their
parents if they do not like the way they are raising them—or, more
precisely (as the above letter suggests), parents would be sued by any
number of "child advocacy" organizations that would rise up in greater
numbers even than now to help "vindicate" children's internationally-
guaranteed rights. There is a great danger, even in the absence of the
U.S. Senate's continued unwillingness to consent to the Convention's
ratification, that the Convention may be thrust on the U.S. by judicial
action as part of the growing movement in international law circles in
support of "customary international law." The latter holds that "when the
vast majority of nations agree on a principle of law" it is binding on all
nations—"even without their consent." Customary international law
supposedly can also be fashioned by international law experts, such as
those from the International Law Association who work closely with the
UN. Since it has been ratified by most nations, the Convention would
seem to qualify as customary international law. In fact, one federal
district court already has held that on that basis it is binding on the
U.S.[183]

In Catholic circles, some have claimed that the Convention cannot be
problematical since the Holy See was one of its early ratifiers, The
context of the Holy See's support must be looked at more closely,
however. In my online column, "Neither Left nor Right but Catholic" in
2011, I pointed out that what the Holy See ratified was a document that it
saw as protecting the true dignity of children—both born and unborn—
not the anti-parent, anti-family manifesto it has turned out to be. In some
respects, what has happened with the Convention has been like what
happened after Vatican Council II in the Western world: false

interpretation and faulty implementation replaced the true meaning of the Council and its actions. In both cases, too, the distortion was/has been ideologically-driven and often orchestrated. Not long ago, Pope Benedict XVI called for a "correct application" of the Convention. As it was, when the Holy See ratified the document, it included a number of reservations, or clarifications about how it understands and interprets the Convention. Most critically, the Holy See said that it interpreted the Convention in a way that "safeguards the primary and inalienable rights of parents." It also interpreted such a provision as that calling for family planning and education services for children as only those that are morally acceptable (e.g., natural family planning), and viewed the Convention as a means of protecting the rights of the unborn child. If the Holy See had foreseen the troublesome interpretations of the Convention and how some on the international scene have used it as a wedge to justify a wholesale subversion of parental rights and regimentation of the family, one wonders if the Holy See would have ratified it at all.[184]

Children and Families Harmed by the Current Child Protective System

There are some who contend, usually denying the scope of the problem of false allegations, that the abuses of the child protective system—even the damage done to families—are the price we must pay to protect children from harm and lifelong damage. It is *also* evil, however, when even one person is falsely accused when something could have been done about *that*—to say nothing about a massive number of people. Only a committed utilitarian ("subject one person to injustice so that the community as a whole can benefit"[185]) would think otherwise. Be that as it may, the question is this: Does the current system succeed in protecting children? It is worth considering Besharov's comment:

> Th[e] high level of state intervention might be acceptable if it were necessary to enable child protective agencies to fulfill their basic mission of protecting endangered children. Unfortunately, it does just the opposite; children in real danger of serious maltreatment get lost in the press of the minor cases flooding the system.[186]

In other words, as Pride puts it, "If *all* parents are guilty, or could be guilty" (which, as we have said, seems to be the upshot of the current child abuse laws and agency attitudes) "then resources end up spread thinly. There is no way to separate the criminals from the average Joes....A system that fails to distinguish crimes from unfashionable childrearing practices cannot protect children."[187] After all, state agencies have only so many personnel—they frequently complain that they are understaffed and overworked, even while justifying more and more intervention into families—and funds do not flow so freely in a period of governmental belt tightening. The unprecedented high level of intervention into families has not produced particularly impressive results in protecting children. In 2000, Besharov cited studies revealing that in the then roughly 25 years since the enactment of CAPTA 30-55% of deaths due to abuse or neglect involved children known about by a child protective agency.[188]

Another way in which current practices threaten children is by consigning them in ever-larger numbers to the troubled foster care system—sometimes after taking them from their parents without good cause.[189] As with intervention into the family in the first place, Besharov writes that "there are no legal standards governing the foster care decision" and often no time limits as to how long children remain in what is supposed to be a "short term remedy."[190] The result is that children frequently are away from their parents for years, shifted from foster home to foster home. This by itself is one way that children can be harmed by foster care. As Besharov states, "Long term foster care can leave lasting psychological scars...it can do irreparable damage to the bond of affection and commitment between parent and child."[191]

A more obvious way that children are harmed by foster care is when they are placed in undesirable foster homes with potentially abusive and neglectful foster parents. Pride discusses cases of children being assaulted, neglected, and even dying in foster care and gives the startling statistic that the death rate for children placed in foster care in Florida is more than double that of children in the general population.[192] Pride also says that so-called "emergency shelters," run by state agencies for children to be placed in immediately after removal from their homes, have also been responsible for abuse.[193] In some places, allegedly abused and neglected children are actually placed in jail or a detention center while social workers try to arrange a foster placement. There, they are faced with real danger from juvenile or adult offenders.[194]

Scott, writing in the mid-1990s, gives some additional startling statistics: in Massachusetts, 60% of the state's criminals came from backgrounds of foster care or state children's institutions; in California, it is 69%.[195] Surveys conducted in 1986 and 1990 by the National Foster Care Education Project found that foster children were 10 times more likely to be abused than children in the general public.[196] Studies cited by Wexler's National Coalition for Child Protection Reform give a further disturbing picture about the treatment of children in foster care and

institutional care. One in Baltimore showed that the number of
"substantiated" cases of sexual abuse of children in foster care was four
times higher than in the general population. An Indiana study revealed
that children in group homes experienced more than 10 times the rate of
physical abuse and more than 28 times the rate of sexual abuse of than
those in the general population. A Georgia study found that 34% of
children in foster care had experienced abuse, neglect, or other harmful
conditions.[197] There are ongoing accounts of abuse in both the foster care
and state group home situations.[198] While there are many decent and
upright foster parents,[199] it is clear that some people become foster
parents for an economic motive. How much the latter truly care about the
children they take in or desire to provide adequately for them is
questionable; they know foster parentage can be lucrative and they seek
to exploit the system.[200] Not all the abuse in foster care is by foster
parents, however. Some is perpetrated by other foster children in the
foster home.[201]

As mentioned above, it is not just the unscrupulous or opportunistic
foster parent who brings a financial motive to the foster care system. It is
also in many cases the cpa's, since foster-care programs bring in more
funds than in-home programs do.

Another way that children are harmed by the system, even if they are
not taken away from their parents or are taken away only for a short
period of time, is by the psychological and physical effects and damage
done to their relationship with their parents. This is intensified in the face
of their sometimes undergoing long, repeated interrogations by social
workers—and the outright intimidation that sometimes accompanies
them—forced physical and sexual examinations in some cases to
determine if they have been sexually abused, and (essentially) forced
therapy by psychologists, counselors and the like. The Jordan, Minnesota
case related above is a vivid and extreme example of this, but it is all too
typical in the annals of child abuse law enforcement.[202] Incidentally, the
Society of Catholic Social Scientists' *amicus curiae* brief to the U.S.
Supreme Court in *Camreta v. Greene/Alford v. Greene* (2011), which
was drafted by the present author, argued that such interrogations could
be considered torture under prevailing international human rights law
and should also be banned under U.S. constitutional law precedent.[203]
Even short of that, a CPS investigation of an innocent family—perhaps
triggered by an anonymous report—can lead to emotional strain, anxiety,
fear, insecurity in children and their parents, and an increasing tendency
of children to be out of control. The children can become distrustful of
outsiders, neighbors, and those in authority. They can have their ability
to form attachments compromised and suffer psychological

consequences. Strains can also develop between the parents. Parental anger toward their children can result (the very kind of thing the CPS claims it wants to stop). The orderly flow of a family's life can be disrupted, and this is often not easily overcome (especially if it is facing ongoing CPS monitoring). Children are also obviously hurt by the financial harm that can occur to their families from extended legal battles with agencies. Sometimes, the strains on parents by unwarranted, ongoing CPS intrusion into the family lead to marital break-ups with the obvious harm that causes to children.[204]

A Generation of Criticism of Current Policy and the CPS, but Little Change

In an article I published in 2007, I surveyed the writings of the leading critics of the American laws on child abuse and the CPS.[205] Most of these writers have either published books on the subject or have published several noteworthy scholarly articles in law reviews or other journals. I discussed ten writers—some of whom have been referred to in this article—besides myself (the present article essentially presents my work on the subject): Douglas J. Besharov, a lawyer and one of the architects of CAPTA who later became by all accounts the leading critic of the CPS; Mary Pride, a noted Christian homeschooling author who wrote the first critical book-length study of the laws and the CPS in the mid-1980s; Brenda Scott, a journalist who wrote what may have been the second overarching critical book on the CPS a decade later; Richard Wexler, previously mentioned, has written extensively (including a book) on the topic and has for many years been involved in trying to reform child protection; Joseph Goldstein, Anna Freud, and Albert J. Solnit, distinguished scholars and professionals in the field of family studies who teamed up on two well-known books in the 1970s; Lawrence D. Spiegel, a psychologist who wrote a 1980s book exposing the CPS after being personally victimized by it; Dana Mack, whose book-length study in the late 1990s addressing various societal forces undermining parents and the family, was devoted partly to a critique of the false child abuse/neglect issue and the CPS; Allan C. Carlson, a historian of the family and culture who is certainly one of the leading pro-family scholars in the U.S. and who (as seen above) put the CPS into the broader context of the history of child-saving in America; HSLDA has both published numerous pieces about the threat from the CPS and has played a major role (as mentioned above) in litigation against the CPS around the country; and Paul Chill, a specialist in juvenile law who has written especially on the CPS's readiness to remove children from their homes and the lack of due process for parents.

These writers or sources came to a number of common conclusions and broadly agreed about certain matters or themes. Some stressed certain points and some others, and in spite of their common criticism of the current arrangements to prevent and address putative child maltreatment they disagreed about the value of the current CPS. Virtually all discuss over-reporting as a central problem, and the vague laws as a major cause. Most cite the figure of nearly two-thirds of reports being outright unfounded (although some suggested that the figure could be at the higher levels that we have seen, as more recent data has indicated). Most, explicitly or implicitly, indicate that the grounds for CPS intervention into families must be narrowed. Some address exaggerated claims of sexual abuse, specifically. Many explain how the current CPS, despite the word "protective," fails to protect many children who truly are in need. Some also speak about the problems of foster care. A number mention "defensive" social work, etc. and the one-sided liability issue concerning CPS operatives and mandated reporters. Most accuse the CPS of anti-parent and anti-family bias. Some of the writers mention the harm to both children and families by unwarranted intervention, and believe that the CPS is largely oblivious to it. Some note the confusion of the CPS itself about what constitutes child maltreatment, the very thing that it is supposed to be protecting against. Some speak about the problem of how even many "substantiated" reports involve only minor or insignificant matters, which most reasonable people would not consider truly to constitute abuse or neglect. Some speak of the problem of anonymous reports, and would like to see them no longer be the grounds for triggering a CPS investigation. The majority point to the fact that parents accused by a cpa have few due process or related rights. Several point to financial and other incentives that the CPS and those connected with it have in maintaining present arrangements. Some point to the lack of qualifications and experience of CPS operatives, even in the most basic matter of raising children. A few mention the suggestive and pressuring interrogation techniques used by the CPS and its therapists to get children to accuse their parents. A number offer similar advice to parents on how to go about their lives to try to avoid a CPS investigation or how to deal with one when it begins, and most present proposals for legal and CPS reform. A few call for using informal—instead of legal or governmental—means to deal with some maltreatment and to generally prevent it. A couple of the writers call for the dismantling of the current CPS and the substitution of other approaches to deal with child abuse; a few others indicate that there are fundamental, intrinsic problems with the CPS. I highlight below the particularly noteworthy points of each of these different writers.

The godfather of critics of the current child protective regimen, Besharov, does not oppose the existence of the current system of specialized governmental cpa's with their therapeutic, instead of outright coercive, focus. He believes that the current system—the "basic infrastructure of laws and agencies" largely spawned by CAPTA—has saved thousands of children from death or serious injury,[206] and he does not want to fundamentally change it. The main focus of his criticism has been the tendency of the CPS, as structured, to encourage massive over-reporting of abuse and neglect. The root of this problem, he believes, has been two prominent themes I have talked about: the vagueness of the laws and a lack of consensus among professionals and CPS personnel about what the terms "abuse" and "neglect" mean. In spite of this criticism, Besharov does not make a substantial legal critique of the child abuse/neglect laws. He does suggest that it is problematical that courts have refused to apply overbreadth and vagueness analysis to them.[207] He also says, revealingly (and there is not much doubt that he is correct here, since he was right there helping to fashion them), that it was not accidental that the laws are so vague about which parental behaviors are abusive or neglectful. The experts who pushed for CAPTA and its state legislative progeny sought laws that would be open-ended so as to, in their minds, make it easier to prevent child abuse and neglect. They sought "unrestricted preventive jurisdiction" to supposedly stop any *possible* child abuse. The laws, in effect, were set up to enable agencies and courts not only to track down abusers, but to supposedly identify *potentially* abusive parents and to predict whether parents would become abusive toward their children. Besharov says that this is "unrealistic," and no social worker, judge, psychologist, or clinician can predict with certainty that someone will become an abuser.[208] Even though he does not want to dispense with the CPS or perhaps even fundamentally change it, he gives the impression of an ineffectual and even counterproductive system. He mentions how reports keep increasing as substantiated cases keep decreasing,[209] how even most of the minority of cases in which abuse or neglect is "substantiated" involve minor matters (such as slapping and poor housekeeping).[210] Another significant point he makes was noted above: the disturbingly high number of children found dead from abuse whose situations were already known about by the CPS.[211]

Mary Pride was one of the first major authors to call attention to the distorted statistical information concerning child abuse, which this paper has discussed. She said that many statistics that are put out by organizations or reported in the media are only estimates or, as she puts it, "somebody's *guess*."[212] If anyone examined them carefully enough, he would have realized how outrageous some of the statistical claims have been: One source's estimates would have meant that over 200% of girls will be raped by age 18. The upshot of another source, which extrapolated from the typical claim that those who are abused will inevitably grow up to abuse their own children, is that the number of current child abusers would have been double the population of the U.S. and Canada at the time that she writes in the 1980s.[213] She identified the "doctrines" that I said above the CPS operates on.[214] She sees the arbitrariness caused by the uncertain legal standards and CPS confusion about what constitutes child maltreatment as being the basis of the problem of the massive number of false reports.[215] She points to a couple of the most extreme proposals that have come forth from some authorities as a way to deal with the presumed epidemic of child abuse: the registration from birth of all children in a health-care "home" and then the regular, mandatory monitoring of all households with children by various professionals, and permitting only persons licensed by the state to become parents.[216] She calls for an end to hotlines and to foster care as we know it, with a notion of "clan care"—where a needy child is taken care of by relatives or friends, as these situations were addressed earlier in American history—to take its place. She identifies as the causes of true abuse the anti-child attitudes spawned by such contemporary moral and legal developments as abortion, pornography, sexual infidelity, and no-fault divorce.[217]

Brenda Scott says that the hysteria created by the media, the mandated reporter laws, and the legal immunity of reporters have primarily been responsible for the over-reporting problem.[218] She also speaks about how the federal funding arrangements supporting foster care, as opposed to in-home treatment, stimulate the removal of children from their homes (she is also one of the writers who discusses the much greater likelihood of children being abused in foster care than in their own homes), and how the tendency in some places to assign certain prosecutors to focus just on child abuse cases and the availability of substantial government funding for therapists creates an incentive to try to find more abuse even if it is not there.[219] She accuses the CPS of systemic abusive behavior, including: the arrogant and overbearing treatment of parents by CPS operatives,[220] the suggestive interrogation techniques to get children to accuse parents of abuse,[221] illegal searches of families' homes by operatives, hiding behind confidentiality laws, and the effective use of self-incrimination when parents—often forcibly—are sent to therapists who then get them to essentially accuse themselves.[222] She raises the possibility—now confirmed, as we have seen—that the number of false reports could have been as high as 80%.[223] To be sure, it is possible that both Mary Pride and Brenda Scott generalize too much about some aspects of the CPS and its operatives' actions without presenting hard data, even while they point to practices and abuses that have been frequently seen and pointed to by other writers and critics.

I previously mentioned how Richard Wexler saw the statistics on child abuse reports breaking down, with only perhaps under ten of every 100 reports constituting genuine abuse. Anticipating the growth of the percentage of false reports to the apparent levels of very recent years, he, like Scott, said in the early 1990s that their number could be as high as 80%.[224] He gives such startling, hard statistics as how in one six-month period in Florida, 92% of the indicated determinations were overturned.[225] He believes that the reason some of the earlier National Incidence Studies showed an increase in child maltreatment was simply because they used a looser definition of the term and put more and more things into the realm of what it encompassed.[226] He is extremely skeptical of categories of maltreatment such as "emotional abuse," which the influential American Humane Association defines as children being "'denied normal experiences that produce feelings of being loved, wanted, secure, and worthy'"—a hopelessly subjective standard.[227] He, too, speaks about the structural bias of the CPS against family preservation, which is caused by 1) an ideology that downgrades the importance of the family and thinks that the state should play a significant role in raising children and 2) perverse financial incentives (i.e., the more abuse an agency finds, the more state money it gets to provide services).[228] Wexler, a journalist by profession, comments as Scott does that the media has aided in the disinformation about child abuse/neglect. The media played a significant role in making the public think that there was a crisis. This was because of its tendency to rush to supposed experts in the field, who usually had an anti-family bias and had developed media savviness.[229]

Goldstein, Freud, and Solnit wrote their most important material on this subject in the 1970s. They were early academic opponents of the children's rights movement and called for a respect for parental rights and a restrained approach to state intervention into the family. They called for a standard of non-intervention into the family unless "probable and sufficient cause for the coercive action has been established in accord with limits prospectively and *precisely defined* by the legislature." This would apply before even an initial inquiry or investigation could commence. Effectively, they called for the probable cause standard of the criminal law to apply in CPS investigations. A yet higher level of proof would be necessary for the CPS to proceed on to more intrusive stages of intervention. If the state does not have a means of helping the situation, it should not intervene and if it does have the means its intervention should be kept to the minimum necessary to deal with the situation. Goldstein, Freud, and Solnit recognized early on that children would be harmed by any infringement of "parental autonomy" and could create the very familial conditions that an intervention supposedly sought to stop.[230] Effectively, they understood the wisdom of the ages about such a matter. They seemed to have a preference for what I call for below: instead of the twilight area of the law that child abuse now occupies, genuine child abuse should be handled under the criminal law with its higher evidentiary standards. They also made clear that they would limit the definition of child maltreatment under the law to parents inflicting serious bodily injury upon a child or sexual abuse (something like corporal punishment would not qualify, nor would such vague notions as "psychological abuse" or "denial of proper care").[231] If Goldstein, Freud, and Solnit's standards would have been embraced by the early CPS in the decade the Mondale Act was first being put into effect, it is likely that the systemic abuses we witness today would not have emerged and child protection in the U.S. would have pursued a more reasonable course. When one considers the utopian-like ambitions of those pushing the Mondale Act, however, it is very unlikely that they would have accepted this.

Spiegel, like Scott, extends his critique beyond the CPS to prosecutors who work with them (even while, as mentioned, most accused parents never face criminal charges so prosecutors never become involved). He raises the other problem mentioned above that has helped to fuel false reporting: a societal attitude that has taken hold that believes that if one is merely accused of child abuse—especially sexual abuse—he necessarily must be guilty. There is also an attitudinal structure within the CPS itself that encourages over-reporting because of the belief of their operatives—which has taken on almost an ideological character within the CPS, but may not be true—that abuse routinely was not reported in the past. He emphasizes the lack of public and even legislative accountability of the CPS. He sees how the very structure of incentives in the CPS and associated prosecutorial authorities encourages an attitude of finding child maltreatment even if none is there: the more investigations done and the more prosecutions undertaken—even if unmerited—is the indicia of effectiveness. It is a "numbers game," much like those police departments that evaluate officers on the basis of how many arrests they make or traffic tickets they write. He does not speak of the one-sided liability of CPS operatives, but simply says that the agencies' fear of being seen as incompetent if they do not find abuse in a case motivates them to continue to investigate and keep it open for a prolonged period. They are more concerned about "covering themselves" than protecting children (as previously mentioned). He also mentions the overzealousness of CPS operatives and therapists, and also—he makes this evaluation as a psychologist himself—how therapists often do an inadequate job of assessing children so as to provide the CPS with conclusions they want.[232] As with a few other of these writers, he gives advice about what an innocent person should do if confronted with a CPS investigation. As part of this, he mentions that certain situations are especially ripe for false charges—as he found out personally—such as troubled marriages or cohabitation situations when children are present or single-divorced parent households where there are teenage discipline problems (teenagers have learned that to cry abuse can achieve a custody change that they prefer).[233]

Dana Mack's 1997 book, *The Assault on Parenthood*,[234] is a discussion of how many different contemporary societal forces undermine the role and authority of parents and threaten the family. While she sees CAPTA as valuable and seems to think that it has helped reduce child abuse—though she does not forge a precise cause-effect relationship—she indicates that the vague laws that it spawned have been the reason for the large number of false allegations.[235] Like Besharov and Wexler, she says that a very small percentage of actual cases of abuse involve serious danger to a child.[236] She also echoes Besharov's claim about the counterproductivity of the CPS: it is so deluged by false reports that it cannot adequately respond to the real cases of abuse. The one-sided liability of mandatory reporters is partially responsible for this.[237] The most striking fact she presents came out of hundreds of interviews and focus groups with parents done by the Institute for American Values, the think tank with which she is connected. Today's American parents take it for granted that the state has absolute power to monitor their families, shape their childrearing practices, and even remove their children from them.[238] She makes the point that advocates of reform of the child abuse laws and the CPS have not made much headway with politicians who are fearful of appearing to be oblivious to "teeming masses of suffering children," and says that change will not come until the "powerful elite" of therapists, government officials, and the media develop a more positive view of the family. Still, I believe that the fact that she says that the same parents who take state intervention for granted "seem to sense instinctively that child abuse is not as widespread as the media makes it appear"[239] offers hope for change in the future. After all, those parents are voters.

The social historian Carlson explains (as we saw above) how the
current CPS emerged from a history of what he—with Wexler—calls
"child-saving" in America, how it was shaped by other—larger—social
currents, and what current factors and perspectives are fueling it. Child-
saving efforts in America went back to colonial times, and later on were
seen in such efforts as the reform school movement, the use of summary
justice to seize and institutionalize children (even when they had
committed no crime), the juvenile justice movement, and finally the anti-
child abuse movement. Most of this was done at the local level until the
federal government began to expand its reach into more and more areas
of American life (on child abuse/neglect, of course, it did so with the
Mondale Act). The Constitution does not mention the family, and for a
long time federal constitutional law afforded no significant protections to
the family from the threats posed to it by the child-savers (until some
significant Supreme Court cases in the twentieth century). As mentioned,
he says that child-saving was done historically under the sanction of the
transformed legal doctrine of *parens patriae*. Carlson says that the
crusade against child abuse was influenced by the new anti-traditional
family attitudes that were taking hold among social scientists and social
workers and getting a hearing in the popular media (he is thus one more
writer who speaks about the role of the media in all this). The perspective
developed that there was something constitutionally wrong with the
family, and child abuse was said to be a significant part of this. In light
of this, the state laws that began to be changed before the Mondale Act
(mentioned above) featured troubling erosions of such traditional legal
protections as husband-wife and physician-patient privilege, the
presumption of innocence until proven guilty, and precluding a recourse
to the civil or criminal law for those falsely accused.[240] Contrary to the
claim of the contemporary child-savers that abuse is a universal
phenomenon, Carlson makes the point that within intact families (i.e.,
with both natural parents, married, present) it is very uncommon. It is
disproportionately high in female-headed families (especially where the
father of an illegitimate child from a current union or a live-in boyfriend
are present) and where there are stepparents. We noted this above, and it
is mentioned by Pride and some of these other writers. Carlson is also
another of the writers who anticipates the most recent data when he
writes, in the late 1980s, that almost 80% of abuse reports are unfounded.
He also points out that there are a number of realities that are ignored by
the CPS and other child-savers because they do not fit their
ideologically-fashioned paradigm: the abuse mentioned above in foster
care and institutional settings, "the growing problems of real neglect"
caused by the high divorce rate and phenomenon of latch key children,

and the link between child abuse and the abortion rate. He cites a noted Canadian study about the latter, and says that various conditions connected with abortion—"diminished restraints on rage, a devaluation of children, an increase in guilt, heightened tensions between the sexes, and ineffective bonding between mothers and subsequent children"— easily spill over into future abusive behavior. He suggests that the views of the "main players" in this area—the social work profession—have to change before there can be a change in policy and practice (his view here is similar to Mack's: the attitudes of an elite element concerned with this subject have to change before policy can change). He does not seem sanguine about this, however, as he says that since the 1960s the social work profession has overwhelmingly embraced anti-family, anti-middle class views.[241] I might just observe that the latter may seem a bit paradoxical, since it has sometimes been said that the CPS wants to impose middle class norms on the often lower-income families with which it deals.

HSLDA has been involved in much litigation against the CPS, especially growing out of contacts that their member homeschooling families sometimes have with it. They have especially been involved in critical Fourth Amendment litigation concerning the warrantless entry of CPS operatives into private homes pursuant to (often anonymous) complaints. That is the topic of James R. Mason, III's paper in this volume. Homeschoolers have particularly been easy victims because of anonymous child abuse hotlines around the country,[242] and they have faced a range of (often ridiculous) allegations.[243] HSLDA advocates eliminating anonymous reports as a basis for starting a CPS investigation (or at least establishing that such reports should not be sufficient grounds for a judge to order removal of children from their homes or grant a search warrant),[244] clarifying the meaning of "abuse" and "neglect" in the laws, and, of course, eliminating any suggestion that homeschooling is a form of "educational neglect."[245] HSLDA worked successfully for the changes that were made to CAPTA in 2003 that require CPS operatives to inform parents on first contact of the nature of the allegation against them, that they undergo training in the Fourth Amendment and other constitutional protections of parents, and that citizen advisory boards be set up to hear complaints against overly aggressive CPS operatives.[246] Like a number of the writers, HSLDA provides practical advice to parents about what to do when a CPS operative shows up at their door, urging them to stand up for their Fourth Amendment rights and alerting them about the best ways to cooperate without allowing the operative access to their homes and children.[247]

Paul Chill's writing focuses especially on the CPS's removing of children from their homes in the face of allegations of abuse. He echoes some of the other writers in saying that the CPS is not sufficiently attentive to the harm done to children and families by unnecessary removal (including the dangers of foster care).[248] He also gives a unique insight into three different topics (which have been discussed above, referring to his writing): 1) how in legal proceedings in juvenile court following a removal, parents are at a considerable disadvantage regardless of their innocence;[249] 2) just as there is routine "defensive social work" with the CPS erring against parents because of the incentives discussed, there is routine "defensive judging" in juvenile court with judges mostly siding with the CPS;[250] and 3) how the Adoption and Safe Families Act of 1997, as noted, has had the effect of making it easier for the state to terminate parental rights even when not merited.[251]

Proposals for Legal and Policy Change

In my 1988 article, I called for the enactment of a number of legal reforms that would protect innocent parents from the abuses of the CPS. They were as follows. First, the anonymous hotlines, which have been an open door to false reporting, should be eliminated. Secondly, I said that the laws should be altered so they spell out more specifically what "child abuse" and "child neglect" are. I called for the elimination of provisions that infringe or could be interpreted to infringe upon the parent's right to choose the childrearing practices he or she wishes, including reasonable corporal punishment. Thirdly, child abuse and neglect should be treated as criminal matters to be dealt with in regular courts, where accused persons have the full range of due process and other constitutional rights. I said that due process guarantees should be established by statute for persons involved in any related matters that are indeed more appropriately dealt with in juvenile court. For example, non-criminal neglect should perhaps receive a hybrid status under the law—not a criminal matter, but no longer treated as a civil matter—but with the accused person's constitutional rights fully protected. I insisted that part of the reform in this area should include permitting accused persons to waive confidentiality in child abuse proceedings; sometimes the very thing needed to protect rights and guard against state abuse is the watchful eye of the public. Also, strict requirements should have to be met before state agencies can remove children from their homes. Children should not be removed, even temporarily, unless authorities can *conclusively* prove in a proceeding before an impartial judge that they are in danger. In the case of emergency removals, authorities should have to supply this proof to a judge within twenty-four hours, or automatically be required to return the child. Actually, I said, perhaps Pride made an even more preferable proposal: simply removing the *perpetrator*, as would be done with any criminal offense. I also said that government agencies should not be allowed to retain records of unsubstantiated or false complaints. The statutory changes of recent decades that have permitted the admission into court of hearsay evidence and videotaped testimony (and generally give the child the overwhelming benefit of the doubt against the accused) should be repealed; child abuse should be dealt with like any other crime. Next, I called for safeguards to be put in place to insure against manipulation of children by prosecutorial authorities, psychologists, and other interrogators. I said that perhaps besides providing free legal counsel for needy accused persons in child abuse cases,[252] the state should also provide free psychologists and psychiatrists to counter the ones that the CPS brings in.[253]

I also said that the laws should be changed to outright discourage and even make it risky for people to file false and malicious child abuse complaints. The laws should require something like probable cause be established before an agency has the authority *even to commence an investigation*. This seemed reasonable because, after all, we are dealing with the natural rights of parents and with an intrusion into the most basic human institution, the family, and one of the most intimate of human relationships, that between parent and child. If someone makes a malicious or intentionally false complaint, I said that he should be liable to suit in tort by the accused party. If a person has to face a trial or other legal proceedings as a result of a knowingly false or malicious charge of child abuse and is exonerated, reversal of attorney's fees should be permitted. Generally, American law does not permit this, but exceptions have been made when a person is the victim of some particularly outrageous conduct.[254]

Finally, I insisted on reversing the "one-sided liability" discussed. Social workers and agencies should not be subject to suit or prosecution for non-removal unless their conduct is clearly outrageous and/or in bad faith. I said that they *should* be subject to suits by parents and legal guardians for wrongful removal, but only if they violate legal provisions—presuming the laws would have been tightened up to prevent the easy removals which are now occurring—or act recklessly or maliciously. Local or state prosecutorial authorities should also be subject to suit if they act in such a manner.[255]

It should be noted that so far no significant trends have emerged to promote the adoption of any of these changes (I mentioned some very limited movement in the probable cause area). The increasing search and seizure protections are encouraging, and the 2003 CAPTA amendments helpful but (as mentioned) limited. Another positive development in certain states has been the enactment of statutory changes which subject to criminal prosecution anyone who knowingly makes a false child abuse/neglect report.[256] The latter probably resulted from the substantial number of false abuse allegations that were being made in child custody battles connected to divorces.[257]

In Scott's book, she lists the following additional sound proposals for change: the required videotaping of all interrogations of children by authorities and the making of these immediately available to the accused; the presence of a friendly adult advocate to be with the child (presumably someone of the parents' choosing) when being questioned; the setting up of independent review boards to hear complaints of the accused (this in some form was done by the 2003 CAPTA amendments); insuring that relatives receive the first consideration in a foster care placement if children are removed from their home, that parents be allowed daily phone calls and visits to children removed, and that if more than one child is removed from a home they be kept together; the elimination of the routine practice of some agencies of forcing children in every case taken up by the agency to undergo therapy; and the elimination of intrusive searches and physical examinations of alleged child-victims.[258]

All of the above ideas are worth pursuing; they would certainly go some distance toward ending the grave abuses and injustices of the system. I came to the conclusion, however, after a decade more of observation and reflection following my 1988 article, that the best course of action—and one that I believe is attainable given the deepening suspicion of government and the heightened attention to this whole problem—is simply to dismantle the current CPS and scrap the child abuse and neglect laws that are now forty or more years old. Specialized cpa's have not proven that they are needed; there is no evidence that the problem of child maltreatment would be dealt with any less effectively in other ways.

In an article I wrote in 2005 (which grew out of a paper I presented at a Society of Catholic Social Scientists seminar on Capitol Hill in Washington, D.C.), I elaborated on why I think that the CPS is conceptually and structurally incapable of carrying out what it claims its purpose is. I said that its basic problem is that it is a *therapeutic* system—although coercively therapeutic. Its structuring and the very nature of that kind of system suggests the following drawbacks: 1) it sees true child maltreatment too much as a condition to be remedied by treatment, instead of a moral evil and criminal act to be punished; 2) while it commendably believes in prevention, it wrongly believes that state action can universally bring that about without also creating universal regimentation and a monstrous tyranny; 3) it is routinely manned by people whose education and training has not made them particularly sympathetic to the family or aware of its basic, natural, and irreplaceable value; 4) the confusion among CPS operatives about what constitutes child maltreatment also reflects their training in contemporary relativistic social science with its ever-changing notions, theories, and even definitions for words (so, even with more precise legal definitions of abuse and neglect, we could expect cpa's would still finds grounds to infringe on legitimate parental actions); 5) it is beleaguered by the rigidities, limitations, self-interestedness/self-protectiveness, and inanities of bureaucratic institutions everywhere; 6) it is beset by the basic contradiction of providing social services and assistance on the one hand and being an enforcement arm on the other—and not only are social workers not trained for the latter, but help and coercion do not readily go together under the same institutional roof; and 7) a specialized agency, with a particular focus, often goes to an extreme in carrying out its mission. It tends to see problems where they do not exist, and overemphasizes the significance of those that it finds. It easily loses its sense of balance, and that tendency is not moderated by additional perspectives or factors that otherwise would come into play.

In short, what I have shown about the CPS is that it does not know clearly what it is supposed to stop, a big percentage of what it investigates is nothing that needs to be investigated in the first place, it ends up hurting children with its interventions supposedly on their behalf and even sometimes fails to stop true cases of maltreatment, is inattentive to parental rights, its failures have been ongoing and consistent, and its attempt to monitor and control vast numbers of people in the minutest of details about how they conduct their lives and raise their children is more than a touch of totalitarianism. It is difficult to conclude that such a system should be continued.

In my judgment, the entire matter simply ought to be turned over to the criminal law—in spite of the police and prosecutorial abuses detailed above in the Jordan and Wenatchee cases, and more recently the Cressy case—and dealt with by current or expanded statutes concerning murder, assault, rape, statutory rape, incest and the like. Carefully drafted criminal child neglect statutes—spelling out *clearly and unambiguously* what the proscribed offenses are, and not including anything resulting from poverty or disadvantage or concerning reasonable parental educational choices—ought to be added to address this aspect of the problem. It must be remembered that this is the primary way the law dealt with child maltreatment for most of American history, and there has been no showing that it was not adequate. Moreover, besides their stronger investigative skills, law enforcement personnel tend not to have been schooled in the intellectual environment of academic social work and related fields that is laced with an anti-parental authority and anti-traditional family ideology and the ethos of "we 'experts' know better." Also, some of the abuses by law enforcement agencies would likely be eliminated if their personnel were no longer trained in this area by the CPS and if there were not cooperative inter-agency arrangements such as those seen in the current child advocacy center movement through which the "CPS perspective" is disseminated.[259]

Ending the current laws and system would also largely overcome the vagueness about what abuse and neglect and all related categories are and help insure that the law would only treat as abuse or neglect actions or omissions which the community—and common sense—widely regard as such. It would also, correspondingly, guarantee that families not be targeted for innocent or trivial actions. It would, additionally, get the state out of the business—for which it has no competency—of dictating to parents preferred methods of childrearing. Further, all of the usual constitutional protections would also almost automatically attach. It would also insure that the *truly* guilty would be punished, as most people think they should be, instead of given therapy (as too often happens).[260]

As I have indicated, an epidemic of abuse and neglect did not exist before the introduction of the current laws. While almost certainly there is not an epidemic today either, there *is* probably more child maltreatment than there was, say, seventy-five or a hundred years ago (this has occurred *despite* the existence of the current laws and child protective apparatus). This is for the same reason—as some scholars, professionals, and politicians and the general public are slowly coming to realize—that there is more illegitimacy, divorce, abortion and the like: the social, moral, and spiritual decay which has occurred in America and the general decline of the family that is part of it.

There is one *fundamental* legal change in the states that would also help protect parental and family rights. This involves the movement for parental rights constitutional amendments that has been witnessed in some state legislatures in recent decades.[261] Even though the generally broad language of constitutional amendments does not afford the specific protections of statutes, and this kind of amendment would probably be most geared to protecting the educational rights of parents, it would give a renewed emphasis to the old common law preference for parental rights. It would also afford a fundamental legal principle that could be appealed to in courts to at least help ameliorate especially serious threats to parental rights, and help to re-insulate the family from the excessive reach of the state. There is now also a movement underway on the national level for a similar amendment to the U.S. Constitution, which would likely help to eliminate the blind spot regarding the family which Carlson argues is found in federal constitutional law. The movement has been fueled by the specter of the Convention on the Rights of the Child (discussed above) and the position of Justice Antonin Scalia in *Troxel v. Granville* (2000) that parental rights cannot be constitutionally enforced because they are not specifically provided for in the document.[262] Curiously, such an amendment has at least the potential to gain broad support. General constitutional language in support of parental rights might be hard politically for lawmakers to refuse to support, especially when it would not be clear about all the specific areas to which it might apply.

On the international level, in light of the above analysis, it goes without saying that the U.S. Senate should not ratify the U.N. Convention on the Rights of the Child (it was pushed by the Clinton Administration, but not by George W. Bush's and now under the Obama administration there has been a renewed effort to get it ratified). If approved, as a treaty it would become the supreme law of the land and, unless specific reservations were made to it, would supersede American domestic law that, at least in certain cases, would seem to afford more protection to parental rights. Even if American judges would not be ready to embrace some of its more extreme principles, it is likely that its overall effect would be to further erode parental rights.[263]

While legal change would surely eliminate a major part of the threat posed to the family in this matter, it would be a delusion to believe that it would entirely eliminate it. There will still be false abuse and neglect reports made to the police (who would then become the major enforcers) and in response to public pressure other public policies would probably be enacted, as they have been throughout American history, which will tread on the legitimate, natural law prerogatives of the family. Thus, there must be a reevaluation of the nagging traditional attitudes of Americans that make them think that they are justified in telling their neighbor that they know better than him about how to raise his children. Being "thy brother's keeper" does not mean interfering with his legitimate childrearing efforts—even if monitoring families and excessively regimenting the lives of individuals both have a long history in the U.S.[264] People must remember that they "should remove the plank from their own eye" before insisting that their brother "remove the speck" from his. Indeed, the CPS is very much an extension of this flawed attitude: the *main thing* it winds up doing is not fighting child abuse and neglect in any true sense of the word, but imposing its views about childrearing practices. The entire problem of false child abuse/neglect allegations and the animating attitudes of the CPS indicate a need to reinvigorate a spirit of liberty that has long since ebbed in the United States, and that will not be easy.

The monitoring and regimenting of families' childrearing practices has to be put into the context of the expanded, intensified attempts by different levels of government in recent decades to monitor and manage many aspects of people's lives generally. This confirms Alexis de Tocqueville's expectation that as time went on the citizens of democratic republics would continue to be free in big things—e.g., they would continue to elect their leaders—but in the everyday things of life they would become increasingly regimented by government.[265] With the issue of child abuse/neglect and the CPS, that regimentation occurs to a massive extent on one of the most intimate aspect of life. Other recent trends are also manifested in this issue. One is the view, going back to the Progressive Era, that holds that technical experts of some sort simply know better, and so should be the ones to manage our politics, society, and lives.[266] So, if one has a social work or counseling or human services degree, he or she almost by definition is seen as more qualified even than parents to say how a child should be raised—irrespective of: 1) the fact that technical knowledge is not by its nature so pertinent to something like childrearing; 2) the unique affection, noted above, that a parent has for one of his or her own and the connatural knowing that a parent gains for one in his or her care, so as to know best how to address the needs of that particular child; and 3) whether he or she has any direct experience in childrearing.[267] Finally, this issue exemplifies the trend of government in recent history to give people help but only with a *quid pro quo*. So, since most of these cases may actually be poverty cases, government gives financial assistance or social services but says that, "we think you are being neglectful, so we have to manage your childrearing or even take your children away and raise them ourselves."

I am inclined to agree with Mary Pride and Dana Mack that when parents need to seek assistance with childrearing and when our political society wants to address what has gone into this big grab-bag of "child abuse," "child neglect," "child dependency" and the like (at least when they are not truly serious and criminal acts), informal, traditional "family and community support structures," instead of government agencies, should be turned to.[268] These would include the extended family and friends, but also churches and clergymen, voluntary associations (it should be within this context that social workers do their main work, non-coercively, to assist families in need), family physicians and certain other professionals (once they have had the legal strictures removed from them that encourage them to over-report abuse and neglect). If the argument is made that the family cannot often be relied on because it is too weak, then efforts should be undertaken to strengthen it (and probably there is little that can be done effectively by government—in contrast to these other entities—in this regard). If the reliance were to be mostly upon informal mechanisms, there is no evidence that the abuse/neglect problem—where it genuinely *does* exist—would get worse, and we would gain the enormous advantage of greater parental and family freedom. At least good parents would then not be stymied and threatened in the name of alleged "child protection." The last paragraph of the article I wrote in 2005 on false abuse/neglect and the CPS makes this point vividly: "If child protection laws that encourage the neighborhood busybody to spy on and report parents were eliminated, maybe we would begin to see the restoration of a true neighborly spirit of looking out for children, knowing and interacting with the family next door and down the street, and kindly and charitably assisting them and bringing problems to their attention. A kindly but firm Widow Douglas and Miss Watson taking care of an abused Huck Finn is much preferable to a cold, impersonal, distant government agency. It perhaps *does* take a village to raise a child, but not in the sense Hillary Clinton and others mean. Rather, it means community respect and support for the family, helping parents—while fully aware of their prior natural rights *as parents*—in their difficult God-given task of childrearing instead of interfering with and undermining them."[269]

I am not sanguine about change in this area being brought about easily. As Richard Wexler wrote me in a personal communication, most people know what needs to be done in the field of child welfare "but decline to face up to it or to act on it."[270] As Mack suggests, legislators and other public officeholders are afraid to make changes in the child abuse laws or the CPS because they are afraid of appearing to the voting public to be "soft on child abusers." This means an even more intensive educational effort by the Wexlers and Scotts and HSLDA, et al. to help the public to see that the image created by the media and ideologically-driven professionals and academics is not the correct one. With so many parents now attuned—as Mack says—to the fact that the state is trying to regiment them, their efforts may bear more fruit in the future than they might expect. It also means ongoing—even accelerated—efforts by the HSLDAs, the Family Defense Centers,[271] etc. to further parental rights and legally limit the sweeping, arbitrary powers of the CPS. It also means a consideration of completely legal mass public action to convince public decisionmakers that the CPS needs to be changed or, preferably, eliminated in its current form. Besides more citizen communication and lobbying with their legislators to secure legal change and media criticism of the current laws and CPS (e.g., in "letters to the editor" columns in newspapers), anti-CPS rallies in state capitals and in Washington would call broader attention to a systemically abusive system.

Finally, I must drive home the point again that whenever religious and moral sanctions decline, as has happened overwhelmingly in America in the last few generations, moral problems such as child abuse and neglect almost inevitably become greater. The positive law then tries to pick up the slack. Government becomes bigger, more active, and more intrusive in trying to solve the problems—and usually creates an entirely new set of problems and abuses. The most reliable, long-term guarantee for protecting parents from false abuse/neglect charges and similar threats—and to protect children too—is to simply have very little actual child maltreatment and very little desire among individuals in the population to do it. This will involve men's renewing the effort that classical antiquity and the world's great religious traditions have all told us was central, but which democratic man by his nature finds difficult and the liberalism which has completely subsumed the American tradition has little time for: to put the soul in right order. As Plato, Aristotle and other great political thinkers observed, law will always be needed, but a community of good men will need relatively few laws. We can put the current American condition, illustrated by the problems of child maltreatment and the mountain of false accusations, in perspective when we look back to the words of the greatest commentator on the American democratic republic, Tocqueville: "Religion is...needed...in democratic republics most of all. How could society escape destruction if, when political ties are relaxed, moral ties are not tightened? And what can be done with a people master of itself if it is not subject to God?"[272]

Notes

[1] See Douglas J. Besharov, "'Doing Something' About Child Abuse: The Need to Narrow the Grounds for State Intervention," *Harvard Journal of Law and Public Policy*, vol. 8 (Summer 1985), 543-544, quoting 42 U.S.C. §§5101-5106 (Supp. V 1975) (CAPTA). CAPTA has subsequently been amended—there were some significant amendments in 2003—but its basic features remain largely unchanged.

[2] On the latter point, see Stephen M. Krason, *The Transformation of the American Democratic Republic* (Piscataway, N.J.: Transaction Publishers, 2012), 418.

[3] Besharov "'Doing Something'...," 545; Stephen M. Krason, "Child Abuse: Pseudo-Crisis, Dangerous Bureaucrats, Destroyed Families," in Stephen M. Krason and Robert J. D'Agostino, eds, *Parental Rights: The Contemporary Assault on Traditional Liberties* (Front Royal, Va.: Christendom College Press, 1988), 167-173.

[4] Besharov, "'Doing Something'...," 543.

[5] Sophie Quinton, "Senators Ask Whether All Adults Should Be Required to Report Child Abuse," *National Journal* (Dec. 13, 2011), http://www.nationaljournal.com/healthcare/senators-ask-whether-all-adults-should-be-re-quired-to-report-child-abuse-201 11213; Internet (accessed Dec. 28, 2011).

[6] Allan C. Carlson, *Family Questions: Reflections on the American Social Crisis* (New Brunswick, N.J.: Transaction Publishers, 1988), 242. This position of the common law reflected its strong endorsement of parental rights, which it viewed as "fundamental" (see Bruce Hafen, "Children's Liberation and the New Egalitarianism: Some Reservations About Abandoning Youth to Their Parents," *Brigham Young University Law Review* [1976], 605), "sacred" (see *In re Hudson*, 126 P.2d 765, 771 [Wash., 1942]), and "natural" (see *People ex rel Portnoy v. Strasser*, 104 N.E.2d 895, 896 [N.Y., 1952] and *Lacher v. Venus*, 188 N.W. 613, 617 [Wis., 1922]).

[7] Carlson, 242.

[8] Ibid., 243.

[9] Ibid., 244-245.

[10] Ibid., 244.

[11] Ibid.

[12] For example, one thinks of the Doris Duke Charitable Foundation and the Child Abuse Prevention Foundation in Southern California. Some of the efforts of the latter, which was founded by restaurant magnate Jackson W. Goodall, were much criticized for creating undue hysteria (see *The Washington Times*, Nov. 7, 1993, A1, A10).

[13] 4 Wharton Pa. 9, cited in Carlson 254.

[14] Ibid., quoted in Carlson 245.

[15] Carlson, 245.

[16] For a discussion of the grounding of the U.S. Constitution in the English common law background, see Russell Kirk, *The Roots of American Order* (Malibu, Calif.: Pepperdine Univ. Press, 1974), 187, 191-192, 368-374.

[17] Carlson, 242-243, 245.

[18] Ibid., 247.

[19] Ibid., 248.

[20] For a good defense of the notion of the natural rights of parents to exercise authority over their children grounded on commonsensical and philosophical argumentation, see Raphael T. Waters, "The Basis for the Traditional Rights and Responsibilities of Parents," in Krason and D'Agostino, 13-38.

[21] Carlson, 248, quoting Miriam Van Waters in her book *Parents on Probation* (N.Y.: New Republic, 1927).

[22] On such licensing proposals, see, e.g., Jeane Westin, *The Coming Parent Revolution* (Chicago: Rand McNally, 1981), 46 (noting such a proposal by psychologist Jerry Bergman of Bowling Green State University); Waters, in Krason and D'Agostino, 35 (noting the proposal by Eddie Bernice Johnson, a high-ranking official in the Department of Health, Education, and Welfare in the Carter Administration and later a Congresswoman from Texas); and Don Feder's syndicated column which appeared in *The Washington Times*, Oct. 18, 1994, A15 (noting the position taken by Dr. Jack C. Westman, psychiatry professor at the University of Wisconsin, in his book, *Licensing*

Parents: Can We Prevent Child Abuse and Neglect? [N.Y.: Plenum Press, Insight Books, 1994]).

[23] 268 U.S. 510, 535.

[24] Carlson, 249.

[25] That was the term given to the Warren Court's expansion of procedural due process guarantees, especially in criminal justice cases, by CBS journalist and lawyer Fred Graham. See Fred P. Graham, *The Due Process Revolution: The Warren Court's Impact on Criminal Law* (originally entitled *The Self-Inflicted Wound*; N.Y.: Hayden, 1970).

[26] 383 U.S. 541.

[27] 387 U.S. 1.

[28] Carlson, 249.

[29] Ibid., 250.

[30] Ibid.

[31] Besharov, "'Doing Something'...," 542.

[32] Ibid., 545.

[33] Douglas J. Besharov, "Unfounded Allegations–A New Child Abuse Problem," *Public Interest*, vol. 83 (1986); 19.

[34] Trevor Armbrister, "When Parents Become Victims," *Reader's Digest* (April 1993),101.

[35] Brenda Scott, *Out of Control: Who's Watching Our Child Protection Agencies?* (Lafayette, La.: Huntington House Publishers, 1994), 29, citing statistics compiled by the American Humane Association.

[36] Douglas J. Besharov, "Symposium: Violence in the Family: Child Abuse Realities: Over-Reporting and Poverty," *Virginia Journal of Social Policy and the Law*, vol. 8 (Fall 2000), 176.

[37] "Childhelp," http://www.childhelp.org/pages/statistics; Internet (accessed Dec. 28, 2011).

[38] *The Washington Times*, June 4, 1993, A6.

[39] "President Bush Signs National Child Abuse Registry into Law," http://www.childhelp.org/press-releases/entry /president-bush-signs-national-child-abuse-registry-into-law; Internet (accessed Feb. 7, 2012).

[40] *The Washington Times*, June 4, 1993, A6.

[41] *The Family Defender* (no. 5, Winter 2012), p. 12. For Illinois, the article cites *Dupuy v. McDonald*, 141 F. Supp. 2d 1090 (N. D. Ill. 2001), aff'd in relevant part, 397 F. 3d 493 (7th Cir. 2005); for Pennsylvania, the citation is: http://datacenter.kidscount. org/data/bystate/Trend.aspx?state=PA&order=a&loc=40&ind=5088&dtm=11521&ch=1 108&tf=15%2c16%2c17%2c18%2c35%2c38%2c133; Internet (accessed March 20, 2012).

[42] Besharov, "'Doing Something'...," 556, citing U.S. National Center on Child Abuse and Neglect, *National Analysis of Child Neglect and Abuse Reporting* (1978), 36.

[43] William D. Slicker, "Child Sex Abuse: The Innocent Accused," *Case and Comment*, vol. 91, no. 6 (1986), 14, citing Scott Kraft, *The Kansas City Times*, Feb. 11, 1985.

[44] Slicker, citing a *Wall Street Journal* article (Oct. 10, 1985), which reported on a paper given by Dr. Diana Schetsky and Howard Boverman at the 1985 Annual Meeting of the American Academy of Psychiatry and the Law.

[45] Douglas J. Besharov, "Afterword," in Lawrence D. Spiegel, *A Question of Innocence; A True Story of False Accusation* (Parsippany, N.J.: Unicorn Publishing House, 1986), 265, 268.

[46] Besharov, "Child Abuse Realities," 176, 179, 190.

[47] Ibid., calculated from the chart he provides at 182. This was a large increase in the total number of children (750,000) who were the subject of unfounded reports in 1978, which data he provides in one of his earlier articles (see Besharov, "'Doing Something...,'" 556). The near two-thirds figure of unsubstantiated reports, in his estimation, remained the same (see ibid., "Child Abuse Realities," 179-180), so there were obviously many more total reports. This does not mean that there were more *actual cases* of abuse and neglect, however, since the CPS could have been using looser criteria for what is "substantiated," or the number of unsubstantiated complaints could already have been much higher than two-thirds (which clearly was the case within a decade).

[48] Besharov, "Child Abuse Realities," 171-172. Most children in substantiated cases of physical abuse suffered what is called "moderate" injuries or impairments: bruises, depression, or emotional distress which persisted more than two days.

[49] Besharov, "'Doing Something'...," 578.

[50] Besharov, "Child Abuse Realities," 172.

[51] Ibid., 176,

[52] Besharov, "'Doing Something...," 540.

[53] Michael P. Farris, "Protecting Our Children from the Statistics," *The Home School Court Report*, vol. viii, no. 5 (Sept.-Oct. 1992), 3.

[54] Cited in Paul Craig Roberts, "Parents in the Pillory?" *The Washington Times*, April 29, 1996, A20.

[55] *The Washington Times*, March 6, 1994, A16. In the second quotation, the article quotes the opinion.

[56] Armbrister, "When Parents Become Victims," 106.

[57] William J. Bennett, *The Index of Leading Cultural Indicators*, vol. 1 (1993), 12, citing Richard Gardner, clinical professor of child psychiatry at Columbia University.

[58] "Dear Abby" column, *The Washington Times*, July 11, 1993, D6.

[59] *The Family Defender* (no. 5, Winter 2012), p. 12, citing the HHS data that appears at: http://www.acf.hhs.gov/ programs/cb/ pubs/cm09/pdf.

[60] Prevent Child Abuse America, "Frequently Asked Questions," http://www.preventchildabuse.org/about_us/faqs.shtml#indicated; Internet (accessed Feb. 8, 2012). See also: National Exchange Club Foundation, "About Child Abuse: Frequently Asked Questions," http://preventchildabuse.com/abuse.shtml; Internet (accessed Feb. 8, 2012). It should be noted that some people also try to draw a distinction between "false" or "unfounded" and "unsubstantiated" reports. I think that there is no true distinction. If we are to be true to our eminently sensible tradition of Anglo-American law that holds that one is innocent until proven guilty, and that there has to be some evidence to find a person guilty, I do not see how a distinction between these terms is valid. I believe that some who have made the distinction—and are also ready to distinguish "substantiated" from " indicated" cases—are just unwilling to accept the fact that the incidence of child abuse/neglect is not as great as the conventional wisdom—which has never been based on hard facts, anyhow—holds.

[61] Armbrister, "When Parents Become Victims," 106.

[62] See Carlson, 241-242; E. Michael Jones, "Abuse Abuse: The Therapeutic State Terrorizes Parents in Jordan, Minnesota," *Fidelity* 4 (Feb. 1985), 28-33.

[63] National Public Radio report, Dec. 17, 1994.

[64] See Mary Pride, *The Child Abuse Industry: Outrageous Facts About Child Abuse and Everyday Rebellions Against a System that Threatens Every North American Family* (Westchester, Ill.: Crossway, 1986), 94-95. Pride is a well-known author on religious, educational, and family questions.

[65] This, of course, is the title of Scott's book above. Scott is an investigative and religious writer, with a background in the fields of criminology and domestic abuse.

[66] *The Intelligencer* (Wheeling, W.Va.), March 9, 1992, 8. The suicide attempt is mentioned in David Gorgan, "A Time for Healing," *People*, vol. 38, no. 14 (Oct. 5, 1992), 133; http://www.people.com/people/archive/article/ 0,,20108755,00.html; Internet (accessed March 17, 2012).

[67] *The Washington Times*, Nov. 7, 1993, A1, A10.

[68] *The Intelligencer,* March 9, 1992, 8; *The Washington Times*, Nov. 7, 1993, A10.

[69] Pride, 19-20.

[70] Ibid., 18-19.

[71] Ibid., 15-16.

[72] Ibid., 37.

[73] Ibid., 95.

[74] Ibid., 233. It is embarrassing that this incident happened at a Catholic hospital, which should have taken more seriously the Church's teaching about the natural rights of parents. For example, in the encyclical *Rerum Novarum,* Pope Leo XIII states that "[t]he contention...that the civil government should at its option intrude into and exercise intimate control over the family and the household is a great and pernicious error...[I]f within the precincts of the household there occur grave disturbance of mutual rights, public authority should intervene to force each party to yield to the other its proper due...[b]ut the rulers of the commonwealth must go no further" (*Rerum Novarum,* 14). In the Holy See's *Charter of the Rights of the Family* (1983), the following is stated: "The activities of public authorities and private organizations which attempt in any way to limit the freedom of couples in deciding about their children constitute a grave offense against human dignity and justice" (Art. 3) and "Public authorities must respect and foster the dignity, lawful independence, privacy, integrity, and stability of every family" (Art. 6).

[75] Armbrister, "When Parents Become Victims," 103-104.

[76] Ohio Administrative Code, Chap. 5101: 2-35-19 (3) (a) (Division of Social Services Regulations).

[77] Personal communication from Dr. Carlson to this author.

[78] Michael P. Farris, "Do Parental Rights Stop at the Door?" *Home School Court Report*, vol. xxviii, no. 2 (Spring 2012), 9-11.

[79] Pride, 14.

[80] Scott, 32.

[81] Ibid., 45-46.

[82] Edward Grimsley, "Courage Beyond the Call to Jury Duty," *The Washington Times*, Feb. 3, 1996, C3.

[83] *The Washington Times*, Aug. 4, 1993, B1, B2.

[84] Scott, 48.

[85] Ibid., 48-49.

[86] Pride, 232, apparently citing statements of the authorities as quoted in the *St. Louis Globe-Democrat,* March 16-17, 1985, 1.

[87] Scott, 170, citing Richard Wexler, *Wounded Innocents* (Buffalo: Prometheus Books, 1990), 100.

[88] Scott, 170-171.

[89] Paul Craig Roberts, "Justice Under Siege in Sex Frenzy?" *The Washington Times*, Oct. 10, 1995, A16; *The Wall Street Journal*, Sept. 29, 1995.

[90] Roberts, ibid.

[91] *Time*, Nov. 13, 1995, 89.

[92] Ibid.

[93] Ibid., 89-90; *The Wall Street Journal*, Sept. 29, 1995 and Oct. 13, 1995; Roberts column, *Washington Times*, Oct. 10, 1995, A16.

[94] See Trevor Armbrister, "Justice Gone Crazy," *Reader's Digest* (Jan. 1994), 33-40.

[95] *The Washington Times*, Feb. 3, 1996, A2.

[96] "Arrested for Homeschooling," *The Home School Court Report*, vol. xxvii, no. 2 (Mar.-Apr. 2011), 7-9, 32-33. The quotes are from 8.

[97] Guggenheim, quoted in Richard Wexler, "Invasion of the Child Savers," *The Progressive* (Sept. 1985), 19.

[98] Scott, 19.

[99] Scott 33, quoting Wexler, *Wounded Innocents*, 17. Besharov concurs with Wexler, saying that a substantial number of the "confirmed" cases (involving about 800,000 children and 470,000 families each year in 2000, when he writes) are really poverty cases (Besharov, "Child Abuse Realities," 181-182).

[100] Gary B. Melton, "Mandated Reporting: A Policy without Reason," *Child Abuse and Neglect*, vol. 29 (2005), 11.

[101] Even when there is genuine sexual abuse—which, as we have said, is a small minority of abuse/neglect cases overall—there are indications that the abuse in many such cases does not involve something on the order, say, of rape or incest. For example, in 1984 in New Jersey almost half of the sexual abuse cases were classified by the Division of Family and Youth Services as "mild fondling" (Pride, 238, citing Nancy Hass, "Other Victims in Child-Abuse Cases: Parents," *North Jersey News*, Jan. 13, 1986).

[102] Pride, 26.

[103] David Finkelhor, Lisa Jones, and Anne Shattuck, "Updated Trends in Child Maltreatment, 2009," short publication of the Crimes Against Children Research Center, 2. They say that there is "no consensus in the child maltreatment field about why sexual abuse and physical abuse have declined so substantially over the longer term" (3). They also note that from 1992-2009 child neglect declined much less, only 10% (2). If most of the neglect cases are really poverty cases as Wexler says this much lesser increase is not surprising. This publication is available at www.unh.edu/ccrc/pdf.

[104] Jeanne M. Giovannoni and Rosina M. Becerra, *Defining Child Abuse* (N.Y.: Macmillan [Free Press], 1979), 2.

[105] Besharov, "Child Abuse Realities," 195, 196.

[106] Armbrister, "When Parents Become Victims," 106.

[107] Craig R. Ducat and Harold W. Chase, eds., *Constitutional Interpretation* (5th edn.; St. Paul, Minn.: West, 1992), G10, G6; Steven H. Gifis, *Law Dictionary* (Woodbury, N.Y.: Barron's Educational Series, 1975), 145.

[108] We can note a number of state judicial decisions that rejected such vagueness and/or overbreadth claims: In 1989, the Minnesota Supreme Court held that the state's child abuse/neglect statute, which subjects certain professionals to criminal misdemeanor liability if they fail to file a report, is *not* unconstitutionally vague or overbroad (*State v. Grover*, 437 N.W. 2d 60 [1989]). In 2002, the Florida Supreme Court held that the provision of that state's criminal child abuse statute referring to "mental injury" was not unconstitutionally vague (*DuFresne v. State*, 826 So.2d 272). In 2008, the Massachusetts Supreme Judicial Court brushed aside a challenge to that state's child endangerment statute on vagueness grounds (*Commonwealth v. Hendricks*, 452 Mass. 97). In 2011, the North Dakota Supreme Court held that that state's child abuse statute was not unconstitutionally vague (*Simons v. State*, 803 N.W.2d 587). A lower-level appellate court in Virginia did declare a portion of that state's child endangerment law unconstitutional vague in 1995 (*Commonwealth v. Carter*, 462 S.E.2d 582).

[109] Ohio Rev. Code Annotated, Sec. 2151.03.

[110] For example, Sec. 2907.01 (B) says that "[s]exual contact means any touching of an erogenous zone of another, including without limitation the thigh, genitals, buttock, pubic region, or, if the person is a female, a breast, for the purpose of sexually arousing or gratifying either person." If an agency or a prosecutor wants to ignore or downplay the latter phrase, they might be able to make a case against a parent for wholly innocent touches of a child, say, for hygienic purposes or to express normal affection (i.e., patting a baby on his bottom). 2907.01 (H) defines "[n]udity" as "the showing, representation, or depiction of human male or female genitals, pubic area, or buttocks with less than a full, opaque covering, or of a female breast with less than a full, opaque covering of any portion thereof below the top of the nipple." This possibly could be interpreted to include the innocent taking of a picture of a baby or small child in a bathtub. In fact, there have been cases like this in which parents have been accused of child abuse (see Donna Whitfield, "Tyranny Masquerades as Charity: Who Are the Real Child Abusers?" *Fidelity* 4, No. 3 [Feb. 1985], 26).

[111] Ohio Rev. Code Annotated, Sec. 2919.22 (A).

[112] Ibid., Sec. 2151.031.

[113] Ibid., Sec. 2919.22 (B) (3), (4).

[114] See the discussion in Richard W. Cross, "The Problem of Spanking: The Vexing Question of Childhood Discipline in the Development of Conscience," in Paul C. Vitz and Stephen M. Krason, eds., *Defending the Family: A Sourcebook* (Steubenville, O.: Catholic Social Science Press, 1998), 195-235.

[115] For example, for a good, brief discussion of the "political" nature of the American Psychiatric Association's famous 1973 decision to declare that homosexuality was no longer to be viewed as abnormal, see Judith A. Reisman and Edward W. Eichel, *Kinsey, Sex, and Fraud: The Indoctrination of a People* (Lafayette, La.: Huntington House, 1990), 141-145.

[116] See Waters, in Krason and D'Agostino, 26-28.

[117] Ohio Rev. Code Annotated, Sec. 2151.03.

[118] Ibid., Sec. 2151.04.

[119] Ibid., Sec. 2151.05.

[120] See Stephen M. Krason, "Parental Rights and Minor Children's Health Care Decisions," *Ethics and Medics*, 19, no. 7 (July 1994), 3-4.

[121] On the academic excellence of homeschooled pupils, see the reports about standardized test results in the following issues of *The Home School Court Report*: vol. viii, no. 6 (Nov.-Dec. 1992), 19, 26; vol. x, no. 4 (Jul.-Aug. 1994), 11-12; vol. x, no. 5 (Sept.-Oct. 1994), 17; vol. x, no. 6 (Winter 1994-1995). Vol. x, no. 5 (18) also reports on a study of learning-disabled pupils that showed that those who were being homeschooled were progressing better than those in public schools.

[122] Joseph Sobran, "Reminding Parents Who's in Charge," *The Washington Times* (Feb. 4, 1995), A13.

[123] See: Armbrister, "When Parents Become Victims," 105; *The Home School Court Report*, vol. ix, no. 5 (Sept.-Oct. 1993), 5.

[124] Besharov, "'Doing Something'...," 570.

[125] Pride, 60-61, 68-69. The publications Pride refers to are *What Everyone Should Know About Child Abuse* (Jefferson City, Mo.: Missouri Division of Family Services, 1976, 1980) and *Foster Family Care in Missouri: An Assessment*, published by the Missouri Coalition on Foster Care under grants from the Missouri Division of Family Services and the U.S. Department of Health and Human Services.

[126] Scott, 52-53.

[127] Pride, 230; Besharov, "'Doing Something'...," 569-570.

[128] Pride, 241.

[129] Scott, 58.

[130] Ibid., 59-60.

[131] Armbrister, "When Parents Become Victims," 105.

[132] Scott, 55. She writes that on one of the standard risk assessment forms used by many agencies, produced by Norman Polansky and associates, the items range from the trivial—e.g., whether meals have courses that "go together"—to those embodying ideological preferences—e.g., whether the toys in the home have a traditional gender orientation (e.g., dolls for girls, trucks for boys). Apparently, on the latter if the parents have not had their consciousness sufficiently raised by feminism to break away from such traditional practices, their children will be concluded to be "at risk."

[133] Pride, 44, 48.

[134] Hollida Wakefield and Ralph Underwager, unpublished manuscript on the child witness and sexual abuse, Institute for Psychological Therapies, quoted in Slicker, 18.

[135] Pride, 44.

[136] Ibid., 46.

[137] Pride, 11, 33, 236 (one of her sources is a study reported in the *St. Louis Post-Dispatch* [Oct. 30, 1985]; another is Pamela D. Mayhall and Katherine Eastlack Norgard, *Child Abuse and Neglect: Sharing Responsibility* [N.Y.: John Wiley & Sons, 1983], 11).

[138] Wexler, "Invasion of the Child Savers," 22.

[139] Besharov, "'Doing Something'...," 570, citing R. Nagi, "Child Abuse and Neglect Programs: A National Overview," *Children Today* 13, 17 (1975). A study reported by United Press International in January 1994, which had been conducted by Ohio State University at Children's Hospital in Columbus, Ohio, and published in the *Journal of Child Abuse and Neglect*, likewise discovered a great deal of disagreement among physicians about what medical neglect is and when it should be reported to authorities. The study also reported that there were no guidelines for physicians to follow in determining what is neglect (*The Home School Court Report*, x, no. 1 [Jan.-Feb. 1994], 21, 23).

[140] Besharov, "'Doing Something'...," 568-569. The court cases that he cites as examples of this view being expressed are the following: *In re Stilley*, 363 N.E.2d 873 (Ill., 1977); *In Interest of Nitz*, 368 N.E.2d 1111 (Ill., 1977).

[141] There is some dispute about the actual percentage of reports that are anonymous. The Home School Legal Defense Association (HSLDA), which does much litigating on false abuse/neglect reports, told this writer that they believe that 60-70% of reports are from anonymous sources, though they acknowledge that this figure is not based on a systematic study but from anecdotal information such as the experiences of their members and others who they have defended and discussions with social workers (phone conversation with HSLDA, July 30, 2004). The Children's Bureau of HHS claims that about 10% are anonymous (see Children's Bureau, U.S. Dept. of Health and Human Services, *Child Maltreatment 2002* (Wash., D.C.: U.S. Government Printing Office, 2004), 6. One of my former university colleagues who worked in a cpa in Ohio for a time found that perhaps 50% of the reports to his county agency were anonymous, although one cannot know if this is typical. My own years of research and gathering of anecdotal information indicate to me that the HHS figure is definitely much too low. There is some problem with duplicate reporting, and it is also likely that the organization of their data puts what are essentially anonymous reports into other categories of sources of reports based, perhaps, only on the reporter's stating some relationship to or association with the

person he is accusing without actually identifying himself (which is rather typically done when reporters contact cpa's). Thus, in its 2002 report HHS says 8% of reports are from another relative other than a parent (the latter would probably mostly be non-custodial parents during custody disputes) and about 6% are from friends or neighbors. Among "nonprofessional sources" of reports, HHS lists almost another 18% in the category of "other" or "unknown or missing." Thus, if we assumed that virtually all of the reports in these additional categories came from people who did not specifically identify themselves (my knowledge of the issue suggests to me that this is a reasonable assumption), this would be 42% It is also fair to assume that there are a not insignificant number of reports made from two of the categories of "professional sources" listed—educational personnel and medical personnel (which together make up 32% of the overall number of reports)—without the person specifically identifying himself (e.g., a nurse simply calls a local cpa saying she is a staff member at the emergency room of hospital X). Let's assume it is 5%, which is probably low. This would bring the overall total of, effectively, anonymous reports to 47%, which is close to the percentage mentioned by my colleague. It is at least reasonable to conclude that a sizable minority of reports are anonymous. Actually, the percentage of anonymous reports is almost certainly higher than even 50%. The HHS data indicates that the categorization of referrals is compiled only from referrals that have not been "screened out." HHS's numbers show that fully 32% were screened out. It is very likely that the screened out reports were overwhelmingly from nonprofessional sources and also quite likely that most of these were anonymous (which according to any rational screening procedure would make reports less reliable).

[142] Whitfield, 25.

[143] See Ohio Rev. Code Annotated, Secs. 2151.99 (A) and 2151.421 (A).

[144] The Ohio statutory provision cited (ORC Sec. 2151.421) specifies that a "reasonableness" standard should apply regarding the mandatory reporting of child abuse/neglect (i.e., if there is "reasonable cause to suspect based on facts that would cause a reasonable person in a similar position to suspect..."). My observation for a quarter of a century and much anecdotal evidence, however, indicates that the "reasonableness" standard is not typically operative. Mandatory reporters make reports irrespective of this standard, apparently believing that they should report if there is any possibility—no matter how unlikely—that there could be abuse or neglect. Thus, the standard becomes arbitrary or open-ended; that is, no standard at all. The same applies to the attitudes and practices of the CPS when receiving reports, as this article makes clear.

[145] On these points, see also: Melton,14.

[146] Armbrister, "When Parents Become Victims," 106; Scott, 142-143 (Scott notes, inter alia, that this curtain of confidentiality was even the grounds for the San Diego County agency's refusing to cooperate with the investigating grand jury referred to above).

[147] Armbrister, "When Parents Become Victims," 106.

[148] Ibid.

[149] Even fewer involve criminal charges, where parents allegedly run afoul of criminal child maltreatment laws.

[150] See Paul Chill, "Burden of Proof Begone: The Pernicious Effect of Emergency Removal in Child Protective Proceedings," Family Court Review, vol. 41 (Oct. 2003), at http://web.lexis-nexis.com/universe/document?; Internet (accessed March 5, 2012), 459.

[151] Ibid., 461.

[152] Ibid., 463.

[153] Armbrister, "When Parents Become Victims,"106.

[154] See, e.g., *Pierce v. Society of Sisters*, 268 U.S. 510, 535 (1925); *Prince v. Massachusetts*, 321 U.S. 158, 166, 168 (1944); *Wisconsin v. Yoder*, 406 U.S. 205, 232 (1972), and *Troxel v. Granville*, 530 U.S. 57, 66 (2000). The first three of these cases are cited in Robert J. D'Agostino, "State Intervention in the Family and Parental Rights: A Legal Assessment," in Krason and D'Agostino, 149. The current writer was co-author of an *amicus curiae* brief, on behalf of the Society of Catholic Social Scientists, on the side of the parent in *Troxel*. This is reprinted in *The Catholic Social Science Review* V (2000), 349-369 and as an appendix in this book.

[155] This data is from the mid-1980s.

[156] Pride, 169.

[157] We are aware that state statutes do not necessarily guarantee the right to appeal— or at least not the right to have an appeal taken up—but they establish the procedures and mechanics for it. In criminal matters, at least, there is a liberal view about allowing appeals to be filed and even heard.

[158] Pride, 229.

[159] Ibid., 160-161, 228-229.

[160] Chill, 458.

[161] For example, in 1985, a U.S. district court decision in Illinois held that searches of a family's home without a warrant by that state's Department of Children and Family Services did not violate the Fourth Amendment (Pride, 228, citing Stephen Chapman's op-ed column in the *St. Louis Post-Dispatch* and the *Jefferson City [Mo.] Post-Tribune*, March 28, 1985, and April 5, 1985, respectively). We see contrary later rulings following in the text.

[162] Scott, chap. 9.

[163] In *White v. Illinois*, 502 U.S. 346 (1992), the Supreme Court upheld the admission of hearsay testimony from third parties in child abuse trials. On the subject of admitting hearsay evidence, Armbrister discusses one Washington State case in which a Christian husband and wife were convicted of sexually abusing their three-year-old daughter. The child and her friend supposedly confided the story of her abuse to a day-care worker. The day-care worker and her supervisor became the chief witnesses against the parents. There was no corroboration of any kind of the two day-care center employees' testimony, nor was any physical evidence entered into the record that showed that any sexual molestation had, in fact, occurred. A physical examination after the trial showed that almost certainly the child could not have been raped (this is what the parents were alleged to have done; they were convicted of statutory rape). The cpa suppressed the examination. The day-care worker who first came forth with the allegations claimed in a post-trial interview that she had been herself abused for over twenty years, saying that almost anyone who came near her abused her. She also said that most people were "sex perverts" and that every other house in her neighborhood had abuse going on inside it. She said she had on numerous other occasions tried to turn in supposed sex offenders, and hated men. Besides such seeming paranoia, she admitted that she was a daily drug user. The trial judge refused to permit any effort to impeach this witness's character. Harvard Law School evidence professor, Charles Nesson, examined the case and later filed an *amicus curiae* brief in the appeal to the Ninth U.S. Circuit Court of Appeals in support of the parents in which he wrote that the case was "the most extreme example of erosion of the confrontation clause of which I am aware" (Armbrister, "When Parents Become Victims," 101-103). Nevertheless, the Ninth Circuit sustained the convictions (*Swan v. Peterson*, 6 F.3d 1373 [1993]).

[164] The grand jury in San Diego County specifically charged that its CPS had shifted the burden of proof in sexual abuse cases from the state to the alleged perpetrator (Scott, 84).

[165] See, for example, Elizabeth Loftus and Katherine Ketcham, *The Myth of Repressed Memory: False Memories and Allegations of Sexual Abuse* (N.Y.: St. Martin's Press, 1994). More recently, the tide seems to have turned in the courts, with people who have born the brunt of allegations of abuse, supposedly turned up in repressed memory therapy, winning damage judgments after convincing juries that the therapists actually manufactured the "memories" by the suggestive character of their therapy (see *The Washington Times*, Dec. 17, 1994, A1, A14).

[166] The Alabama case is discussed in *The Home School Court Report*, vol. viii, no. 5 (Sept.-Oct. 1992), 1, 4 and ix, no. 2 (Mar.-Apr. 1993), 1, 24. The New York case is discussed in *The Home School Court Report*, x, no. 6 (Winter 1994-1995), 1. The Maryland case was discussed in *The Home School Court Report*, vol. ix, no. 5 (Sept.-Oct. 1993), 5. This author received further information about the latter case from constitutional lawyer Vieira by personal communication.

[167] *The Home School Court Report*, xx, no. 4 (July-Aug. 2004), 7.

[168] See "The *Stumbo* Decision: Turning the Tide," *Home School Court Report*, vol. xix, no. 4 (July/Aug. 2003), 33.

[169] The case was *Matter of Smith Children*, NN-22728-32/09 (2009), discussed in Mark Fass, "Judge Rejects Home Visit in Child Welfare Investigation" (Dec. 17, 2009), http://nccr.info; Internet (accessed Feb. 14, 2012). The New York statute that was involved had been amended in 2006, however, to make it easier for the CPS to carry out an investigation when parents will not cooperate with them, so it does not seem that this decision represented some kind of trend in the state to protect parental rights.

[170] *The Home School*, xx, no. 4 (July-Aug. 2004), 10.

[171] "President Bush Signs Keeping Children and Families Safe Act of 2003," *Home School Court Report*, vol. xix, no. 4 (July-Aug. 2003), 38.

[172] "Congressional Breakthroughs in CAPTA Reform," *Home School Court Report*, vol. xviii, no. 5 (Sept.-Oct. 2002), 24.

[173] See "Mississippi: CAPTA Legislation Enacted," Home School Legal Defense Association website, May 2, 2007; http://www.hslda.org/hs/state/ms/200705020.asp; Internet (accessed March 15, 2012).

[174] "Foster Care," http://en.wikipedia.org/wiki/Foster_father#cite_note-22; Internet (accessed March 4, 2012). The first case was *Rogers v. County of San Joaquin*, No. 05-16071; the second was *Fogarty-Hardwick v. County of Orange, et al.*, United States Supreme Court, Docket # 10-857.

[175] Pride, 229.

[176] See Krason, in Krason and D'Agostino, 186-190. The extent of such an emotional, unreasoned response to this was seen by the fact that one major newspaper poll—taken at the height of the national hysteria about the child abuse "epidemic"—found that nearly half of the respondents indicated they were willing to either throw people off buildings or lynch them if they were merely *accused* of child abuse (see *Minneapolis Star and Tribune*, May 19, 1985, cited in Farris, "Protecting Our Children from the Statistics").

[177] Philip Jenkins, "Believe the Children? Child Abuse and the American Legal System," *Chronicles* (Jan. 1993), 22.

[178] On the point about the assumptions and outlook of contemporary social scientists, see Stephen M. Krason, "What the Catholic Finds Wrong About Secular Social Science," *Social Justice Review*, vol. 84, no. 1 (Jan.-Feb. 1993), 5-11.

[179] Jenkins, 22.

[180] Pride, 252-253. Programs seeking to identify "potentially abusive parents" when they have babies and force them to undergo parenting training have already been put into effect in different parts of the country (Pride, 253; Scott, 175).

[181] Society of Catholic Social Scientists' letter to members of the U.S. Senate on the United Nations Convention on the Rights of the Child, April, 1995.

[182] Jean E. Smith, *The Constitution and American Foreign Policy* (St. Paul, Minn.: West Publishing Co., 1989), 107.

[183] Michael P. Farris, "A Deeper Understanding of the Threat of International Law," *The Home School Court Report*, vol. xxiii, no. 6 (Nov.-Dec. 2007), 5-9. The quotations are from 6.

[184] See Stephen M. Krason, "The Church and the UN Convention on the Rights of the Child" ("Neither Left nor Right but Catholic" column, September 1, 2011); http://skrason.wordpress.com/; Internet; accessed Feb. 14, 2012. The quotations are from a telegram by Pope Benedict XVI in June 2009 (see "Pope's Promo for UN Child Rights Convention Must Be Read in Context of Vatican Reservations: Vatican," by LifeSiteNews.com (John-Henry Westen), June 12, 2009; http://www.lifesitenews.com/news/archive/ldn/2009/jun/09061210; Internet [accessed March 15, 2012]).

[185] Daniel J. Sullivan, *An Introduction to Philosophy* (rev. edn.; Milwaukee: Bruce, 1964), 168.

[186] Besharov, "'Doing Something'...," 562.

[187] Pride, 55. It should be noted that it has *not* been accidental that the child protective system investigates parents for all sorts of actions, so many of which are completely innocuous. Besharov tells us that the experts who pushed for CAPTA and its state legislative progeny wanted "unrestrictive preventive jurisdiction," which would supposedly enable them to identify even *potentially* abusive parents to predict whether parents would become abusive toward their children. They wanted to stop any *possible* abuse. This in spite of the fact that, as Besharov makes clear, no clinician, psychologist, or other expert can predict with certainty that someone will become a child abuser (Besharov "'Doing Something'...," 574-575).

[188] Besharov, "Child Abuse Realities," 192. See the article for his citations.

[189] Although there are some indications that the number of children in foster care in the U.S. has dropped just in the last few years, a report on ABC's "Prime Time" in 2006 stated 800,000 children per year come into contact with the foster care system (apparently about 520,000 of these because of abuse and neglect allegations). The latter was double the number in the early 1980s (which would be consistent with the sharp rise in child abuse reports nationally). In 2004, a record number of 304,000 children entered the system (this increase was thought to be due to parental drug abuse problems) (ABC "Prime Time" [May 30, 2006], http://abcnews.go.com/Primetime/FosterCare/story?id=2017991&page=1#.Tzb2OuBw9e4; Internet [accessed Feb. 11, 2012]).

[190] Besharov, "'Doing Something'...," 584, 560.

[191] Ibid., 560. Even with the Adoption and Safe Families Act of 1997, the Department of HHS reported that as of July 2010 children stay in the foster care system for an average of 31 months. Nearly 20% are in the system for five or more years (cited in: "Foster Hope, Foster a Child," http://www.achildshopeintl.org/FosterCare.html; Internet [accessed March 17, 2012]).

[192] Pride, 77-79, 81.

[193] Ibid., 20-21. See also Whitfield, 26.

[194] Pride, 81-83.

[195] Scott, 101.

[196] Timothy W. Maier, "Suffer the Children," *Insight on the News* (Nov. 24, 1997), 11, cited in "A Critical Look at the Foster Care System: How Widespread a Problem?" http://www.liftingtheveil.ord/foster04.htm; Internet (accessed March 17, 2012).

[197] See National Coalition for Child Protection Reform, "Foster Care vs. Family Preservation: The Track Record on Safety and Well-Being" (Issue Paper 1 - Jan. 3, 2011). The studies are cited in the Paper, and are apparently from the 1980s and early 1990s. Chill contends that the number of "emergency removals" of children from families in the U.S.—i.e., they are removed supposedly because they are threatened with harm from their parents—doubled to 555,000 over the twenty years just prior to when he was writing in 2003. He says that the number of erroneous removals "is alarmingly large"; in 2001, for example, of 100,000 children removed, more than a third were later determined not to have been maltreated (Chill, 458).

[198] See "Foster Care." This article shows that the problems of child abuse in the foster care and institutional care systems continue. An Internet search of the subject of child abuse in foster care also shows many recent cases.

[199] Sometimes these decent people wind up becoming victims of the system themselves. Some children who have bounced around the foster care system for years have come to learn how to use it to their advantage and have sometimes falsely accused such decent foster parents of abuse, and gotten them unjustly into trouble (e.g., Pride, 21, 232-233; personal communication of this author with a Franklin County, Ohio, family who experienced this).

[200] See: Pride, 111; Scott, 106-106. Scott mentions that the San Diego County grand jury mentioned above in the text concluded this same thing about many foster parents.

[201] See National Coalition for Child Protection Reform, "The Most Common Lie in Child Welfare (It's the One About the Rate of Abuse in Foster Care)" (May 24, 2010), http://www.nccprblog.org/2010/05/most-common-lie-in-american-child.html; Internet (accessed March 15, 2012).

[202] See, e.g: Whitfield, 25, 26; Scott, chap. six; Besharov, "'Doing Something'...," 557.

[203] See *amicus curiae* brief of Society of Catholic Social Scientists in *Camreta v. Greene/Alford v. Greene*, 16-17.

[204] On these points, see: Joseph Goldstein, Anna Freud, and Albert Solnit, *Beyond the Best Interests of the Child* (N.Y.: Free Press, 1973), 25, 72-74; Besharov, "'Doing Something...," 586; Chill, 457, 462.

[205] Stephen M. Krason, "The Critics of the Current Child Abuse Laws and the Child Protective System: A Survey of the Leading Literature," *The Catholic Social Science Review* XII (2007), 307-350.

[206] See: Besharov, "'Doing Something'...," 550; Douglas J. Besharov (with Lisa A. Laumann), "Child Abuse Reporting: The Need to Shift Priorities from More Reports to Better Reports," in *Social Policies for Children*, ed. Irwin Garfinkel, Jennifer L. Hochschild, and Sara S. McLanahan (Wash., D.C.: Brookings Institution, 1996), 258-259.

[207] Besharov, "'Doing Something'...," 570.

[208] Ibid., 574-575.

[209] Besharov, "Child Abuse Realities,"179.

[210] Besharov, "'Doing Something'...," 578.

[211] Besharov, "Child Abuse Realities," 192.

[212] Pride, 25. Emphasis is in the book.

[213] Ibid., 24-25, 28.

[214] Ibid., 41-50.

[215] Ibid., 14, 30.

[216] Ibid., 113-117, 120.

[217] Ibid., 140-143, 152.

[218] Scott, 33-35.

[219] Ibid., 39-42.

[220] Ibid., 57-59.

[221] Ibid., chap. 8.

[222] Ibid, 137-141, 142-143, 145-146.

[223] Ibid., 45.

[224] Wexler, *Wounded Innocents*, 85.

[225] Ibid.

[226] Ibid., 88.

[227] Ibid., 86.

[228] Ibid., 81-84.

[229] Ibid., 266.

[230] Joseph Goldstein, Anna Freud, and Albert J. Solnit, *Before the Best Interests of the Child* (N.Y.: Free Press, 1979), 25. Emphasis is in the book.

[231] Ibid., 72-74.

[232] Spiegel, 243-247.

[233] Ibid., 261-264.

[234] Dana Mack, *The Assault on Parenthood: How Our Culture Undermines the Family* (N.Y.: Simon and Schuster, 1997).

[235] Ibid., 60.

[236] Ibid., 31.

[237] Ibid., 60.

[238] Ibid., 62.

[239] Ibid., 77-78.

[240] Carlson, 250.

[241] Ibid., 251-254.

[242] Christopher Klicka, *The Right Choice—Homeschooling* (rev. edn.; Gresham, Oreg.: Noble, 1995), 272.

[243] See ibid., 271-284.

[244] Klicka, 294; see also: "The *Stumbo* Decision: Turning the Tide," *Home School Court Report*, vol. xix, no. 4 (July-Aug. 2003), 30-34.

[245] These positions of HSLDA are apparent when going through back issues of its publication, *The Home School Court Report*, and checking its website.

[246] Stephen McGarvey, "President Bush Signs Keeping Children & Families Safe Act of 2003," *Home School Court Report*, vol. xix, no. 4, 38.

[247] See the HSLDA website and various issues of *The Home School Court Report*.

[248] Chill, 457-459, 462, 463, 468.

[249] Ibid., 459.

[250] Ibid., 462.

[251] Ibid., 463.

[252] This was not meant just to include the poor but many middle-class people who simply cannot bear the massive cost of a legal defense in one of these cases.

[253] The proposals recounted in this paragraph were in Krason, in Krason and D'Agostino, 192-194.

[254] Ibid., 194.

[255] Ibid., 194-195.

[256] See, e.g., Ohio Rev. Code Annotated, Sec. 2921.14, enacted in 1991. This makes the knowing filing of a false abuse/neglect report a first-degree misdemeanor. It apparently does not apply to mandated reporters.

[257] For a discussion of how serious this problem had become, *see* Pride, 54, 239; Slicker, 16; *U.S. News and World Report*, Vol. 98 (April 1, 1985), 66. Prior to the adoption of Sec. 2921.14 (see note 256 above), the Ohio courts had held that if an ex-spouse made a false report, even knowingly and in bad faith, there was no legal recourse for the accused (*Hartley v. Hartley*, 537 N.E. 2d 706 [1988]).

[258] Scott, 183-184.

[259] Child advocacy centers began in the mid-1980s. What they seek to do is to better coordinate the efforts of the CPS, the law enforcement and criminal justice community, and medical and mental health professionals to deal with child abuse. The National Children's Advocacy Center (NCAC) in Alabama trains professionals from around the U.S. and other countries to, it says, learn "how to recognize and support endangered children" (see National Children's Advocacy Center website, http://www.nationalcac.org/history/history.html; Internet [accessed March 8, 2012]). Various local communities around the country have these centers, which provide such training on a localized level and say they aim to help children who allegedly have been abused to not be also "victimized" by the system investigating and dealing with abuse (e.g., by having children interrogated by a cpa, and then law enforcement, and then health care providers in intimidating surroundings, etc.) and also making easier a coordinated agency response to the alleged abuse and facilitating the provision of various therapeutic and other services to the children. Some of the subjects that the CACs are concerned about—as judged, say, from the NCAC's spring 2012 National Symposium on Child Abuse (see ibid.)—indicate a focus on some legitimate traditional moral questions that indeed involve or can lead to child maltreatment, such as child pornography and pornography generally, sex trafficking, sex tourism, sexual experimentation among children, and illicit drug use. The dominance of child welfare professionals and child abuse prosecutors and the absence of parental rights advocates among the speakers and the NCAC's seeming ready acceptance of such problematical legal developments as permitting young child witnesses in cases—which, as noted, contravened traditional criminal law practices—makes one think that the CACs, however, essentially espouse the mind-set of the CPS. This is further reinforced when one goes to the websites of various local CACs, which feature some of the typical CPS claims that this article has shown are questionable or false (e.g., intra-family sexual abuse crosses—and implicitly is equally prevalent within—all socio-economic groupings; one in three females and one in four males experience sexual abuse before age eighteen; that spanking is bad for children; that genuine physical abuse of children is common; that children rarely lie about abuse; that aggressive or disruptive behavior, or passive, withdrawn, or emotionless behavior, or frequent urinary tract or yeast infections are signs of abuse (of course, they are more typically signs of things that have nothing to do with abuse) (see, e.g., the websites of CAC of Springfield, Mo., http://www.childadvocacycenter.org/about-child-abuse.php; Athens County, Ohio CAC, http://www.athenscac.org/; Dallas Children's Advocacy Center, http://www.dcac.org/reportingchildabuse. aspx; all Internet and accessed March 8, 2012). The website of the National Children's Alliance, which accredits CACs, claims that in 2009 763,000 American children were determined to be victims of abuse or neglect. That would be a substantiation rate of 23%, whereas as we have seen HHS data indicates that it is only 14%. It correctly says that most of the substantiated cases were for neglect, but says nothing about how most of these were actually poverty matters. It also claims that many

entirely innocent child behaviors are signs of abuse. (See website of National Children's Alliance, http://www.nationalchildrensalliance.org/; Internet [accessed March 8, 2012].)

[260] Pride cites sources and studies that show that therapy has a very questionable record of effectiveness in deterring genuine child abusers from further abusive actions (see Pride, 256-257).

[261] See Thomas Sowell's syndicated column in *The Washington Times*, Nov. 6, 1994, B1.

[262] See "Parental Rights: Why Now is the Time to Act," *Home School Court Report*, vol. xxii, no. 2 (Mar.-Apr. 2006), 8.

[263] The present author is on the Board of Directors of ParentalRights.org, an organization set up by Michael Farris (the founder of HSLDA) and others whose main objectives are to work to stop ratification of the Convention on the Rights of the Child by the U.S. Senate and to build up support for a draft Parental Rights Amendment to the U.S. Constitution. Further information and a petition to support the amendment can be found at the organization's website: http://parentalrights.org/.

[264] About this latter point, see Krason, *The Transformation of the American Democratic Republic*, 16.

[265] Alexis de Tocqueville, *Democracy in America* (ed. J.P. Mayer; Garden City, N.Y.: Doubleday [Anchor], 1969), vol. II, pt. iv, 692-694.

[266] See Krason, *The Transformation of the American Democratic Republic*, 147, 154, 180, 194, 217.

[267] See Waters, in Krason and D'Agostino, 26-28.

[268] See: Pride, 61-62; Mack, 73-76.

[269] Stephen M. Krason, "Child Abuse and Neglect: Failed Policy and Assault on Innocent Parents," *The Catholic Social Science Review* X (2005), 225.

[270] Email from Richard Wexler to this author, March 22, 2011.

[271] The Family Defense Center, based in Chicago, says it mission is to advocate for justice for families in the child welfare system, especially families threatened with losing their children to foster care. It says further that it is "a legal advocacy organization that provides high level systemic advocacy and grass-roots activities for families treated unfairly by state child protection agencies, and defends children who can be safely raised in their own families and helps families preserve their right to raise their own children" (Family Defense Center website, http://www. familydefensecenter.net/; Internet; accessed Feb. 14, 2012).

[272] Tocqueville, vol. I, pt. ii, 294.

The Family and Parental Rights in Light of Catholic Social Teaching and International Human Rights Law: A Convergence

By William L. Saunders

I am examining both human rights law and Catholic social teaching as each bears upon the family and parental rights. Obviously, I cannot treat either topic in depth. However, my aim is to provide a backdrop for consideration and evaluation of the child protective system ("CPS"), which is the focus of this book. I will begin with human rights law, then turn to Catholic social teaching, and end by trying to draw forth some principles that might productively guide reflection upon the CPS.

Human Rights: Preliminary Considerations

Some preliminary points should be noted before we examine human rights law.

First, when I speak of "human rights," I am referring to "rights" recognized in an international system of agreements. In other words, they are neither indeterminate nor subjective. We can examine written documents to discern the content of the rights. Thus, human rights are not what someone asserts they are. Rather, they are what the documents say they are.

Second, if we speak of human rights *law*, we are referring to a *legally binding* obligation. In other words, nations must be required to obey it.

Third, there are two ways in which such obligation might be created—by a treaty or by custom. Under the U.S. Constitution, treaties are the supreme law of the law, ranking just below the text of the Constitution itself in authority.[1] Generally, a treaty requires the enactment of laws to make it binding (though some treaties could be *self-executing*, that is, they might immediately go into legal effect and change existing law). The United States has not ratified some treaties (such as the Convention on the Rights of the Child,[2] or "CRC"), and has conditioned its ratification of others (such as the International Covenant on Civil and Political Rights,[3] or "ICCPR") so that domestic law is not changed.[4]

Thus, and fourth, I am not limiting my consideration to laws that bind the United States. Rather, since my charge is to provide a context about how to think about the CPS, I am examining *the principles* that can be discerned in the documents of the international human rights system.

Human Rights Principles

Following the terrors of the World War II—the destruction of civilian populations, the murder of people in camps, the cruel and inhumane experiments on prisoners—there was a strong desire among nations—and among ordinary people—to put something in place to prevent the repetition of such horrors. It was believed that only by protecting these basic rights could the world be certain to avoid a *third* world war.[5] Shortly after the formation of the United Nations, a statement was issued declaring basic human rights.

The document issued was the Universal Declaration of Human Rights (hereafter, the "Declaration" or the "UDHR").[6] It was contemplated at the time that its principles would be put into legal force through a series of human rights treaties. I will return to those treaties subsequently, but let us turn our attention to what the first and most basic human rights document says about the family and parental rights.

Regarding the family, Article 16 states: "Men and women...have a right to marry and to found a family....The family is the natural and fundamental group unit of society and is entitled to protection by society and the State." Thus, the family is the foundation; everything else is built upon it. It precedes not only the State (i.e., the national political unit) but the larger community ("society"). Both are obligated to support it.

Regarding parental rights, Article 26 (3) states: "Parents have a prior right to choose the kind of education that shall be given their children." This is not a limited right (or a limited role) for parents—education is defined quite broadly in Article 26 (2): "Education shall be directed to the full development of the human personality and to the strengthening of respect for human rights and fundamental freedoms. It shall promote understanding, tolerance, and friendship among all nations, racial or religious groups, and shall further the activities of the United Nations for the maintenance of peace." Further, we should note that this primacy for the parental role in education (again, "education" broadly conceived) was an absolutely essential right so far as the framers of the UDHR were concerned. Believing that World War II and it associated horrors were due, in large part, to the growth of totalitarian regimes, they identified the separation of children from the oversight of their parents as a fundamental reason for the growth of those regimes. Once the State separated the child from the parent, the State could indoctrinate the child. They were determined to prevent that.[7] Hence, the State role is supportive and subordinate.

Regarding the child, the UDHR says: "Motherhood and childhood are entitled to special care and assistance."[8] This recognizes the necessarily dependent state of children (as well as the important role motherhood plays in society).

Not surprisingly, these principles were echoed in what is sometimes called "the first generation" of human rights treaties.

For example, in the ICCPR, Article 18 (4) states: "The States Parties...undertake to have respect for the liberty of parents...to ensure the religious and moral education of their children in conformity with their own convictions." Article 23 repeats the language about the family and marriage from the UDHR (see Article 16 above).

The ICCPR also states a principle about children: "Every child shall have...the right to such measures of protection as are required by his status as a minor, on the part of his family, society and the State."[9]

The second treaty of the first generation—the International Covenant on Economic, Social & Cultural Rights (or "ICESCR")—has similar provisions. Article 10 requires the State to provide "the widest possible protection and assistance...to the family, which is the natural and fundamental group unit of society, particularly...while it is responsible for the care and education of dependent children." Likewise, Article 13 provides for "the liberty of individuals and bodies to establish and direct educational institutions." Further, it obligates the States to "undertake to have respect for the liberty of parents...to choose for their children schools, other than those established by the public authorities...and to ensure the religious and moral education of their children in conformity with their own convictions."

What is clear from these documents is that they recognize the importance of the family—the family is natural and fundamental and precedes not only the State, but also society. Consequently, the State—as well as society—is obligated to undertake positive measures to protect it.

Similarly, parental rights are paramount. While every child has "the right to...measures of protection" from exploitation, which rights the State must guarantee, the priority of the parents in the supervision of the child is clear. They are the ones who have the right to guarantee the "education" of their own child—and "education," as we have seen, is very broadly defined. It is the parents, not the State, who are the fundamental guardians of the child.

Since these family and parental rights are basic principles of human rights, a State that fails to ensure them may be seen to be violating its international obligations.

It may be that the "human rights document" most people think of when considering the care and protection of children is the CRC. This treaty has been ratified by every nation except the United States and Somalia.[10] Thus, while the U.S. is not bound by the CRC through treaty ratification, is it bound by "customary international law"? As noted, "custom" is the second way by which international legal obligations may be formed.[11]

It seems unlikely. Under traditional notions of customary international law, which requires consistent practice among the nations, it would be impossible to demonstrate that nations are *actually following* the requirements of the CRC and have, thereby, created a *custom* of doing so.

But whether the U.S. is formally bound by the terms of the CRC, those terms are influencing the opinions of the Supreme Court Justices. For instance, in *Roper v Simmons*,[12] a 5-to-4 decision which found the juvenile death penalty to be unconstitutional, the majority cited the provisions of the CRC favorably (the CRC "contains an express prohibition on capital punishment for crimes committed by juveniles under 18"[13]), suggesting it has persuasive weight (even if not technically binding).[14]

Certainly, the CRC has many provisions that elevate children's rights, and seem to render the parents' supervisory role as, at best, secondary. See, for instance, Articles 12 (right of a child to be heard "in all matters affecting the child"), 13 ("the right to seek, receive and impart information and ideas of all kind, regardless of frontiers...through any ...media of the child's choice"), 15 (right to "freedom of association and ...peaceful assembly"), and 16 (right to privacy).

There are also articles that deal with separating the child from his parents that elevate the State's role to an extreme degree. Article 9 says: "States...shall ensure that a child shall not be separated from his or her parents against their will, except when competent authorities subject to judicial review determine...that such separation is necessary for the best interests of the child....States...shall respect the right of the child who is separated from one or both parents to maintain personal relations and direct contact with both parents...except if it is contrary to the child's best interests. Where such separation results from any action initiated by a State...that State shall...provide the parents, the child or...another family member with the essential information concerning the whereabouts of the absent member(s) of the family unless the provision of the information would be detrimental to the well-being of the child." This gives the State a dominant role, and takes away with one hand (the State's right to determine the best interests of the child) what it gives with the other (e.g., the right of parents to maintain contact).

Since the question I am considering is what are the human rights *principles* that bear upon our evaluation of the CPS, the issue arises whether the CRC is inconsistent with the other human rights principles, which have been discussed above and which recognize parental rights and the importance of the family. To the extent it is inconsistent, it does not state true principles of human rights. My conclusion is that the CRC may be understood as containing important principles we identified from UDHR, ICCPR, and ICESCR, though those principles have been compromised and obscured, by other principles in the CRC that distort the State's role and minimize parental/family oversight.

First, this is the logical conclusion that follows when one considers the design of the international human rights system. All human rights treaties—including the CRC—are conceived as descended from the principles established in the UDHR; it is hardly conceivable that newer treaties would contradict the UDHR (or that they would contradict the first generation treaties, the ICCPR and the ICESCR); if they do, then they are not legitimate developments or elaborations of those principles.

In fact, the Preamble of the CRC expressly cites certain of the provisions I discussed above: "childhood is entitled to special care and assistance" and "the family, as the fundamental group of society and the natural environment for the growth and well-being of all its members and particularly children, should be afforded the necessary protection and assistance."

The Preamble does not, however, mention parental rights. While it is true that the growth of governmental programs displaces parental rights as a practical matter and should always be limited to those strictly necessary, what I am considering is whether the *actual terms* of the CRC do so. There is evidence both ways. Article 5 requires States to "respect the responsibilities, rights and duties of parents," but conditions that upon "the evolving capacities of the child." Article 18 recognizes that "[p]arents...have the primary responsibility for the upbringing and development of the child."[15] However, by saying "the best interests of the child shall be their basic concern," the CRC opens room for the State to argue that it knows better than the parents what the "best interests of the child" in question are. (Article 3: "In all action concerning children, whether undertaken by public or private social welfare institutions, courts of law, administrative authorities or legislative bodies, the best interests of the child shall be a primary consideration.") Article 19, which is aimed at protecting the child from abuse, nonetheless defines abuse very broadly ("all forms of physical or mental violence or abuse, neglect or negligent treatment, maltreatment or exploitation"). It also notes the State can protect the child "while in the care of parent(s)."

It must be noted that interpretations of CRC articles that are hostile to the family and parental rights have often been announced by the very body entrusted under the CRC with monitoring State compliance, the CRC Committee.

Every "human rights" treaty, whether the first generation or the second, contains provisions for the election of a committee to make advisory recommendations. The CRC Committee, which holds three sessions a year, and is comprised of eighteen "experts" in human rights and international law and juvenile justice, has urged States to give minor children the following: the right to privacy, even in the household; the right to professional counseling without parental consent or guidance; the full right to abortion and contraceptives; the right to full freedom of expression at home and in school; and the legal mechanisms to challenge in court their parents' authority in the home.

For example, in 1995 the United Kingdom was specifically rebuked by the CRC committee for allowing parents to withdraw their children from sex-education classes if they disagreed with the content.[16] The CRC committee report to Belize recommended that the government set up legal mechanisms to help children challenge their parents, including making an "independent child-friendly mechanism" accessible to children "to deal with complaints of violations of their rights and to provide remedies for such violations."[17] The report goes further, asserting it is "concerned that the law does not allow children, particularly adolescents, to seek medical or legal counseling without parental consent, even when it is in the best interests of the child."[18] The CRC committee told Austria, "Austrian Law and regulations do not provide a legal minimum age for medical counseling and treatment without parental consent."[19]

Likewise, the CRC committee recommended the Japanese government "guarantee the child's right to privacy, especially in the family."[20] The committee urged the Ethiopian government to change its laws so that "the limitation of the right to legal counsel of children be abolished as a matter of priority."[21]

The committee periodically issues "general comments" intended to flesh out the commitments inherent in the CRC treaty itself. In 2003, the committee's General Comment No. 4 expounded upon "adolescent health and development in the context of the Convention on the Rights of the Child." This comment asserts the right of children "to access appropriate information" regarding "family planning." It instructed States to allow minors to receive confidential medical care. Minors should have "access to appropriate information [regarding HIV/AIDS and STDs], regardless of their marital status and whether their parents or guardians consent." States should, according to the committee, "take measures to remove all barriers hindering the access of adolescents to information, preventative measures such as condoms, and care."[22] Such measures, if implemented, would also increase the availability of abortion for adolescents.

My own review of the reports from thirty countries, chosen more or less at random, from 2007-2012 showed that the Committee in nearly every instance called upon the reporting country to ban all forms of corporal punishment and to increase the opportunities for the child to express his views.[23] Further, during this period, it called upon several nations from this group of thirty—Argentina, Chile, El Salvador, Uruguay, Venezuela, Ukraine, Korea—to liberalize restrictive abortion laws for adolescents,[24] *despite the facts that (a) the CRC does not mention abortion and (b) many of these nations have constitutional provisions or national laws restricting or banning abortion.*

From this brief review, the ideological biases of the Committee are clear. All of these recommendations also quite clearly undermine both the parental role and the family.

It is important to remember that there are contending cultural forces at work, and they battle over the meaning of the language used. Some of these forces believe it advances the cause of freedom to undermine the

family, which they regard as oppressive and patriarchal.[25] However, that
need not be the way in which all provisions of the CRC are understood.[26]
This is clear if we consider the history of the CRC.

The CRC was unveiled at the World Summit on Children in 1989.
At the *second* World Summit, which was held at the UN in 2001/02,[27]
nations gathered to assess a decade on international efforts on behalf of
children. They concluded that much remained to be done. For example,
one area where more was needed was education.

The statement adopted upon the close of the World Summit
(officially designated the UN Special Session on Children) noted many
remaining problems faced by children. Regarding education, the chief of
which may have been that "more than 100 million children of primary
school age, the majority of them girls, are not enrolled in school...and
one third of all children do not complete five years of schooling, the
minimum required for basic literacy."[28] The resolution called for an array
of programs and efforts, by governments and by civil society, to meet
this problem. *Even so*, the nations gathered at the UN recognized, in the
official statement, that it was parents who are "the primary caretakers of
children" and they pledged to "strengthen their capacity to provide
optimum care, nurturing and protection."[29] Thus, the statement called for
government programs to support parents and families.

The public position taken by the United States at the Summit, I
believe, rightly identified the "human rights" principles concerning
parental rights, and personified the orientation toward these matters that
stakeholders should always employ. In its official, written "explanation
of position,"[30] which explained how the United States understood certain
terms in the statement, the United States stated the following: "The
United States understands that 'children's rights' are [to be] seen at all
times in relation to the rights, duties and responsibilities of parents, who
have the primary responsibility for their children's education and well-
being. In this regard, the United States emphasizes the importance it
attaches to the involvement of parents in decisions affecting children and
adolescents in all aspects of sexual and reproductive health and in all
aspects of their lives and education for which they have the primary
responsibility." This identifies the parents as *primarily* responsible, and
the State in a *secondary or supportive* role. Children's "rights" are not
highly individualized rights of autonomy; rather, they are located within
a context of parental duties, rights, and responsibilities and all are located
within the social unit of "the family."

To summarize, from an examination of human rights principles and
law, we have identified the following: 1) the family, founded upon
marriage, is fundamental, natural and essential to the health of society; 2)

the State must make efforts to support—not to undermine—the family; 3) parental rights in the formation and education (broadly conceived) of the child are paramount and the State is to *supplement* their efforts; 4) the child is entitled to protection from abuse and exploitation. These are the principles that go all the way back to the UDHR; they are basic principles of human rights. Principles to the contrary in the CRC are simply not consistent with basic human rights.

Catholic Social Teaching

Although any and all teaching of the Catholic bishops might be regarded as "Catholic social teaching" ("CST")—because it is a) teaching, b) by authority figures (i.e., bishops), c) within the Catholic Church, and d) about social life—that term is properly reserved for the body of teaching of a more authoritative nature, both in a) encyclicals (letters) from one of the popes and b) documents from ecumenical councils (that is, of the bishops from around the world, including the pope). While any encyclical and any document from councils would qualify under such a definition, "Catholic social teaching" is usually reserved for the teaching, by encyclical and council, which marks the Church's engagement with modernity, that is, from the 1890s to the present.

The first such document was *Rerum Novarum* (*On the Condition of the Working Classes*), issued by Pope Leo XIII in 1981. In *Rerum Novarum*, the Church first systematically responded to the problems of the modern era. In *Rerum Novarum*, Pope Leo XIII set forth many principles that would be subsequently developed by the teaching Magisterium of the Church, particularly at Vatican Council II (1962-1965) and during the pontificate of John Paul II (1978-2005). The success of Leo XIII in identifying the principles for the engagement with the modern world may be gauged by the comment of a subsequent pontiff, Pius XI, who, in *Quadragesimo Anno* (*Reconstructing the Social Order*) in 1931, called *Rerum Novarum* "the *magna carta* on which all Christian activities in social matters are ultimately based."[31]

Indeed, when preparing this article, it became clear to me that it is probably no exaggeration to say that *all* of the essential principles that will help us to evaluate the CPS were identified in *Rerum Novarum*. Vatican II, functioning at the highest teaching level of the Church, embraced these principles, and they were developed in detail by John Paul II, but the essentials were all in *Rerum Novarum*, and it is to that document that I will now turn.

The encyclical insisted on the right to marriage.[32] It also emphasized that the right to own property was integral to the fulfillment of parental duties.[33]

Rerum Novarum taught that the family was "the society of the household," which existed *prior to* the State.[34] Consequently, the State was obliged to respect the inherent rights and integrity of the family. "If citizens, if families, after becoming participants in common life and society, were to experience injury in a commonwealth instead of help, impairment of their rights instead of protection, society would be something to be repudiated rather than to be sought after."[35] Thus, "the civil power" may not "enter arbitrarily into the privacy of the home."[36]

There are, however, certain situations in which the State is justified in intervening in family life. "If a family perchance is in such extreme difficulty and is so completely without plans that it is entirely unable to help itself, it is right that the distress be remedied by public aid, for each individual family is a part of the community. Similarly, if anywhere there is a grave violation of mutual rights within the family walls, public authority shall restore to each his right for this is not usurping the rights of citizens, but protecting and confirming them with just and due care."[37] But State intervention must stop there, for "nature does not permit [the civil authorities] to go beyond these limits."[38] Central to this conception of the relationship of the State and the family is the role of the parents, their rights and responsibilities. "Paternal authority is such that it can be neither abolished nor absorbed by the State."[39]

This brief review of *Rerum Novarum* establishes the following principles, relevant to our evaluation of the CPS: 1) the family predates the State and society, and is founded upon marriage; 2) society and the State are obligated to support, and not to undermine, the family; 3) parental authority is fundamental and the State may not displace it; and 4) there are limited situations—defending basic human rights—in which State intervention is appropriate.

As noted, these principles were endorsed at Vatican II. I will look at two important documents from the Council, *Gravissimum Educationis* and *Guadium et spes*.

In *Gravissimum Educationis* (*Declaration on Christian Education*), the Council Fathers emphasized the irreplaceable role of parents in the education of children. "As it is the parents who have given life to their children, on them lies the gravest obligation of educating their family....The role of parents in education is of such importance that it is almost impossible to provide an adequate substitute."[40]

This reference to education does not envision a limited role for parents. In other words, it is not a narrow definition of education;

"education" is not limited to what a child might learn in classroom. Rather it is about all the habits and virtues necessary for the child to grow to know God and to serve his fellow man. Thus, the parental role is very broad because education encompasses what we might identify as the moral formation of the child and preparation of him to be a good citizen. As the document says, "the family is…the principal school of social virtues which are necessary to every society."[41]

The civil and political authorities "should recognize the duties and responsibilities of parents…and provide them with the requisite assistance. In accordance with the principle of subsidiarity, when the efforts of the parents and of other organizations are inadequate, it should itself undertake the duty of education, with due consideration, however, for the wishes of the parents."[42]

Thus, in the *Declaration on Christian Education*, the Church asserted that a) the parents are the primary educators of children, b) that such education prepares children to take their place in society and in the Church, and c) that the role of the State is to *assist*—not to substitute for—parents in this task.

Guadium et spes (*The Pastoral Constitution on the Church in the Modern World*) complements what the Declaration says about parents. It contains an important chapter on "The Dignity of Marriage and the Family."[43] The document notes that man is inherently made for relationship (i.e., is a *social* being) and that marriage is the first form of communion between persons.[44] By teaching its members about self-giving, love and cooperation, and thereby preparing them for life among others (i.e., for life in *society*), the family is "the basis of society."[45] Therefore, "Civil authority should consider it a sacred duty to acknowledge the true nature of marriage and the family, [and] to protect and foster them…."[46]

The pontificate of John Paul II, who, as a bishop, was a participant at Vatican II, was devoted to expounding and exploring the themes from the Council. The most systematic treatment of the family and the role of parents is found in *Familiaris Consortio* (*The Role of the Family in the Modern World*) (1981).

The Pope began by proclaiming, "Marriage and the family were willed by God in the very act of creation."[47] Thus, there is nothing in human existence that is more fundamental. It is in the family that love finds expression. "[And] love is the fundamental and innate vocation of every human being."[48] God made human beings to love. "The only place in which this self-giving in its whole truth is made possible is marriage…whereby man and woman accept the intimate community of life and love willed by God."[49]

As man and woman encounter each other and learn to love one another in marriage, they also form the first human society. "The family is the first and fundamental school of social living: as a community of love, it finds in self-giving the law that guides it and makes it grow. The self-giving that inspires the love of husband and wife for each other is the model and norm...."[50] This "experience of communion and sharing that should characterize the family's daily life represents its first and fundamental contribution to society."[51] The family teaches its members to love others with whom they are joined in community, and, thereby, to deepen that community. This model of love as self-giving will then be taken by members of the family into their other relationships in the wider society. Thereby, the entire society benefits.

The State is not entitled to substitute itself for the family: "By virtue of this principle (subsidiarity), the State cannot and must not take away from families the functions that they can just as well perform."[52] The proper role of the State is, rather, to *assist* the family: "The public authorities must do everything possible to ensure that families have all those aids—economic, social, educational, political, and cultural assistance—that they need in order to face all their responsibilities in a human way."[53]

Yet, the situation in the modern world is far from this ideal. As John Paul II puts it, "[i]n fact,...the situation experienced by many families in various countries is highly problematical, if not entirely negative; institutions and laws unjustly ignore the inviolable rights of the family...; and society, far from putting itself at the service of the family, attacks it violently in its values and fundamental requirements. Thus the family, which in God's plan is the basic cell of society and a subject of rights and duties before the State or any other community, finds itself the victim of society...even of its blatant injustice." John Paul proclaimed, in order to counter this, that "the Church openly and strongly defends the rights of the family against the intolerable usurpations of society and the State." He listed fourteen "rights of the family," including "the right...to educate children" and "the right to bring up children in accordance with the family's own traditions and religious and cultural values."[54]

These rights were collected, expanded, and issued two years later as *The Charter of the Rights of the Family*.[55] Certain provisions are particularly relevant in the context of evaluating the CPS: Preamble E ("the family constitutes, much more than a mere juridical, social and economic unit, a community of love and solidarity, which is uniquely suited to teach and transmit cultural, ethical, social, spiritual and religious values, essential for the development and well-being of its own members and of society"); Preamble I ("society, and in a particular manner the State and International Organizations, must protect the family through measures of a political, economic, social and juridical character, *which aim at consolidating the unity and stability of the family...*" [emphasis added]); Article 4 (d) ("Children...have the right to special protection and assistance..."); and Article 5 ("Since they have conferred life on their children, parents have the original, primary and inalienable right to educate them; hence they must be acknowledged as the first and foremost educators of their children....Parents have the right to educate their children in conformity with their moral and religious convictions...[T]hey should also receive from society the necessary aid and assistance to perform their educational role properly").

Conclusion

It is seems clear there are many principles relevant to the family and the parental role that are common to both human rights law/principles and Catholic social teaching, and which are also relevant in evaluating the CPS. Among these are: 1) the right of men and women to marry; 2) the right to found a family; 3) the importance of the family to society and the State, both of which it predates; 4) the essential (primary) role of parents in the upbringing and education of children (with education being very broadly conceived); 5) the obligation of society and the State to provide assistance to parents as needed; 6) the principle that the State is never permitted to substitute itself for the family or for parental functions (e.g., even as regards "education," the State role is supplementary to that of the parents); and 7) the recognition that children, unlike adults, need "special care and assistance." Thus, the burden of proof, we might say, is upon the State to justify its intervention. Both human rights law/principles and CST acknowledge there can be instances where State authorities are entitled (even required) to infringe upon the family unit to protect the child from abuse. But, even so, such intervention must be limited. To paraphrase Leo XIII, the State role is "restorative." The State must act so that its actions tend—over all the cases, if not every particular one—to reinforce the family. This necessarily means not undermining the role of parents. The State's role is secondary, subsidiary, and supportive. When it begins to take a primary role, or to permanently displace parents, it has gone too far. On this, I would say both accepted human rights principles and CST agree.

Notes

[1] Article VI: This Constitution, and the Law of the United States that shall be made in Pursuance thereof; and Treaties made, or which shall be made, under the Authority of the United States, shall be the supreme Law of the Land.

[2] Convention on the Rights of the Child, Art. 37, Nov. 20, 1989, 1577 U.N.T.S. 3, 28 I.L.M. 1448, 1468–1470 (entered into force Sept. 2, 1990).

[3] International Covenant on Civil and Political Rights (ICCPR), December 19, 1966, 999 U.N.T.S. 175.

[4] Senate Committee on Foreign Relations, International Covenant on Civil and Political Rights, S. Exec. Rep. No. 102–23 (1992).

[5] See, for example, Preamble of the Universal Declaration of Human Rights, paragraphs 1 and 3: "[R]ecognition of the inherent dignity and of the equal and inalienable rights of all members of the human family is the foundation of freedom, justice and peace in the world," and "[I]t is essential, if man is not to be compelled to have recourse...to rebellion against tyranny and oppression, that human rights should be protected by the rule of law."

[6] Universal Declaration of Human Rights, Dec. 10, 1948, G.A. Res. 217A(III), UN Doc. A/810, (1948) (available at http://www.un.org/en/documents/udhr).

[7] Mary Ann Glendon, *A World Made New* (Random House: New York, 2001), at page 159 (hereafter, *World Made New*).

[8] Article 25 (2)

[9] Article 24

[10] In the text that follows, I am not advocating that the United States ratify the CRC. For reasons that will become apparent, ratification would pose significant legal problems for the U.S. and for families in the U.S. Indeed, nations who have ratified the CRC should consider repudiating it and withdrawing from it.

[11] Curtis A. Bradley & Jack L. Goldsmith, "Customary International Law as Federal Common Law: A Critique of the Modern Position, 110 *Harvard Law Review* 815 (1997).

[12] 543 U.S. 551 (2005)

[13] 543 U.S., at 576.

[14] This reliance upon an unratified treaty was vigorously challenged in a dissent written by Justice Antonin Scalia (see 662 and following).

[15] Article 18 goes on to say: "States...shall render appropriate assistance to parents...in the performance of their child-rearing responsibilities...".

[16] CRC Committee, 8th Session, Concluding Observations of the Committee on the Rights of the Child: United Kingdom of Great Britain and Northern Ireland, CRC/C/15/Add.34, February 15, 1995. "Insufficient attention has been given to the right of the child to express his/her opinion, including in cases where parents in England and Wales have the possibility of withdrawing their children from parts of the sex education programs in school. In this as in other decisions, including exclusion from school, the child is not systematically invited to express his/her opinion and those opinions may not be given due weight, as required under article 12 of the Convention."

[17] CRC Committee, 20th Sess. (1999), "Report on Belize," paragraph 11.

[18] Ibid, paragraph 14.

[19] CRC Committee, 20th Sess. (2000), "Report on Austria," paragraph 15.

[20] CRC Committee, 19th Sess. (1998), "Report on Japan," paragraph 36.

[21] CRC Committee, 14th Sess. (1998), "Report on Ethiopia," paragraph 27.

[22] CRC Committee, General Comment No. 4 (2003), sections 9, 11, 28, and 30.

[23] Countries reviewed over this period were Argentina, Bolivia, Chile, Ecuador, Paraguay, Uruguay, Venezuela, El Salvador, Honduras, Dominican Republic, Belarus, Czech Republic, Georgia, Kazakhstan, Azerbaijan, Pakistan, Moldova, Montenegro, Romania, Serbia, Slovakia, Ukraine, Belgium, United Kingdom, Finland, the Netherlands, Korea, and New Zealand. Reports at: http://www2.ohchr.org/english/bodies/crc/sessions.htm.

[24] Ibid.

[25] UN Population Fund representative, Arie Hoekman, for instance, lauded high divorce rates and high out-of-wedlock births as a victory for human rights. See M. Aguirre and A. Wolfgram, "United States Policy and the Family: Redefining the Ties that Bind," *B.Y.U. Journal of Public Law*, p. 23

[26] Note, of course, that even if some of the language of the CRC can be understood in a way that is consistent with human rights principles established previously, that would not eliminate the problems posed by the CRC. One such problem is the understanding of "human rights" by officials (such as those discussed from the Committee) that is used to undermine parental authority and the family.

[27] The author was a "private sector" member of the official United States delegation, the first UN delegation under President George W. Bush.

[28] "A World Fit for Children," UN General Assembly, A/Res/S-27/2 (October 11, 2001), at paragraph 38 (hereafter, "World Fit").

[29] See, "World Fit," at, e.g., paragraphs 6 and 31-1.

[30] "United States of America Explanation of Position," 5/1/2001.

[31] *Quadregessimo Anno* I-3.

[32] "No law of man can abolish the natural and primeval right of marriage" (*Rerum Novarum 19*).

[33] *Rerum Novarum* 17-20.

[34] "Behold...the family, or rather the society of the household, a very small society indeed, but a true one, and older than any polity." *Rerum Novarum* 19.

[35] *Rerum Novarum* 20.

[36] *Rerum Novarum* 21.

[37] Ibid.

[38] Ibid.

[39] Ibid.

[40] *Gravissimum Educationis* 3.

[41] Ibid.

[42] Ibid.

[43] Part Two, Chapter 1 (paragraphs 47-52)

[44] Paragraph 12

[45] Paragraph 52

[46] Ibid.

[47] Ibid.

[48] *Familiaris Consortio* 11.

[49] Ibid.

[50] Ibid. 37.

[51] Ibid. 43.

[52] Ibid. 45.

[53] Ibid. 45.

[54] Quotations in the preceding paragraph in the text are all from paragraph 46 of *Familiaris Consortio*.

[55] Pontifical Council for the Family, The Charter of the Rights of the Family (1983), http://www.vatican.va/roman_curia/pontifical_councils/family/documents/rc_pc_family_ doc_19831022_family-rights_en.html.

Child Protective Services and Police Interference with Family Relations: A Constitutional Perspective

By Michael E. Rosman*

The United States Constitution protects the rights of families and family relationships. It is, we are told, the oldest and most important "fundamental right" that is loosely ascribed to the doctrine known as "substantive due process."

Lawsuits that have reached the Supreme Court relating to these rights usually involve what protections families have in court: what standard of proof might be necessary to permit a judge to interfere with, or diminish, the rights of parents to make decisions involving their children or to sever the parent-child relationship altogether.

Frequently, though, interference with familial relations takes place outside of the courtroom, either without the involvement of a judge or without the family being given a chance to make their case in court. This article examines one subset of this phenomenon: when social workers from a Child Protective Services ("CPS")[1] agency or the police decide, on their own, that a child should be removed for a period of time from the custody of his or her parents, or that the relationship should, in some other way, be altered. A social worker perhaps decides that a parent presents a threat of abuse to a child right away and takes the child out of his or her home. Or a doctor may conclude that a child needs emergency medical treatment right away and provides it without parental consent (or over parental objections). A judicial hearing likely will follow, but even the temporary alteration of the parent-child relationship is consequential and subject to the United States Constitution.

*The author thanks Diane Redleaf for carefully reading and commenting on this paper.

The liberty interest in familial relationships governs these situations as well. Most of the law in these situations, however, has been created by the lower courts; the Supreme Court has not yet provided any guidance. Moreover, the cases expounding on these fundamental rights are not only fact-specific, but seem to vary from court to court and judge to judge. If the police suspect a parent of sexual abuse, how solid must the evidence be before they can remove the child from the home without a hearing in which the parent disputes the charge? Does it matter that the evidence is of infrequent abuse so that the chances of any harm occurring before a judicial proceeding, where the parent can defend herself, can be commenced is slim? These questions have not been given any consistent answer.

My goal in this paper is to introduce the reader to the application of the Constitution to situations in which a state actor has interfered with a family's right to be together, or a parent's right to make decisions for a child, prior to the family (or parent) having the opportunity to defend itself (or himself) in court. I suggest that, given the speed with which judicial hearings can be held in this day and age, there are few instances in which such hearings are properly delayed. The right to family integrity is too frequently violated by overzealous members of the child protection community, with few or inadequate checks from the judiciary.

In Part I of this article, I introduce the concept of "due process" under which familial rights litigation is frequently conducted. In Part II, I describe how "due process" applies to temporary disruptions of the family relationship and/or the rights of parents, and describe a few other legal issues related to such cases. Part III addresses cases involving the most common means of independent (i.e., without judicial imprimatur) interference by CPS social workers and the police—the temporary removal of children from their parents' custody—and Part IV addresses other kinds of independent interference. Part V briefly identifies the way in which social workers and police, or even the system as a whole, can violate families' constitutional rights even when judges are involved in some tangential way (but before a full-fledged hearing). I offer a few concluding thoughts in Part VI.

I

An Introduction to "Due Process" and Family Rights

In relevant part, the Fourteenth Amendment to the United States Constitution provides:

No State shall make or enforce any law which shall abridge the privileges or immunities of citizens of the United States; nor shall any State deprive any person of life, liberty, or property, without due process of law .... [2]

The Fifth Amendment to the United States Constitution has somewhat similar language, albeit in the passive voice.[3] The Supreme Court has held, not without some controversy, that the protection against deprivations of life, liberty, or property without due process has a "substantive" component.[4] That is, it provides heightened protection against government interference with certain "fundamental" rights and liberty interests.[5]

The "controversy," of course, is twofold. First, the phrase and notion of "substantive due process" is a bit odd. It applies to acts of legislatures that interfere with the identified fundamental rights, and it is strange that a "law" can violate "due process of law."[6] Second, the Court has used "substantive due process" to find constitutional rights that are not deemed fundamental by a substantial portion of the population—most notably, the right to an abortion.[7] Basically, substantive due process means that a law cannot be enacted if it interferes with a fundamental right.

That being said, the notion that the Constitution protects the interest of parents in the care, custody, and control of their children has provoked little controversy, and certainly not the controversy associated with other rights found under the "substantive due process" rubric. The Court has said that parental rights are "the oldest of the fundamental liberty interests recognized,"[8] tracing back to decisions from the 1920s.[9] The Court has, for example, declared unconstitutional a Nebraska law that prohibited the teaching of any language other than English to students who have not passed the eighth grade.[10] It was deemed "materially to interfere with the calling of modern language teachers, with the opportunities of pupils to acquire knowledge, and with the power of parents to control the education of their own."[11] The Court declared unconstitutional an Oregon law (adopted by voter initiative) requiring all children who had not completed the eighth grade to go to public school.[12] That law, the Court said, "unreasonably interferes with the liberty of parents and guardians to direct the upbringing and education of children under their control."[13]

More recently, the Court has declared unconstitutional an Illinois procedure in which children could be declared wards of the state despite the existence of a father (unmarried to the child's deceased mother) whose competence as a parent had not been adjudged.[14] The Court held that the Illinois statute that excluded unwed fathers from the definition of "parent" (whose competence would have to be adjudged before a child could be declared a ward of the state) violated due process.[15] Ten years later, the Court concluded that a State seeking to sever permanently a parent's relationship with a child could not do so by showing, as New York's statutes permitted, by a mere preponderance of the evidence that the parent was negligent. Rather, the Constitution required that the state's burden be at least showing negligence by clear and convincing evidence.[16] Finally, the Court has declared unconstitutional a state law that permitted any person to seek "visitation rights" with a child, and a court to order such visitation, upon a showing of the "best interests of the child."[17] The law violated due process not because "the [state court] intervened, but that when it did so, it gave no special weight at all to [the mother's] determination of her daughters' best interests."[18]

The foregoing demonstrates that it is sometimes difficult—perhaps to the point of being artificial—to distinguish between substantive and procedural due process in this area (procedural due process means that certain legal procedures must be followed to determine if there is good cause for a person's rights can be taken away before this or if such infringement can be allowed to stand. *Santosky v. Kramer*, for example, the case involving the level of proof of negligence that a state needed to show to sever the parent-child relationship, used the basic analysis of procedural due process.[19] But the first part of that analysis assessed the importance of the "private interest" affected by the state proceeding, and concluded that the "private interest affected is commanding."[20] That conclusion could not help but be influenced by the Court's earlier statement that "freedom of personal choice in matters of family life is a fundamental liberty interest protected by the Fourteenth Amendment."[21] Similarly, *Troxel v. Granville* is usually considered a case involving "substantive due process," the parents' right to determine when and where others could visit with their children.[22] But the holding of the Court did not state that such a right was inviolable. Rather, it held that the state court proceeding had failed to give sufficient weight to the parent's determination before it overruled it.[23] This certainly sounds like the state failed to provide procedures adequate to protect the important interest at stake, the very heart of procedural due process.

Regardless of labels, the earlier cases precluded the state from substituting its judgment, through legislation, for the parents' educational determinations, while the modern cases have not precluded the state from affecting the parent-child relationship. Rather, they have limited its ability to modify that relationship with procedures that fail to take into account the importance of the relationship.

II
Temporary Deprivations

The cases that have reached the Supreme Court concerning family relations and parental rights all have involved relatively long-term and substantial changes in those relations and rights: e.g., the inability to send one's child to private school (*Pierce v. Society of Sisters*), the right to control who visits the child (*Troxel*), or the complete severance of the parent-child relationship (*Santosky*). None have yet considered the role of the Constitution in more temporally ephemeral changes in the relationship. For example, a court might temporarily preclude a parent from living with a child while charges of abuse are investigated and/or litigated.

It is relatively clear, however, that such temporary infringements on the parent-child relationship are subject to constitutional challenge. Beginning in 1969, the Court has addressed temporary deprivations of *property* interests usually affected as part of an ongoing legal proceeding. Thus, for example, a state law may permit a plaintiff beginning a lawsuit to "garnish" the wages (essentially "freeze" them by requiring an employer to hold on to the earned but unpaid wages) of a defendant without notice or a hearing on the propriety of the underlying claim.[24] Or a statute may give the seller of goods with financing to the buyer the right to ask the sheriff to repossess them if the buyer defaults on a payment.[25]

When addressed by the Court, the constitutional fate of such laws has depended upon a whole series of factors, including the type of property involved,[26] whether a judge was involved in issuing the process that led to the temporary deprivation,[27] whether the standard that ultimately would be at issue was factually complex,[28] whether the person seeking to encumber the property of another had an interest in that property (like a lien or contractual right to repossess),[29] whether procuring the encumbrance requires the assertion of facts based upon personal knowledge,[30] whether the party seeking the encumbrance is required to post a bond (or whether the defendant can remove it by posting a bond),[31] and whether there is a post-deprivation hearing that takes place soon.[32]

None of these factors appear dispositive, and they need not detain us for long. Although there may be some analogies in the context of interference with familial relationships, the importance of the *Sniadach v. Family Finance Corp.* line of cases is that they establish that there is no minimum period of time for a state-imposed or state-aided deprivation of property to qualify as a constitutional deprivation.[33] To be sure, the Court has stated that the time of the deprivation may influence what procedures are needed.[34] But the right to notice and a hearing remain intact regardless of how long the deprivation is. The lower courts generally have concluded that temporary deprivations of the right to custody implicate due process concerns.[35]

Indeed, the Court has said that a pre-deprivation hearing—that is, a hearing that takes place before the loss of a right or property interest—is the presumptive requirement. That presumption is only overcome in "emergencies."[36] Nonetheless, the Court has acknowledged a whole host of such "emergencies." A search warrant, of course, is issued without a prior hearing for the party being searched (although there must be judicial authorization).[37] And the Court has never suggested that a prior hearing must be held before a person can be arrested; indeed, there is no general requirement of judicial authorization for arrests.[38] When the state itself is so substantially involved in a temporary deprivation of property or liberty, it would appear that the standard for postponing the hearing is lower.

And this brings us to interference with familial relations without a hearing. The circumstances under which the state can interfere are myriad, and the analysis of whether such interference violates the Constitution is usually quite fact-specific. But the basic rule should apply: in the absence of an emergency, almost always involving the well-being of a child, the state ought not to be permitted to act without the minimal due process requirements of notice and a hearing. Further, because families frequently, even in this day and age, involve more than one parent and more than one child, a second set of questions ought to be (but frequently is not) asked: Whose well-being is threatened and what needs to be done to protect it?

The standards vary from federal judicial circuit to circuit, but generally (at least as articulated) come fairly close to the standard just suggested. The Ninth Circuit has perhaps the most detailed statement of the standard (and, in my view, the best, were it consistently applied): state officials cannot interfere in the parent-child relationship unless the information they possess at the time of the interference is such "as provides reasonable cause to believe that the child is in imminent danger of serious bodily injury and that the scope of the intrusion is reasonably necessary to avert that specific injury."[39]

Here are a few of the possible circumstances in which this test, or quite similar tests in other circuits, might be applied: state officials (that is, police or CPS social workers) take a child into custody because a parent is accused of abusing or mistreating a child, or of failing to provide a child with necessary medical care; state officials, in seeking to protect a child, have interfered with the ability of a non-abusive parent to provide for his/her child; state officials take a position in a custodial battle; or state officials make false allegations in an effort to obtain an *ex parte* order for certain actions they wish to take. Each of these situations can raise constitutional issues, as can the existence of a prompt post-deprivation hearing. In the next few sections, we will consider and examine how various factual scenarios are analyzed under the Constitution's due process clause.

Before doing so, I briefly make three preliminary notes on legal doctrine. (Those less interested in the niceties of legal doctrine should feel free to skip the rest of this section and go right to Part III.)

The first (and briefest) doctrinal note is on the defense of "qualified immunity." When state officials are sued for damages for violations of the Constitution, they can assert an affirmative defense of qualified immunity. Under this defense, a state official is not liable for damages unless he or she violated "clearly established" law.[40] I mention this solely so the reader will understand some of the case citations. Frequently, courts will hold that a state official violated the Constitution (or, on summary judgment, that there is a genuine issue of material fact as to whether the state official violated the Constitution), but that the state official is entitled to dismissal of the claim because the law was sufficiently unclear at the time that the official acted that the defense of "qualified immunity" should be upheld.

Second, it deserves mention that the lower courts not only treat situations in which state officials intervene in family situations differently at times, but they also apply different rubrics. More particularly, the doctrine of "substantive due process" has different standards in different courts, particularly as to executive conduct (that is, the acts of executive branch officials like CPS social workers and police). Some courts require a showing that the executive conduct "shocks the conscience."[41] Others view that as just one of several possible tests, and, at least theoretically, are open to apply "fundamental rights" analysis to the conduct (requiring the conduct to meet "strict scrutiny," i.e., a compelling governmental interest and means that are narrowly tailored).[42]

Further, as we saw in reviewing the Supreme Court's jurisprudence, the line between substantive and procedural due process in this general area is sometimes difficult to discern. So, too, with the specific analyses of temporary interferences with parental rights and family relations, especially (but not necessarily) when courts employ a "fundamental rights" analysis. Thus, where courts analyze "substantive due process" by subjecting the government interference with the family relations to strict scrutiny, they ask whether there was a "compelling governmental interest," usually involving the state's right to protect children from harm, to interfere with that substantive right, and whether the removal was narrowly tailored to meet that interest. Procedural due process analysis depicts the issue as one involving whether the "emergency" conditions for omitting the normally required pre-deprivation notice and hearing under "procedural due process" are met. In some cases, both are asserted and the standards—or, at least, the results—look quite similar.[43]

Even when the standards for the two doctrines are different, the ultimate constitutional outcome may not change much because the procedural due process inquiry follows the basic rule. The Second Circuit Court of Appeals, for example, analyzes the removal of a child from a parent under substantive due process quite differently from procedural due process. The former requires that the removal "shock the conscience" to violate substantive due process.[44] It accordingly asks whether the removal would have been constitutional even if the plaintiffs had been given full process (presumably meaning after notice and a hearing before a judge).[45] Temporary separations are insufficiently severe to constitute a deprivation of substantive due process.[46] Nonetheless, when addressing the same set of facts under procedural due process, the Second Circuit uses a standard quite similar to the one that has been identified here: notice and a hearing are required except in an emergency, and an emergency exists if something significantly bad will happen to the child before the appropriate process can be effected.[47]

Similarly, in the Seventh Circuit, the courts have adopted the "probable cause" standard for arrests to determine whether a child's seizure without court approval violates substantive due process—an additional justification beyond an emergency of some kind.[48] But that court still requires an "emergency" of some kind under a procedural due process analysis before state officials can dispense with the otherwise-required notice and hearing.[49]

Finally, some judges using the "shock the conscience" standard for substantive due process have found that removal of children without an immediate threat to the child's welfare *does* shock the conscience.[50]

The last doctrinal note involves the Fourth Amendment. The Fourth Amendment of the United States Constitution states:

> The right of the people to be secure in their persons, houses, papers, and effects, against unreasonable searches and seizures, shall not be violated, and no Warrants shall issue, but upon probable cause, supported by Oath or affirmation, and particularly describing the place to be searched, and the

persons or things to be seized.[51]

Although the text of the Fourth Amendment restricts the government's ability to search private places, to search individuals, and to seize individuals, the Court has provided greater protections for the first, particularly when the private place is a person's home. Thus, while a person can be arrested based upon probable cause that they have committed a crime, and without a warrant,[52] searches of people's homes and other private effects generally require a warrant.[53] Thus, a search of a home without a warrant for evidence of child neglect or child abuse, or the entry into a home in order to seize a child, will be subjected to Fourth Amendment review. Not all such warrantless searches are unconstitutional. Several of the exceptions to the warrant requirement relate to "emergency" situations, and are thus similar to those exceptions involved in determining whether state officials violated someone's right to "due process" by failing to provide a pre-deprivation hearing.[54]

That being said, one important distinction, often ignored by the courts, deserves mention.[55] Whether something is an "emergency," either for determining whether a search is unreasonable or whether someone's due process rights have been violated, may be dependent upon what the standard procedure is.[56] Something *ought* to be defined as an emergency if there is a substantial threat of something bad happening and the standard procedure—the constitutionally-required procedure—would take too long to prevent it.[57] Furthermore, the standard procedures for searches of a home under the Fourth Amendment and for interference with familial relationships and parental rights under the due process clause are not the same. The standard procedure for a government-sponsored search is a warrant. The standard procedure—that is, the "due process"—for interference with a property or liberty interest is notice and a hearing prior to the deprivation. It is frequently—although, as we shall see, not universally—the case that a warrant can be obtained more quickly than a judicial hearing. This, of course, is at least in part because warrants can be obtained *ex parte*—the police go to a judge or a magistrate and apply for a warrant without anyone else there to contradict the evidence that they put forth to support one.

On the other hand, while an *ex parte* warrant based upon probable cause can justify a search of the home under the Fourth Amendment, it ought not, by itself, justify interference with the parent-child relationship. *That*, under the due process clause, requires notice and some kind of pre-deprivation hearing, which the *ex parte* warrant procedure plainly does not provide. To be sure, the reasons justifying the warrant may be sufficient in many cases also to justify the circumvention of the notice and hearing requirement (just as the reasons for a warrantless search of a home can also justify the removal of children from their parents). A warrant can be issued based on probable cause that a crime has taken place (or, in the case of a CPS investigation, that an abused or neglected child is on the premises).[58] Past neglect or abuse, by itself, does not demonstrate that there is an emergency, and the fact that police or social workers are lawfully on the premises does not necessarily mean that they can interfere with familial relations by removing children or otherwise.

Further, when a child is seized (regardless of where), it also raises Fourth Amendment claims for the child.[59] Thus, in analyzing the propriety of such a seizure, courts will frequently consider claims by the child under the Fourth Amendment and the parents under the due process clause of the Fourteenth Amendment, and this is true even where the seizure takes place outside the home. Generally speaking, the courts tend to employ the same analysis in determining whether children's or parents' constitutional rights were violated by such a seizure.[60]

The point, then, is that 1) searches, including entries in to the home, 2) seizures, and 3) interference with familial relationships or parental rights must be separately analyzed. Thus, for example, the Ninth Circuit separately analyzed a coerced entry into a home and a strip search of a three-year old in a case involving both.[61] Although the court did not really analyze in depth the constitutional theory that prohibited the strip search in its 1997 decision, and never even mentioned due process at all (as opposed to the Fourth Amendment), some of its analysis resonates with the rhetoric of, and likely today would be understood as falling under, the familial rights rubric:

> There is not much reason to be concerned with the privacy and dignity of the three year old whose buttocks were exposed, because with children of that age ordinarily among the parental tasks is teaching them when they are not supposed to expose their buttocks. But there is a very substantial interest, which forcing the mother to pull the child's pants down invaded, in the mother's dignity and authority in relation to her own children in her own home. The strip search as well as the entry stripped the mother of this authority and dignity. The reasonable expectation of privacy of individuals in their homes includes the interests of both parents and children in not having government officials coerce entry in violation of the Fourth Amendment and humiliate the parents in front of the children. An essential aspect of the privacy of the home is the parent's and the child's interest in the privacy of their relationship with each other.[62]

III
Removing Custody or Control

The most common temporary interference with parent-child relationships by CPS social workers and the police—or, at least, the most-commonly litigated—is the temporary removal of the children from the custody or physical control of the parent or parents. The circumstances under which that takes place is the focus of this section.

I have argued that the courts should require those acting prior to a hearing to point to credible evidence of some kind of emergency involving the child's health or well-being that justifies dispensing with notice and a hearing. So, in the normal case, when their decision to remove children from the custody of their parents is challenged in court, state officials will generally point to evidence of abuse (and, less often, neglect) by one or both parents.

The cases involving such scenarios are many, and they raise a distinct set of issues. First, is every instance of abuse an "emergency" involving (to use the Ninth Circuit's words) a "serious bodily injury"? One would think not, given the broad definition of abuse, and there are indeed some cases in which the allegations on which state officials based their interference have been deemed insufficient.[63] Yet other courts have indicated that virtually any kind of abuse can form the basis of an "emergency."[64] Indeed, several circuits state as the standard for circumventing the constitutional requirements evidence of an instance of past abuse *or* evidence of imminent danger.[65] The disjunction is difficult to understand; it is unclear why normal procedures to remove parental custody cannot be followed for a child for whom there is some evidence of past abuse but no evidence of imminent danger.

One clear sign that the allegations of abuse are not that urgent is if the social workers themselves do not treat them as if they were. Thus, if they have delayed investigating after receiving a complaint, or have begun an investigation and then gone back to their office to think about what to do next for a few days, courts will often (but, alas, not always) conclude that the situation was not an emergency that would justify circumventing the required procedures.[66] Similarly, it is a bad litigation tactic for a police officer or social worker to concede that the child was unlikely to suffer a serious consequence very soon, that there was time to hold a hearing or get some other kind of judicial authorization, or that the evidence was in equipoise.[67]

Where the allegations seem to focus more on neglect than abuse, courts have been a bit more vigilant in policing the constitutional boundary, perhaps because neglect seems to involve more long-term than immediate harm. First, the element of probability must be considered (as it only sometimes is in abuse cases). The neglect must be such that a bad result to the child has a good chance of occurring soon.[68] The courts have held, in both neglect and abuse cases, that the mere possibility of harm to the child is not enough.[69] Thus, the facts that an infant has been left home with a 12-year old,[70] that the mother is obese and may be unable to care fully for an infant,[71] or that the children have multiple bruises and bottle rot, are missing teeth, have thinning hair, and are soon to be locked in a room at the auto shop where their parents work,[72] are not reasons sufficient to permit social workers to take children into custody without the prerequisites of notice and a hearing. Dangerous situations in which there is a small chance that serious harm will result, at least when neglect allegations are concerned, do not seem to justify dispensing with the requirements of notice and a hearing.

Also in the "low risk" category are those cases where there is evidence of a *very* serious harm happening very soon—but the evidence itself is weak. In a seminal Ninth Circuit case, *Wallis v. Spencer*, police and social workers removed children from their home after receiving information that the father was going to sacrifice one of them in a satanic cult ritual.[73] This information was conveyed by the mother's sister, who had a long history of psychiatric problems; she conveyed it to a therapist in the hospital who, as a "mandated reporter" of child abuse under California law, relayed that information to the local Child Protective Services.[74] The Court concluded that "[u]nder the circumstances, a jury could reasonably conclude that the information possessed by the officers was insufficient to give rise to reasonable cause [that the children were in imminent danger of serious bodily harm]."[75] Of course, the evidence was almost surely of imminent danger of serious bodily injury (the child's sacrifice to Satan was to take place in a day or two.) It just was not very good evidence.

Good evidence of a dangerous situation, but in which nothing bad is likely to happen very soon (as in *Rogers*), is very much like weak evidence of almost certain and soon-to-happen death (as in *Wallis*). Mentally unstable people are not *invariably* wrong. So, in both cases, the evidence suggests a possibility of something serious and harmful happening soon, but one whose likelihood is so low that it should preclude dispensing with the standard constitutional requirements.[76]

Wallis raises two other issues that are frequently seen in the cases. First, the Court noted that, even granting some credibility to the information received, the father was supposed to only sacrifice one of his two children (his son). This, the court stated, suggested that perhaps there was no basis for believing that the other child (his daughter) was in danger.[77] One sees similar fact patterns all too often in the cases. Allegations, even credible allegations, are made that a parent is abusing one child—or even a child not his own—and social workers immediately move to take any and all children away from that parent.[78]

Second, the *Wallis* court noted that there were two parents, and only one of them was accused of wanting to sacrifice the son. Indeed, the "tip" from the mother's mentally unstable sister suggested that the mother likely did not know about the father's plan to sacrifice his son to Satan.[79] So, too, in a number of other cases, especially in the Ninth Circuit, courts have questioned whether children needed to be removed because of the alleged conduct of one parent.[80] This has even been extended to protect the rights of a parent with legal, but not physical, custody of the child.[81]

Indeed, one could well ask the following question: If one parent has engaged in abuse or neglect, why not just arrest him or her? Child abuse and child neglect are crimes in most states.[82] After the arrest, the children can just stay at home with the other parent. Wouldn't this be to the benefit of the children?

Part of the answer may have something to do with levels of proof required—that is, the evidentiary standard (as opposed to the substantive standard that the evidence might need to meet, like "imminent danger of serious bodily harm"). Arresting someone for a crime requires "probable cause."[83] The level of evidence of an emergency needed to remove children from their parents (or otherwise interfere with their relationship) varies from jurisdiction to jurisdiction, and has been variously described as "reasonable suspicion" and "reasonable cause," with just the occasional reference to "probable cause."[84] The "reasonable suspicion" standard is generally assumed to be something less than probable cause.[85] So, one answer to the "why not just arrest one parent" question may be that the evidence is sufficient to protect children, but not to arrest anyone for neglect or abuse.

But that answer does not wholly satisfy because, after all, if the goal is to protect children, one can simply remove the possible abuser from the home on a lower standard, much in the way that protective orders are commonly issued.[86] It seems unlikely that an order to not be in a particular place would constitute a "seizure" for purposes of the Fourth Amendment,[87] and so it is at least possible that there would be no constitutional requirement of "probable cause" (as there *might* be when children are seized).[88] Some states have statutes that specifically provide for such removal,[89] and those that do not ought to be able to rely upon whatever "protect the children" justification they use to seize and remove children, since removing just one parent is a constitutionally narrower disruption of the family than removing the chidlren.[90] Indeed, in some cases, the alleged offender *volunteers* to leave the home in the hopes that the children can be left with the remaining parent.[91] One can very well question the "voluntariness" of such offers given the coercive nature of the process.[92] But even if the removal of a parent is coerced and unconstitutional under due process, it is still *less* intrusive than removing a child from *both* parents.

Whatever may be motivating police and social workers, the courts have been less than diligent in requiring police and social workers to consider that alternative.[93] The social workers will often justify their actions by claiming that they believed that the non-abusing parent would not "protect" the child if the child remained in the home, perhaps because the non-abusing parent did not completely believe the allegations of abuse.[94] The courts' evident acceptance of this excuse is baffling (and basically unexplained). Protect the children from whom? If the abusing parent is being removed from the home, the source of danger from which protection might be needed is no longer there. Are the social workers concerned that the abusing parent will escape from jail? Be released on bond? Ignore an order requiring separation from the children? That there is another unknown abuser lurking in the shadows? These concerns, if that is in fact the motivation of the social workers, would be particularly odd where the alleged abuser has voluntarily offered to leave the home and the children temporarily. Alas, we do not know what the concerns might be because the courts explain neither the social workers' rationale nor their own (other than the obviously inadequate "inability to protect" excuse).

Keep in mind, as discussed in part V, that, even when justified by emergency circumstances, the social workers' actions must be followed fairly shortly by the hearing that was dispensed with prior to the children's removal. So, the "inability to protect" that motivates the social workers must be an "inability to protect" over a very short period of time (days). After the constitutionally-required notice and hearing, a judge might conclude that the children do indeed need to be removed from the non-abusing parent for some reason. Assuming the hearing has the constitutionally-required indicia of fairness, that presents no problem under the due process clause. However, removal of children by social workers or police from a non-abusing, non-negligent parent without a better explanation than "inability to protect" presents a constitutional problem.

IV
Other Kinds of Temporary Interference

The temporary removal of children from their parents' custody is the most common act whereby CPS social workers and/or the police interfere with the parent-child relationship, but it is not the only way. This section addresses a few of the other means that the cases have addressed.

The most common form of interference after temporary removal, and one closely connected to it, is subjecting the child to some medical examination or treatment without the parents' knowledge or consent. It is closely connected to temporary removals for the obvious reason that state would find it difficult to perform a medical examination, or provide medical treatment, without seizing the child and taking it somewhere.[95]

The courts have generally deemed parents' ability to make medical decisions for their children as part of the liberty interest protected by the due process clause.[96] They have also held that, as with removal, subjecting children to a medical examination for investigative purposes requires notice and a hearing unless there are important reasons to dispense with this requirement. In *Wallis*, the court identified two: "a reasonable concern that material physical evidence might dissipate" and an "urgent medical problem . . . requiring immediate attention."[97] Thus, where a police officer had (after removing them several days earlier), picked children up from the state institution where they were being kept and subjected them to an examination to determine whether they had been sexually abused, all without court imprimatur, the court held that there were issues of fact as to whether she had violated the Constitution.[98]

When one considers the two exceptions proffered by *Wallis*, though, they suggest different concerns and different kinds of medical procedures. A concern with the dissipation of evidence is not related to the immediate health of the child; rather, it concerns the state's efforts to conduct an effective investigation. Indeed, the courts have been particularly troubled by medical exams designed only to facilitate an investigation, no doubt in part because facilitating an investigation is not the kind of "emergency" that might justify the dispensing of constitutionally required procedures like notice and a hearing. A medical examination to assess whether a child has been sexually abused is not undertaken because there is an emergency, but rather to determine whether a serious situation requiring some kind of state intervention exists.

Such examinations obviously implicate the Fourth Amendment as well. They are both seizures and searches. (And since, as I have suggested, searches seem to be subject to greater constitutional protection than seizures, it is best to characterize them as both.) Whether they are reasonable for Fourth Amendment purposes may depend upon the scope of the examination. Several cases have dealt with brief visual examinations; a full discussion of such cases lies beyond the scope of this article. Suffice it to note that the courts in those cases have indicated that such examinations must still satisfy the Fourth Amendment standard of reasonableness. Precisely what that standard will mean in practice is not yet clear.[99] Even less clear is how the concomitant interference with familial relations will be assessed.[100] When courts are dealing with a full-fledged, poking and prodding medical examination, as in *Wallis*, the obligation that it be preceded by notice and a hearing seems more settled.

Moving back to the second limited exception identified in *Wallis* to medical procedures without consent or a court order—an urgent medical problem requiring immediate attention—it seems unrelated to the usual medical *examination*, but highly related to medical *treatment*. (To the extent that it relates to an examination at all, it must relate to an examination looking for a specific serious disease or condition that seems likely to be present.) But here, an urgent medical problem requiring immediate treatment sounds very much like the "emergency" that justifies the dispensing of constitutional requirements in the removal cases. The standard really ought to be the same standard: Will something bad happen prior to the constitutionally-required notice and a hearing that justifies dispensing with them and having the state intervene to order treatment?

Cases involving treatment are less frequent than cases involving examinations for abuse, but what little case law there is suggests that the courts do conflate the "imminent danger" and "urgent medical problem" standards. In one such case, a newborn was being treated in a hospital when his biological grandmother and her husband received a temporary order of adoption; a social worker immediately placed the child in state custody because the husband had been found to have sexually abused his wife's daughter (the newborn's mother). The infant died at the age of eight days.[101] The Ninth Circuit reversed summary judgment on qualified immunity grounds for the social worker. It held that the prospective adoptive parents had the right to make medical decisions for the child, and concluded: 1) that the social worker could not reasonably have believed that the child was in "imminent danger" of sexual abuse from the husband and 2) that the child was being cared for at a hospital.[102]

Thus, the court used the "removal" standard of imminent danger and reasonable necessity to avert that danger instead of the "urgent medical problem" standard to determine whether the social worker's actions were unconstitutional.[103]

In yet another case, *Mueller v. Auker*, a mother took her 5½-week-old infant into the hospital because it had a modest fever. The doctor advised various tests and treatment; the mother refused certain of them, viz., a lumbar puncture (to test for bacterial meningitis) and the prophylactic administration of antibiotics. The doctor advised a police officer that there was a small chance (3-5%) that the child had a serious bacterial infection, and that *could* be fatal if untreated.[104] The court concluded that there were issues of fact over whether the child was in imminent danger of serious bodily injury—again using that locution rather than the "urgent medical problem" phrase.[105]

One important aspect of the *Mueller* case is that there was a state procedure that permitted medical professionals to call up a judge and get an order for treatment over the phone, even over a parent's objection.[106] That provision required the judge to hear from the objecting parents if time permitted,[107] and the court concluded that there was an issue of fact over whether there was time to call a judge.[108] Thus, *Mueller* suggests that, on occasion, some kind of "notice and a hearing"—even if not the full-fledged hearing that might be required were more time available— can be procured quite quickly, even faster than one normally can obtain a warrant. As set forth earlier, since an "emergency" ought to be defined as a situation where something bad reasonably could happen before the constitutionally-required procedure can be completed, an "emergency" concerning medical treatment should almost never happen in a state that has such a "call the judge" procedure.

Finally, one case, *Doe v. Lebbos*,[109] which involved a dispute over the question of whether something was an examination or treatment, does little to clarify the standard. After a four-year-old was taken into custody, a state dependency court hearing was held in which a judge expressed concern about the girl's vaginal pain and discharge. A social worker, based upon those comments and evidence of sexual abuse, referred the girl for a sexual abuse examination.[110] In determining whether that examination, done without parental consent or a formal court order, violated the due process clause, the court held that the social worker was not entitled to summary judgment on the underlying constitutional violation, but was entitled to qualified immunity because she reasonably could have believed that the court's concern about the girl's health was the necessary authorization for an examination.[111] The dissent argued that the court had been concerned about getting *treatment* for a *condition* causing the girl pain; that she never got that treatment, but rather a sexual abuse examination instead; and that the examination took place five days after the court's comments, strongly suggesting that no one considered it an "urgent medical problem."[112] The analogy to those cases where the court views a slow reaction time as inconsistent with a child being in "imminent danger" should be apparent.[113]

Two other issues deserve brief mention. First, several courts have suggested that the right to care, custody, and management of children also includes the right to be apprised of important facts about them. Thus, when social workers failed to inform a parent with legal, but not physical, custody of the fact that his daughter had been taken into state custody and placed with another, the court held that there were issues of fact as to whether his right to substantive due process was violated.[114] Indeed, simply interviewing children without notifying parents or targeting the parents as the subjects of abuse investigations without a reasonable suspicion of abuse can violate parental rights.[115]

Finally, the courts have looked with care at efforts by social workers to obtain "consent" from the parents to take action that diminishes family rights. A threat to remove a child from parents' custody can implicate the liberty interest in familial relations.[116] Those familiar with child protective services know of the "safety plans" that those employed by those agencies try to get parents to agree to by suggesting that they will seek court orders. Courts will occasionally conclude that such plans were "coerced" and thus provide no protection to social workers who impose them and then carry them out.[117] The Seventh Circuit has been most active in identifying when a safety plan has been coerced; there, a "coerced" safety plan is one where the social workers have made threats about a future course of action that has little or no legal basis.[118]

V

Ex Parte Procedures and the Prompt Hearing Requirement

The discussion to this point has focused on actions of CPS workers and police that do not involve courts. To close the loop, this section takes a brief look at how the constitutional rights of parents and children can be violated even when the CPS workers and police have involved the courts in some way.

The most obvious way for CPS to use the courts—and where much mischief can occur—is to get a judge to sign an *ex parte* order that sanctions whatever it is CPS would like to do. A review of cases suggests that this is a fairly easy thing to get judges to do.[119] But such an order does not immunize the social workers. Courts have held that obtaining such orders by distortion or material omissions can violate the Constitution.[120]

What is less clear is whether true but obviously inadequate representations to a judge can also render a social worker liable for subsequent seizures or violations of familial relationships. In *Malley v. Briggs*,[121] the Supreme Court held that police officers who apply for an arrest warrant with facts plainly inadequate to constitute probable cause for an arrest could be sued for Fourth Amendment violations despite the fact that a judicial officer signed the arrest warrant. The Court rejected the argument that the officers were "shielded from damages liability because the act of applying for a warrant is *per se* reasonable, provided that the officer believes that the facts alleged in his affidavit are true."[122] If a reasonable officer should have known that his affidavit was insufficient to establish probable cause, then his conduct violated the Constitution and was not shielded by qualified immunity.[123]

I am unaware of any cases in which *Malley* has unambiguously been applied to a social worker seeking an *ex parte* order.[124] But it should. The *ex parte* order for a child's protection and the arrest warrant are analogous. And since an *ex parte* order plainly does not entail the notice and hearing to which procedural due process entitles families, except in the case of an emergency, an application for an *ex parte* order of removal under circumstances that *do not* constitute an emergency should violate due process.[125]

Ex parte procedures should be subject to constitutional scrutiny for precisely this reason: that they circumvent the notice and hearing required by due process *before* a deprivation of liberty. Unfortunately, there is little case law on this question, and the likelihood of its development is diminished by various technical considerations regarding where one can sue and who should be responsible. In the one lawsuit I am aware of addressing the general requirements for *ex parte* orders affecting parental rights, the defendant was a state court judge—an unusual situation, to say the least.[126] That case, *Blazel v. Bradley*, relying on the Supreme Court's *Sniadach* line of cases concerning temporary deprivations of property,[127] held that an *ex parte* procedure that deprived a parent of custodial rights had to involve a judicial officer, have a prompt post-deprivation hearing, and permit the issuance of an order only on sworn and detailed allegations based on personal knowledge, demonstrating a risk of immediate and irreparable harm.[128] It held that the state statute invoked by the judge was facially constitutional under those criteria, but that the procedure used to issue temporary restraining orders against the plaintiff violated the Constitution because the affidavit did not allege immediate harm.[129]

One of the constitutional criteria identified in *Blazel*—the requirement of a prompt post-deprivation hearing—has been addressed by a few other courts, although usually in the context where the police and/or social workers acted on their own (i.e., without any judicial imprimatur, even an *ex parte* order). The requirement for a prompt post-deprivation hearing seems to derive from a similar requirement for arrestees—i.e., the requirement of a prompt (within 48 hours) "probable cause" review of the basis for a warrantless arrest.[130] But only one court of which I am aware has suggested that the same 48-hour rule should apply to the needed post-deprivation hearing after an interference with familial relations.[131] The other courts that have discussed the issue have permitted more time, and there is no consistent answer to when such a hearing must take place.[132] Moreover, whether the same rules for a prompt post-deprivation hearing would apply if there had been some *ex parte* judicial involvement prior to the deprivation, cannot really be determined from the current meager case law to date.

VI
Conclusion

The reader who bothered to carefully review the citations in the footnotes of this article no doubt noticed that there are numerous citations of cases that do not seem to follow the general rule that the procedures of notice and a hearing required by due process should be dispensed with only in an emergency. Or, to put it more kindly, some cases define "emergency" in a rather idiosyncratic way that has little to do with an immediate threat to life or limb.

Unfortunately, many judges—not just state court judges assessing an ongoing situation, but even federal judges viewing the facts in retrospect—seem to lean towards giving CPS workers and the police a great deal of slack in this area. They emphasize the difficult situations that such workers face and the importance of protecting the children.[133] They often give inadequate weight to the harm that befalls children (especially young ones) when the children are wrested from the only homes and families that they have known. They fail to acknowledge the importance of the rights at issue.[134]

More astute jurists acknowledge that the simplistic tendency to support CPS social workers and the police is misguided if the goal is to protect children: "'[W]e must be sensitive to the fact that society's interest in the protection of children is, indeed, multifaceted, composed not only with concerns about the safety and welfare of children from the community's point of view, but also with the child's psychological well-being, autonomy, and relationship to the family.'"[135] There is a "critical difference between necessary latitude and infinite license,"[136] and "if officers of the State come to believe that they can never be questioned in a court of law for the manner in which they remove a child from her ordinary care, custody and management, it is inevitable that they will eventually inflict harm on the parents, the State, *and* the child."[137]

The words of Judge Kleinfeld's dissent in *Lebbos* deserve repeating:

> Overzealousness by government agents taking children away from their parents can have (and in this case apparently did have) devastating consequences, consequences not ameliorated in the slightest by self-righteous confidence of government agents sure that they are doing good. We do children no good by overindulging government agents who take them away from their families with immunity beyond what the facts and the law justify.[138]

Noting that the child who was removed from her father in *Lebbos*, immediately after that removal, had been observed as a pleasant and sociable child, Judge Kleinfeld noted:

> After being bounced around in the agency and foster-parent bureaucracy for over a year, Lacey was quite a different little girl. She was "diagnosed with Post Traumatic Stress Disorder, hearing voices, and suicidal ideation." She was put on anti-psychotic medication. She had taken to smearing feces and to other abnormal and highly disruptive behavior. Though Lacey had somehow held her personality together through her mother's death, her father's lack of financial success, and the move back to California, what the county did to her to "protect" her apparently destroyed her. Something in this experience, perhaps being ripped away from her father for whom she consistently expressed love during the whole miserable period, perhaps having strangers strip her and search her heretofore private parts, perhaps being put with caretakers instead of her father, amounted to a trauma that was too much for her.[139]

This article has tried to identify the limits that the law at least theoretically places on the CPS social workers and the police when they choose to act without affording any due process to the family. The stated rule is generally that that should happen only in an emergency, when serious harm is likely to happen quite soon, before any hearing can take place. Hopefully, as people (and their attorneys) learn their rights, and as the courts articulate them, that principle will be internalized by judges, and social workers and police required to adhere to it. That "should not deter their concern for the well-being of children and families, but heighten their awareness of their proper role within these boundaries."[140] Only then will the kinds of harms inflicted by the overzealous government agents be kept to manageable proportions.

Notes

[1] I use "CPS" in this article to describe any agency whose objective is to investigate child abuse or neglect, regardless of what name the agency might actually have in a given jurisdiction. Similarly, the term "social workers" is used in this article merely to identify those who work for such agencies, and is not intended to signify any kind of special education, training, or certification. I use that phrase primarily because it is one that courts frequently use.

[2] U.S. Const. amend XIV, § 1.

[3] U.S. Const. amend. V ("No person shall . . . be deprived of life, liberty, or property, without due process of law . . . "). From an early time in our history, the Fifth Amendment was held to apply only to the federal government. *Barron v. Baltimore*, 32 U.S. (7 Pet.) 243 (1833). An excellent recent discussion of the use of the passive voice in the Fifth Amendment, and the Constitution more generally, can be found in Nicholas Quinn Rosenkranz, *The Objects of the Constitution*, 63 Stan. L. Rev. 1005, 1010-15, 1041-43 (2011).

[4] *E.g., Troxel v. Granville*, 530 U.S. 57, 65 (2000).

[5] *Id.*

[6] A recent law review article has collected the various pejoratives used by some academics and judges against the notion of "substantive due process." Ryan C. Williams, *The One And Only Substantive Due Process Clause*, 120 Yale L.J. 408, 411 & nn. 1-7, 414 n. 18 (2010). Williams's article identifies the various kinds of "due process," both substantive and procedural, *id.* at 419-27, in order to examine the general understanding of the phrase "due process of law" when the Fifth and Fourteenth Amendments were adopted. He argues that, regardless of whether it is linguistically counterintuitive, the understanding of "due process" at the time of the enactment of the Fourteenth Amendment (but not the Fifth) included some substantive rights.

[7] *Roe v. Wade*, 410 U.S. 113 (1973).

[8] *Troxel*, 530 U.S. at 65.

[9] *Id.*

[10] *Meyer v. Nebraska*, 262 U.S. 390 (1923).

[11] *Id.* at 401.

[12] *Pierce v. Society of the Sisters of the Holy Name of Jesus and Mary*, 268 U.S. 510 (1925).

[13] *Id.* at 534-35.

[14] *Stanley v. Illinois*, 405 U.S. 645 (1972).

[15] *Id.* at 650.

[16] *Santosky v. Kramer*, 455 U.S. 745 (1982). Curiously, Justice Blackmun wrote the opinion in *Santosky*. He had previously dissented in *Stanley* and joined an opinion that would have upheld Illinois's inclusion of unwed mothers, but not unwed fathers, in the definition of "parent" on "the basis of common human experience, that the biological role

of the mother in carrying and nursing an infant creates stronger bonds between her and
the child than the bonds resulting from the male's often casual encounter." *Stanley*, 405
U.S. at 665 (Burger, C.J., dissenting).

[17] *Troxel v. Granville*, 530 U.S. 57 (2000).

[18] *Id.* at 69.

[19] *Santosky*, 455 U.S. at 754 (citing the three-part procedural due process analysis of
Mathews v. Eldridge, 424 U.S. 319 [1976], in which the Court weighs and balances
"the private interests affected by the proceeding; the risk of error created by the State's
chosen procedure; and the countervailing governmental interest supporting use of the
challenged procedure").

[20] *Id.* at 758.

[21] *Id.* at 753.

[22] *E.g.*, *McCurdy v. Dodd*, 352 F.3d 820, 826 (3rd Cir. 2003); *Doe v. Heck*, 327 F.3d
492, 519 (7th Cir. 2003).

[23] *See* the quotation in the text of this article pertaining to note 18, *supra*.

[24] *Sniadach v. Family Finance Corp. of Bay View*, 395 U.S. 337 (1969). Some years
later, Chief Justice Rehnquist opined that *Sniadach* and its progeny "represented
something of a revolution in the jurisprudence of procedural due process." *Connecticut v.
Doehr*, 501 U.S. 1, 27 (1991) (Rehnquist, C.J., concurring). *See also Fuentes v. Shevin*,
407 U.S. 67, 72 n. 5 (1972) ("Since the announcement of this Court's decision in
[*Sniadach*] summary prejudgment remedies have come under constitutional challenge
throughout the country").

[25] *Fuentes v. Shevin*, 407 U.S. 67 (1972).

[26] *Sniadach*, 395 U.S. at 340 (noting that wages are "a specialized type of property
presenting distinct problems in our economic system"); *id.* at 341-42 ("a prejudgment
garnishment . . . may as a practical matter drive a wage-earning family to the wall").
But see Fuentes, 407 U.S. at 89 (procedural due process not limited to wages and
similarly crucial forms of property).

[27] *Mitchell v. W.T. Grant Co.*, 416 U.S. 600, 616 (1974) (upholding Louisiana writ
of sequestration which permitted a seller of goods to seek an order having the court
constable take possession of certain disputed property; "The Louisiana law provides for
judicial control of the process from beginning to end"); *id.* at 615 (distinguishing the
Florida law involved in *Fuentes*, which "authorized repossession of the sold goods
without judicial order, approval, or participation"); *North Georgia Finishing Inc. v.
Di-Chem*, 419 U.S. 601, 607 (1975) (finding Georgia writ of garnishment statute used to
garnish defendant's bank account unconstitutional where, *inter alia*, "[t]he writ is
issuable, as this one was, by the court clerk, without participation by a judge").

[28] *Mitchell*, 416 U.S. at 617-18 (comparing "fault-like" standard of laws at issue in
Fuentes with the simple issue of default at issue in the Louisiana statute before the
Court); *Doehr*, 501 U.S. at 12-13 (holding Connecticut attachment statute
unconstitutional where attachment required assessment of the underlying merits of
plaintiff's assault case against defendant).

[29] Compare *Mitchell*, 416 U.S. at 608-09 (noting that the seller of goods on an
installment plan had an important lien in the goods that the State could properly protect),
with *Doehr*, 501 U.S. at 16 ("The plaintiff had no existing interest in Doehr's real estate
when he sought the attachment").

[30] Compare *Mitchell*, 416 U.S. at 605 (writ could be issued only when supported by
specific facts sworn under oath) with *North Georgia Finishing*, 419 U.S. at 607
(distinguishing *Mitchell* because the statute permitted garnishment based upon attorney's
affidavit without personal knowledge and using conclusory assertions) and *Doehr*, 501

U.S. at 14 ("[O]nly a skeletal affidavit need be, and was, filed. . . . It is self-evident that the judge could make no realistic assessment concerning the likelihood of an action's success based upon these one-sided, self-serving, and conclusory submissions").

[31] *Mitchell*, 416 U.S. at 608 (noting that the seller/plaintiff "was required to put up a bond to guarantee the buyer against damage or expense, including attorney's fees, in the event the sequestration is shown to be mistaken or otherwise improvident. The buyer is permitted to regain possession by putting up his own bond to protect the seller"). *But cf. Fuentes*, 407 U.S. at 83 ("The minimal deterrent effect of a bond requirement [imposed on the plaintiff seeking to encumber the defendant's property] is, in a practical sense, no substitute for an informed evalution by a neutral official"); *id.* at 85 (fact that statutes permitted defendant to recover possession of the property by posting a bond did not alone render them constitutional because "[w]hen officials . . . seize one piece of property from a person's possession and then agree to return it if he surrenders another, they deprive him of property. . . "); *Bell v. Burson*, 402 U.S. 535, 536 (1971) (holding unconstitutional a state law that suspended the driver's license of "an uninsured motorist involved in an accident...unless he posts security to cover the amount of damage claimed by aggrieved parties in reports of the accident").

[32] Compare *Mitchell*, 416 U.S. at 610 (noting that "the debtor may immediately have a full hearing on the matter of possession following the execution of the writ, thus cutting to a bare minimum the time of creditor- or court-supervised possession") with *North Georgia Finishing*, 419 U.S. at 607 (distinguishing *Mitchell* because the statute had "no provision for an early hearing at which the creditor would be required to demonstrate at least probable cause for the garnishment").

[33] *E.g.*, *Fuentes*, 407 U.S. at 84-85 ("[I]t is now well settled that a temporary, nonfinal deprivation of property is nonetheless a 'deprivation' in the terms of the Fourteenth Amendment"); *id.* at 86 ("The Fourteenth Amendment draws no bright lines around three-day, 10-day or 50-day deprivations of property. Any significant taking of property by the State is within the purview of the Due Process Clause."); *Doehr*, 501 U.S. at 15 ("It is true that a later [post-deprivation] hearing might negate the presence of probable cause, but this would not cure the temporary deprivation that an earlier [pre-deprivation] hearing might have prevented").

[34] *Fuentes*, 407 U.S. at 86 ("While the length and consequent severity of a deprivation may be another factor to weigh in determining the appropriate form of hearing, it is not decisive of the basic right to a prior hearing of some kind.").

[35] *Brittain v. Hansen*, 451 F.3d 982, 988 (9th Cir. 2006) ("[O]ur later precedents expanded this protection [from *Santosky*] so that a custodial parent could not be deprived of physical custody on a temporary basis without either an emergency or a pre-deprivation hearing"); *Roska ex rel. Roska v. Peterson*, 328 F.3d 1230, 1245 (10th Cir. 2003) ("This circuit has applied *Santosky*'s holding . . . to the temporary seizures of children and has held that notice and a hearing are required before a child is removed except for extraordinary situations where some valid governmental interest is at stake that justifies postponing the hearing until after the event.") (internal quotation marks and citations omitted); *Ram v. Rubin*, 118 F.3d 1306, 1311 (9th Cir. 1997) ("[N]otice and a hearing are required before the children can be removed, even temporarily, from the custody of their parents"). *But see Neaves v. City of San Diego*, 70 Fed. Appx. 428, 432, 2003 WL 21500201, *3 (9th Cir. 2003) ("the brief period during which [child] was separated distinguishes her seizure from an unlawful seizure . . . . A brief separation of a few days from both parents . . . is not excessively intrusive"); *Terry v. Richardson*, 346 F.3d 781, 786 (7th Cir. 2003) (questioning whether non-custodial parent, who was told by social worker that he could not exercise his visitation rights with his four-year-old

daughter while an investigation was pending, had suffered a constitutional deprivation of liberty).

[36] *Burson*, 402 U.S. at 542 ("it is fundamental that except in emergency situations (and this is not one) due process requires that when a State seeks to terminate an interest such as that here involved, it must afford 'notice and opportunity for hearing appropriate to the nature of the case' before the termination becomes effective."); *Fuentes*, 407 U.S. at 90-91 (noting that extraordinary situations may justify postponing a hearing where the government has an important interest, there is a special need for very prompt action, and the State has kept strict control over its monopoly of legitimate force).

[37] *Fuentes*, 407 U.S. at 93 n. 30 ("a writ of replevin is entirely different from the seizure of possessions under a search warrant"; the interest of the government (the apprehension of criminals) is greater, the situation generally demands prompt action and might be undermined if the suspect were given notice, and the procedure requires that a state official provide probable cause to a magistrate or judge).

[38] *Gerstein v. Pugh*, 420 U.S. 103, 113 (1975) ("[W]hile the Court has expressed a preference for the use of arrest warrants when feasible…it has never invalidated an arrest supported by probable cause solely because the officers failed to secure a warrant."). Arrest warrants are required for arrests in the home. *See* note 53, *infra*.

[39] *Wallis v. Spencer*, 202 F.3d 1126, 1138 (9th Cir. 2000).

[40] *Pearson v. Callahan*, 555 U.S. 223, 231 (2009).

[41] *Cox v. Warwick Valley Central School Dist.*, 654 F.3d 267, 275 (2d Cir. 2011) ("To state a claim for a violation of this substantive due process right of custody, a plaintiff must demonstrate that the state action depriving him of custody was 'so shocking, arbitrary, and egregious that the Due Process Clause would not countenance it even were it accompanied by full procedural protection.'") (citation omitted); *Studli v. Children & Youth and Families Central Regional Office*, 346 Fed. Appx. 804, 811, 2009 WL 2873306, *4 (3rd Cir. 2009) ("a substantive due process violation by a social worker must be 'so clearly arbitrary' that it 'can properly be said to shock the conscience.'") (citation omitted).

[42] See *Hernandez v. Foster*, 657 F.3d 463, 479 (7th Cir. 2011) (rejecting the "shock the conscience" test for child removal substantive due process claims); *Pittman v. Cuyahoga County Dep't of Children and Family Services*, 640 F.3d 716, 729 n. 6 (6th Cir. 2011) (district court improperly analyzed substantive due process claim of father, asserting interference with his relationship with child, under the "shock the conscience" test); *T.E. v. Grindle*, 599 F.3d 583, 589 (7th Cir. 2010) (noting that there are "two types of substantive due process violations"; one occurs when the state actor's conduct shocks the conscience and the second occurs when the state actor violates an identified liberty or property interest protected by the due process clause); *Seegmiller v. Laverkin City*, 528 F.3d 762, 767-68 (10th Cir. 2008) (identifying the "two strands of the substantive due process doctrine" and rejecting the proposition that executive branch action is subject only to the "shocks the conscience" strand); *Coontz v. Katy Independent School Dist.*, 159 F.3d 1355, 1998 WL 698904, *5 (5th Cir. 1998) (strands of substantive due process are "conceptually distinguished but . . . intertwined"; plaintiff can prove case by showing deprivation of a fundamental right in a manner that does not survive strict scrutiny or conduct that shocks the conscience); *Brown v. Nix*, 33 F.3d 951, 953 (8th Cir. 1994) ("substantive due process claims are analyzed under two tests," the fundamental liberty/ strict scrutiny test and the shock the conscience test); *O'Donnell v. Brown*, 335 F. Supp. 2d 787, 821 n. 16 (W.D. Mich. 2004) (rejecting proposition that "shock the conscience" test was only applicable substantive due process test for removal of children from parents' custody).

[43] See *Doe v. Heck*, 327 F.3d 492, 527 (7th Cir. 2003) (where police wanted to investigate potential abuse charges of children in private school, court concludes that the procedural due process balancing test "was essentially subsumed into our analysis of the plaintiffs' underlying constitutional claims, all of which required a balancing of the plaintiffs' interests against those of the government"); *Darryl H. v. Coler*, 801 F.2d 893, 901 n. 7 (7th Cir. 1986) (noting that both doctrines, as well as Fourth Amendment analysis, are essentially the same); *Hernandez v. Foster*, 2009 WL 1952777, *5-6 (N.D. Ill. July 6, 2009) (denying motion to dismiss substantive and procedural due process claims based upon social workers' having taken a 15-month old child because of an arm fracture unlikely to have been caused by abuse); *Mueller v. Auker*, 2007 WL 627620, *15-17 (D. Idaho Feb. 26, 2007) (finding that there was an issue of fact as to whether police officer violated parents' procedural due process right to a judicial hearing, and, for the same reasons, concluding that there was an issue of fact as whether police officer violated parents' substantive due process rights); *cf. id.* at *9-12 (discussing parameters of both doctrines). *Cf. O'Donnell v. Brown*, 335 F. Supp. 2d 787, 810 (W.D. Mich. 2004) (asserting that a substantive due process claim "requires a deprivation of greater severity"); *id.* at 812 (holding that removal of children left in the care of older siblings violated procedural due process because the "process . . . was constitutionally inadequate" in part because of the absence of exigent circumstances); *id.* at 821 (denying defendants' motion for summary judgment on substantive due process grounds because the absence of exigent circumstances meant that the defendants could not establish a compelling governmental interest as a matter of law).

[44] *E.g.*, *Southerland v. City of New York*, 2012 WL 1662981, *19 (2d Cir. 2012) ("To establish a violation of substantive due process rights, a plaintiff must demonstrate that the state action was 'so egregious, so outrageous, that it may fairly be said to shock the contemporary conscience.'") (internal citation omitted).

[45] *Id.*

[46] *Id.*

[47] *Id.* at 109.

[48] *E.g.*, *Hernandez v. Foster*, 657 F.3d at 474-75 (noting that, against a claim of substantive due process by parents, social workers did not seek to justify removal of child by exigent circumstances, but rather probable cause).

[49] *Id.* at 486 ("The danger must be imminent, or put another way, the circumstances must be exigent."). The court concluded that its precedents were sufficiently unclear prior to that time that the defendants were entitled to qualified immunity.

[50] *Martin v. St. Mary's Dept. of Social Services*, 346 F.3d 502, 507 (4th Cir. 2003) (Traxler, J., dissenting) (social worker who directed the removal of two children because of concerns about "mental injury" to one of them had engaged in an egregious abuse of official power that shocked the conscience in violation of the due process clause); *Doe v. Fayette County Children and Youth Services*, 2010 WL 4854070, *11 (W.D. Pa. Nov. 22, 2010) (finding that prohibiting father from having any contact with his children, based on allegations that he had sex with an unrelated, perhaps underage, teenager and for no reason other than agency protocol, shocks the conscience). *Cf. Croft v. Westmoreland County Children and Youth Services*, 103 F.3d 1123, 1126 (3rd Cir. 1997) (interference with parental rights can be justified only by an objectively reasonable suspicion of abuse; "Absent such reasonable grounds, governmental intrusions of this type are arbitrary abuses of power.").

[51] U.S. Const., amend IV. Although the Fourth Amendment's proscriptions apply only to the federal government and its agents, they have been incorporated against state actors through the Fourteenth Amendment. *Wolf v. Colorado*, 338 U.S. 25 (1949).

[52] *United States v. Watson*, 423 U.S. 411 (1976).

[53] *Id.* at 427-28 (Powell, J., concurring) (noting that there are just a few narrow exceptions to the warrant requirement for searches, but that arrests traditionally have been made without warrants). A warrant *is* required when an arrest is made *in* the home. But that rule is designed to protect the sanctity of the home more than to protect a person's right to freedom from restraint by the state. *New York v. Harris*, 495 U.S. 14, 20 (1990) (holding that the Fourth Amendment's exclusionary rule does not require the suppression of statements made in the police station after a warrantless, unconstitutional arrest in the home; "The warrant requirement for an arrest in the home is imposed to protect the home . . . ").

[54] *E.g., Kentucky v. King*, 131 S. Ct. 1849, 1856 (2011) (identifying three kinds of "exigencies" that will authorize a warrantless entry into a person's home: where entry is needed to protect against imminent injury, where the police are chasing a fleeing suspect, and where there is concern that the occupants might destroy evidence before a warrant can be obtained). It is the first of these exceptions—the so-called "emergency aid" exception—which is most likely to arise in a case involving children's welfare.

[55] Occasionally, courts have applied an "emergency" standard from Fourth Amendment cases in analyzing seizures of the child against the due process clause, even where the child is not seized at home and the warrant requirement likely inapplicable. *Burke v. County of Alameda*, 586 F.3d 725, 731-32 (9th Cir. 2009) (citing standard for taking a child from the home without a warrant even though the child was in police headquarters when seized).

[56] *Doe v. Kearney*, 329 F.3d 1286, 1294 & n. 10 (11th Cir. 2003) ("The issue boils down to how we define an emergency"; "The term 'emergency' as used in this context is synonymous with 'exigency' and 'imminent danger.' We have found that courts use them interchangeably"). The 11th Circuit was certainly correct in suggesting that courts have used these terms interchangeably, and the seriousness of the threat to the child is certainly the same regardless of which constitutional provision is at issue. The point of this paragraph is that the time element may differ because the standard process needed to satisfy the Constitution is different.

[57] This definition is not always adopted. *Id.* at 1297 ("We agree that the sole focus should not be whether there is time to obtain a court order.").

[58] *Southerland v. City of New York*, 2012 WL 1662981, *13 (2d Cir. 2012). In the Second Circuit, "a Family Court order is equivalent to a search warrant for Fourth Amendment purposes." *Id.* at *12 n. 15. The Fourth Amendment states that search warrants can only issue on probable cause.

[59] Since those seizures are properly analyzed under the Fourth Amendment, the children themselves do not have due process claims associated with those seizures (at least not the initial seizures). *E.g., Southerland v. City of New York*, 2012 WL 1662981, *26 (2d Cir. 2012); *Dubbs v. Head Start, Inc.*, 336 F.3d 1194, 1203 (10th Cir. 2003). Of course, other conduct accompanying or following the seizure may separately violate the Constitution, *Doe v. Heck*, 327 F.3d 492, 518 n. 23 (7th Cir. 2003) ("If a plaintiff's sole purpose in bringing a familial relations claim is to recover damages for a physical seizure, then that claim is more appropriately analyzed under the Fourth Amendment. . . . On the other hand, if . . . a familial relations claim specifically alleges that the government's physical seizure coincided with other conduct amounting to an interference with the parent-child relationship (*e.g.*, custodian interview of child by government official without the consent of his parents and without reasonable suspicion that parents were abusing the child or that the child was in imminent danger of abuse), that allegation of harm constitutes a separate and distinct violation of a separate fundamental constitutional

right and both claims may therefore be maintained."); *Brokaw v. Mercer County*, 235 F.3d 1000, 1018 n. 14 (7th Cir. 2000) (noting uncertainty as to whether four-month separation should be deemed a seizure, but declining to decide the issue because the result of the analysis "under the Fourth Amendment or substantive due process . . . is the same").

[60] *E.g., Hernandez v. Foster*, 657 F.3d 463, 474 (7th Cir. 2011); *Gates v. Dep't of Protective and Regulatory Services*, 537 F.3d 404, 434-35 (5th Cir. 2008); *Wallis v. Spencer*, 202 F.3d 1126, 1137 n. 8 (9th Cir. 2000); *Darryl H. v. Coler*, 801 F.2d 893, 901 n. 7 (7th Cir. 1986). *But see Roe v. Texas Dep't of Protective and Regulatory Services*, 299 F.3d 395, 411-12 (5th Cir. 2003) (concluding that mother did not have separate due process claim based upon strip search of daughter).

[61] *Calabretta v. Floyd*, 189 F.3d 808 (9th Cir. 1997).

[62] *Id.* at 820. *Cf. Darryl H. v. Coler*, 801 F.2d 893, 901 (7th Cir. 1986) ("A child of very tender years may not exhibit a subjective expectation of privacy in the same sense as an older child. He is, however, a human being entitled to be treated by the state in a manner compatible with that human dignity. Also at stake, of course, are the closely related legitimate expectations of the parents or other caretakers, protected by the fourteenth amendment, that their familial relationship will not be subject to unwarranted state intrusion").

[63] *Mabe v. San Bernardino County, Dept. of Public Social Services*, 237 F.3d 1101, 1108 (9th Cir. 2001) (where allegations were that stepfather had touched 14-year old's breasts and crotch area through her clothing at night, but had not done so in the past month, court holds that there was a dispute of fact as to whether there were exigent circumstances warranting removal of daughter without a hearing; "[T]he type of abuse here is qualitatively different than that [in past cases]. Here, the allegations were not of physical beatings that could happen at any time of the day . . . ."); *Moodian v. County of Alameda Social Services Agency*, 206 F. Supp. 2d 1030, 1035 (N.D. Cal. 2002) (holding that removal of children without a hearing on the basis of social worker's conclusion that there was imminent danger of emotional harm violated due process; "Unlike physical harm, such as a beating, which can have immediate and dire consequences, emotional harm by its nature does not carry the same immediacy"). I cite *Moodian* here because in many cases of abuse, especially cases of sexual abuse, the primary harm would seem not to be physical, but emotional. Thus, for example, the sexual abuse alleged in *Mabe* does not appear to be of the sort that would have resulted in any serious *physical* harm to the stepdaughter.

[64] *Burke v. County of Alameda*, 586 F.3d 725, 730, 732 (9th Cir. 2009) (distinguishing *Mabe* because the allegations regarding inappropriate touching were that it happened every few days (although not in the nine days prior to the child's removal) and were not limited to a particular time of day; thus, whether stepdaughter's allegation that stepfather "pinched her on the buttocks on several occasions and repeatedly grabbed her breasts when he hugged her" was sufficient to justify removal from parents would be for a jury to decide); *Doe v. Lebbos*, 348 F.3d 820, 827 (9th Cir. 2003) (affirming summary judgment for social worker who kept four-year old girl in state custody based "on the redness observed around [child's] vaginal area, [her] complaints of vaginal discharge, and [father's] alleged alcohol abuse and general neglect . . . [Child's] case qualified as an 'emergency' situation").

[65] *Hatch v. Dept. for Children, Youth and Their Families*, 274 F.3d 12, 21 (1st Cir. 2001) (asserting that "most" courts "have concluded that a case worker . . . may place a child in temporary custody when he has evidence giving rise to a reasonable and articulable suspicion that the child has been abused or is in imminent peril of abuse");

Croft v. Westmoreland County Children and Youth Services, 103 F.3d 1123, 1126 (3rd Cir. 1997) ("a state has no interest in protecting children from their parents unless it has some reasonable and articulable evidence giving rise to a reasonable suspicion that a child has been abused or is in immediate danger of abuse"). Whether the *Hatch* decision accurately states (or stated at the time) the law for "most courts" can be debated, but it appears to be the standard in the First Circuit. *Suboh v. District Attorney's Office of the Suffolk District*, 298 F.3d 81, 92 (1st Cir. 2002) (stating that, in the absence of a court order, state may place a child in temporary custody only "when it has evidence giving rise to a suspicion that the child has been abused or is in imminent danger"). *Cf. Terry v. Richardson*, 346 F.3d 781, 787 (7th Cir. 2003) (substantive due process requires that "caseworkers who come between parents and their children . . . must have evidence to support a 'reasonable suspicion' of past or imminent abuse."); *Doe v. Kearney*, 329 F.3d 1286, 1298 (11th Cir. 2003) (affirming grant of summary judgment to social worker who removed children from home based on two allegations of sexual contact by father against other children, one four years old and the other five, and the father's criminal record from an even earlier time).

[66] *Anderson-Francois v. County of Sonoma*, 415 Fed. Appx. 6, 9, 2011 WL 195570, *2 (9th Cir. 2011) (affirming denial of qualified immunity for police detective for removal of children where investigation had been going on for six weeks); *Mabe v. San Bernardino County, Dept. of Public Social Services*, 237 F.3d 1101, 1104-05, 1108 n. 2 (9th Cir. 2001) (reversing grant of summary judgment to social worker where social worker interviewed family nearly one month after allegations that stepfather had molested 14-year old stepdaughter had been made, and did not remove stepdaughter until four days later; "The failure to remove [stepdaughter] on [date of interview] is the strongest evidence in the record that [social worker] did not believe the circumstances were exigent"); *Tenenbaum v. Williams*, 193 F.3d 581, 594 (2d Cir. 1999) (reversing summary judgment for City where report of possible abuse to handicapped five-year old was made on a Friday, not investigated until the following Monday, and the child not removed until Tuesday); *Calabretta v. Floyd*, 189 F.3d 808, 813 (9th Cir. 1997) ("The facts in this case are noteworthy for the absence of emergency. The social worker and her department delayed entry into the home for fourteen days after the report, because they perceived no immediate danger of serious harm to the children"); *Wolf v. County of San Joaquin*, 2006 WL 1153755, *1 (E.D. Cal. April 28, 2006) (denying social workers' motion to dismiss where plaintiff-mother's complaint alleged that daughter's allegations that mother's ex-boyfriend had touched her inappropriately was first classified as a "ten day response" case before being reclassified as an "immediate response" case, that social worker did not respond to mother's request to meet, and that a week went by before social worker met with family). *Cf. Gomes v. Wood*, 451 F.3d 1122, 1125 (10th Cir. 2006) (concluding that there was an issue of fact as to whether a removal of a nine-month old baby with a skull fracture, four days after the child's pediatrician reported it, was justified by emergency circumstances).

[67] *Franet v. County of Alameda Social Services Agency*, 291 Fed. Appx. 32, 35 2008 WL3992332, *1 (9th Cir. 2008) (affirming jury award against social worker who removed children from home based upon belief that father was sexually molesting daughter where social worker "admitted she would have had time to obtain a warrant"); *Rogers v. County of San Joaquin*, 487 F.3d 1288, 1295 (9th Cir. 2007) (social worker conceded that "she could have obtained a warrant within hours" for three- and five-year old children who were suffering from bottle rot with teeth missing, were still in diapers, and were thin and pale; court reverses summary judgment in social worker's favor and orders district court to grant partial summary judgment to parents even though "if the...

parents' conduct was not modified within a reasonable period of time, [it could] lead to long-term harm"); *Roska ex rel. Roska v. Peterson*, 328 F.3d 1230, 1238 n. 3 (10th Cir. 2003) (noting that social worker testified that she did not think that child would die within a week); *Croft v. Westmoreland County Children and Youth Services*, 103 F.3d 1123, 1127 (3rd Cir. 1997) ("Most damaging . . . is [social worker's] . . . testimony that, after the interviews, she had no opinion one way or the other whether sexual abuse had occurred.").

[68] *Rogers*, 487 F.3d at 1295 (reversing grant of summary judgment to social workers where parents, *inter alia*, took their three- and five-year old children to their place of work, an auto shop, and locked them in a room there; "The chances of accidental injury . . . during the few hours that it would take [social worker] to obtain a warrant were very low. So remote a risk does not establish reasonable cause to believe that the children were in immediate danger"); see generally *Mueller v. Auker*, 2007 WL 627620, *11 (D. Idaho Feb. 26, 2007) (holding that there was an issue of fact as to whether a 5½ week old baby with a fever, for whom a doctor concluded has a small chance of a serious bacterial infection, was in imminent danger of serious bodily injury; "'imminent danger' . . . has both a time and probability component. It means that a danger is likely [the probability component] to occur at any moment or immediately [the time component]").

[69] *E.g., Roska*, 328 F.3d at 1245 ("'Valid governmental interests' include 'emergency circumstances which pose an immediate threat to the safety of a child'.....[T]he 'mere possibility' of danger is not enough to justify a removal without appropriate process" [citations omitted]); *Hurlman v. Rice*, 927 F.2d 74, 81 (2d Cir. 1991) (presence of person with a history of abuse or endangerment did not justify child's removal; "[i]f the mere 'possibility' of danger constituted an emergency, officers would "always" be justified in making a forced entry and seizure of a child whenever the child was in the presence of a person who had such a history"). *Roska* is probably best thought of as an abuse case rather than a neglect case. The social workers in *Roska* feared that the child's mother was suffering from Munchausen syndrome by proxy, a disorder whereby a person (usually a mother) inflicts physical harm upon a child in order to gain sympathy and attention. *Id.* at 1238. It is interesting, then, to contrast *Roska* to cases of sexual abuse, where the courts have been more willing to assume that the possibility of such abuse happening must mean that it could happen right away. Obviously, a person suffering from the mother's alleged disease might inflict a serious injury on her child at any time, including the time that it would take to hold a hearing. That possibility, though, did not permit the social workers to claim any kind of "exigent circumstances" authorizing a warrantless entry into the home or taking a child into custody. *Id.* at 1240-41, 1246.

[70] *O'Donnell v. Brown*, 335 F. Supp. 2d 787, 805 (W.D. Mich 2004) (fact that small children were left home alone with twelve-year old in charge did not constitute "exigent circumstances" permitting policemen's entry into home; "[t]hese facts perhaps raise reasons for concern, but they do not reach to the level of exigent circumstances to support a warrantless entry" that resulted in the removal of the children); *id.* at 809-13 (for the same reason, policemen violated procedural due process); *id.* at 810, 819-22 (although "the substantive [due process] claim requires a deprivation of greater severity" than a procedural due process claim, defendants were not entitled to summary judgment on substantive due process claim because exigent circumstances were lacking).

[71] *Brown v. Montana*, 442 F. Supp. 2d 982, 994-95 (D. Montana 2006) (denying defendants' motion for summary judgment where newborn was taken from mother on basis that, *inter alia*, mother was so obese that she could only hold the baby for ten minutes and, thus, could not take proper care of it, and that there was an unresolved child neglect case, involving another child, in Alaska).

[72] *Rogers*, 487 F.3d at 1291-93, 1295 (granting summary judgment to parents where the social worker conceded that "she could have obtained a warrant within hours" and "[t]here is no indication in the record that so short a delay could have resulted in a significant worsening of the children's physical conditions or an increase in the prospects of long-term harm"); *id.* at 1297 (acknowledging that "the . . . children [may have been] in a sorry state and suffering from neglect of a type that could, if their parents' conduct was not modified within a reasonable period of time, lead to long-term harm," but that "the conditions here did not present an imminent risk of serious bodily harm").

[73] *Wallis v. Spencer*, 202 F.3d 1126, 1131 (9th Cir. 2000).

[74] *Id.* at 1131-32.

[75] *Id.* at 1140.

[76] *E.g., Ram v. Rubin*, 118 F.3d 1306, 1311 (9th Cir. 1997) (finding that social worker and police officer were not entitled to summary judgment where they temporarily removed father's adopted and foster children to conduct physical examinations based on allegations of sexual abuse by a different minor that had been previously investigated and found to lack credibility).

[77] *Wallis*, 202 F.3d at 1139 n. 10 ("This part of the tip suggests that there was never any reasonable cause to remove [daughter] even if there were reason to remove [son].").

[78] *Robinson v. Tripler Army Medical Center*, 2009 WL 688922, *4 (9th Cir. March 17, 2009) (reversing summary judgment favoring social worker who removed newborn from prospective adoptive parents, one of whom was the child's biological grandmother, on the ground that prospective adoptive father had sexually abused the newborn's mother; although evidence of abuse frequently can justify removing a child "that is not always the case, especially when the allegations of abuse are not specific to the child who is allegedly in danger"); *Franet v. County of Alameda Social Services Agency*, 291 Fed. Appx. 32, 35, 2008 WL 3992332, *1 (9th Cir. 2008) (affirming jury award against a social worker for removing children from mother based on allegations that divorced father was sexually abusing the daughter; "there was no evidence even to suggest that the father had abused the son"); *Ram*, 118 F.3d at 1311 (concluding that summary judgment for social worker and police officer were premature where father's adopted and foster children, despite their denial of abuse, were taken into custody based upon allegations of sexual abuse from a child outside the family); *Hurlman v. Rice*, 927 F.2d 74, 81 (2d Cir. 1991) (rejecting the assertion that the presence of a person with "a history of conduct constituting sexual abuse or endangerment of a child" constituted an emergency for any child in the household); *Doe v. Fayette County Children and Youth Services*, 2010 WL 4854070, *11 (W.D. Pa. Nov. 22, 2010) (finding that prohibiting father from having any contact with his young children, based on allegations that he had sex with an unrelated, perhaps underage, teenager violated substantive due process; "[W]hile there was an allegation that Plaintiff had sexual contact with a minor that was not his child, Defendants had no evidence that Plaintiff had abused or mistreated his children."); *Brown v. Montana*, 442 F. Supp. 2d 982, 994-95 (D. Montana 2006) (denying defendants' motion for summary judgment where newborn was taken from mother based in part on allegations that there was an unresolved child neglect case, involving another child, in Alaska). *But see Doe v. Kearney*, 329 F.3d 1286, 1298 (11th Cir. 2003) (affirming grant of summary judgment to social worker who removed children from home based on two allegations, one four years old and the other five, of sexual contact by father against other children, and the father's criminal record from an even earlier time).

[79] *Wallis*, 202 F.3d at 1131 (psychiatric facility patient told therapist that her sister was not in the cult and might not know about her husband's cult membership); *id.* at 1138

(concluding that there were issues of fact about whether it was necessary to take children away from mother); *id.* at 1142 n. 14 ("[T]he claims of each family member must be assessed separately. Here, nothing in the record before us suggests that [mother] was anything other than a fit and loving mother. . . .The government may not, consistent with the Constitution, interpose itself between a fit parent and her children simply because of the conduct—real or imagined—of the other parent").

[80] *Fredenburg v. County of Santa Clara*, 407 Fed. Appx. 114, 115, 2010 WL 5393868, *1 (9th Cir. 2010) (affirming denial of summary judgment to police officer where "although [he] had reasonable cause to remove the children from [mother], he failed to determine or even consider whether [father] posed a threat to the children before removing the children from him and placing them with a social worker"); *Franet v. County of Alameda Social Services*, 291 Fed. Appx. 32, 34-35, 2008 WL 3992332, *1 (9th Cir. 2008) (affirming jury award for mother where only father was suspected of sexually molesting preschool-aged daughter).

[81] *Burke v. County of Alameda*, 586 F.3d 725, 733 (9th Cir. 2009) (reversing summary judgment on father's claim against county where police officer had taken 14-year old into custody based on allegations of abuse against stepfather and had not consulted father before doing so or informed him for several days afterwards).

[82] *See* http://www.ndaa.org/ncpca_state_statutes.html (last viewed on May 9, 2012).

[83] *United States v. Watson*, 423 U.S. 411, 417-21 (1976).

[84] These various standards are discussed in a number of cases. *E.g., Gomes v. Wood*, 451 F.3d 1122, 1129-30 (10th Cir. 2006) (categorizing the courts that have followed a "reasonable suspicion" standard, and those, including the 9th and 11th Circuits, requiring reasonable or probable cause; "In our view, the reasonable suspicion standard appropriately balances the interests of the parents, the child, and the state"); *Hatch v. Dept. for Children, Youth and Their Families*, 274 F.3d 12, 21-22 (1st Cir. 2001) (rejecting the 9th Circuit's standard of "reasonable cause to believe that the child is in imminent danger of serious bodily injury," which "borders on an obligatory showing of probable cause (or something fairly close to probable cause)" because it "sets the bar too high"; concluding instead that "the Constitution allows a case worker to take temporary custody of a child, without a hearing, when the case worker has a reasonable suspicion that child abuse has occurred [or, alternatively, that a threat of abuse is imminent]"); *Brown v. Montana*, 442 F. Supp. 2d 982, 994-95 (D. Montana 2006) (concluding that the Ninth Circuit standard in *Wallis* "leaves open the question whether 'reasonable cause' means reasonable suspicion, probable cause, or something else"). Several courts have explicitly adopted a "probable cause" standard for Fourth Amendment analysis of seized children, although, even there, it is unclear whether that standard is the same as the "probable cause" standard for criminal law. *Tenenbaum v. Williams*, 193 F.3d 581, 602-03 (2d Cir. 1999) (probable cause is the standard for determining whether a seizure of a child is "reasonable" under the Fourth Amendment although "[p]robable cause is a flexible term" without any specific tests to meet); *Doe v. Kearney*, 329 F.3d 1286, 1295 (11th Cir. 2003) ("a state may not remove a child from parental custody without judicial authorization unless there is probable cause to believe the child is threatened with imminent harm"). The facts of *Kearney*—in which children were removed from a home based on old allegations of sexual abuse by the father against other children—casts doubt on whether the 11th Circuit was actually applying the stated standard.

[85] *E.g., Griffin v. Wisconsin*, 483 U.S. 868, 878 (1987) (although tip from a policeman that probationer might have guns in his apartment was sufficient to meet the "reasonable grounds" standard of Wisconsin statute providing for warrantless searches of probationers' homes, and statute met constitutional requirements because of the "special

needs" of the state in operating a probation system, "it is most unlikely that the unauthenticated tip of a police officer. . .would meet the ordinary requirement of probable cause"); *Hernandez v. Foster*, 657 F.3d 463, 478 (7th Cir. 2011) (stating standard for substantive due process as requiring a reasonable suspicion of past or imminent danger of abuse before a child could be taken into custody; "A reasonable suspicion requires more than a hunch but less than probable cause.") (internal quotation marks and citations omitted). Cases like *Gomes* and *Hatch*, discussed in the last note, assume that the standard they are adopting is something less than probable cause.

[86] Of course, removal of the parent must still pass muster under due process and thus requires some evidence that a child is in danger, even if less than probable cause. *Croft v. Westmoreland County Children and Youth Services*, 103 F.3d 1123, 1126 n. 4 (3rd Cir. 1997) (demanding that father leave home while investigation continued violated due process).

[87] *Cf. Walker v. City of Orem*, 451 F.3d 1139, 1149 (10th Cir. 2006) ("We note that *detaining* the plaintiffs is a different matter from *excluding* them from the crime scene itself. Thus, even if plaintiffs had no right to cross the crime scene tape . . . this does not necessarily mean that the police had the right to detain them, even in their own home.") (emphasis in original).

[88] Some courts analyze the Fourth Amendment claim of the child under the same standards as the Fourteenth Amendment due process claims of the parents. *See* note 60, *supra*. To the extent that the "reasonable cause to believe" standard for the due process and Fourth Amendment claims in those courts is something less than "probable cause" standard, *see* discussion in note 84, *supra*, they require less evidence for seizure of a child than for the arrest of a criminal suspect.

[89] I.C. § 16-1608 (1) (b) ("An alleged offender may be removed from the home of the victim of abuse or neglect by a peace officer, without an order . . . only where the child is endangered and prompt removal of an alleged offender is necessary to prevent serious physical or mental injury to the child").

[90] The Ninth Circuit standard described earlier requires that state officials believe that their action is "reasonably *necessary*" to avert the harm. *See* text accompanying note 39, *supra*. If removal of a child into state custody is not necessary to protect the children because an alleged offender may be removed from the home or in some other way kept away from the child until a hearing can be had, then removal of the child ought to be constitutionally infirm. Diane Redleaf has suggested to me that one possible explanation for the phenomenon described is that CPS workers do not have state law authority to order removal. Perhaps so, but that only raises the question as to whether such a state scheme is constitutional. A state, after all, must justify its laws that impinge on fundamental rights and are subject to strict scrutiny by showing that they are narrowly-tailored to meet a compelling state interest. If a less intrusive option is ignored, that lends strong weight to the argument that the scheme is not narrowly-tailored. *Cf. Heffron v. Int'l Society for Krishna Consciousness, Inc.*, 452 U.S. 640, 658 (1981) (holding that when government regulation impinges on free speech rights, the burden is on the government to show that it has a compelling interest that cannot be achieved by less intrusive means).

[91] *Mabe v. San Bernardino County, Dept. of Public Social Services*, 237 F.3d 1101, 1105 (9th Cir. 2001) (accused stepfather "told [social worker] that he was willing to leave the house if necessary to allow [daughter] to remain in her mother's home"); *Complaint in Raykin v. Arapahoe County Dept of Human Services*, D. Colo. Civ. No. 10-cv-00908-LTB-KLM (filed April 22, 2010) ¶ 41. In the interests of full disclosure, I was an attorney representing the plaintiffs in the *Raykin* matter.

[92] *See* the discussion of coerced "safety plans" accompanying the text at notes 116-118, *infra.*

[93] *E.g., Neaves v. City of San Diego,* 70 Fed. Appx. 428, 432, 2003 WL 21500201, *3 (9th Cir. 2003) (affirming grant of qualified immunity on claim that child was seized from both parents even though only mother was suspected of abuse because "[t]he officers knew that [child's] parents were married and that placing [her] with her father would not necessarily remove [her] from the risk of her mother, who was a suspect in the child abuse investigation").

[94] *E.g., Burke v. County of Alameda,* 586 F.3d 725, 732-33 (9th Cir. 2009) (concluding that removal of child from both allegedly abusing stepfather and mother was reasonable where mother had "repeatedly denied abuse and accused [daughter] of lying," had "admitted that [stepfather] ignored her requests to stop," and had "repeatedly blamed [daughter]."); *Doe v. Kearney,* 329 F.3d 1286, 1291 (11th Cir. 2003) (after social worker interviewed each member of the family, she "concluded the children were in danger of abuse from [father]" and "that [mother] was incapable of protecting the children and that the children would need to be temporarily removed for their safety"); *Tower v. Leslie-Brown,* 326 F.3d 290, 294 (1st Cir. 2003) (after the father was arrested for assaults on his eldest daughter and teenage stepchildren, social worker waited for the mother and then removed the couple's young children from her custody; mother's "conversation with the [social workers] led them to doubt her ability to protect the children, and the caseworkers decided to remove all five children from the home"); *Mabe v. San Bernardino County, Dept. of Public Social Services,* 237 F.3d 1101, 1110 (9th Cir. 2001) (affirming grant of summary judgment to social worker as to scope of the removal based on removal of 14-year old daughter from home because of allegations that stepfather had molested her; social worker concluded that mother "was not protecting [stepdaughter] in light of how she reacted to [stepdaughter's] report of the stepfather's alleged misconduct" in that she "did not believe [the] allegations" and "was verbally abusive of [stepdaughter] during the removal, harassing [stepdaughter] within inches of her face."). *Cf. Franet v. County of Alameda Social Services,* 291 Fed. Appx. 32, 34, 2008 WL 3992332, *1 (9th Cir. 2008) (affirming jury award for mother where only father was suspected of sexually molesting preschool-aged daughter even though social worker "found the mother's failure to take the daughter to a doctor indicative of [her] inability to protect her children from abuse").

[95] *Tenenbaum v. Williams,* 193 F.3d 581, 592 (2d Cir. 1999) (where social worker removed handicapped child from school to subject her to sexual abuse examination in order to rule out sexual abuse, court separately analyzes the removal and the examination).

[96] *P.J. v. Wagner,* 603 F.3d 1182, 1197 (10th Cir. 2010) ("[W]e do not doubt that a parent's general right to make decisions concerning the care of her child includes, to some extent, a more specific right to make decisions about the child's medical care."); *Wallis v. Spencer,* 202 F.3d 1126, 1141 (9th Cir. 2000) ("The right to family association includes the right of parents to make important medical decisions for their children, and of children to have those decisions made by their parents rather than the state."); *Van Emrik v. Chemung County Dept. of Social Services,* 911 F.2d 863, 867 (2d Cir. 1990) ("We believe the Constitution assures parents that, in the absence of parental consent, x-rays of their child may not be undertaken for investigative purposes at the behest of state officials unless a judicial officer has determined, upon notice to the parents and an opportunity to be heard, that grounds for such an examination exist and that the administration of the procedure is reasonable under all the circumstances"); *In re Baby K,* 832 F. Supp. 1022, 1030 (E.D. Va. 1993). *Cf. Kia P. v. McIntyre,* 235 F.3d 749, 757 n. 3

(2d Cir. 2000) ("Neither we nor the Supreme Court have . . . marked the boundaries of a parent's right to control the medical treatment of his or her child," but noting dicta in an earlier case that such a right exists). *But see Franet v. County of Alameda Social Services Agency*, 291 Fed. Appx. 32, 35, 2008 WL3992332, *2 (9th Cir. 2008) (reversing jury award based on social worker's taking daughter to a sexual assault examination without mother's consent or knowledge because "the law on this right was not clearly established"); *Roska ex rel. Roska v. Peterson*, 328 F.3d 1230, 1246-47 & n. 14 (10th Cir. 2003) (expressing no opinion on whether such a right exists, noting that "[p]laintiffs point us to no authority or argument supporting an extension of such a right [to direct medical care] to a temporary deprivation such as that suffered by the Roskas" and concluding that the defendants did not violate the right, if it exists, because they did not seek "to alter the child's medical program"). *Franet* is particularly difficult to understand since the events in question took place in 2001, one year after *Wallis* had been decided. *Cf. Doe v. Lebbos*, 348 F.3d 820, 828 n. 11 (9th Cir. 2003) (*Wallis* established law of the circuit in November 1999 when first opinion came out even though opinion was subsequently amended).

[97] *Wallis*, 202 F.3d at 1141.

[98] *Id.* at 1134-35, 1142.

[99] *Dubbs v. Head Start, Inc.*, 336 F.3d 1194, 1203 (10th Cir. 2003) (visual inspections of pre-school children in Head Start program were warrantless searches that were presumptively unconstitutional without consent); *Darryl H. v. Coler*, 801 F.2d 893, 902 (7th Cir. 1986) (concluding that visual inspections for sexual abuse at school were searches under the Fourth Amendment, but not subject to the requirement that there be probable cause or a warrant; court affirms denial of preliminary injunction but questions whether child protection agency's standards would result in "reasonable" searches in all instances). *But see Michael C. v. Gresbach*, 526 F.3d 1008, 1017 (7th Cir. 2008) (distinguishing *Darryl H.*, limiting it to searches taking place on public school property, and affirming denial of summary judgment on qualified immunity grounds to social worker who conducted visual inspection of children at a private school); *id.* at 1015 (holding that, for searches and seizures of young children, "it is more appropriate [than considering the privacy expectations of the children] to consider whether the parents manifested a subjective expectation of privacy in the premises within which the search took place"). An argument might be made that a very brief visual inspection is analogous to a *Terry* stop, a brief stop and search of a suspect that the Court has held may be effected with something less than probable cause. *Terry v. Ohio*, 392 U.S. 1 (1968).

[100] *Dubbs*, 336 F.3d at 1204 ("Given the particular posture of this case, we decline to resolve the difficult questions regarding the standard to be applied to this [substantive due process] claim . . . "); *Darryl H.*, 801 F.2d at 901 n. 7 (due process and Fourth Amendment should be assessed together under the same standards).

[101] *Robinson v. Tripler Army Medical Center*, 2009 WL 688922, *1 (9th Cir. March 17, 2009).

[102] *Id.* at *4. The social worker apparently did not argue that "prospective adoptive parents" had fewer rights than biological and custodial parents, and the court assumed that they had the same rights. *Id.*

[103] Indeed, since the child died shortly after the state took custody, it seems likely that the child *did* have an "urgent medical problem." The court nonetheless (and wisely, in my view) ignored that possibility—or even whether the child was in "imminent danger of serious bodily injury" *in general*—and focused on whether it was "reasonably necessary" to remove custody from the adoptive parents in order to protect the child. Since the court did not mention any evidence that the prospective parents had interfered

in the child's treatment at the hospital, it seems most likely that it was not reasonably necessary.

[104] *Mueller v. Auker*, 2007 WL 627620, *3 (D. Idaho Feb. 26, 2007), *rev'd in part on other grounds*, 576 F.3d 979 (9th Cir. 2009). The 9th Circuit viewed the evidence as the doctor claiming a small chance of a serious bacterial infection and a small chance of death if the infant had one particular infection (*viz.*, meningitis) and was left untreated. *Mueller v. Auker*, 576 F.3d 979, 984 (9th Cir. 2009) (doctor said that the child had a 3-5 percent chance of a serious bacterial infection and that, if a child had meningitis and went home untreated, there was up to a 5 percent chance she "could potentially die"). I should disclose that I represent the plaintiffs in the *Mueller* case.

[105] *Mueller v. Auker*, 2007 WL 627620, *16 (D. Idaho Feb. 26, 2007). The court nonetheless concluded that the police officer who removed the newborn's mother was entitled to qualified immunity. *Id.* at *19.

[106] *Id.* at *12.

[107] *Id.*

[108] *Id.* at *16.

[109] 348 F.3d 820 (9th Cir. 2003).

[110] *Id.* at 824.

[111] *Id.* at 830.

[112] *Id.* at 833 (Kleinfeld, J., dissenting in part).

[113] *See* cases discussed in note 66, *supra*.

[114] *James v. Rowlands*, 606 F.3d 646, 654-56 (9th Cir. 2010). The court held that "public officials may encourage and facilitate a transfer of a minor's physical custody without notifying a parent with shared legal custody only if they have reasonable cause to believe that such notification would put the child in imminent danger of serious bodily injury." *Id.* at 655. The court nonetheless held that the social workers were entitled to qualified immunity.

[115] *Doe v. Heck*, 327 F.3d 492, 524 (7th Cir. 2003). The investigation concerned possible corporal punishment in a private school. The court also held that the parents' liberty interest included the right to use corporal punishment, if not excessive, and to delegate that authority to a private school. *Id.* at 523.

[116] *Id.* at 524-25.

[117] *Hernandez v. Foster*, 657 F.3d 463, 481-84, 486-87 (7th Cir. 2011) (reversing summary judgment on substantive and procedural due process claims where social worker told parents that they had no parental rights and could not see already-removed child if they did not sign safety plan); *Doe v. Fayette County Children and Youth Services*, 2010 WL 4854070, *4-5 (W.D. Pa. Nov. 22, 2010) (granting summary judgment to plaintiff where social worker removed children and required their father and his mother (who had already been given temporary custody) to sign safety plan based upon father's having allegedly had sexual relations with an unrelated 16-year old girl; father's mother was told that children would be assessed for protective custody if she did not sign and father knew that mother already had signed an agreement precluding him from having contact with his children before social worker asked him to sign his own safety plan).

[118] *Hernandez*, 657 F.3d at 482 ("where an official makes a threat to take an action that she has no legal authority to take, that is duress"); *see also Croft v. Westmoreland County Children and Youth Services*, 103 F.3d 1123, 1125 n. 1 (3rd Cir. 1997) ("The threat that unless [father] left his home, the state would take his four-year-old daughter and place her in foster care was blatantly coercive."). *Cf. Heck*, 327 F.3d at 524 ("defendants' threat to remove [son] and his sister from the custody of their parents violated the [plaintiffs'] right to familial relations . . . .Although it is true the defendants

did not make good on their threat, the threat alone implicates the [plaintiffs'] liberty
interest in familial relations.").

[119] *Southerland v. City of New York*, 2012 WL 1662981, *4 n. 5 (2d Cir. 2012)
(quoting affidavit that was used to procure family court order which listed: 1) attempted
suicide by one 16-year old child and 2) the father's refusal to allow CPS into the home to
speak to the other children as reasons to believe that the children were abused or
neglected). *Cf. Malik v. Arapahoe County Dept. of Social Services*, 191 F.3d 1306, 1311
(10th Cir. 1999) (County attorney "had previously contacted Magistrate Yoder [who
handled all of the Department of Social Service's dependency and neglect cases]
regularly concerning other cases, and had never failed to receive a verbal order from him
allowing her to pick up a child"). For a description of domestic abuse orders that are
frequently issued with similar ease, see *Blazel v. Bradley*, 698 F. Supp. 756, 758-59 (W.D.
Wisc. 1988) (noting how wife procured temporary restraining order ("TRO") against
husband, failed to show up at the injunction hearing six days later leading to the dismissal
of the case, but obtained a second TRO from a different judge on the same day).

[120] *Southerland, supra*, at *15-*17 (concluding that there were issues of fact as to
whether social worker had made knowing or reckless misstatements of fact to a family
court judge to obtain a removal order); *Brokaw v. Mercer County*, 235 F.3d 1000, 1012
(7th Cir. 2000) (holding that defendants violated the Fourth Amendment for removal of
children "to the extent the defendants knew the allegations of child neglect were false, or
withheld material information"); *Malik v. Arapahoe County Dept. of Social Services*, 191
F.3d 1306, 1311-12, 1315 (10th Cir. 1999) (affirming denial of summary judgment
motion by social workers where they had procured a verbal order to pick up a child after
describing to magistrate pictures that allegedly showed bruising, but neglected to mention
that the pictures were five months old and had been taken by an uncle, that the mother
had been interviewed voluntarily, that a police officer had cancelled a
previously-scheduled interview, and that one member of the Department doubted that the
photos indicated bruising; "an *ex parte* hearing based on misrepresentation and omission
does not constitute notice and an opportunity to be heard").

[121] 475 U.S. 335 (1986).

[122] *Id.* at 345.

[123] *Id.* at 345-46 ("It is true that in an ideal system an unreasonable request for a
warrant would be harmless, because no judge would approve it. But ours is not an ideal
system, and it is possible that a magistrate, working under docket pressures, will fail to
perform as a magistrate should"); *id.* at 346 n. 9 ("If the magistrate issues the warrant in
such a case [where no application should have been made in the first place], his action is
not just a reasonable mistake, but an unacceptable error indicating gross incompetence or
neglect of duty. The officer then cannot excuse his own default by pointing to the greater
incompetence of the magistrate.").

[124] *Cf. Austin v. Borel*, 830 F.2d 1356, 1362 (5th Cir. 1987) (holding that Louisiana
social workers filing a verified complaint were not entitled to absolute, but only qualified,
immunity because their filing of the verified complaint was analogous to police filing a
probable cause affidavit, which was given only qualified immunity in *Malley*). In *Malik*,
the 10th Circuit made several statements suggesting that the social worker and police
officer did not subjectively believe that the situation warranted an *ex parte* order. *Malik*,
191 F.3d at 1315 ("The facts . . . support a conclusion that defendants did not believe that
the child faced such danger to warrant seeking temporary protective custody in an ex
parte proceeding"); *id.* at 1315 n. 5 (citing the "district court's finding that '[d]efendants
acknowledged [daughter] was in no imminent danger at the time they sought the
order . . . '"). Of course, a subjective belief that the facts were inadequate is not the same

as the *Malley* standard (that a reasonable officer would not believe that they were adequate), and, in any event, the court in *Malik* also focused to a significant degree on the existence of material omissions in the application. *Id. Cf. Southerland*, 667 F.3d at 106 (noting that if social worker did not knowingly make false and misleading statements, "that would entitle [him] to qualified immunity, but would not necessarily render his underlying conduct lawful"). The court in *Southerland* did not identify the characteristics of true statements to a judge in an application for a child protection order that would nonetheless violate the Constitution (but, apparently, not clearly established constitutional law).

[125] *Blazel v. Bradley*, 698 F. Supp. 756, 761 (W.D. Wisc. 1988) (so holding). The temporary restraining order issued by a state court judge in question in *Blazel* had been for domestic abuse against a wife, but since the TRO required that the husband stay out of the marital home and, thus, away from his children, it implicated his parental rights as well. *Id.* at 762.

[126] *Id.* at 757. The plaintiff in *Blazel* only sued one of the two judges who had issued an *ex parte* temporary restraining order against him. *Id.* at 758 n. 1. Judges do not have immunity from lawsuits seeking declaratory judgments. *Pulliam v. Allen*, 466 U.S. 522, 541-42 (1970). There are more problematic procedural hurdles in such cases. One is that the plaintiff is not likely to be subjected to the constitutional harm by the same judge in the future, a requirement for standing in federal courts under Article III. *Los Angeles v. Lyons*, 461 U.S. 95 (1983) (plaintiff did not have standing to seek forward-looking injunctive relief against police department for chokehold; chances of him suffering same chokehold again in the future were too slim to warrant invocation of federal jurisdiction); *Bauer v. Texas*, 341 F.3d 352, 358 (5th Cir. 2003) (individual for whom defendant judge had appointed a temporary guardian did not have standing to challenge the Texas law permitting such appointments in a lawsuit against the judge; because "there have been no such proceedings since November 2001, and [the state guardianship proceeding] was transferred from [defendant judge] to Judge Wood, there does not exist a 'substantial likelihood' and a 'real and immediate' threat that [plaintiff] will face injury from [defendant judge] in the future"). Another is that lower federal courts have interpreted Section 1983—42 U.S.C. § 1983, the primary statute used to sue state officials in federal court for violations of federal law, especially the Constitution—to prohibit suing judges in their adjudicative capacities. *In re Justices of the Puerto Rico Supreme Court*, 695 F.2d 17, 21-23 (1st Cir. 1982). Neither of these problems was addressed in *Blazel*.

[127] *See* notes 24-34 and accompanying text, *supra*.

[128] *Blazel*, 698 F. Supp. at 764.

[129] *Id.* at 768 (allegation of an assault two weeks earlier, without any allegation that husband would attack her in the near future, was inadequate and issuance of TRO violated husband's constitutional rights). *Blazel* was decided several years before the Supreme Court's decision in *Connecticut v. Doehr*, 501 U.S. 1 (1991), in which the Court emphasized that the factually-complex nature of the underlying dispute there militated in favor of requiring a pre-deprivation hearing. *Id.* at 14. *See* note 28, *supra*.

[130] *County of Riverside v. McLaughlin*, 500 U.S. 44 (1991). *McLaughlin*, it deserves mention, did not establish any requirement of a *hearing*, in which the arrestee could state her version of events. Rather, it established only the necessity of a review by a judicial officer of the basis for the arrest, to determine whether it met the requirement of probable cause. Of course, other cases, involving temporary deprivations of property interests in lawsuit initiated by private parties, do require a prompt post-deprivation hearing. *See* note 32, *supra*.

[131] *Brown v. Montana*, 442 F. Supp. 2d 982, 996 n. 14 (D. Montana 2006) (dicta)

(subsequent order by state judge, three days after custody of child was taken and finding probable cause for the removal, did not justify initial constitutional deprivation; citing *County of Riverside* for proposition that "a *judicial determination* of probable cause must occur within 48 hours of a warrantless arrest, *including* weekends and holidays, except in truly extraordinary circumstances") (emphasis in original).

[132] *Jordan by Jordan v. Jackson*, 15 F.3d 333, 344-53 (4th Cir. 1994) (hearing held on Monday for child seized on Friday afternoon met constitutional standards; while 48-hour rule of *County of Riverside* was useful as a guide, different state interests meant that a somewhat longer time would be permitted); *Egervary v. Rooney*, 80 F. Supp. 2d 491, 503 & n. 8 (E.D. Pa. 2000) ("Although there is no bright-line rule for deciding whether a post-deprivation custody hearing is sufficiently prompt, a survey of the case law shows that the delay should be measured in hours and days, not weeks and months"), *rev'd on other grounds*, 366 F.3d 238 (3d Cir. 2004); *Campbell v. Burt*, 949 F. Supp. 1461, 1468 (D. Hawaii 1996) (one-week delay too long).

[133] *E.g.*, *Hatch v. Dept. for Children, Youth and Their Families*, 274 F.3d 12, 22 (1st Cir. 2001) ("When presented with evidence of apparent child abuse, a case worker must have a fair amount of leeway to act in the interest of an imperiled child—and it is better to err on the side of caution than to do nothing and await incontrovertible proof"); *Darryl H. v. Coler*, 801 F.2d 893, 904 (7th Cir. 1986) (concluding that the balance of harms, for purposes of reviewing the district court's denial of a preliminary injunction, favors affirmance because the cost of granting an injunction would be some child abuse going undetected); *E.Z. v. Coler*, 603 F. Supp. 1546, 1559 (N.D. Ill. 1985) ("Even assuming that most abuse situations are not life-threatening, this court finds that the life of even one child is too great a price to pay for the possible increased degree of parental privacy through additional preliminary investigation which plaintiffs' proposed procedure would demand"), *aff'd sub. nom.*, *Darryl H. v. Coler*, 801 F.2d 893 (7th Cir. 1986).

[134] *Jordan by Jordan v. Jackson*, 15 F.3d 333, 343 (4th Cir. 1994) ("Through these relationships, our children—indeed, we, as parents—are strengthened, fulfilled and sustained. The bonds between parent and child are, in a word, sacrosanct, and the relationship between parent and child inviolable except for the most compelling reasons.").

[135] *Tenenbaum v. Williams*, 193 F.3d 581, 595 (2d Cir. 1999) (quoting *Franz v. Lytle*, 997 F.2d 784, 793 (10th Cir. 1993)).

[136] *Tenenbaum*, 193 F.3d at 595.

[137] *Id.* (emphasis in original).

[138] *Doe v. Lebbos*, 348 F.3d 820, 833 (9th Cir. 2003) (Kleinfeld, J., concurring and dissenting).

[139] *Id.* at 834 (citations omitted). Judge Kleinfeld closed by quoting Justice Brandeis's dissent in *Olmstead v. United States*, 277 U.S. 438, 479 (1928) (Brandeis, J., dissenting) to the effect that "[e]xperience should teach us to be most on our guard to protect liberty when the government's purposes are beneficent." *Lebbos*, 348 F.3d at 835 (Kleinfeld, J., concurring and dissenting).

[140] *Franz v. Lytle*, 997 F.2d 784, 793 (1993).

Fourth Amendment Litigation in CPS Cases

By James R. Mason, III

One of the first questions you might be asking yourself is, "How does a lawyer from Home School Legal Defense Association (HSLDA) know anything useful about Fourth Amendment litigation in CPS cases?" One law student noticed our involvement in this area of the law and wrote a journal article entitled, "Standard Bearers of the Fourth Amendment: The Curious Involvement of Home School Advocates in Constitutional Challenges to Child Abuse Investigations."[1] While the title states the issue, the article casts little light on the answer.

The Battle for the Front Door

In the early days of the modern homeschooling movement, say from the mid-1970s through the early-1990s, homeschooling was thought to be illegal in many states. Additionally, homeschooling as an educational option was not as well known then as it is now and far fewer children were being homeschooled. So it was not surprising that the pioneering homeschoolers would be sought out by school districts and truant officers.

What may not seem as apparent is that in many cases homeschoolers found an investigative social worker at the front door. They were typically investigating anonymous tips that the children were being abused or neglected for reasons that often went something like this: "The children are always home, don't go to school, and the family seems really religious."

Three factors combined to draw homeschooling advocates into what we call, "The Battle for the Front Door." First, in the early days, homeschooling pioneers, Michael Farris and J. Michael Smith, both lawyers and homeschooling dads, defended homeschoolers as their *pro bono* time permitted. As the need grew, they founded Home School Legal Defense Association in 1983, quit private practice, and devoted their considerable full-time energy to helping homeschoolers and the homeschooling movement. One of the services HSLDA provided to its members (and still provides) is 24/7 access to a lawyer for relevant legal emergencies.

Second, in 1974, Congress passed the Child Abuse Prevention and Treatment Act, commonly referred to as CAPTA.[2] In CAPTA, Congress dangled federal money in front of states in exchange for adopting policies and procedures to prevent, investigate, and remediate child abuse and neglect. This sounds good in principle, but in practice it helped create a monstrous bureaucracy, which bears directly on the battle for the front door.

While state laws differ in the particulars they generally share the same features. Every state has a "hotline" to encourage the reporting of suspected abuse or neglect. Many of the tips received by these hotlines are made anonymously. Tips are screened and most are eventually assigned to an investigative social worker.

"Storming the Castle to Save the Children"

In her seminal article, "Storming the Castle to Save the Children," Duke Law Professor Doriane Coleman notes that, under CAPTA, states are actively encouraged to adopt a "'take no chances' approach to defining and screening-in cases" for CPS to investigate.[3] Social workers widely believe that the state laws enacted in response to CAPTA *require* them to interview the child and inspect the home whenever they receive any allegations of maltreatment—no matter how baseless.

In an effort to "ferret out" as many instances of abuse as possible, states have developed their laws on the assumption that there is a "child-welfare exception to the Fourth Amendment."[4] Such an exception, they assume, grants case workers "broad discretion in their conduct on the assumption that the particularized warrant that would otherwise fetter them is not required in this context."[5] Armed with the apparent authority of the state, caseworkers routinely "storm the castle, opening closed bedroom doors to find, talk to, examine, and remove the children; opening and looking through refrigerators and cupboards to see if the children have sufficient food to eat; opening and searching closets and drawers to check if the children have enough clothing and that no inappropriate disciplinary methods are being used in the family."[6] These home "visits," which "epitomize deep intrusion[s] in both symbolic and actual respects," can shatter the innocence of even the youngest of children, exposing them to a broad range of emotional responses, including "trauma, anxiety, fear, shame, guilt, stigmatization, powerlessness, self-doubt, depression, and isolation."[7]

In 2010, the most recent year for which data is available, state investigations intruded into the private lives of more than 3 million children, only to conclude that their incursions were unnecessary in more than 73% of cases.[8] Without clear constitutional guidelines, millions of children each year confront "a disturbingly overbroad scheme that wrongfully captures hundreds of thousands of children within its auspices each year."[9]

Even though states investigate millions of reports of child maltreatment each year, the Supreme Court has yet to decide whether these investigations must comply with the Fourth Amendment, while the Court has addressed the Fourth Amendment rights of criminal defendants in dozens of cases. More than one Circuit Court of Appeals has opined that the fractured state of the law is due, at least in part, to the lack of clear constitutional guidelines from the Supreme Court.

In the absence of clear constitutional standards, "it is the children who primarily pay the price for the states' investigatory policies"[10] as caseworkers wield discretionary authority "similar in scope to that given colonial authorities under the universally abhorred general warrant."[11] Enter the Fourth Amendment.

The Fourth Amendment provides: "The right of the people to be secure in their persons, houses, papers, and effects, against unreasonable searches and seizures, shall not be violated, and no warrants shall issue, but upon probable cause, supported by oath or affirmation, and particularly describing the place to be searched, and the persons or things to be seized."

The Supreme Court has adopted a clear, consistent, bright-line standard that "searches and seizures inside a home without a warrant are presumptively unreasonable."[12] While this standard has long been clearly understood in the context of police officers investigating crime, it has been an uphill legal battle to persuade courts that this standard also applies when social workers are investigating reports of child neglect.

The third factor that bears on why homeschooling advocates became involved in the battle for the front door has tactical origins. When a report is screened for investigation, the first stop of many investigators is at the child's public school, where school officials routinely allow the child to be interviewed without parental knowledge or consent.[13] In other words, going to the school first is tactically the path of least resistance. But where homeschooled children are involved the school is the home and the administrators are the parents. Add to the mix immediate access to lawyers to provide timely legal advice about Fourth Amendment rights and it is easy to see how the battle for the front door is joined.

It goes without saying that investigative social workers have an important job in detecting and intervening when real abuse or neglect is involved. But it should also go without saying that respecting the constitutional rights of families in their own homes from unnecessary intrusion and disruption is also paramount. As the U. S. Court of Appeals for the Ninth Circuit has put it, "The government's interest in the welfare of children embraces not only protecting children from physical abuse, but also protecting children's interest in the privacy and dignity of their homes and in the lawfully exercised authority of their parents."[14]

But the one-size-fits-all bureaucratic approach spawned by CAPTA has led to maddening results. Each of the lawyers at HSLDA fields calls where an investigative social worker is at the door. One of my favorite after-hours calls illustrates just how maddening these encounters can sometimes be. I call it:

The Case of the Missing Pool

One evening the answering service called me with the following message, "Mrs. Smith has a social worker at the front door who is investigating a report that she regularly leaves her very young children unattended around the pool in the backyard."

"So, Mrs. Smith," I said, "these allegations sound serious if true."

"But, Mr. Mason," she said, "There are at least two problems. First, I don't have young children."

"Really," I responded. "What's the second problem?"

"Well . . . ," she hesitated and then in a loud voice for the benefit of the social worker shouted, "I DO NOT HAVE A POOL!"

Jaded though I may be, even I thought that the logic of Mrs. Smith's position would lead to a quick conclusion of the investigation. I advised her to allow the social worker to verify that there was no pool and then spoke with him.

"As I'm sure you'll agree," I said with lawyerly confidence, "The report you received was absolutely false, so I'm certain you will want to close your investigation."

Undaunted, he replied, "Yes, I can see that the report about the pool is false, but my policy manual requires me to interview each of the children and inspect the inside of the home before I can close the investigation."

How Does CPS Litigation Arise?

Sadly, this anecdote, while more outrageous than most, recurs in contour on a regular basis. HSLDA attorneys field hundreds of calls involving trivial allegations every year. Parents in these situations find themselves in a dilemma: On the one hand, they have nothing to hide, but they do have a constitutional right to be free from unjustified intrusion into their home and family; on the other hand, if they assert their rights the situation could escalate, either creating a scene at the front door, or landing them in court. And even more frightening, they sometimes face the possibility that failure to cooperate could result in their children being taken into state custody.

Those families who go along with the social worker's request often do so in the belief that cooperation is the best way to end the situation quickly. Sometimes it works out that way, but not always. Homeschoolers learned long ago that cooperation can expose their frightened children to pop quizzes in math and reading conducted on the spot by unqualified investigators. Also, cooperation sometimes subjected their children to probing questions about sexual matters, child-rearing philosophy, and methods of correction. This kind of intrusion can damage a child's perception of safety and security even if both the dramatic scene and the courthouse are avoided.

And in the old days, when homeschooling was thought by investigators to be neglectful *per se* no matter how well the children thrived, the results of those pop quizzes sometimes found their way into juvenile-court petitions. Other choice allegations that tended to recur with regular frequency were, "piles of clean laundry on the living room furniture," "unwashed dishes in the kitchen," and the near universal catch-all, "clutter."

As the result of these experiences, HSLDA and many homeschoolers determined to mount a more spirited defense of the front door. Those who assert their rights sometimes do so successfully, avoiding both the scene and the courthouse. This is especially true when a lawyer knowledgeable in the Fourth Amendment is involved early.

But standing up for one's rights can land one in court in one of two ways. The officials at the door may take "no" for an answer and leave the home only to file papers in the juvenile court asking a judge to order cooperation. This posture would be defensive litigation.

Sometimes the officials at the front door refuse to take no for an answer, call for back-up, and then force their way into the home. This can open the way for litigation on offense if the official's actions violated the Fourth Amendment.

CPS Litigation on Defense

Three cases HSLDA handled illustrate both the typical practices of investigative social workers and how defensive litigation can change those practices. They are from the HSLDA case files.

The Case of the Rubber Stamp[15]

After the birth of the Gauthier's daughter at home in in Pennsylvania, Susquehanna County Services for Children and Youth received a ChildLine referral for "possible medical neglect."

During the investigation the social worker spoke with the parents and several doctors at the hospital where the child had been treated shortly after birth for a respiratory problem. No medical neglect was discovered.

After the hospital discharged the baby to return home, the social worker asked to visit the Gauthier's home "to complete the investigation." The social worker told the Gauthiers that she must complete a home "visit" in all investigations before they can close the file.

The Gauthiers declined the social worker's request to enter their home, citing their state and federal constitutional right to be free from unreasonable searches and seizures. Not only did the social worker have enough information from the doctors to close the investigation and determine that the accusations were unfounded, but a search of their home would not cast any light on possible medical neglect allegations.

This is an all-too-common scenario. Social workers around the country believe that they must search a home before they can close an investigation, even when the caseworker knows that no abuse or neglect occurred.

After the Gauthiers declined the social worker's request to search their home, Susquehanna County filed a petition in juvenile court to compel them to cooperate. The Gauthiers received no notice of the petition and only learned of it when they received a court order in the mail directing them to "cooperate with the completion of a home visit within ten days."

The Gauthiers immediately called HSLDA. Review of the court file revealed that the petition recited no facts other than the ChildLine referral for possible medical neglect had been received, that the Gauthiers refused to allow the social worker into their home, and that the social worker needed to complete at least one home visit before she could close the file.

The juvenile court literally rubber-stamped the social worker's petition even though it contained no facts at all.

HSLDA immediately appealed and sought an emergency stay of the search order in the juvenile court, the Pennsylvania Superior Court and the Pennsylvania Supreme Court, all of which were denied in less than a week.

The social worker completed the home "visit," closed the file and determined that the accusations were unfounded. But the appeal on the Fourth Amendment issue proceeded on the merits.

Susquehanna County argued on appeal that the Fourth Amendment simply does not apply to social-worker investigations. One of the judges seemed persuaded. At oral argument she asked me why I kept referring to the "home visit" as a search.

"A government agent," I replied, "has gone to court and obtained an order requiring my clients to allow them into their home without their consent so the agent can look around for evidence of child abuse or neglect. By any definition, that is a search."

Much to my surprise after what I perceived to be an unfavorable oral argument, the three-judge panel of the Pennsylvania Superior Court agreed that it was a search and ruled that it violated the Fourth Amendment. "However, C & Y's responsibilities under the DPW regulations and the CPSL to investigate each and every allegation of child abuse/neglect, including visiting the child's home at least once during its investigation, do not trump an individual's constitutional rights under the Fourth Amendment."[16]

The Court further explained that before juvenile courts may issue search orders, the social worker "must file a verified petition alleging facts amounting to probable cause to believe that an act of child abuse or neglect has occurred and evidence relating to such abuse will be found in the home."[17]

We viewed this case as tremendous victory for Pennsylvania families because it halted an unconstitutional practice for the whole state. Obviously, real child abuse should be prosecuted to the fullest extent of the law. But the social workers in this case spent a lot of time trying to fulfill a technical requirement that wasn't needed when they should have been focusing on more serious matters.

The Case of the Junior Lady Godiva[18]

The Stumbos' troubles began in September 1999 when their two-year-old daughter slipped outside halfway through dressing—without any clothes—to chase her new kitten. Although an older sibling retrieved her a few minutes later, it was too late. A passerby anonymously reported the family to social services.

Two hours later, a social worker showed up at the Stumbos' door, demanding to enter their home and privately interview all of their children. Based on HSLDA's advice, the Stumbos refused to let the social worker in.

Despite having no probable cause for entry or private interviews, the social worker convinced a judge to issue a court order forcing the family to comply. HSLDA immediately challenged the order, but the North Carolina Court of Appeals upheld it by a 2 to 1 vote, deciding that the order did not constitute a "search" under the Fourth Amendment. HSLDA then appealed to the North Carolina Supreme Court, which heard the case in February 2002.

The North Carolina Supreme Court ruled 7 to 0 against the Department of Child Protective Services declaring that the department did not have a legitimate basis to even begin an investigation of the Stumbo family, much less compel them to open their front door.

The *Stumbo* case is important because the court found that social workers have an obligation to examine the reports they receive to make sure they rise to the level of neglect or abuse as defined by statue *before* initiating an investigation.

Justice Robert Orr called the *Stumbo* case "a circumstance that probably happens repeatedly across our state, where a toddler slips out of a house without the awareness of the parent or caregiver—no matter how conscientious or diligent the parent or caregiver might be."

Justice Orr further stated that, "such a lapse does not in and of itself constitute 'neglect.'"

The main opinion did not address the Fourth Amendment issue but three justices issued a concurring opinion indicating that the Fourth Amendment applies in child abuse investigations. And in this case, there was not sufficient evidence to justify the search order.

Again, a case of defensive litigation resulted in changing the common practice of investigative social workers in an entire state. And the opinion went a long way to helping another North Carolina family in a later case.

The Case of the Nine-year-old Babysitter[19]

The case began in August when the Department of Social Services (DSS) received a false report that the Boyds (name changed) had removed their nine-year-old from public school to care for his younger siblings all day every day. The Boyds did not have a nine-year-old child. They had left their five-year-old in the care of a twelve-year-old for a few hours after Mrs. Boyd had been unexpectedly admitted to the hospital. The Boyds had been legally homeschooling all of their children for over four years.

The Boyds' ordeal began on a Monday evening in August when Mrs. Boyd began experiencing severe pains in her back. Her husband took her to the emergency room. They took their three sons, ages 12, 11 and 5 to the emergency room with them. Around eleven o'clock the hospital admitted Mrs. Boyd and scheduled an MRI for the next morning.

On Tuesday morning Mr. Boyd stayed home with the children, hoping that the MRI would be concluded so that he could bring his wife home. Unfortunately, the test was delayed to the next day and Mrs. Boyd had to stay at the hospital.

Mr. Boyd left for work after lunch, leaving instructions with his older boys to watch the five-year-old and to call him at work if they needed him. Mr. Boyd was always available by phone and if needed could be home in less than ten minutes. He arrived home around 6 p.m., and after dinner took his children to the hospital to visit their mother.

On Wednesday morning, Mr. Boyd left for work at 9:00 a.m., again leaving his older boys to baby-sit. He came home for lunch at 11:00 and stayed home till 1:30 p.m. when he returned to work.

That afternoon, one of the Boyd's sons phoned his dad at work and reported that a stranger had come to the door earlier. They had not answered the door as Mr. Boyd had instructed them. The boy reported that he had just noticed that the stranger was still sitting on the porch close to an hour after she first knocked. Mr. Boyd came home immediately.

When he arrived home, Mr. Boyd was met by DSS worker, Heather Smith (name changed), who told him that DSS had received a report that the Boyd children were left home alone every day in the care of a nine-year-old. Mr. Boyd explained that he does not have a nine-year-old child and that his older boys, ages 12 and 11 were babysitting the five-year-old for a few hours each day due to his wife's unexpected admission to the hospital. He fully explained to Ms. Smith the situation, including the times he was at home on Tuesday and Wednesday and that he worked less than ten minutes away from home.

Nevertheless, Ms. Smith demanded private interviews with each of the children and demanded to search the Boyds' home. Mr. Boyd declined, citing concern for protecting his children from intrusive questioning out of his presence and for the privacy of his home. He did, however, offer Ms. Smith the opportunity to interview the children in his presence. She declined stating that this would not be satisfactory—she had to interview them far enough away from him so that he could not hear the conversation.

Ms. Smith summoned a supervisor who came to the Boyds' home and also demanded that Ms. Smith be allowed to privately interview the children and search the home. When Mr. Boyd again declined, the supervisor asked to see the children. Mr. Boyd called the children to him and the DSS workers could see that they were well-dressed, well-fed and healthy.

On Thursday, a third DSS worker interviewed Mrs. Boyd at the hospital. Mrs. Boyd confirmed that the older boys had babysat on Tuesday and Wednesday and that they were not left home alone every day in the care of a nine-year-old.

On Friday, DSS filed a petition alleging obstruction or interference with a juvenile investigation. The petition cited the allegation about a nine-year-old, but recognized that the two older boys were 12 and 11. You read that correctly. The petition stated that they needed to investigate a report that the children were left with a nine-year-old, and listed each of the boys' birth dates.

DSS asked the judge to issue the order without a hearing, which the judge rejected because North Carolina law requires a hearing unless there is an emergency situation requiring immediate action. HSLDA filed a motion to dismiss the petition arguing that the *Stumbo* case required DSS to close its file once it learned that the allegations were false. The juvenile judge agreed and dismissed the noninterference petition without even holding a hearing. The judge wrote this in his order: "That after having seen the children in person and having talked to both parents it should have been apparent that the report of the children being left alone every day in the care of a nine year old was simply untrue. That after conducting an initial screening the Department should have concluded that a statutorily mandated investigation was not necessary and dismissed the report."

Tragically, some children are abused and neglected. Equally tragic is the fact that DSS's limited resources to protect those children are stretched thin by false reports. In this case, the time and energy of no less than three social workers and a juvenile judge had been needlessly expended because of a false tip.

But DSS also bore some responsibility. Once the social workers learned that the allegations in the report were false that should have ended the matter. In *Stumbo*, the North Carolina Supreme Court held that social workers should be guided by common sense and by the Constitution.

The above three cases from our case files illustrate how defensive litigation can advance Fourth Amendment protections in CPS investigations. But mounting a defense in court is not always possible. CPS investigators at the door sometimes refuse to leave to obtain a court order. These occurrences open the courthouse door to civil rights lawsuits where the parents are on offense and the investigators are on defense.

CPS Litigation on Offense

Sometimes CPS investigators come to the front door without a court order and demand to be allowed to look around inside the home. Sometimes they coerce their way into the home, usually with the assistance of uniformed police officers. When they do this they open themselves up to personal liability for money damages if their entry is later determined to be in violation of Fourth Amendment rights.

The Civil Rights Act of 1871, which is codified at 42 U.S.C. §1983, paved the way for damages lawsuits in CPS litigation. It provides: "Every person who under color of any statute, ordinance, regulation, custom, or usage, of any State or Territory or the District of Columbia, subjects, or causes to be subjected, any citizen of the United States or other person within the jurisdiction thereof to the deprivation of any rights, privileges, or immunities secured by the Constitution and laws, shall be liable to the party injured in an action at law, Suit in equity, or other proper proceeding for redress...."

These "Section 1983" lawsuits have proven to be a valuable tool in defining, protecting, and advancing the rights of parents who find themselves confronted by a determined CPS investigator at the front door.

Section 1983 lawsuits are often settled before a court can write a published opinion, which is good for the family involved, but does little to advance the ball for others. Sometimes, though, the case proceeds far enough that a federal court writes a published opinion, which helps everyone in future cases as well. One of the earliest Section 1983 cases HSLDA handled illustrates the point.

The Case of the Cry in the Night[20]

Jill Floyd, a social worker for the Yolo County (California) Department of Social Services (DSS), had the "goods" on the Calabretta family. An anonymous tipster had heard a child's voice yelling "No, Daddy, no" late at night. Another time the tipster had heard a child's voice yelling "No, no, no" from the backyard. Additionally, the tipster knew that the Calabrettas homeschooled their children and were very religious.

Ms. Floyd went to the home four days after DSS received this report. She demanded entry. Shirley Calabretta, a member of Home School Legal Defense Association who had been instructed in her rights under the Fourth Amendment, graciously said "no." The Calabretta children were observed by the social worker when Shirley opened the door. Later that day, the social worker wrote that the children "did not appear to be abused or neglected."

Ms. Floyd went on a ten-day vacation. She hoped that another worker would complete the investigation while she was away. But when she returned, she found the file still sitting, uncompleted. She then called for a policeman to accompany her to the home. Not for her protection, but to "encourage cooperation" by Mrs. Calabretta.

Officer Nicholas Schwall knew nothing more than that children had been heard crying in the home. When Mrs. Calabretta opened her door he said, "We will get into your home one way or another." Mrs. Calabretta calmly replied that she did not consent to them coming into her home, but she would not resist if they came in against her will.

Once inside, Ms. Floyd insisted on segregating the two girls, then ages 12 and 3. She asked the twelve-year-old whether the children were spanked. The girl gave a remarkably mature description of biblical discipline and said that they were sometimes spanked with a short, thin dowel and other times with a Lincoln Log roofing piece. The girl denied any abuse or bruises.

Nonetheless, Ms. Floyd insisted on strip-searching the three-year-old. She demanded that the twelve-year-old remove the younger sister's pants. The older girl refused and the little girl began to scream in the tug-of-war that ensued. Mrs. Calabretta came into the bedroom, despite having been told to stay out.

When she found out what the social worker was demanding, Mrs. Calabretta removed the little girl's pants to show the social worker a perfectly normal child's bottom without a hint of bruising. The investigator and police officer left the home and the investigator closed the investigation, determining that there was no abuse or neglect.

HSLDA filed a civil-rights lawsuit for the Calabretta family in the federal district court in Sacramento. We argued that the Fourth Amendment prohibits social workers and police officers from coercing entry into a family's home without a warrant or probable cause evidence of an emergency.

The social worker and police officers argued that the normal rules of the Fourth Amendment do not apply to child welfare investigations. Additionally, they argued that the law concerning child welfare investigations was not clear and they were entitled to the good faith immunity defense for government officials who act in an area where the law is murky.

The federal trial court ruled in favor of the Calabrettas on all points. Unsurprisingly, the government agents appealed this decision to the U. S. Court of Appeals for the Ninth Circuit.

The Ninth Circuit issued an extraordinarily strong decision affirming the Fourth Amendment rights of family's and the right of privacy of the family home. The court held that neither social workers nor police officers can coerce their way into a home unless they have either a warrant or probable cause that there is an emergency situation. Anonymous tips like the one here simply do not qualify.

The court said, "The reasonable expectation of privacy of individuals in their homes includes the interests of both parents and children in not having government officials coerce entry in violation of the Fourth Amendment and humiliate the parents in front of the children. An essential aspect of the privacy of the home is the parent's and the child's interest in the privacy of their relationship with each other."[21]

The court concluded on a strong philosophical note. "The government's interest in the welfare of children embraces not only protecting children from physical abuse, but also protecting children's interest in the privacy and dignity of their homes and the lawfully exercised authority of their parents."[22]

This published opinion of a federal appeals court is now controlling law in thirteen western states. Moreover, decisions of other federal courts have also concluded since *Calabretta* that there is no social-worker exception to the Fourth Amendment.[23]

Conclusion

Fourth Amendment litigation in CPS cases can be a trying and challenging proposition. It involves real parents, real children, and very real interests in protecting the sanctity of the home and the family. Sometimes it can't be avoided. Sometimes it is a choice a family makes to right a wrong for their own family and to correct a system that sometimes runs amok.

To paraphrase Benjamin Franklin, we have Fourth Amendment rights—if we can keep them.

Notes

[1] Note, 73 UMKC L. Rev. 137 (2005).

[2] *Child Abuse Prevention and Treatment Act* as amended by the *Keeping Children and Families Safe Act of 2003*, 42 U.S.C. 5101 *et seq.*; 42 U.S.C. 5116 *et seq.* (2003).

[3] Doriane L. Coleman, *Storming the Castle to Save the Children: The Ironic Costs of a Child-welfare Exception to the Fourth Amendment*, 47 Wm. & Mary L. Rev. 413, 444 (2005).

[4] *Storming the Castle*, 47 Wm. & Mary L. Rev. at 458.

[5] *Id.*

[6] *Id.* at 518.

[7] *Id.* at 520.

[8] U.S. Department of Health and Human Services, Administration For Children, Youth and Families, "Child Maltreatment 2010" 20 (2011), *available at* http://www.acf.hhs.gov/programs/cb/pubs/cm10/cm10.pdf#page=17, visited June 27, 2012.

[9] *Storming the Castle*, 47 WM. & MARY L. REV. at 444.

[10] *Id.* at 529.

[11] *Id.* at 534.

[12] *Payton v. New York*, 445 U.S. 573, 586 (1980).

[13] *See, e.g. Greene v. Camreta*, 588 F.3d 1011 (9th Cir. 2009) (holding that such interviews violate the Fourth Amendment, vacated as moot by 131 S.Ct. 2020 [2011]).

[14] *Calabretta v. Floyd*, 189 F.3d 808, 820 (9th Cir. 1999).

[15] *In re Petition to Compel Cooperation with Child Abuse Investigation*, 875 A.2d 365 (Pa. Super. 2005).

[16] *Id.* at 379.

[17] *Id.* at 377.

[18] *In re Stumbo*, 357 N.C. 279 (N.C. 2003).

[19] This case resulted in an unpublished juvenile-court decision. Copies are on file with the author. A redacted copy may be provided on request.

[20] *Calabretta v. Floyd*, 189 F.3d 808 (9th Cir. 1999).

[21] *Id.* at 820.

[22] *Id.*

[23] *See e.g., Gates v. Texas Dept. of Protective and Regulatory Services*, 537 F.3d 404 (5th Cir. 2008); *Doe v. Heck*, 327 F.3d 492 (7th Cir. 2003). *Roska v. Peterson*, 304 F.3d 982, 989 (10th Cir.2002); *Walsh v. Erie County Dept of Jobs and Family Services*, 240 F.Supp.2d 731 (N.D. Ohio 2003).

The Effects of Family Structure on Child Abuse

By Patrick F. Fagan, Anna Dorminey, and Emily Hering

Introduction

Family brokenness is pervasive in the United States. The Second Annual Index of Family Belonging and Rejection, an analysis of the U.S. Census Bureau's American Community Survey, showed that only 45.8 percent of American children reach the age of 17 with both their biological parents married.[1] Intact families are indicative and generative of family belonging and cohesion; broken families are indicative and generative of rejection, which is often cyclical and intergenerational.[2]

It is important to note, in light of the fact that family brokenness is widespread, that the incidence of child abuse is not randomly distributed; rather, *it strongly correlates with "disrupted and disturbed families."*[3] Conversely, intact marriage is protective against both child abuse and intimate partner violence, as we demonstrate below.

Incidence of Spousal and Intimate Partner Violence

Marriage is protective against both physical and emotional abuse for men and women, as is older age.[4] Analysis of the Fragile Families and

Child Well Being study found that married mothers are less likely to be abused by their childen's father than are cohabiting mothers, dating mothers, or mothers who are not in any sort of relationship with their child's father. Their relationships with the fathers of their children are also marked by the lowest level of relational conflict.[5]

Figure 1: (DOJ) Rate of spousal and intimate partner violence against mothers over age 20 with children under 12 (per 1,000)

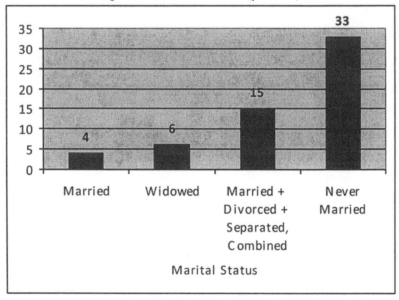

Incidence of Intimate Partner Violence by Type

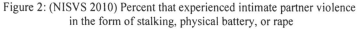

Figure 2: (NISVS 2010) Percent that experienced intimate partner violence
in the form of stalking, physical battery, or rape

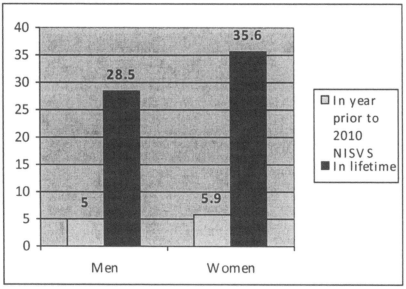

Whereas over one third of female victims experienced multiple forms of victimization, 92.1 percent of male victims experienced solely physical victimization, and 6.3 percent were both stalked and physically victimized. Most men and women (53 percent and 69 percent, respectively) who suffer intimate partner violence experience it for the first time before reaching the age of 25.[6]

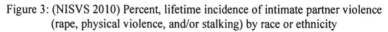

Figure 3: (NISVS 2010) Percent, lifetime incidence of intimate partner violence
(rape, physical violence, and/or stalking) by race or ethnicity

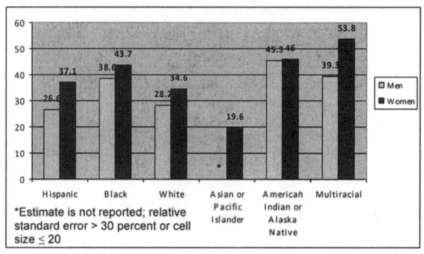

Lifetime incidence of intimate partner violence is highest among
those of multiracial, American Indian or Alaska Native, and Black race
or ethnicity.[7] The variance of intimate partner violence across ethnicity is
similar to the incidence of family brokenness: Only 16.7 percent of Black
adolescents, 27.5 percent of American Indian adolescents, and 35.7
percent of multiracial adolescents aged 15 to 17 live with biological
parents who are married to one another.[8]

Figure 4: (NISVS 2010) Percent, age at time of first IPV[9] experience among men and
women who experienced rape, physical violence, and/or stalking by an intimate partner

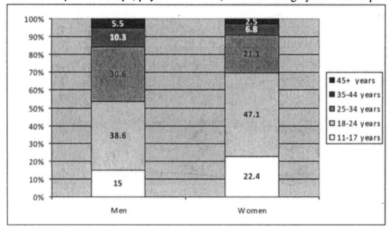

Psychological Aggression and Stalking

Intimate partner violence in the form of psychological aggression[10] is common among both men and women: 48.8 percent of men and 48.4 percent of women, over the course of their lifetime, experience psychological aggression by an intimate partner.[11] Stalking[12] is a similarly pernicious problem: An estimated 10.7 percent of females and 2.1 percent of males have experienced intimate partner violence in the form of stalking over the course of their lives. Among stalking victims, 66.2 percent of females and 41.4 percent of men were stalked by a current or previous intimate partner.[13]

Physical Abuse

Nearly one quarter of women and 13.8 percent of men have experienced intimate partner violence in the form of severe physical assault, such as being beaten or hit with a fist, over the course of their lifetime.[14]

Rape and Sexual Violence

Over 9 percent of American women have been raped by an intimate partner during their lifetime, and 51.1 percent of female rape victims were raped by an intimate partner. Estimates of men who suffered rape at the hands of an intimate partner could not be produced because too few men reported rape by an intimate partner.[15]

Nearly 5 percent of American men have been forced, over the course of their lifetime, to penetrate another individual; 44.8 percent reported that this forced penetration took place at the hands of an intimate partner. In their lifetime, an estimated 16.9 percent of females and 8 percent of males have suffered intimate partner violence in the form of sexual violence other than rape.[16]

Figure 5: (NISVS 2010) Percent, overlap of lifetime intimate partner rape, stalking, and physical violence among male victims

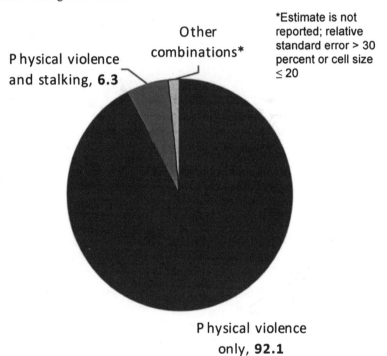

Figure 6: (NISVS 2010) Percent, overlap of lifetime intimate partner rape, stalking, and physical violence among female victims

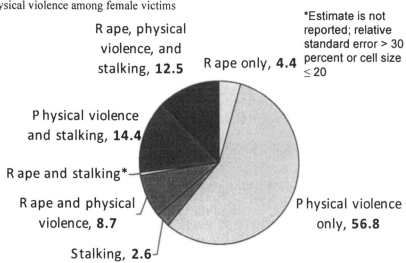

Rape, physical violence, and stalking, **12.5**

Rape only, **4.4**

*Estimate is not reported; relative standard error > 30 percent or cell size ≤ 20

Physical violence and stalking, **14.4**

Rape and stalking*

Rape and physical violence, **8.7**

Stalking, **2.6**

Physical violence only, **56.8**

Gender and Spousal and Intimate Partner Violence

A New Zealand study, whose sample included university students, prisoners, and members of the general population, found that women are more likely than men to perpetrate intimate partner abuse while not experiencing abuse; men are more likely than women to report only being victimized by their partner, not victimizing.[17] Female abusers are more likely to kick, push, shove, or throw something at their partner, whereas male abusers are more likely to choke their partner.[18] More women (46.7 percent) than men (30.2 percent) report emotional abuse from a spouse or cohabiting partner.[19] One study's findings indicated the existence of equal rates of perpetrated partner aggression among men and women; however, male-perpetrated abuse is more physically damaging than female-perpetrated abuse.[20]

Pregnancy and Childbearing

One study of women in northern Israel (a sample of 270 women, 95 percent of whom were married) seeking gynecological care found that pregnant women and women who are not pregnant are at a similar risk of domestic abuse. This study found physical attacks on pregnant women's abdomens to be the least common form of abuse, occurring among 5.4

percent of the women surveyed. Sexual coercion was slightly more common (5.6 percent), followed by severe physical abuse (8.1 percent), minor physical abuse (17 percent), and psychological abuse (24 percent).[21] A Brazilian study of 1,045 pregnant women found psychological abuse to be the most common form of spousal or cohabiting partner abuse during pregnancy, whether it occured alone or in addition to physical or sexual abuse.[22] A British study of 200 women receiving antenatal or postnatal care found that women who reported having suffered intimate partner violence were more likely than women who had never suffered intimate partner violence to report having experienced at least one other traumatic event (e.g., childhood sexual abuse, "rape or attempted rape," a "[s]erious incident, fire, or explosion," military combat, imprisonment).[23]

10 percent of men in one study reported that 13 or more circumstances justified hitting or slapping a wife; 15 percent of the men surveyed reported that hitting and slapping were unjustifiable under all circumstances. (The sample included 47 men aged 21 to 45, recruited from employment agencies, 70 percent of whom were Caucasian and 77 percent of whom were always single.) Items for which hitting or slapping received relatively high justification among these men were (by order of mean justification rating): "she comes at [her husband] with a knife" (3.47 mean justification rating), "she physically abuses their child" (2.53), "in an argument, she hits [her husband] first" (1.81), "[her husband] catches her in bed with another man" (1.77), and "[her husband] learns that she is having an affair" (1.17).[24]

Figure 7: Reasons for hitting or slapping a wife that received relatively high justification

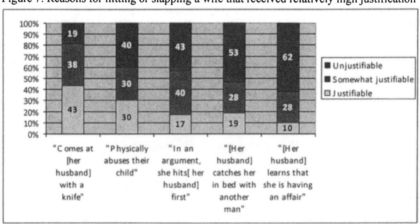

Environment and Correlates of Spousal and Intimate Partner Violence

Alcohol and Drug Abuse

Analysis of the National Educational Longitudinal Survey found that adolescents from recently divorced single-parent families are more likely to drink heavily (to consume five or more alcoholic beverages frequently) and to consume alcohol while at school.[25] This increased likelihood of persons from broken families to consume alcohol heavily is significant because one study of over 400 Rhode Island batterers found that problems with alcohol directly contribute to intimate partner physical abuse, as well, or indirectly, through psychological aggression.[26] Jealous individuals who do not have anger control problems are likelier to exhibit severe physical abuse against their spouses or cohabiting partners when they exhibit problematic levels of drinking. (This increase is nonexistent for those with jealousy and anger control problems, because they exhibit aggression toward their spouses or partners even while sober.)[27]

The relationship between intimate partner violence and alcohol is constant across socioeconomic groups, while the relationship between intimate partner violence and marijuana use is much stronger in the lower socioeconomic group than in the higher group.[28] Analysis of a sample of over 19,000 individuals surveyed in the 2001 National Household Survey on Drug Abuse found that perpetration of or subjection to intimate partner violence and the occurrence of serious emotional abuse, yelling, and insults in a household are strongly linked to more than one drug or alcohol dependence or abuse problem and with dependence upon or abuse of marijuana.[29]

Those who have mental health problems, receive welfare, have lower educational attainment, or live in a "drug supportive environment" are more likely to yell at and insult each other.[30] (A drug supportive environment was one in which "most or all of their friends smoke marijuana or were drunk once a week...reported selling illegal drugs...reported that illicit drugs were fairly or very easy to obtain and they had fewer than three friends who cared about them or would support them in financially hard times."[31]) The relationship between marijuana use and intimate partner violence is mediated by low-income marijuana users' increased tendency to yell at and insult one another.[32] Persistent mental abuse is more commonly inflicted on those who live in a "drug supportive culture."[33] The relationship between drug use and intimate partner violence is not moderated by an individual's residing in a drug supportive community.[34] The relationship between drug use and intimate partner violence is stronger among those who did not complete high school and are unemployed than among those who did not complete high school and are employed.[35]

Among female prostitutes, those who use heroin or who engage in sexual activity in "crack houses" are more likely to be abused than those who do neither.[36] A woman's frequent exchange of sex for money or drugs increased her chances of being physically abused by one of her paying partners.[37]

Community Drug Use

Interviews of fifty women eligible for TANF (Temporary Assistance to Needy Families) found that women living in communities marked by substance abuse and social disorder were at greater risk of intimate partner violence because the incidence of substance abuse and disorder contributed to a greater general level of violence in the community to which these women were exposed.[38]

Personal Characteristics

Acts of intimate partner violence are less common among individuals with a large number of friends,[39] while male abusers (more than female abusers) report having antisocial traits.[40]

One study found that men specifically designated as batterers (118 men brought to a "a cognitive behavioral, psycho-educational group batterers treatment program at the UMass/Memorial Medical Center") had more problems in school as adolescents: They got into more fights, beat up other children more often, skipped school more often, and got into trouble with the law more often than men in the "general public" group.[41]

These characteristics are correlated with home life in childhood: A different study found that children whose mothers smoke while pregnant, whose mothers began having children early, whose mothers have "a history of anti-social behavior during their school years," and whose parents have serious difficulty living together or have low income have the largest risk "of not learning to regulate physical aggression in early childhood."[42] One study of abuse in a rural setting found educational attainment to be unrelated to incidence of physical and emotional violence among spouses and cohabiting partners.[43]

Effects of Intimate Partner Violence
and Spousal Abuse

Spousal or Partner Relationship

Men and women (in the aforementioned New Zealand study of university students, prisoners, and the general population) who had perpetrated or suffered physical violence were found to differ widely from those who had not experienced violence in their "communication problems, dominance, hostility to men, hostility to women, partner blame, and explicit gender role beliefs."[44] Although abused women report enjoying significantly less marital satisfaction than their abusive husbands,[45] extremely victimized husbands report less marital satisfaction than extremely victimized wives.[46]

Analysis of a sample of 3,519 married or cohabiting men and women surveyed in the 1994 National Comorbidity Survey found that, of those with "excellent" relationships, almost 30 percent experienced some "mutual mild violence" in their relationship and that 16.2 percent reported "severe mutual violence." Furthermore, 27 percent of those in violent relationships described their relationship as excellent,[47] leading another author to conclude, ironically, that "it is unclear whether marital discord or marital satisfaction is more highly related to IPV [intimate partner violence]."[48]

Health

Poor physical health, persistent pain and headaches, trouble sleeping, limited activity, and poor mental health were commonly reported among men and women who experienced physical violence by an intimate partner, or stalking or rape at the hands of any perpetrator. Women who experienced physical intimate partner violence (or who experienced stalking or rape by any victimizer) also more often reported suffering irritable bowel syndrome, asthma, and diabetes.[49]

Psychological Problems

Emotionally abused women reported more physical, psychological, and social support problems than women who had not suffered emotional abuse.[50] In a sample of over 500 mostly African-American individuals selected from an urban hospital emergency department, increases in physical and psychological aggression diminished mental health among women who suffered intimate partner violence, whereas for males who suffered intimate partner violence, worsening mental health issues were contingent on increased psychological aggression.[51] Women who are victims of severe assault suffered four times as much depression, six times as many suicide attempts, and twice as many headaches as women who were not so assaulted.[52] One Brazilian study found that women who experienced frequent psychological abuse by their intimate partner during pregnancy were more likely to suffer postnatal depression. The earlier-cited study of pregnant women in Brazil found that women were at the highest risk of postnatal depression when they had experienced physical or sexual abuse by a spouse or cohabiting partner during pregnancy, in addition to psychological violence.[53] Analysis of data from the Dunedin Multidisciplinary Health and Development Study, a longitudinal study in New Zealand (a sample of over 900), found that women in a "clinically abusive relationship" were at a greater risk of generalized anxiety disorder, major depressive episodes, post-traumatic stress disorder (PTSD), and dependence on marijuana (even after controlling for baseline functioning at age 18 and for conduct disorder). No such relationship was found among men after controls.[54]

According to the National Intimate Partner and Sexual Violence Survey, almost 3 in 10 women and one in 10 men have experienced some intimate partner violence in the form of stalking, physical battery, or rape, and reported experiencing post-traumatic stress disorder symptoms; fear or concern for their safety; contacting a crisis hotline; needing legal, victim's advocate, or housing services; needing healthcare; injury; or missing one or more days of work or school.[55]

A study of a sample of 79 battered women found that those women who had also suffered physical abuse as girls developed obsessive-compulsive tendencies as "a concerted effort to change her environment to prevent further assault."[56]

Figure 8: (NISVS 2010) Percent, distribution of IPV-related impacts among male victims of rape, physical violence, and/or stalking by an intimate partner

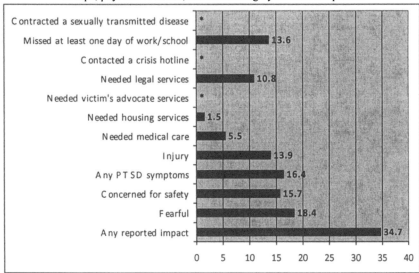

*Estimate is not reported; relative standard error > 30 percent or cell size ≤ 20

Figure 9: (NISVS 2010) Percent, distribution of IPV-related impacts among female victims of rape, physical violence, and/or stalking by an intimate partner

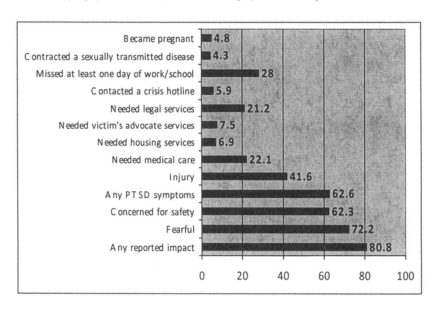

The Effects of Intimate Partner Violence and Spousal Abuse on Children

It is clear that children are affected when their parents exhibit aggression toward one another. Children exposed to intimate partner violence and spousal abuse exhibit more behavioral problems and are more likely themselves to later commit intimate partner violence and spousal abuse. Some begin to abuse their parent(s), or alternately, others feel compelled to intervene to prevent the abuse of a parent. Furthermore, children in homes marked by domestic violence are often the victims of compromised parenting or of direct abuse. Intimate partner violence and spousal abuse, simply put, misshape family dynamics and personality and character formation.

Behavioral Problems

Analysis of a sample of 2,020 female caregivers (approximately 95 percent of whom were the biological mothers of the children in question) obtained from the National Survey of Child and Adolescent Well-Being found that severe intimate partner violence is associated with internalizing behaviors (depression, anxiety) and externalizing behaviors (aggression, hostility) in children.[57] One study, whose participants were drawn from the Minnesota Parent-Child Project (a 25-year longitudinal study of poor mothers and their first children; of the mothers, 83 percent were Caucasian, 62 percent were single, and 60 percent had completed high school), found that boys' exposure to intimate partner violence in middle childhood and preschool is linked with externalizing behavior in adolescence and middle childhood, respectively. Girls' exposure to intimate partner violence in preschool is associated with internalizing behavior in adolescence. This study also found that early childhood exposure to intimate partner violence (as well as life stress) was found to be the most influential variable shaping behavior problems at age 16.[58]

Spousal and Intimate Partner Abuse

Children who witness physical violence between their parents exhibit significantly worse outcomes than children who witness other forms of conflict between their parents.[59] Young adults exposed to severe intimate partner violence between their primary caregiver (95 percent of whom were their biological mothers or "mother figures") and his or her partner are themselves more likely to later engage in intimate partner violence and severe intimate partner violence, according to an analysis of data from the Rochester Youth Development Study (a longitudinal study of 1,000 urban adolescents, the majority of whom were male and African-American),[60] though the witnessing of violence between parents may only have a small though significant effect on the child's later likelihood to commit spousal abuse or to abuse a cohabiting partner.[61] "[C]hildren who witness domestic violence may show inappropriate attitudes about violence as a means of resolving conflict, a greater willingness to use violence themselves, and stronger beliefs about being responsible for their parent's violence."[62] The earlier-cited analysis of 118 abusive men at the University of Massachusetts Memorial Medical Center found that abusers are more likely than the general population to report having seen their fathers drunk or having seen their fathers hit their mothers.[63] Nearly one fourth of a randomly selected group of 1,368 male municipal workers in Cape Town, South Africa, had seen their mother abused, which was associated with harmful or destructive behaviors, such as involvement in violence and gang activity; arrest; arrest as a result of violence, theft, or illegally possessing a firearm; and incarceration. Having witnessed the abuse of one's mother was associated with commission of intimate partner violence, particularly the use of physical violence.[64] The South African authors wrote, "Our findings suggest that the violent behavior engaged in by male respondents in adulthood might have been prevented or diminished had they not witnessed the abuse of their mothers as children. These childhood experiences appeared to be strongly predictive of both physical violence against partners and possible violent crime."[65]

Abuse of Parents

Many children or adolescents who abuse a parent have witnessed domestic violence or have themselves been victims of physical or sexual abuse.[66] Often after an abusive parent has left the home, the child or adolescent begins to take on the role of victimizer by continuing to abuse his or her long-abused parent.[67]

Intervention During Parent Abuse

Some children, instead of repeating the abuse themselves, may intervene to prevent the abuse of a parent. Abused mothers surveyed in one study reported that this occurred in various ways. 52 percent reported that their children shouted from another room, 53 percent reported that their child shouted from within the same room, 21 percent reported that their children called for help, and 23 percent reported that their child had physically intervened during abuse [whether "occasionally," "frequently," or "very frequently").[68] Children who were biologically related to their mother's abuser were less likely to intervene during her abuse than children who are not biologically related to their mother's abuser.[69] Children of married mothers intervened *less* than children of unmarried mothers.[70]

Dysfunctional Family Dynamics

The effects of familial abuse ripple out into further and more deeply misshapen family dynamics. Children who witness abuse are also likely to have experienced "harsh discipline, lack of emotional support and affection, and poor parental supervision," all of which are detrimental to children's psychological and social well-being and which themselves correlated with more violence.[71] One qualitative study of the effects of domestic violence on family dynamics found that a child, for example, may blame his mother for his father leaving, or the child may take on an adult role and intervene during abuse. Many children's relationships with their father were negatively affected because the child came to distrust or fear him. When angry with their partners, some fathers compromised their parent-child relationship by exhibiting aggression toward their children. Similarly, some mothers would hit or shout at their children when they felt stressed by their relationship with their partners. Others reported that their children fought as they had seen their parents do, or that one child "assumed a parental role to protect younger siblings." Some mothers said that though they eventually became aware of the negative effects of the violence on their children's welfare and development, while they were still living with the abusive partner, they either "were not aware of, or minimized, the effects of the domestic violence on their children."[72]

Compromised Parenting

Intimate partner violence or spousal abuse may be accompanied by "compromised parenting": One author posits that domestic violence produces parental inability to protect their children and help their children understand and deal with an experience like abuse.[73] Analysis of the northwest subset of the Longitudinal Studies of Child Abuse and

Neglect, a sample of 261 children who had experienced neglect or abuse and had subsequently been referred to child protective services, found that domestic violence affects family functioning and the welfare and health of caregivers, as well as their relationship with a child (all of which, in turn, affect a child's behavior and health).[74] Mothers, as a result of living in constant fear and anxiety will be unable to provide their children with a sense of basic trust in their parents, and thus deprive them of the experience of healthy emotional development and normal transitions through the stages of such development.[75]

Relayed Child Abuse

Finally, abused mothers may be more likely to hurt their children as a result of being hurt themselves,[76] though some data contradicts this.[77] Homes characterized by intimate partner violence are often characterized by child neglect and abuse.[78] As Louise Dixon of the School of Psychology at the University of Birmingham and colleagues write, "It is evident from this study that both mothers and fathers can aggress against their partner, child or both. Therefore, this lends support for the need to explore violent families from a more holistic perspective in both research and practice, considering the overlap of child and partner maltreatment and the effects of intimate partner violence upon all members of the family rather than exclusively considering the violent man."[79] We address the incidence and effects of child abuse in the sections that follow.

Anaylsis of Family Structure on Abuse and Neglect

As noted in this article's Introduction, the incidence of child abuse is not randomly distributed. Neither is it linked to race or economic status. It is most prevalent among single-parent and reconstructed families;[80] and, as one author wrote, "mounting divorce rates, soaring nonmarital births, and the ubiquity of cohabitation combine to create a profoundly negative consequence...."[81]

Figure 10: (NIS-4) Age differences in incidence rates for all Harm Standard maltreatment, abuse, and neglect (per 1,000 children)

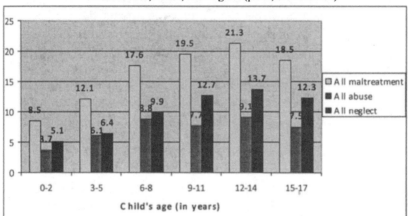

Ed. Note: NIS-4, from which this data is taken, is the most recent of the periodic Congressional-mandated studies of child abuse data around the country (published in 2010). These studies have used two standards to determine how much child maltreatment has occurred: the Harm Standard and the Endangerment Standard. The former is relatively stringent in that it generally requires that an act or omission result in demonstrable harm in order to be classified as abuse or neglect. The Endangerment Standard counts children who were not yet harmed by abuse or neglect if a sentinel thought that the maltreatment endangered the children or if a CPS investigation substantiated or indicated their maltreatment (which as this book shows may not actually mean something that most people would truly consider maltreatment or is based on vague definitions of "abuse" and "neglect" in the laws). The Harm Standard is viewed as more objective of the two.

One study of 176 low-income African-American and Caucasian women in their early twenties found child physical abuse to be far more common in that income bracket than child sexual abuse. Whereas 63 percent reported "at least rarely" suffering physical abuse as girls, 25 percent reported "at least rarely" suffering sexual abuse, and 20 percent reported having "at least rarely" suffered both forms of abuse. Women who reported experiencing sexual abuse as children frequently also reported having suffered physical abuse; however, women who report having been subjected to childhood physical abuse infrequently report also being subjected to sexual abuse as children.[82] Childhood psychological abuse is commonly accompanied by parental antipathy, neglect, and sexual abuse, as well as physical abuse.[83] Analysis of a sample of over 55,000 pregnant Norwegian women (the Norwegian Mother and Child Cohort Study by the Norwegian Institute of Public Health) found that, among those women who reported experiencing abuse as a child (whether physical, emotional, or sexual), 31 percent reported being subjected to two or more forms of abuse. Analysis of this sample found that women who had suffered abuse as girls had less education and were less likely to be employed.[84]

Approximately one-fifth of female stalking victims were teenagers between the ages of 11 and 17.[85] Among female rape victims, 42.2 percent were first raped before reaching 18 years of age; among male rape victims, 27.8 percent were raped before reaching age 10.[86]

The average age at initial abuse among one sample of female sexual abuse victims (99 female undergraduate university students with an average age of 21, the majority of whom were Caucasian, had never been married, and came from "the midrange of family income") was 8.5 years old. Abuse lasted, on average, 1.3 years and resulted in sexual intercourse or penetration for approximately 40 percent of respondents. Most reported being coerced; over half of those surveyed reported that their abuser used or threatened to use violence or force.[87]

Figure 11: (NIS-4) Incidence of Harm Standard maltreatment by family structure and living arrangement (per 1,000 children)

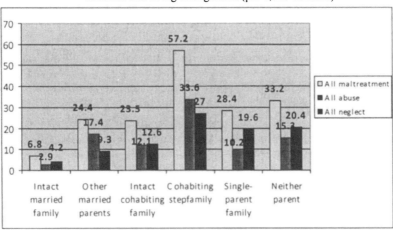

Figure 12: (NIS-4) Incidence of Harm Standard abuse by family structure and living arrangement (per 1,000 children)

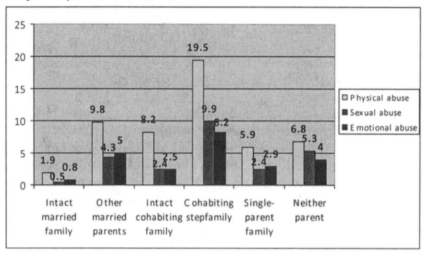

Figure 13: (NIS-4) Incidence of Harm Standard neglect by family structure and living arrangement (per 1,000 children)

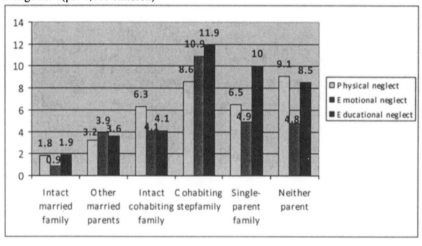

Figure 14: (NIS-4) Incidence of outcomes from Harm Standard maltreatment by family structure and living arrangement (per 1,000 children)

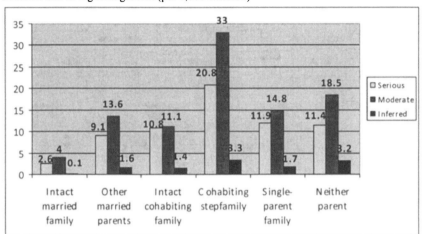

Intact Families

The NIS-4 shows that all forms of Harm Standard maltreatment are rarest in intact married families (see above). The rates of Harm Standard abuse (physical, sexual, and emotional) and Harm Standard neglect (physical, emotional, and educational) are lowest in households with married biological parents.[88] Furthermore, the incidence of serious, moderate, and inferred outcomes is by far the rarest in intact married families[89]

A large Icelandic study found that adolescents (particularly girls) living with two biological parents are less likely to experience sexual abuse than those living in any other family structure (with a single mother, a mother and stepfather, a single father, a father and stepmother, or "other" [with grandparents, relatives, siblings, alone, etc.]).[90]

Stepfamilies

According to the NIS-4, by the Harm Standard, children in all kinds of non-biological married families (including stepfamilies) are significantly more likely to experience maltreatment than those in intact married families. Physical abuse is relatively high in non-biological married families.[91] Furthermore, children in non-biological married families suffer far worse outcomes than children in intact married families.[92]

According to an analysis of the Developmental Victimization Survey (a random national sample of 1,000 children aged 10 to 17 and 1,030 caregivers of children aged 2 to 9), children in stepfamilies are more likely to experience sexual victimization, physical assault, child maltreatment, and peer/sibling victimization than children in single-parent homes or biologically intact families.[93] Biological parents in biologically intact families (7 percent) and single-parent families (8.5 percent) victimize their children at approximately the same rate; however, biological parents in stepfamilies are significantly more likely to victimize their children (18.1 percent).[94] Children in stepfamilies are substantially more likely (63 percent) to be victimized by a family member than children from single-parent homes (38.7 percent) or biologically intact families (38.6 percent).[95] Furthermore, children in stepfamilies (79 percent) and single-parent families (73.9 percent) are at significantly greater risk than children in intact biological families (60 percent) of victimization by a person outside their family.[96] This study's analysis of victimization encompassed "a relatively broad category of events, including criminal offenses against minors (such as robbery and aggravated assault), violations of child welfare statutes (such as physical abuse and neglect), and other aggressive and sexual behaviors against children (such as bullying and sexual harassment),"[97] and was organized by instances of child maltreatment, physical assault, sexual victimization, peer/sibling victimization, property crime, and witnessing/indirect victimization.[98]

Robin Fretwell Wilson, of the Washington and Lee University School of Law, wrote that "[i]t is likely that a parent beginning a new relationship, however well intentioned, will see his or her new partner through rose-colored glasses: 'even when signs of abuse are more obvious, many [parents] find it more difficult to think that their [spouse, lover], or other trusted person could actually be a sexual offender, or even that sexual abuse could occur in their family.'"[99] One researcher found that girls living with stepfathers are seven times more likely to be abused than girls living with both their biological parents.[100] Another study found that stepfathers accounted for 41 percent of all sexual abuse, almost four times what would be expected based upon the number of children cared for by non-biological fathers.[101]

Girls who live with a single mother are at a significantly greater risk of sexual exploitation than girls who live in an intact family, but the transition from a single-mother family to a stepfamily with a stepfather further increases a girl's risk.[102]

Single-Parent Families

According to the NIS-4, by Harm Standard measures, the rate of abuse in single-parent families is relatively low, though the rate of abuse in intact married families is significantly lower.[103] Single-parent families have the second-highest rate of educational neglect.[104]

Analysis of the Developmental Victimization Survey (cited above) showed that children from single-parent homes or stepfamilies experience more sexual assault, maltreatment, violence, and "non-victimization adversity" (e.g., experiencing a major disaster, an accident or illness that required hospitalization, constant teasing) and witness more family violence than children living in biologically intact or two-parent adoptive families.[105]

Half of all girls living in a father-only household reported experiencing sexual abuse.[106] Households with an absent mother (whether she has passed away or is absent due to hospitalization or mental illness) report increased sexual abuse.[107] Boys who live with one parent are more likely to experience sexual abuse than boys who live with two parents, particularly after controlling for childhood socioeconomic status. Those boys from single-parent families who experienced sexual abuse were disproportionately likely to have a female abuser or an abuser who is not part of their family.[108]

Intact Cohabiting Families

The NIS-4 finds that, by Harm Standard measures, rates of sexual and emotional abuse are relatively low in intact cohabiting families, though they are higher than in intact married families.[109]

Cohabiting Stepfamilies

Cohabiting families, as shown by NIS-4 Harm Standard measures, are a dangerous place for children. Rates of all three types of abuse are highest in cohabiting stepfamilies, particularly physical abuse.[110] Emotional and educational neglect is highest in cohabiting stepfamilies, and only families in which children live with neither parent have higher rates of physical neglect.[111] Finally, children in cohabiting stepfamilies have the highest rates of severe, moderate, and inferred outcomes.[112]

Low Socioeconomic Status

The NIS-4 found that children in families of low socioeconomic status (SES) were at greater risk for Harm Standard abuse and neglect than children who were not. (Children were classified as being in low SES families if any member of their family received "subsidized school breakfasts or lunches, Temporary Assistance for Needy Families (TANF), food stamps, public housing, energy assistance, and public assistance," if their household income was below $15,000 per year, or if their parents' attained less than a high school education.)[113] The differences are sharpest in the categories of emotional abuse, physical neglect, and educational neglect.[114]

Figure 15: (NIS-4) Differences related to family socioeconomic status in incidence rates and outcomes of Harm Standard maltreatment (per 1,000 children)

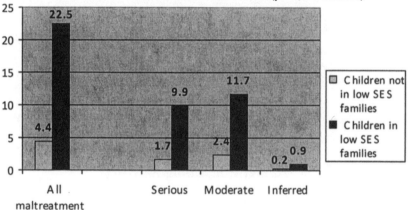

Figure 16: (NIS-4) Differences related to family socioeconomic status in incidence rates of Harm Standard abuse and neglect (per 1,000 children)

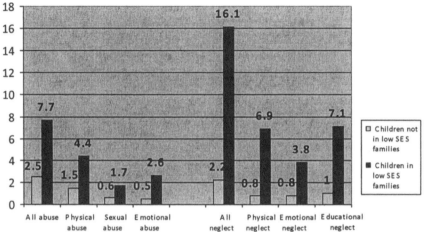

Siblings

Some children suffer victimization at the hands of their own siblings. Children with siblings as "targets for physical aggression" are four times as likely to be classified as highly aggressive as children without siblings.[115]

One study of 203 undergraduate students found that nearly half of respondents had experienced aggressive behavior by a sibling and that 41 percent had directed physical aggression at a sibling. Almost 31 percent of victims of sibling abuse notified an authority figure about the matter; in almost all cases, the authority figure intervened, and thereafter, the majority (63.4 percent) of sibling abuse decreased. However, in the situations in which an authority figure was not notified about the sibling abuse, the behavior subsided only 20 percent of the time. Approximately half of perpetrators described the aggression they leveled at their siblings as "mild" and "rare."[116]

Figure 17: Percent, incidence of committed or received sibling aggression and its perception as abuse

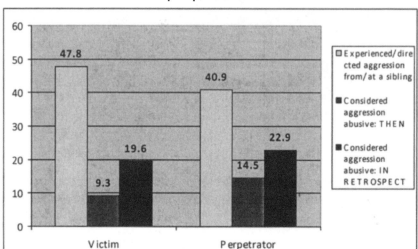

Notably, an analysis of 1,000 adolescents in the Developmental Victimization Survey (cited earlier) found sibling victimization to be more common in stepfamilies than in single-parent or biologically intact families (see Figure 21).[117] The study of undergraduate students referenced above also found that victims and perpetrators of physical sibling assault and respondents who reported engaging in sexual activity with siblings "reported more stressful changes in the family" (measured by nine factors, including divorce or affairs and physical or sexual abuse in the home).[118]

Figure 18: Percent, incidence of sibling victimization by family structure

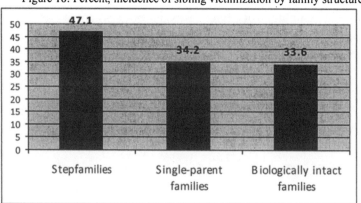

Other Correlates of Child Maltreatment

Females aged 10 to 17 reported experiencing more sexual victimization than males.[119] Young men (particularly those aged 12 and younger) are significantly more likely to be sexually assaulted than adult men.[120] Daughters are more likely than sons to be abused by a parent. Children (aged 8 to 11) who are sexually abused are more likely than adolescents (aged 12 to 15) to be threatened, but adolescents are more likely to suffer forced sexual abuse, to be abused frequently, and to be abused by a parental figure.[121]

Lower parental educational attainment and family income is correlated with increased exposure to family violence and child maltreatment, compared to families whose parents are more educated or earn higher incomes.[122] A larger number of children are sexually abused in urban areas; however, the rate of child sexual abuse is higher in rural areas.[123]

Effects of Child Neglect and Abuse

Victims of childhood maltreatment are most frequently deeply shaped by their suffering. Though the emotional and behavioral symptoms of child sexual abuse were previously thought to manifest themselves approximately one year after the abuse occurrs, more recent research suggests that symptoms may even lie latent until adulthood.[124] As we will demonstrate below, the abuse affects the child concerned profoundly and in a variety of ways.

Perpetration of Abuse

Studies of the intergenerational effects of abuse make it very clear that children often model the behaviors that their parents exhibit. An abused child may repeat the same behavior to which he or she was subjected. A study of inmates in state and federal correction facilities showed that "offenders model specific behaviors to which they have been exposed." The authors of this study found that male inmates who had suffered physical abuse as children were more likely to commit physical violence; likewise, those who had suffered childhood sexual abuse were more likely to commit sexual offenses (particularly against children).[125] The connection between experiencing child abuse and committing spousal abuse in adulthood is slight but significant.[126]

Physical Abuse

Analysis of the National Youth Survey shows that those who suffer physical abuse in adolescence are twice as likely to commit minor intimate partner violence and over five times as likely to commit serious intimate partner violence.[127] One small study found that almost half of the men sampled who had experienced severe violence growing up (e.g., "kick, bit, or hit you with a fist," "hit or tried to hit you with something," "burned or scalded you," "used a knife or a gun") had physically abused a partner and that 90 percent of those men had emotionally abused a partner. (The sample included 47 men aged 21 to 45, recruited from employment agencies, 70 percent of whom were Caucasian and 77 percent of whom were always single.) Among men who had not been subjected to such victimization in their family of origin, 12 percent physically abused a partner and 50 percent emotionally abused a partner.[128] This study also found that among men who believe physical aggression against their partner is justifiable, suffering abuse while growing up and exhibiting physical and emotional aggression against a partner are strongly associated. No such association was found among men who do not condone physical aggression.[129] The above-cited study of 118 abusive men at the University of Massachusetts Memorial Medical Center found that batterers were more likely to report having been beaten by their mothers and to report bad relationships with their parents than was the sample representing the general population.[130]

Sexual Abuse

Analysis of the Christchurch Health and Development study, a longitudinal study (from birth to age 30) of a sample of over 900 in New Zealand, found child sexual abuse to be correlated with increased commission of intimate partner violence, earlier and more frequent cohabitation, earlier parenthood, and lower satisfaction and investment in relationships.[131] Child sexual abuse is not directly associated with later perpetration of intimate partner violence among females, but it is the largest direct predictor of intimate partner violence commission among males.[132]

Increased Victimization

Those victimized as children are more likely to be victimized in other relationships. The authors of one small quantitative study of a group of women receiving treatment for drug addiction, all of whom, as girls, had been witness to parental intimate partner violence or had been physically or sexually abused, wrote that "[t]he women also all spontaneously told the interviewer that they realized that there were similarities in how they raised their children and how they were raised. The women said things like 'history repeats' and 'what goes around comes around.'"[133]

Physical Abuse

The earlier-cited sample of 79 battered women found that such women were more likely to remain in abusive relationships if they had experienced physical abuse as girls.[134] Physically abused girls were more likely to be in multiple abusive relationships when they grew up (83 percent) than were women who had not been physically abused as girls (55 percent).[135] Furthermore, battered women who were physically abused as girls sought help much later than battered women who were not physically abused as girls.[136]

Sexual Abuse

Individuals with a history of childhood sexual abuse involving attempted or completed intercourse are more likely to be sexually victimized after age 16, are more likely to engage in a variety of unhealthy and risky sexual behaviors, such as early sexual debut, and are more likely to contract sexually transmitted diseases.[137] The Norwegian study cited earlier found that one-third of women who were abused in girlhood were also abused as adult women. 27 percent of women who reported suffering emotional abuse in childhood also suffered emotional abuse as adult women; 12.6 percent of those who were subjected to physical abuse as girls were also subjected to physical abuse as adult women; and 10.4 percent of women who were sexually abused as girls were also sexually abused as adults.[138]

Family

Sexual Behavior

Those who were sexually abused as children report more sexual partners than those who were not sexually abused.[139] A survey of mainly Caucasian girls in eighth, tenth, and twelfth grade found (after controlling for age) that those girls who had been sexually abused had a tripled likelihood of having had sexual intercourse and a doubled likelihood of making their sexual debut by age 15.[140]

Divorce

Children who experience physical abuse, rape, or serious physical assault are more likely to also experience marital disruption (i.e., divorce or separation) as adults than children who do not.[141]

Conflicted Parent-Child Relationship

In males and females, childhood verbal maltreatment (such as being insulted, humiliated, or publicly embarrassed by one's father or mother) is associated with anxious attachment and avoidant attachment (a relationship to the parent characterized by indifference) to both father and mother. In males, childhood physical maltreatment by one's parents was positively associated with anxious attachment in their relationships with their mothers and strongly and positively associated with avoidant attachment in their relationships with their fathers. In females, childhood physical maltreatment was positively and strongly associated with anxious attachment and "avoidant attachment" in their relationships to their mothers, as well as avoidant attachment in their relationships to their fathers.[142] Expectant teenage mothers who have experienced greater degrees of physical abuse from family members tended to report later that they experienced less joy in their relationships with their babies, that they did not feel equal to the task of parenting, and that they experienced "greater disappointment with infant responsiveness." The relationship between abuse and these results was mediated by the perceptions of caregiver-child relationships that these women had previously developed. However, this relationship was only true among adolescents who did not have a strong romantic partnership.[143]

Aggression

In boys, maltreatment tends to produce physical aggressiveness ("starts fights, says mean things, pushes or hits others"), and in girls, maltreatment may produce relational aggressiveness ("when s/he is mad at someone, refuses to play or talk to the person, will try to get others not to like the person, will spread rumors or talk behind the person's back").[144] Childhood physical abuse generated physical aggression; however, "girls who were sexually abused exhibited lower levels of physical aggression than nonsexually abused girls (p< .01)."[145] Sexual abuse tended to generate relational aggression in girls.[146]

Income

Analysis of the above-noted sample of 79 battered women found that those who had been physically abused as girls earned, on average, $97 per month less than those who had not been physically abused as girls.[147] The mean income of those who had not been sexually abused as girls to be $1200, whereas the mean income of those who suffered childhood sexual abuse was $620.[148]

Crime

Delinquency

Anger resulting from sexual abuse is a strong predictor of delinquent behavior. This relationship is twice as strong among boys.[149] Abused girls are more likely to participate in delinquent and criminal activity, and are thus more likely to use drugs as women.[150] Girls who experience victimization in their communities (being threatened, beaten up, attacked sexually, etc.) who have strong support from a guardian are less likely than girls with low guardian support to exhibit delinquent behavior.[151]

Alcohol Problems

Among both men and women, rejection by a father can contribute to a tendency to drink to cope and results in increased drinking problems.[152] A history of suffering child abuse or neglect predicts excessive drinking in women as adults, but not in men. Women who were abused or neglected as girls report having consumed more alcohol in the past year and more days in the past month in which they consumed eight or more alcoholic beverages than women who were not abused or neglected as girls.[153] The relationship among women between child maltreatment and excessive drinking in middle adulthood was mediated by their relationship to alcohol in young adulthood (whether or not they were diagnosed as alcohol dependent or abusive). No relationship was found among men between neglect or abuse in childhood and their young adulthood alcohol diagnosis or drinking to excess in middle adulthood.[154]

Substance Abuse

Among men, having experienced severe emotional abuse as a child is associated with severe lifetime substance abuse. Among women, having experienced severe maltreatment, emotional abuse, and emotional neglect is also associated with severe lifetime substance abuse.[155] The relationship among women between abuse and neglect in childhood and substance abuses in adulthood is partially mediated by the number of stressful life events they experience and the number of delinquent and criminal behaviors and PTSD symptoms they exhibit.[156]

Health

Child abuse has significant implications for the health of those it affects. An analysis of the National Violence against Women Survey found that respondents who were abused as children were more likely to acquire a mental health condition or sustain a serious injury in adulthood, to abuse a variety of substances (pain killers, tranquilizers, antidepressants, and illegal drugs), or to consume alcohol daily.[157]

Physical Complaints

A child who has suffered five or more adverse experiences (including psychological mareatment, physical abuse, sexual abuse, neglect, substance use or alcohol abuse on the part of the caregiver, caregiver exhibiting symptoms of depression, violence against caregiver, or criminal activity in the home), particularly between ages 6 and 12, is at an increased risk for health problems, for acquiring illnesses that require a doctor, and for somatic complaints (reported by a caregiver).[158]

The earlier cited Norwegian study found that women who reported suffering abuse as children were more likely to report seven or more common complaints (including "nausea and vomiting, pruritus gravidarum, pelvic girdle relaxation, Braxton Hicks contractions, edema, leg cramps, constipation, heartburn, urine incontinence, candidiasis, leucorrhea, urinary tract infections, tiredness, headache, backache, and fear of labor") while pregnant. Those women who had experienced physical, emotional, and sexual abuse as children experienced, on average, nearly 46 percent more complaints than women who did not report childhood abuse. All sixteen complaints examined were "associated with reported childhood abuse."[159]

Various Psychological Problems

Children who are sexually abused exhibit more loneliness, anxiety, depression, and low self-esteem than children who have not been sexually abused.[160] Victims of severe childhood sexual abuse may be predisposed to avoid coping with trauma. This "avoidant coping" is a sign of trauma and a predictor of yet more abuse or neglect for many children.[161] Emotional neglect and abuse, physical neglect and abuse, and sexual abuse are associated with increased psychological distress and substance abuse.[162] Those who experience sexual abuse by an acquaintance or a stranger tend to have fewer internalized problems than those who suffer at the hands of a family member (i.e., the closer the belonging should be, the greater are the violation and its effects).[163]

Incest survivors often must struggle with anger problems, phobic anxiety, and fear of men in adulthood.[164] Women who have been so exploited are also more likely to "experience thoughts of self-harm and lower self-esteem."[165] Among males and females, verbal maltreatment is positively associated with anxiety, depression, and sexual problems, as well as sleep disturbances (though the relationship is much stronger in females). In females (but not males), childhood physical maltreatment is associated with anxiety and sleep disturbances.[166]

Depression

Almost 22 percent of female incest survivors will experience major depression (compared to 5.5 percent of women who have not so suffered).[167] However, women who were emotionally abused or neglected as girls may benefit from the social support of friends and be thereby protected against depression in adulthood.[168]

Those aged 10 to 17 who had experienced victimization (witnessing family violence, experiencing physical abuse or neglect by a caregiver, experiencing sexual abuse, or being exposed to violence) had depression scores and anger and aggression scores 3.3 times higher than those who had not been so victimized (scores of 1.9 and 2.4, respectively).[169]

Another study found that childhood neglect and emotional abuse are more often associated with depression than childhood physical or sexual abuse.[170] Though children removed from their families because of major physical or sexual abuse or neglect deny suffering from depression, their caregivers report major problems.[171]

Suicide

Suicidal thoughts and attempts at suicide are more common among those who are sexually abused as children than those who were not sexually abused as children.[172]

A study of low-income African-American women receiving care at a public, urban hospital (approximately half of whom were receiving care following a nonfatal suicide attempt and half of whom had no history of suicidal behavior and were receiving care for non-emergency problems) found that 54 percent had suffered abuse as a child and that, of those who suffered abuse, nearly half had suffered more than one type (emotional, physical, or sexual). Those who had been abused were more likely to attempt suicide, and those who suffered three types of abuse were more likely to attempt suicide than those who suffered one type of abuse.[173] Figure 19 illustrates this. The reverse also holds: The lower the number of types of abuse, the less likely she is to have attempted suicide.[174]

Figure 19: Percent, relationship between suicide attempt and incidence and number of types of childhood abuse

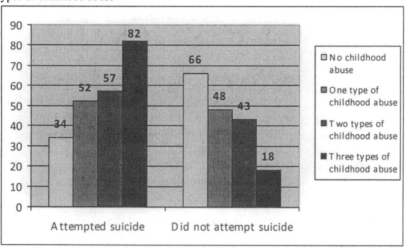

One study of Australian men found those who suffered childhood sexual abuse to be up to ten times more likely to report suicidal ideation than men who suffered no childhood sexual abuse. The study found "self-blame, isolation and physical injuries sustained from the abuse" to be the most important factors in the model they constructed to explain the relationship.[175] A large Icelandic study found that sexual abuse generates depression in girls more than in boys.[176]

Sexual Abuse and Post-traumatic Stress Disorder

Many sexually abused children exhibit symptoms typically associated with post-traumatic stress disorder.[177] Sexually abused children demonstrate more post-traumatic stress disorder, sexually inappropriate and/or antisocial behavior, substance abuse disorders,[178] and depressive mood, as well as loss of companionship and loss of self-esteem.[179]

Contrary Interpretations

Regarding child maltreatment's effects on delinquency, one study's findings suggest that "claims that child maltreatment is the leading cause of delinquency cannot be sustained by available evidence. The vast majority of studies on this topic are too seriously flawed to be of significant policy value. The few rigorous studies that have been completed are either inconclusive or suggest a weak connection at best."[180] An analysis by Alan Horwitz, of the Institute for Health at Rutgers University, as well as Cathy Spatz Widom (of New Jersey Medical School) and Julie McLaughlin and Helene Raskin White (both also of Rutgers University) found that being victimized as a child did not have a direct, strong impact on mental health over the course of one's lifetime, after controlling for stressful life events.[181] However, what this likely suggests is that abuse and many other negative experiences come together.

Sexual Abuse

Perpetrator Identity

Most victims of violence suffer at the hands of one perpetrator, according to the 2010 National Intimate Partner and Sexual Violence Survey.[182]

Most female victims are abused by male perpetrators.[183] Over 98 percent of female rape victims and 92.5 percent of females who suffer other types of sexual violence report abuse exclusively by males.[184]

Approximately half of male stalking victims are stalked by males,[185] and over 93 percent of males who suffer rape and 49 percent of males who suffer "non-contact unwanted sexual experiences" (such as "flashing," exposing one's sexual body parts, or forcing a victim to do so) report victimization exclusively by males. By contrast, almost 38 percent of males who suffer non-contact unwanted sexual experiences, 53.1 percent of males who suffer unwanted sexual contact, 83.6 percent of males who are sexually coerced, and 79.2 percent of males who are forced to penetrate another individual report exclusively female perpetrators.[186]

The study of undergraduate women cited previously found that 44 percent had suffered abuse by a relative; 9 percent were abused by a parental figure. Most (89 percent) were abused by a male, and most (80 percent) were victimized by only one abuser, though some (20 percent) were victimized by multiple abusers.[187]

Child sexual abuse by fathers and stepfathers is far more common than abuse at the hands of other male relatives and nonrelatives: One study of British incest survivors found that "54.2 [percent] of fathers and stepfathers abused their daughters more than fifty times, while only one-third of other family members abused their children at this rate."[188] The least safe environment for young girls is in a household with adult males after her biological parents have separated. "This increased risk held true whether that male was the natural father or someone brought into the family by the child's mother." Girls living in a household with adult males are over seven times more likely to suffer sexual abuse than girls who lived only with women. More than half of girls who live in a post-divorce or post-separaration household with adult males suffer sexual abuse at the hands of either their biological father or another man in the home.[189] Sexual abuse by fathers or stepfathers is significantly more likely to involve penetration or physical contact than abuse committed by others.[190] (If a father figure is the perpetrator of abuse, penetration is the most significant predictor of outcomes and the greatest sign indicating the severity of symptoms. However, if the perpetrator is *not* a father figure, the most substantial predictor of outcomes is the use of force on the victims.[191]) Fathers and stepfathers are more likely to use (or threaten to use) force in their sexual abuse. Force is associated with particularly poor outcomes in victims—according to one study, more so than any other factor.[192]

Figure 20: (NISVS 2010) Percent, lifetime number of perpetrators among female victims of sexual violence

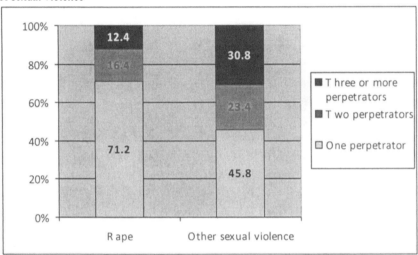

Stalking

The 2010 National Intimate Partner and Sexual Violence Survey found that, in the previous year, approximately 4 percent of women and 1.3 percent of men had been stalked. Over the course of their lifetime, 16.2 percent of women and 5.2 percent of men "have experienced stalking victimization at some point during their lifetime in which they felt very fearful or believed that they or someone close to them would be harmed or killed." The most common method of stalking, repeatedly receiving unwanted calls, voicemails, and text messages, was experienced by 78.8 percent of women and 75.9 percent of men who experienced any form of stalking.[193]

Fagan, Dorminey, and Hering

Figure 21: (NISVS 2010) Percent, lifetime prevalence of stalking victimization by race or ethnicity

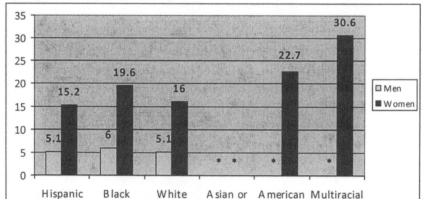

Lifetime incidence of stalking was highest among multiracial non-Hispanic women and Black non-Hispanic men.[194]

Rape and Sexual Contact

According to the 2010 National Intimate Partner and Sexual Violence Survey, in the previous year, 1 percent of women had been raped and 5.6 percent of women and 5.3 percent of men had experienced unwanted sexual contact.[195]

Figure 22: (NISVS 2010) Percent, lifetime incidence of rape, sexual coercion, and sexual contact

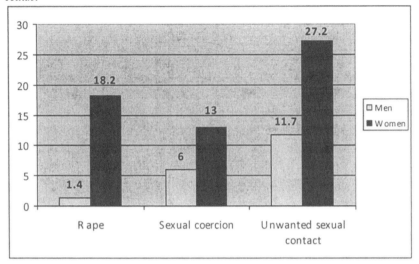

Lifetime incidence of rape and other sexual violence among women was found highest among multiracial non-Hispanic women, at 33.5 percent and 58 percent, respectively. Lifetime incidence of sexual violence among men was highest among multiracial non-Hispanic men, at 31.6 percent.[196]

Figure 23: (NISVS 2010) Percent, lifetime prevalence of rape by race or ethnicity

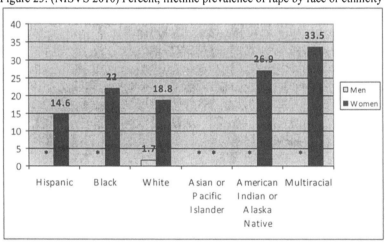

*Estimate is not reported; relative standard error > 30 percent or cell size ≤ 20

Figure 24: (NISVS 2010) Percent, lifetime prevalence of other sexual violence by race or ethnicity

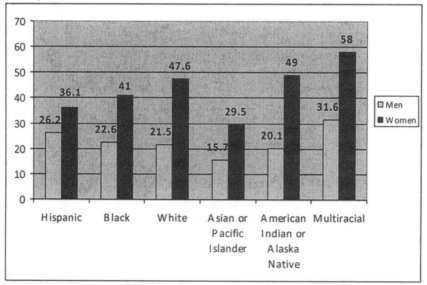

Figure 25: (BI) Number of rapes

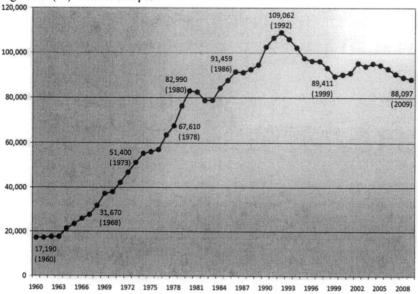

Figure 26: (NISVS 2010) Percent, age at time of first completed rape victimization in lifetime among female victims

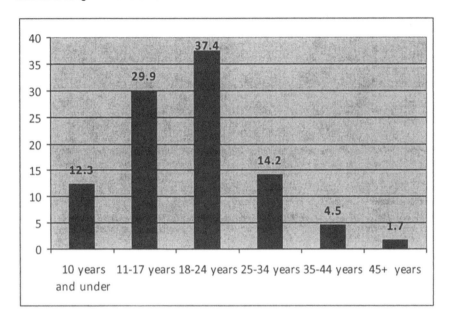

Physical Abuse

Single, divorced, and widowed men with disabilities are four times more likely than married or cohabiting men to report physical abuse by their care provider (whether a family member, friend, or paid caregiver) and ten times more likely to report that that their caregiver demanded substances (alcohol, drugs) or money in exchange for providing care.[197]

Effects of Any Abuse

Even after controlling for treatment received, psychiatric diagnosis, various demographic characteristics, and baseline functioning, one's reported lifetime history of sexual or physical abuse predicts alcohol, drug, psychiatric, medical, legal, and family problems. Though men (in the case of this study of 20,611 veteran patients, almost all of whom were men, over half of whom were separated or divorced, 57 percent of whom were white, 64 percent of whom had one or more comorbid psychiatric disorders, and all of whom had a substance abuse disorder) reported less abuse than women, abuse produced similarly negative effects among both genders.[198]

Pregnant Teenaged Girls

Those who were sexually abused had sexual debuts one year earlier, were less likely to use contraception and were more likely to use drugs or alcohol than were their non-abused counterparts.[199]

Social

Young adults from families marked by conflict tend to have fewer available social supports and more anxiety regarding their personal relationships than young adults whose families are less marked by conflict.[200] Women who reported physical or sexual abuse were at greater risk of experiencing "marginality," or "social isolation within [their] broader culture."[201]

Other research has found that "adolescents who were inclined to approve of aggressive behavior and state more hostile social goals were more likely to have been victims of severe violence."[202] Witnessing domestic abuse as a child is predictive of various physical ("hitting, strangling, threatening to use knife, and pulling hair") and psychological ("cursing, cessation of verbal communication, cessation of marital intercourse, and reprisal") abusive behaviors in adulthood, particularly hitting and cursing.[203]

Health

Women aged 50 to 79 who reported having been physically and/or verbally abused in the past year had a higher mortality risk than women who did not report abuse.[204]

Those who have experienced sexual abuse are more likely to suffer gynecological, gastrointestinal, and panic-related symptoms, as well as headaches. Repeated sexual abuse and sexual abuse in which penetration takes place seem to produce the worst effects. Both men and women suffer from poor health in association with sexual abuse.[205]

Women in the earlier-cited British study of 200 women receiving antenatal or postnatal care with a history of physical or sexual abuse (whether as children or adults) had significantly higher scores on the Post-traumatic Diagnostic Scale, a measure of PTSD and of lifetime exposure to trauma.[206]

In his article in this collection, Stephen M. Krason states that a strongly-held view of those in the child protective system is that all parents are potential abusers. The data that we have recounted in this article shows, *to the contrary*, that the incidence of child abuse strongly correlates with disrupted and disturbed families and that intact marriage is protective against it.

Notes

[1] Patrick F. Fagan and Nicholas Zill, "The Second Annual Index of Family Belonging and Rejection," (2011): 1. Available at http://downloads.frc.org/EF/EF11K28.pdf. Accessed 13 April 2012.

[2] For more on the cyclical nature of family brokenness, see Patrick F. Fagan and Aaron Churchill, "The Effects of Divorce on Children," (2012). Available at http://downloads.frc.org/EF/EF12A22.pdf. Accessed 20 April 2012.

[3] P.E. Mullen, J.L. Martin, J.C. Anderson, S.E. Romans, and G.P. Herbison, "The Long-Term Impact of the Physical, Emotional, and Sexual Abuse of Children: A Community Study," *Child Abuse & Neglect* 20 (1996): 8, as cited in C. Menard, K.J. Bandeen-Roche, H.D. Chilcoat, "Epidemiology of Multiple Childhood Traumatic Events: Child Abuse, Parental Psychopathology, and Other Family-Level Stessors," *Social Psychiatry Psychiatric Epidemiology* 39 (2004): 857.

[4] Susan A. Murty, Corinne Peek-Asa, Craig Zwerling, Ann M. Stromquist, Leon F. Burmeister, and James A. Merchant, "Physical and Emotional Partner Abuse Reported by Men and Women in a Rural Community," *American Journal of Public Health* 93, no. 7 (2003): 1073.

[5] Rachel T. Kimbro, "Together Forever? Romantic Relationship Characteristics and Prenatal Health Behaviors," *Journal of Marriage and Family* 70, no. 3 (2008): 750.

[6] Centers for Disease Control and Prevention, National Center for Injury Prevention and Control, *The National Intimate Partner and Sexual Violence Survey (NISVS): 2010 Summary Report*, by M.C. Black, K.C. Basile, M.J. Breiding, S.G. Smith, M.L. Walters, M.T. Merrick, J. Chen, and M.R. Stevens, 2-3 (Atlanta, Georgia: 2011).

[7] Centers for Disease Control and Prevention, National Center for Injury Prevention and Control, *The National Intimate Partner and Sexual Violence Survey (NISVS): 2010 Summary Report*, by M.C. Black, K.C. Basile, M.J. Breiding, S.G. Smith, M.L. Walters, M.T. Merrick, J. Chen, and M.R. Stevens, 40 (Atlanta, Georgia: 2011).

[8] Patrick F. Fagan and Nicholas Zill, "The Second Annual Index of Family Belonging and Rejection," (2011): 5. Available at http://downloads.frc.org/EF/EF11K28.pdf. Accessed 13 April 2012.

[9] For the purposes of the NISVS, the CDC defines intimate partner violence as including "physical violence, all forms of sexual violence, stalking, psychological aggression, and control of reproductive or sexual health."

[10] Defined by the CDC for the purposes of the NISVS as "expressive aggression and coercive control": "Expressive psychological aggression includes acting dangerous, name calling, insults and humiliation. Coercive control includes behaviors that are intended to monitor and control an intimate partner such as threats, interference with family and friends, and limiting access to money." Centers for Disease Control and Prevention, National Center for Injury Prevention and Control, *The National Intimate Partner and Sexual Violence Survey (NISVS): 2010 Summary Report*, by M.C. Black, K.C. Basile,

M.J. Breiding, S.G. Smith, M.L. Walters, M.T. Merrick, J. Chen, and M.R. Stevens, 9-10 (Atlanta, Georgia: 2011).

[11] Centers for Disease Control and Prevention, National Center for Injury Prevention and Control, *The National Intimate Partner and Sexual Violence Survey (NISVS): 2010 Summary Report*, by M.C. Black, K.C. Basile, M.J. Breiding, S.G. Smith, M.L. Walters, M.T. Merrick, J. Chen, and M.R. Stevens, 2 (Atlanta, Georgia: 2011).

[12] Described by the CDC for the purposes of the NISVS as "a pattern of unwanted harassing or threatening tactics used by a perpetrator and included tactics related to unwanted contacts, unwanted tracking and following, intrusion, and technology-assisted tactics." Centers for Disease Control and Prevention, National Center for Injury Prevention and Control, *The National Intimate Partner and Sexual Violence Survey (NISVS): 2010 Summary Report*, by M.C. Black, K.C. Basile, M.J. Breiding, S.G. Smith, M.L. Walters, M.T. Merrick, J. Chen, and M.R. Stevens, 10 (Atlanta, Georgia: 2011).

[13] Centers for Disease Control and Prevention, National Center for Injury Prevention and Control, *The National Intimate Partner and Sexual Violence Survey (NISVS): 2010 Summary Report*, by M.C. Black, K.C. Basile, M.J. Breiding, S.G. Smith, M.L. Walters, M.T. Merrick, J. Chen, and M.R. Stevens, 2 (Atlanta, Georgia: 2011).

[14] Centers for Disease Control and Prevention, National Center for Injury Prevention and Control, *The National Intimate Partner and Sexual Violence Survey (NISVS): 2010 Summary Report*, by M.C. Black, K.C. Basile, M.J. Breiding, S.G. Smith, M.L. Walters, M.T. Merrick, J. Chen, and M.R. Stevens, 2 (Atlanta, Georgia: 2011).

[15] Centers for Disease Control and Prevention, National Center for Injury Prevention and Control, *The National Intimate Partner and Sexual Violence Survey (NISVS): 2010 Summary Report*, by M.C. Black, K.C. Basile, M.J. Breiding, S.G. Smith, M.L. Walters, M.T. Merrick, J. Chen, and M.R. Stevens, 42 (Atlanta, Georgia: 2011).

[16] Centers for Disease Control and Prevention, National Center for Injury Prevention and Control, *The National Intimate Partner and Sexual Violence Survey (NISVS): 2010 Summary Report*, by M.C. Black, K.C. Basile, M.J. Breiding, S.G. Smith, M.L. Walters, M.T. Merrick, J. Chen, and M.R. Stevens, 1-2 (Atlanta, Georgia: 2011).

[17] Kirsten Robertson and Tamar Murachver, "It Takes Two to Tangle: Gender Symmetry in Intimate Partner Violence," *Basic and Applied Social Psychology* 29, no. 2 (2007): 112, 114-115.

[18] Kirsten Robertson and Tamar Murachver, "It Takes Two to Tangle: Gender Symmetry in Intimate Partner Violence," *Basic and Applied Social Psychology* 29, no. 2 (2007): 113.

[19] Susan A. Murty, Corinne Peek-Asa, Craig Zwerling, Ann M. Stromquist, Leon F. Burmeister, and James A. Merchant, "Physical and Emotional Partner Abuse Reported by Men and Women in a Rural Community," *American Journal of Public Health* 93, no. 7 (2003): 1073.

[20] John Archer, "Sex Differences in Aggression between Heterosexual Partners: A Meta-Analytic Review," *Psychological Bulletin* 126 (2000): 651-680, as cited in Sandra M. Stith, Narkia M. Green, Douglas B. Smith, and David B. Ward, "Marital Satisfaction and Marital Discord as Risk Markers for Intimate Partner Violence: A Meta-Analytic Review," *Journal of Family Violence* 23 (2008): 149.

[21] Menachem Fisher, Dalit Yassour-Borochowitz, Efrat Neter, "Domestic Abuse in Pregnancy: Results from a Phone Survey in Northern Israel," *Domestic Abuse in Pregnancy* 5 (2003): 35.

[22] Ana Bernarda Ludermin, Glyn Lewis, Sandra Alves Valongueiro, Thália Velho Barreto de Araújo, and Ricardo Araya, "Violence Against Women by their Intimate Partner During Pregnancy and Postnatal Depression: A Prospective Cohort Study," *The Lancet* 376 (2010): 906.

[23] Gillian Mezey, Loraine Bacchus, Susan Bewley, Sarah White, "Domestic Violence, Lifetime Trauma, and Psychological Health of Childbearing Women," *BJOG: An International Journal of Obstetrics and Gynecology* 112 (2005): 200.

[24] Holly Garcia O'Hearn and Gayla Margolin, "Men's Attitudes Condoning Marital Aggression: A Moderator Between Family of Origin Abuse and Aggression Against Female Partners," *Cognitive Therapy and Research* 24, no. 2 (2000): 164-166.

[25] William H. Jeynes, "The Effects of Recent Parental Divorce on Their Children's Consumption of Alcohol," *Journal of Youth and Adolescence* 30, no. 3 (2001): 312.

[26] Gregory L. Stuart, Jeffrey C. Meehan, Todd M. Moore, Meghan Morean, Julianne Hellmuth, Katherine Follansbee, "Examining a Conceptual Framework of Intimate Partner Violence in Men and Women Arrested for Domestic Violence," *Journal of Studies on Alcohol* 67 (2006): 102.

[27] Heather M.Foran and Daniel K. Leary, "Problem Drinking, Jealousy, and Anger Control: Variables Predicting Physical Aggression Against a Partner," *Journal of Family Violence* 23 (2008): 147.

[28] Loretta J. Stalans and Jennifer Ritchie, "Relationship of Substance Use/Abuse with Psychological and Physical Intimate Partner Violence: Variations Across Living Situations," *Journal of Family Violence* 23 (2008): 16.

[29] Loretta J. Stalans and Jennifer Ritchie, "Relationship of Substance Use/Abuse with Psychological and Physical Intimate Partner Violence: Variations Across Living Situations," *Journal of Family Violence* 23 (2008): 15.

[30] Loretta J. Stalans and Jennifer Ritchie, "Relationship of Substance Use/Abuse with Psychological and Physical Intimate Partner Violence: Variations Across Living Situations," *Journal of Family Violence* 23 (2008): 19.

[31] Loretta J. Stalans and Jennifer Ritchie, "Relationship of Substance Use/Abuse with Psychological and Physical Intimate Partner Violence: Variations Across Living Situations," *Journal of Family Violence* 23 (2008): 14.

[32] Loretta J. Stalans and Jennifer Ritchie, "Relationship of Substance Use/Abuse with Psychological and Physical Intimate Partner Violence: Variations Across Living Situations," *Journal of Family Violence* 23 (2008): 21.

[33] Loretta J. Stalans and Jennifer Ritchie, "Relationship of Substance Use/Abuse with Psychological and Physical Intimate Partner Violence: Variations Across Living Situations," *Journal of Family Violence* 23 (2008): 20.

[34] Loretta J. Stalans and Jennifer Ritchie, "Relationship of Substance Use/Abuse with Psychological and Physical Intimate Partner Violence: Variations Across Living Situations," *Journal of Family Violence* 23 (2008): 18.

[35] Loretta J. Stalans and Jennifer Ritchie, "Relationship of Substance Use/Abuse with Psychological and Physical Intimate Partner Violence: Variations Across Living Situations," *Journal of Family Violence* 23 (2008): 16.

[36] Nabila El-Bassel, Susan S. Witte, Takeshi Wada, Louisa Gilbert, and Joyce Wallace, "Correlates of Partner Violence Among Female Street-Based Sex Workers: Substance Abuse, History of Childhood Abuse, and HIV Risks," *AIDS Patient Care and STDs* 15, no. 1 (2001): 48.

[37] Nabila El-Bassel, Susan S. Witte, Takeshi Wada, Louisa Gilbert, and Joyce Wallace, "Correlates of Partner Violence Among Female Street-Based Sex Workers:

Substance Abuse, History of Childhood Abuse, and HIV Risks," *AIDS Patient Care and STDs* 15, no. 1 (2001): 47.

[38] Chitra Raghavan, Amy Mennerich, Ellen Sexton, and Susan E. James, "Community Violence and Its Direct, Indirect, and Mediating Effects on Intimate Partner Violence," *Violence Against Women* 12, no. 12 (2006): 1132, 1141-1142.

[39] Loretta J. Stalans and Jennifer Ritchie, "Relationship of Substance Use/Abuse with Psychological and Physical Intimate Partner Violence: Variations Across Living Situations," *Journal of Family Violence* 23 (2008): 20.

[40] Gregory L. Stuart, Jeffrey C. Meehan, Todd M. Moore, Meghan Morean, Julianne Hellmuth, Katherine Follansbee, "Examining a Conceptual Framework of Intimate Partner Violence in Men and Women Arrested for Domestic Violence," *Journal of Studies on Alcohol* 67 (2006): 106.

[41] The violence level of the men in the "general public" group was not measured. Alan Rosenbaum and Penny A. Leisring, "Beyond Power and Control: Towards an Understanding of Partner Abusive Men," *Journal of Comparative Family Studies* (2011): 15.

[42] Richard E. Tremblay, Daniel S. Nagin, Jean R. Seguin, Mark Zoccolillo, Philip D. Zelazo, Michel Boivin, Daniel Perusse, and Christa Japel, "Physical Aggression During Early Childhood: Trajectories and Predictors," *Pediatrics* 114, no. 1 (2004): e48.

[43] Susan A. Murty, Corinne Peek-Asa, Craig Zwerling, Ann M. Stromquist, Leon F. Burmeister, and James A. Merchant, "Physical and Emotional Partner Abuse Reported by Men and Women in a Rural Community," *American Journal of Public Health* 93, no. 7 (2003): 1073.

[44] Kirsten Robertson and Tamar Murachver, "It Takes Two to Tangle: Gender Symmetry in Intimate Partner Violence," *Basic and Applied Social Psychology* 29, no. 2 (2007): 113.

[45] D. Vivian and J. Malone, "Relationship Factors and Depressive Symptomatology Associated with Mild and Severe Husband-to-Wife Physical Aggression," *Violence and Victims* 12 (1997): 3-18, as cited in Sandra M. Stith, Narkia M. Green, Douglas B. Smith, and David B. Ward, "Marital Satisfaction and Marital Discord as Risk Markers for Intimate Partner Violence: A Meta-Analytic Review," *Journal of Family Violence* 23 (2008): 151.

[46] Diana Vivian and Jennifer Langhinrichsen-Rohling, "Are Bi-Directionally Violent Couples Mutually Victimized? A Gender-Sensitive Comparison," *Violence and Victims* 9 (1994): 107-124, as cited in Sandra M. Stith, Narkia M. Green, Douglas B. Smith, and David B. Ward, "Marital Satisfaction and Marital Discord as Risk Markers for Intimate Partner Violence: A Meta-Analytic Review," *Journal of Family Violence* 23 (2008): 150.

[47] Stacey L. Williams and Irene Hanson Frieze, "Patterns of Violent Relationships, Psychological Distress, and Marital Satisfaction in a National Sample of Men and Women," *Sex Roles* 52 (2005): 771-784, as cited in Sandra M. Stith, Narkia M. Green, Douglas B. Smith, and David B. Ward, "Marital Satisfaction and Marital Discord as Risk Markers for Intimate Partner Violence: A Meta-Analytic Review," *Journal of Family Violence* 23 (2008): 150.

[48] Sandra M. Stith, Narkia M. Green, Douglas B. Smith, and David B. Ward, "Marital Satisfaction and Marital Discord as Risk Markers for Intimate Partner Violence: A Meta-Analytic Review," *Journal of Family Violence* 23 (2008): 150.

[49] Centers for Disease Control and Prevention, National Center for Injury Prevention and Control, *The National Intimate Partner and Sexual Violence Survey (NISVS): 2010*

Summary Report, by M.C. Black, K.C. Basile, M.J. Breiding, S.G. Smith, M.L. Walters, M.T. Merrick, J. Chen, and M.R. Stevens, 3 (Atlanta, Georgia: 2011).

[50] John H. Porcerelli, Patricia A. West, Juliann Binienda, and Rosemary Cogan, "Physical and Psychological Symptoms in Emotionally Abused and Non-Abused Women," *The Journal of the American Board of Family Medicine* 19 (2006): 201.

[51] Helen Straus, Catherine Cerulli, Louise Anne McNutt, Karin V. Rhodes, Kenneth R. Conner, Robin S. Kemball, Nadine J. Kaslow, and Debra Houry, "Intimate Partner Violence and Functional Health Status: Associations with Severity, Danger, and Self-Advocacy Behaviors," *Journal of Women's Health* 18, no. 5 (2009): 625.

[52] Richard J. Gelles and Murray A. Straus, *Intimate Violence* (New York, New York: Simon & Schuster, 1988), as cited in Sandra M. Stith, Karen H. Rosen, and Eric E. McCollum, "Effectiveness of Couples Treatment for Spouse Abuse," *Journal of Marital and Family Therapy* 29, no. 3 (2003): 407-426.

[53] Ana Bernarda Ludermin, Glyn Lewis, Sandra Alves Valongueiro, Thália Velho Barreto de Araújo, and Ricardo Araya, "Violence Against Women by their Intimate Partner During Pregnancy and Postnatal Depression: A Prospective Cohort Study," *The Lancet* 376 (2010): 903, 907.

[54] Miriam K. Ehrensaft, Terrie E. Moffitt, and Avshalom Caspi, "Is Domestic Violence Followed by an Increased Risk of Psychiatric Disorders Among Women But Not Among Men? A Longitudinal Cohort Study," *The American Journal of Psychiatry* 163, no. 5 (2006): 889.

[55] Centers for Disease Control and Prevention, National Center for Injury Prevention and Control, *The National Intimate Partner and Sexual Violence Survey (NISVS): 2010 Summary Report*, by M.C. Black, K.C. Basile, M.J. Breiding, S.G. Smith, M.L. Walters, M.T. Merrick, J. Chen, and M.R. Stevens, 2 (Atlanta, Georgia: 2011).

[56] Debra K. Miller, "The Effects of Childhood Physical Abuse or Childhood Sexual Abuse in Battered Women's Coping Mechanisms: Obsessive-Compulsive Tendencies and Severe Depression," *Journal of Family Violence* 21, no. 3 (2006): 192, 194.

[57] Andrea L. Hazen, Cynthia D. Connelly, Kelly J. Kelleher, Richard P. Barth, and John A. Landsverk, "Female Caregivers' Experiences with Intimate Partner Violence and Behavior Problems in Children Investigated as Victims of Maltreatment," *Pediatrics* 117, no. 1 (2006): 99.

[58] Tuppett M. Yates, Michele F. Dodds, Alan L. Sroufe, and Byron Egeland, "Exposure to Partner Violence and Child Behavior Problems: A Prospective Study Controlling for Child Physical Abuse and Neglect, Child Cognitive Ability, Socioeconomic Status, and Life Stress," *Development and Psychopathology* 15 (2003): 207-209.

[59] Cheryl Buehler, Christine Anthony, Ambika Krishnakumar, Gaye Stone, Jean Gerard, and Sharon Pemberton, "Interparental Conflict and Youth Problem Behaviors: A Meta-Analysis," *Journal of Child and Family Studies* 6 (1997): 233-247; William J. Reid and Alida Crisafulli, "Marital Discord and Child Behavior Problems: A Meta-Analysis," *Journal of Abnormal Child Psychology* 18 (1990): 105-117, both as cited in Katherine M. Kitzmann, Noni K.Gaylord, Aimee R. Holt, and Erin D. Kenny, "Child Witnesses to Domestic Violence: A Meta-Analytic Review," *Journal of Consulting and Clinical Psychology* 71, no. 2 (2003): 346.

[60] Timothy O. Ireland and Carolyn A. Smith, "Living in Partner-Violent Families: Developmental Links to Antisocial Behavior and Relationship Violence," *Journal of Youth Violence* 38 (2009): 333.

202

[61] Sandra M. Stith, Karen H. Rosen, Kimberly A. Middleton, Amy L. Busch, Kirsten Lundeberg, and Russell P. Carlton, "The Intergenerational Transmission of Spouse Abuse: A Meta-Analysis," *Journal of Marriage and Family* 62, no. 3 (2000): 645.

[62] P.G. Jaffe, D.J. Hurley, and D. Wolfe, "Children's Observations of Violence: I. Critical Issues in Child Development and Intervention Planning," *Canadian Journal of Psychiatry* 35 (1990): 466-470, as cited in Katherine M. Kitzmann, Noni K.Gaylord, Aimee R. Holt, and Erin D. Kenny, "Child Witnesses to Domestic Violence: A Meta-Analytic Review," *Journal of Consulting and Clinical Psychology* 71, no. 2 (2003): 347.

[63] Alan Rosenbaum and Penny A. Leisring, "Beyond Power and Control: Towards an Understanding of Partner Abusive Men," *Journal of Comparative Family Studies* (2011): 15.

[64] Naeemah Abrahams and Rachel Jewkes, "Effects of South African Men's Having Witnessed Abuse of their Mothers During Childhood on Their Levels of Violence in Adulthood," *American Journal of Public Health* 95, no. 10 (2005): 1811, 1814.

[65] Naeemah Abrahams and Rachel Jewkes, "Effects of South African Men's Having Witnessed Abuse of their Mothers During Childhood on Their Levels of Violence in Adulthood," *American Journal of Public Health* 95, no. 10 (2005): 1814.

[66] Charles W. Peek, Judith L. Fischer, and Jeannie S. Kidwell, "Teenage Violence toward Parents: A Neglected Dimension of Family Violence," *Journal of Marriage and the Family* 47 (1985): 1051-1060; Larry R. Livingston, "Children's Violence to Single Mothers," *Journal of Sociology and Social Welfare* 13 (1986): 920-933; Ellis D. Evans and Luann Warren-Sohlberg, "A Pattern of Analysis of Adolescent Abusive Behaviour toward Parents," *Journal of Adolescent Research* 3 (1988): 201-216; Claire Pedrick Cornell, Richard J. Gelles, "Adolescent-to-Parent Violence," *Urban and Social Change Review* 15 (1982): 8-14; Timothy Brezina, "Teenage Violence toward Parents as an Adaptation of Family Strain," *Youth Society* 30 (1999): 416-444; K.D. Browne and C.E. Hamilon, "Physical Violence between Young Adults and their Parents: Associations with a History of Child Maltreatment," *Journal of Family Violence* 13 (1998): 59-79; Mabel G. Wells, "Adolescent Violence against Parents: An Assessment," *Family Therapy* 14 (1987): 125-133, all as cited in Nicola Kennair and David Mellor, "Parent Abuse: A Review," *Child Psychiatry and Human Development* 38 (2007): 207.

[67] Barbara Cottrell and Peter Monk, "Adolescent to Parent Abuse: A Qualitative Overview of Common Themes," *Journal of Family Issues* 25 (2004): 1072-1095, as cited in Nicola Kennair and David Mellor, "Parent Abuse: A Review," *Child Psychiatry and Human Development* 38 (2007): 207.

[68] Jeffrey L. Edleson, Lyungai F. Mbilinyi, Sandra K. Beeman, Annelies K. Hagemeister, "How Children are Involved in Adult Domestic Violence: Results from a Four-City Telephone Survey," *Journal of Interpersonal Violence* 18, no. 1 (2003): 24-25.

[69] Jeffrey L. Edleson, Lyungai F. Mbilinyi, Sandra K. Beeman, Annelies K. Hagemeister, "How Children are Involved in Adult Domestic Violence: Results from a Four-City Telephone Survey," *Journal of Interpersonal Violence* 18, no. 1 (2003): 25.

[70] Jeffrey L. Edleson, Lyungai F. Mbilinyi, Sandra K. Beeman, Annelies K. Hagemeister, "How Children are Involved in Adult Domestic Violence: Results from a Four-City Telephone Survey," *Journal of Interpersonal Violence* 18, no. 1 (2003): 24.

[71] P.L. Caesar, "Exposure to violence in the families of origin among wife abusers and marital nonviolent men," *Violence and Victims* 3 (1988) 49-63; D.G. Dutton, A.J. Starzomski, and L. Ryan, "Antecedents of Abusive Behavior in Wife Assaulters," *Journal of Family Violence* 11 (1996): 113-132; Mary Carroll Ellsberg, Rodolfo Peña,

Andrés Herrera, Jerker Liljestrand, and Anna Winkvist, "Wife Abuse among Women of Childbearing Age in Nicaragua," *American Journal of Public Health* 89 (1999): 241-244; G.T. Hotaling and D.B. Sugarman, "An Analysis of Risk Markers in Husband to Wife Violence: The Current State of the Knowledge," *Violence Victims* 1 (1986): 101-123, all as cited in Naeemah Abrahams and Rachel Jewkes, "Effects of South African Men's Having Witnessed Abuse of their Mothers During Childhood on Their Levels of Violence in Adulthood," *American Journal of Public Health* 95, no. 10 (2005): 1811.

[72] Wendy L. Haight, Woochan S. Shim, Linda M. Linn, and Laura Swinford, "Mother's Strategies for Protecting Children from Batterers: The Perspectives of Battered Women Involved in Child Protective Services," *Child Welfare* 86, no. 4 (2007): 50-52.

[73] J.E. McIntosh, "Thought in the Face of Violence: A Child's Need," *Child Abuse and Neglect* 26 (2002): 229–241, as cited in Stephanie Holt, Helen Buckley, and Sadhbh Whelan, "The Impact of Exposure to Domestic Violence on Children and Young People: A Review of the Literature," *Child Abuse and Neglect* 32 (2008): 802.

[74] Diana J. English, David B. Marshall, and Angela J. Stewart, "Effects of Family Violence on Child Behavior and Health during Early Childhood," *Journal of Family Violence* 18, no. 1 (2003): 43.

[75] Alytia A. Levendosky, Shannon M. Lynch, and Sandra A. Graham-Bermann, "Mothers' Perceptions of the Impact of Woman Abuse on their Parenting," *Violence Against Women* 6 (2000): 248-272; Alytia A. Levendosky and Sandra A. Graham-Bermann, "Parenting in Battered Women: The Effects of Domestic Violence on Women and their Children," *Journal of Family Violence* 16, no. 2 (2001): 171-192, both as cited in Stephanie Holt, Helen Buckley, and Sadhbh Whelan, "The Impact of Exposure to Domestic Violence on Children and Young People: A Review of the Literature," *Child Abuse and Neglect* 32 (2008): 801.

[76] Carol Coohey, "Battered Mothers Who Physically Abuse their Children," *Journal of Interpersonal Violence* 9, no. 8, (2004): 943-952, as cited in Stephanie Holt, Helen Buckley, and Sadhbh Whelan, "The Impact of Exposure to Domestic Violence on Children and Young People: A Review of the Literature," *Child Abuse and Neglect* 32 (2008): 801.

[77] See G.W. Holden, J. D. Stein, K. L. Richie, S. D. Harris, and E.N. Jouriles, "Parenting Behaviour and Beliefs of Battered Women," in *Children Exposed to Marital Violence: Theory, Research, and Applied Issues*, eds. G.W. Holden, R. Geffner, and E.N. Jouriles (Washington, D.C.: American Psychological Association, 1998), 289–332, as cited in Stephanie Holt, Helen Buckley, and Sadhbh Whelan, "The Impact of Exposure to Domestic Violence on Children and Young People: A Review of the Literature," *Child Abuse and Neglect* 32 (2008): 801.

[78] Joy D. Osofsky, "Prevalence of Children's Exposure to Domestic Violence and Child Maltreatment: Implications for Prevention and Intervention," *Clinical Child and Family Psychological Review* 6, no. 3 (2003): 161.

[79] Louise Dixon, Kevin Browne, Catherine Hamilton-Giachritsis, and Eugene Ostapuik, "The Co-occurrence of Child and Intimate Partner Maltreatment in the Family: Characteristics of the Violent Perpetrators," *Journal of Family Violence* 22 (2007): 685.

[80] John M. Leventhal, "Epidemiology of Sexual Abuse of Children: Old Problems, New Directions," *Child Abuse and Neglect* 22 (1998): 488-489, as cited in Robin Fretwell Wilson, "Children at Risk: The Sexual Exploitation of Female Children after Divorce," *Cornell Law Review* 86 (2000): 262.

[81] Robin Fretwell Wilson, "Children at Risk: The Sexual Exploitation of Female Children after Divorce," *Cornell Law Review* 86 (2000): 281.

[82] Jeremiah A. Schumm, Lisa R. Stines, Steven E. Hobfoll, and Anita P. Jackson, "The Double-Barreled Burden of Child Abuse and Current Stressful Circumstances on Adult Women: The Kindling Effect of Early Traumatic Experience," *Journal of Traumatic Stress* 18, no. 5 (2005): 471.

[83] Antonia Bifulco, Patricia M. Moran, Rebecca Baines, Amanda Bunn, and Katherine Stanford, "Exploring Psychological Abuse in Childhood: II. Association with Other Abuse and Adult Clinical Depression," *Bulletin of the Menninger Clinic* 66, no. 3 (2002): 249-250.

[84] Mirjam Lukasse, Berit Schei, Siri Vangen, and Pal Oian, "Childhood Abuse and Common Complaints in Pregnancy," *Birth* 36, no. 3 (2009): 194.

[85] Centers for Disease Control and Prevention, National Center for Injury Prevention and Control, *The National Intimate Partner and Sexual Violence Survey (NISVS): 2010 Summary Report*, by M.C. Black, K.C. Basile, M.J. Breiding, S.G. Smith, M.L. Walters, M.T. Merrick, J. Chen, and M.R. Stevens, 2 (Atlanta, Georgia: 2011).

[86] Centers for Disease Control and Prevention, National Center for Injury Prevention and Control, *The National Intimate Partner and Sexual Violence Survey (NISVS): 2010 Summary Report*, by M.C. Black, K.C. Basile, M.J. Breiding, S.G. Smith, M.L. Walters, M.T. Merrick, J. Chen, and M.R. Stevens, 2 (Atlanta, Georgia: 2011).

[87] Michelle A. Fortier, David DiLillo, Terri L. Messman-Moore, James Peugh, Kathleen A. DeNardi, and Kathryn J.Gaffey, "Severity of Child Sexual Abuse and Re-victimization: The Mediating Role of Coping and Trauma Symptoms," *Psychology of Women Quarterly* 33 (2009): 314.

[88] U.S. Department of Health and Human Services, Administration for Children and Families, *Fourth National Incidence Study of Child Abuse and Neglect (NIS–4): Report to Congress*, by Andrea J. Sedlak, Jane Mettenburg, Monica Basena, Ian Petta, Karla McPherson, Angela Greene, and Spencer Li, 5-22 (Washington, DC: 2010).

[89] U.S. Department of Health and Human Services, Administration for Children and Families, *Fourth National Incidence Study of Child Abuse and Neglect (NIS–4): Report to Congress*, by Andrea J. Sedlak, Jane Mettenburg, Monica Basena, Ian Petta, Karla McPherson, Angela Greene, and Spencer Li, 5-25 (Washington, DC: 2010).

[90] Inga Dora Sigfusdottir, Bryndis Bjork Asgeirsdottir, Gisli H. Gudjonsson, and Jon Fridrik Sigurdsson, "A Model of Sexual Abuse's Effects on Suicidal Behavior and Delinquency: The Role of Emotions as Mediating Factors," *Journal of Youth and Adolescence* 37 (2008): 707.

[91] U.S. Department of Health and Human Services, Administration for Children and Families, *Fourth National Incidence Study of Child Abuse and Neglect (NIS–4): Report to Congress*, by Andrea J. Sedlak, Jane Mettenburg, Monica Basena, Ian Petta, Karla McPherson, Angela Greene, and Spencer Li, 5-22 (Washington, DC: 2010).

[92] U.S. Department of Health and Human Services, Administration for Children and Families, *Fourth National Incidence Study of Child Abuse and Neglect (NIS–4): Report to Congress*, by Andrea J. Sedlak, Jane Mettenburg, Monica Basena, Ian Petta, Karla McPherson, Angela Greene, and Spencer Li, 5-25 (Washington, DC: 2010).

[93] Heather A. Turner, David Finkelhor, and Richard Ormrod, "Family Structure Variations in Patterns and Predictors of Child Victimization," *American Journal of Orthopsychiatry* 77, no. 2 (2007): 286.

[94] Heather A. Turner, David Finkelhor, and Richard Ormrod, "Family Structure Variations in Patterns and Predictors of Child Victimization," *American Journal of Orthopsychiatry* 77, no. 2 (2007): 287.

[95] Heather A. Turner, David Finkelhor, and Richard Ormrod, "Family Structure Variations in Patterns and Predictors of Child Victimization," *American Journal of Orthopsychiatry* 77, no. 2 (2007): 286.

[96] Heather A. Turner, David Finkelhor, and Richard Ormrod, "Family Structure Variations in Patterns and Predictors of Child Victimization," *American Journal of Orthopsychiatry* 77, no. 2 (2007): 286.

[97] Heather A. Turner, David Finkelhor, and Richard Ormrod, "Family Structure Variations in Patterns and Predictors of Child Victimization," *American Journal of Orthopsychiatry* 77, no. 2 (2007): 282.

[98] Heather A. Turner, David Finkelhor, and Richard Ormrod, "Family Structure Variations in Patterns and Predictors of Child Victimization," *American Journal of Orthopsychiatry* 77, no. 2 (2007): 285.

[99] Elizabeth A. Sirles and Pamela J. Franke, "Factors Influencing Mothers' Reactions to Intrafamily Sexual Abuse," *Child Abuse and Neglect* 13 (1989): 132; Beverly B. Lovett, "Child Sexual Abuse: The Female Victim's Relationship with Her Nonoffending Mother," *Child Abuse and Neglect* 19 (1995): 730, both as cited in Robin Fretwell Wilson, "Children at Risk: The Sexual Exploitation of Female Children after Divorce," *Cornell Law Review* 86 (2000): 306.

[100] Diana E.H. Russell, *The Secret Trauma: Incest in the Lives of Girls and Women* (1986): 234, 255, as cited in Robin Fretwell Wilson, "Children at Risk: The Sexual Exploitation of Female Children after Divorce," *Cornell Law Review* 86 (2000): 267.

[101] Leslie Margolin and John L. Craft, "Child Sexual Abuse by Caretakers," *Family Relations* 38 (1989): 450, 452, as cited in Robin Fretwell Wilson, "Children at Risk: The Sexual Exploitation of Female Children after Divorce," *Cornell Law Review* 86 (2000): 269.

[102] David Finkelhor, Gerald Hotaling, I.A. Lewis, and Christine Smith, "Sexual Abuse in a National Survey of Adult Men and Women: Prevalence, Characteristics, and Risk Factors," *Child Abuse and Neglect* 14 (1990): 24, 25, 25 table 7, as cited in Robin Fretwell Wilson, "Children at Risk: The Sexual Exploitation of Female Children after Divorce," *Cornell Law Review* 86 (2000): 271.

[103] U.S. Department of Health and Human Services, Administration for Children and Families, *Fourth National Incidence Study of Child Abuse and Neglect (NIS-4): Report to Congress*, by Andrea J. Sedlak, Jane Mettenburg, Monica Basena, Ian Petta, Karla McPherson, Angela Greene, and Spencer Li, 5-22 (Washington, DC: 2010).

[104] U.S. Department of Health and Human Services, Administration for Children and Families, *Fourth National Incidence Study of Child Abuse and Neglect (NIS-4): Report to Congress*, by Andrea J. Sedlak, Jane Mettenburg, Monica Basena, Ian Petta, Karla McPherson, Angela Greene, and Spencer Li, 5-24 (Washington, DC: 2010).

[105] Heather A. Turner, David Finkelhor, and Richard Ormrod, "The Effect of Lifetime Victimization on the Mental Health of Children and Adolescents," *Social Science and Medicine* (2005): 7.

[106] David Finkelhor, Gerald Hotaling, I.A. Lewis, and Christine Smith, "Sexual Abuse in a National Survey of Adult Men and Women: Prevalence, Characteristics, and Risk Factors," *Child Abuse and Neglect* 14 (1990): 25 table 7, as cited in Robin Fretwell Wilson, "Children at Risk: The Sexual Exploitation of Female Children after Divorce," *Cornell Law Review* 86 (2000): 256.

[107] Jillian Fleming, Paul Mullen, and Gabriele Bammer, "A Study of Potential Risk Factors for Sexual Abuse in Childhood," *Child Abuse and Neglect* 21 (1997): 49, 55-56, as cited in Robin Fretwell Wilson, "Children at Risk: The Sexual Exploitation of Female Children after Divorce," *Cornell Law Review* 86 (2000): 256.

[108] William C. Holmes, "Men's Childhood Sexual Abuse Histories by One-parent Versus Two-Parent Status of Childhood Home," *Journal of Epidemiol Community Health* 61 (2007): 324.

[109] U.S. Department of Health and Human Services, Administration for Children and Families, *Fourth National Incidence Study of Child Abuse and Neglect (NIS–4): Report to Congress*, by Andrea J. Sedlak, Jane Mettenburg, Monica Basena, Ian Petta, Karla McPherson, Angela Greene, and Spencer Li, 5-22 (Washington, DC: 2010).

[110] U.S. Department of Health and Human Services, Administration for Children and Families, *Fourth National Incidence Study of Child Abuse and Neglect (NIS–4): Report to Congress*, by Andrea J. Sedlak, Jane Mettenburg, Monica Basena, Ian Petta, Karla McPherson, Angela Greene, and Spencer Li, 5-22 (Washington, DC: 2010).

[111] U.S. Department of Health and Human Services, Administration for Children and Families, *Fourth National Incidence Study of Child Abuse and Neglect (NIS–4): Report to Congress*, by Andrea J. Sedlak, Jane Mettenburg, Monica Basena, Ian Petta, Karla McPherson, Angela Greene, and Spencer Li, 5-24 (Washington, DC: 2010).

[112] U.S. Department of Health and Human Services, Administration for Children and Families, *Fourth National Incidence Study of Child Abuse and Neglect (NIS–4): Report to Congress*, by Andrea J. Sedlak, Jane Mettenburg, Monica Basena, Ian Petta, Karla McPherson, Angela Greene, and Spencer Li, 5-25 (Washington, DC: 2010).

[113] U.S. Department of Health and Human Services, Administration for Children and Families, *Fourth National Incidence Study of Child Abuse and Neglect (NIS–4): Report to Congress*, by Andrea J. Sedlak, Jane Mettenburg, Monica Basena, Ian Petta, Karla McPherson, Angela Greene, and Spencer Li, 5-10 (Washington, DC: 2010).

[114] U.S. Department of Health and Human Services, Administration for Children and Families, *Fourth National Incidence Study of Child Abuse and Neglect (NIS–4): Report to Congress*, by Andrea J. Sedlak, Jane Mettenburg, Monica Basena, Ian Petta, Karla McPherson, Angela Greene, and Spencer Li, 5-11—5-14 (Washington, DC: 2010).

[115] Richard E. Tremblay, Daniel S. Nagin, Jean R. Seguin, Mark Zoccolillo, Philip D. Zelazo, Michel Boivin, Daniel Perusse, and Christa Japel, "Physical Aggression During Early Childhood: Trajectories and Predictors," *Pediatrics* 114, no. 1 (2004): e45.

[116] Marjorie S. Hardy, "Physical Aggression and Sexual Behavior Among Siblings: A Retrospective Study," *Journal of Family Violence* 16, no. 3 (2001): 261-262.

[117] Heather A. Turner, David Finkelhor, and Richard Ormrod, "Family Structure Variations in Patterns and Predictors of Child Victimization," *American Journal of Orthopsychiatry* 77, no. 2 (2007): 287.

[118] Marjorie S. Hardy, "Physical Aggression and Sexual Behavior Among Siblings: A Retrospective Study," *Journal of Family Violence* 16, no. 3 (2001): 263.

[119] Heather A. Turner, David Finkelhor, and Richard Ormrod, "The Effect of Lifetime Victimization on the Mental Health of Children and Adolescents," *Social Science and Medicine* (2005): 7.

[120] Grace Mattern, David Laflamme, Sharyn Potter, and Mary M. Moynihan, "Violence Against Men in New Hampshire," *Center for Disease Control and Prevention*: 2.

[121] Candice Feiring, Lynn Taska, and Michael Lewis, "Age and gender differences in children's and adolescents' adaptation to sexual abuse," *Child Abuse and Neglect* 23 (1999): 115-128, as cited in Kimberly A. Tyler, "Social and Emotional Outcomes of Childhood Sexual Abuse: A Review of Recent Research," *Aggression and Violent Behavior* 7, no. 6 (2002): 577.

122 Heather A. Turner, David Finkelhor, and Richard Ormrod, "The Effect of Lifetime Victimization on the Mental Health of Children and Adolescents," *Social Science and Medicine* (2005): 7.

123 Kim S. Ménard and Barry R. Ruback, "Prevalence and Processing of Child Sexual Abuse: A Multi-Data-set Analysis of Urban and Rural Countries," *Law and Human Behavior* 27, no. 4 (2003): 394.

124 Anthony P. Mannarino, Judith A. Cohen, Judith A. Smith, and Susan Moore-Motily, "Six- and twelve-month follow-up of sexually abused girls," *Journal of Interpersonal Violence* 6 (1991): 494-511; Benjamin E. Saunders, Dean G. Kilpatrick, Rochelle F. Hansen, Heidi S. Resnick, and Michael E. Walker, "Prevalence, Case Characteristics, and Long-Term Psychological Correlates of Child Rape among Women: A National Survey," *Child Maltreatment* 4 (1999) 187-200; Cathy S. Widom, "Posttraumatic Stress Disorder in Abused and Neglected Children Grown Up," *American Journal of Orthopsychiatry* 56 (1999): 1223-1229, all as cited in Raymond E. Webster, "Symptoms and Long-Term Outcomes for Children Who Have Been Sexually Assaulted," *Psychology in the Schools* 38, no. 6 (2001): 537.

125 Richard B. Felson and Kelsea Jo Lane, "Social Learning, Sexual and Physical Abuse, and Adult Crime," *Aggressive Behavior* 35 (2009): 489.

126 Sandra M. Stith, Karen H. Rosen, Kimberly A. Middleton, Amy L. Busch, Kirsten Lundeberg, and Russell P. Carlton, "The Intergenerational Transmission of Spouse Abuse: A Meta-Analysis," *Journal of Marriage and Family* 62, no. 3 (2000): 645.

127 Abigail A. Fagan, "The Relationship Between Adolescent Physical Abuse and Criminal Offending: Support for an Enduring and Generalized Cycle of Violence," *Journal of Family Violence* 20, no. 5 (2005): 284.

128 Holly Garcia O'Hearn and Gayla Margolin, "Men's Attitudes Condoning Marital Aggression: A Moderator Between Family of Origin Abuse and Aggression Against Female Partners," *Cognitive Therapy and Research* 24, no. 2 (2000): 166.

129 Holly Garcia O'Hearn and Gayla Margolin, "Men's Attitudes Condoning Marital Aggression: A Moderator Between Family of Origin Abuse and Aggression Against Female Partners," *Cognitive Therapy and Research* 24, no. 2 (2000): 159.

130 Alan Rosenbaum and Penny A. Leisring, "Beyond Power and Control: Towards an Understanding of Partner Abusive Men," *Journal of Comparative Family Studies* (2011): 15.

131 M.D. Friesen, L.J. Woodward, L.J. Horwood, and D.M. Fergusson, "Childhood Exposure to Sexual Abuse and Partnership Outcomes at age 30," *Psychological Medicine* 40 (2010): 679.

132 Xiangming Fang and Phaedra S. Corso, "Gender Differences in the Connections Between Violence Experienced as a Child and Perpetration of Intimate Partner Violence in Young Adulthood," *Journal of Family Violence* 23, no. 3 (2008): 303.

133 Marcia Polansky, Walter Lauterbach, Cheryl Litzke, Becky Coulter, and Linda Sommers, "A Qualitative Study of an Attachment-Based Parenting Group for Mothers With Drug Addictions: On Being and Having a Mother," *Journal of Social Work Practice* 20, no. 2 (2006): 121.

134 Debra K. Miller, "The Effects of Childhood Physical Abuse or Childhood Sexual Abuse in Battered Women's Coping Mechanisms: Obsessive-Compulsive Tendencies and Severe Depression," *Journal of Family Violence* 21, no. 3 (2006): 190.

135 Debra K. Miller, "The Effects of Childhood Physical Abuse or Childhood Sexual Abuse in Battered Women's Coping Mechanisms: Obsessive-Compulsive Tendencies and Severe Depression," *Journal of Family Violence* 21, no. 3 (2006): 190.

[136] Debra K. Miller, "The Effects of Childhood Physical Abuse or Childhood Sexual Abuse in Battered Women's Coping Mechanisms: Obsessive-Compulsive Tendencies and Severe Depression," *Journal of Family Violence* 21, no. 3 (2006): 190.

[137] David M. Fergusson, L. John Horwood, and Michael T. Lynskey, "Childhood Sexual Abuse, Adolescent Sexual Behaviors, and Sexual Revictimization," *Child Abuse and Neglect* 21 (1997): 789-803, as cited in Kimberly A. Tyler, "Social and Emotional Outcomes of Childhood Sexual Abuse: A Review of Recent Research," *Aggression and Violent Behavior* 7, no. 6 (2002): 574.

[138] Mirjam Lukasse, Berit Schei, Siri Vangen, and Pal Oian, "Childhood Abuse and Common Complaints in Pregnancy," *Birth* 36, no. 3 (2009): 194.

[139] Tom Luster and Stephen A. Small, "Sexual Abuse History and Number of Sex Partners among Female Adolescents," *Family Planning Perspectives* 29 (1997): 204-211, as cited in Kimberly A. Tyler, "Social and Emotional Outcomes of Childhood Sexual Abuse: A Review of Recent Research," *Aggression and Violent Behavior* 7, no. 6 (2002): 574.

[140] Jacqueline L. Stock, Michelle A. Bell, Debra K. Boyer, and Frederick A. Connell, "Adolescent Pregnancy and Sexual Risktaking among Sexually Abused Girls," *Family Planning Perspectives* 29 (1997): 200-227, as cited in Kimberly A. Tyler, "Social and Emotional Outcomes of Childhood Sexual Abuse: A Review of Recent Research," *Aggression and Violent Behavior* 7, no. 6 (2002): 571.

[141] Mark A. Whisman, "Childhoood Trauma and Marital Outcomes in Adulthood," *Personal Relationships* 13 (2006): 380.

[142] Duane F. Reinert and Carla E. Edwards, "Childhood Physical and Verbal Mistreatment, Psychological Symptoms, and Substance Use: Sex Differences and the Moderating Role of Attachment," *Journal of Family Violence* 24 (2009): 593.

[143] Stephanie Milan, Jessica Lewis, Kathleen Ethier, Trace Kershaw, and Jeannette R. Ickovics, "The Impact of Physical Maltreatment History on the Adolescent Mother-Infant Relationship: Mediating and Moderating Effects During the Transition to Early Parenthood," *Journal of Abnormal Child Psychology* 32, no. 3(2004): 257-258.

[144] Crystal Cullerton-Sen, Adam R. Cassidy, Dianna Murray-Close, Dante Cicchetti, Nicki R. Crick, Fred A. Rogosch, "Childhood Maltreatment and the Development of Relational and Physical Aggression: The Importance of a Gender-Informed Approach," *Child Development* 79, no. 6 (2008): 1736.

[145] Crystal Cullerton-Sen, Adam R. Cassidy, Dianna Murray-Close, Dante Cicchetti, Nicki R. Crick, Fred A. Rogosch, "Childhood Maltreatment and the Development of Relational and Physical Aggression: The Importance of a Gender-Informed Approach," *Child Development* 79, no. 6 (2008): 1745.

[146] Crystal Cullerton-Sen, Adam R. Cassidy, Dianna Murray-Close, Dante Cicchetti, Nicki R. Crick, Fred A. Rogosch, "Childhood Maltreatment and the Development of Relational and Physical Aggression: The Importance of a Gender-Informed Approach," *Child Development* 79, no. 6 (2008): 1745.

[147] Debra K. Miller, "The Effects of Childhood Physical Abuse or Childhood Sexual Abuse in Battered Women's Coping Mechanisms: Obsessive-Compulsive Tendencies and Severe Depression," *Journal of Family Violence* 21, no. 3 (2006): 190.

[148] Debra K. Miller, "The Effects of Childhood Physical Abuse or Childhood Sexual Abuse in Battered Women's Coping Mechanisms: Obsessive-Compulsive Tendencies and Severe Depression," *Journal of Family Violence* 21, no. 3 (2006): 191.

[149] Inga Dora Sigfusdottir, Bryndis Bjork Asgeirsdottir, Gisli H. Gudjonsson, and Jon Fridrik Sigurdsson, "A Model of Sexual Abuse's Effects on Suicidal Behavior and Delinquency: The Role of Emotions as Mediating Factors," *Journal of Youth and Adolescence* 37 (2008): 707.

[150] Helene R. White and Cathy S. Widom, "Three Potential Mediators of the Effects of Child Abuse and Neglect on Adulthood Substance Use Among Women," *Journal of Studies on Alcohol and Drugs* 69 (2008): 344.

[151] Margaret Rosario, Richard S. Feldman, Suzanne Salzinger, Daisy S. Ng-Mak, "Community Violence Exposure and Delinquent Behaviors Among Youth: The Moderating Role of Coping," *Journal of Community Psychology* 31, no. 5 (2003): 502-503.

[152] Julie A. Patock-Peckham and Antonio A. Morgan-Lopez, "Direct and Mediational Links Between Parental Bonds and Neglect, Antisocial Personality, Reasons for Drinking, Alcohol Use, and Alcohol Problems," *Journal Studies of Alcohol and Drugs* 71 (2010): 99.

[153] Cathy S. Widom, Helene R. White, Sally J. Czaja, and Naomi R. Marmorstein, "Long-Term Effects of Child Abuse and Neglect on Alcohol Use and Excessive Drinking in Middle Adulthood," *Journal of Studies on Alcohol and Drugs* 68 (2007): 317, 325.

[154] Cathy S. Widom, Helene R. White, Sally J. Czaja, and Naomi R. Marmorstein, "Long-Term Effects of Child Abuse and Neglect on Alcohol Use and Excessive Drinking in Middle Adulthood," *Journal of Studies on Alcohol and Drugs* 68 (2007): 317.

[155] Scott M. Hyman, Miguel Garcia, and Rajita Sinha, "Gender Specific Associations Between Types of Childhood Maltreatment and the Onset, Escalation and Severity of Substance Use in Cocaine Dependent Adults," *The American Journal of Drug and Alcohol Abuse* 32 (2006): 661.

[156] Helene R. White and Cathy S. Widom, "Three Potential Mediators of the Effects of Child Abuse and Neglect on Adulthood Substance Use Among Women," *Journal of Studies on Alcohol and Drugs* 69 (2008): 341.

[157] Martie P. Thompson, J.B. Kingree, and Sujata Desai, "Gender Differences in Long-Term Health Consequences of Physical Abuse of Children: Data From a Nationally Representative Survey," *American Journal of Public Health* 94, no.4 (2004): 600-601.

[158] Emalee G. Flaherty, Richard Thompson, Alan J. Litrownik, Adam J. Zolotor, Howard Dubowitz, Desmond K. Runyan, Diana J. English, and Mark D. Everson, "Adverse Childhood Exposures and Reported Child Health at Age 12," *Academic Pediatrics* 9, no. 3 (2009): 150.

[159] Mirjam Lukasse, Berit Schei, Siri Vangen, and Pal Oian, "Childhood Abuse and Common Complaints in Pregnancy," *Birth* 36, no. 3 (2009): 191, 194.

[160] Nadia Garnefski and Ellen Arends, "Sexual abuse and adolescent maladjustment: differences between male and female victims," *Journal of Adolescence* 21 (1998): 99-107, as cited in Kimberly A. Tyler, "Social and Emotional Outcomes of Childhood Sexual Abuse: A Review of Recent Research," *Aggression and Violent Behavior* 7, no. 6 (2002): 576.

[161] Michelle A. Fortier, David DiLillo, Terri L. Messman-Moore, James Peugh, Kathleen A. DeNardi, and Kathryn J.Gaffey, "Severity of Child Sexual Abuse and Revictimization: The Mediating Role of Coping and Trauma Symptoms," *Psychology of Women Quarterly* 33 (2009): 308, 314.

[162] Meeyoung Min, Kathleen Farkas, Sonia Minnes, and Lynn T. Singer, "Impact of Childhood Abuse and Neglect on Substance Abuse and Psychological Distress in Adulthood," *Journal of Traumatic Stress* 20, no. 5 (2007): 833.

[163] Caroline Tremblay, Martine Hébert, and Christiane Piché, "Coping Strategies and Social Support as Mediators of Consequences in Child Sexual Abuse Victims," *Child Abuse and Neglect* 23 (1999): 929-945, as cited in Kimberly A. Tyler, "Social and Emotional Outcomes of Childhood Sexual Abuse: A Review of Recent Research," *Aggression and Violent Behavior* 7, no. 6 (2002): 578.

[164] Joseph H. Beitchman, Kenneth J. Zucker, Jane E. Hood, Granville A. DaCosta, Donna Akman, and Erika Cassavia, "A Review of the Long-Term Effects of Child Sexual Abuse," *Child Abuse and Neglect* 16 (1992): 105-106; "Childhood Abuse Ups Risk for Adult Mental Illness," *Reuters Health News*, available at www.ama-assn.org/insight/gen_hlth/med_news/tmp-news/071410f.htm (accessed 16 July 1999), both as cited in Robin Fretwell Wilson, "Children at Risk: The Sexual Exploitation of Female Children after Divorce," *Cornell Law Review* 86 (2000): 278.

[165] Joseph H. Beitchman, Kenneth J. Zucker, Jane E. Hood, Granville A. DaCosta, Donna Akman, and Erika Cassavia, "A Review of the Long-Term Effects of Child Sexual Abuse," *Child Abuse and Neglect* 16 (1992): 107, as cited in Robin Fretwell Wilson, "Children at Risk: The Sexual Exploitation of Female Children after Divorce," *Cornell Law Review* 86 (2000): 278.

[166] Duane F. Reinert and Carla E. Edwards, "Childhood Physical and Verbal Mistreatment, Psychological Symptoms, and Substance Use: Sex Differences and the Moderating Role of Attachment," *Journal of Family Violence* 24 (2009): 593.

[167] Judith A. Stein, Jacqueline M. Golding, Judith M. Siegel, M. Audrey Burnam, and Susan B. Sorensen, "Long-Term Psychological Sequelae of Child Sexual Abuse: The Los Angeles Epidemiologic Catchment Area Study," in *Lasting Effects of Child Sexual Abuse*, eds. Gail Elizabeth Wyatt and Gloria Johnson Powell (1988), 135, 143 table 8.4, as cited in Robin Fretwell Wilson, "Children at Risk: The Sexual Exploitation of Female Children after Divorce," *Cornell Law Review* 86 (2000): 278.

[168] Abigail Powers, Kerry J. Ressler, and Rebekah G. Bradley, "The Protective Role of Friendship on the Effects of Childhood Abuse and Depression," *Depression and Anxiety* 26 (2009): 46.

[169] Heather A. Turner, David Finkelhor, and Richard Ormrod, "The Effect of Lifetime Victimization on the Mental Health of Children and Adolescents," *Social Science and Medicine* (2005): 8.

[170] Abigail Powers, Kerry J. Ressler, and Rebekah G. Bradley, "The Protective Role of Friendship on the Effects of Childhood Abuse and Depression," *Depression and Anxiety* 26 (2009): 46.

[171] Kerri M. Schneider and Vicky Phares, "Coping with Parental Loss Because of Termination of Parental Rights," *Child Welfare League of America* 34, no. 6 (2005): 832.

[172] Nadia Garnefski and René F.W. Diekstra, "Child Sexual Abuse and Emotional and Behavioral Problems in Adolescence: Gender Differences," *Journal of the American Academy of Child Adolescent Psychiatry* 36 (1997): 323-329, as cited in Kimberly A. Tyler, "Social and Emotional Outcomes of Childhood Sexual Abuse: A Review of Recent Research," *Aggression and Violent Behavior* 7, no. 6 (2002): 569.

[173] Page L. Anderson, Jasmin A. Tiro, Ann Webb Price, Marnette A. Bender, and Nadine J. Kaslow, "Additive Impact of Childhood Emotional, Physical, and Sexual Abuse on Suicide," *Suicide and Life-Threatening Behavior* 32, no. 2 (2002): 135.

[174] Page L. Anderson, Jasmin A. Tiro, Ann Webb Price, Marnette A. Bender, and Nadine J. Kaslow, "Additive Impact of Childhood Emotional, Physical, and Sexual Abuse on Suicide" *Suicide and Life-Threatening Behavior* 32, no. 2 (2002): 134.

[175] Patrick O'Leary and Nick Gould, "Men Who Were Sexually Abused in Childhood and Subsequent Suicidal Ideation: Community Comparison, Explanations and Practice Implications," *British Journal of Social Work* 39 (2009): 950.

[176] Inga Dora Sigfusdottir, Bryndis Bjork Asgeirsdottir, Gisli H. Gudjonsson, and Jon Fridrik Sigurdsson, "A Model of Sexual Abuse's Effects on Suicidal Behavior and Delinquency: The Role of Emotions as Mediating Factors," *Journal of Youth and Adolescence* 37 (2008): 708.

[177] Esther Deblinger, Robert A. Steer, and Julie Lippmann, "Two-Year Follow-up Study of Cognitive Behavioral Therapy for Sexually Abused Children Suffering from Post-Traumatic Stress Symptoms," *Child Abuse and Neglect* 23 (1999): 1371-1378, as cited in Raymond E. Webster, "Symptoms and Long-Term Outcomes for Children Who Have Been Sexually Assaulted," *Psychology in the Schools* 38, no. 6 (2001): 537.

[178] Jon McClellan, Julie Adams, Donna Douglas, Chris McCurry, and Mick Storck, "Clinical Characteristics Related to Severity of Sexual Abuse: A Study of Seriously Mentally Ill Youth," *Child Abuse and Neglect* 19 (1995): 1245-1254, as cited in Kimberly A. Tyler, "Social and Emotional Outcomes of Childhood Sexual Abuse: A Review of Recent Research," *Aggression and Violent Behavior* 7, no. 6 (2002): 578.

[179] Jeremiah A. Schumm, Lisa R. Stines, Steven E. Hobfoll, and Anita P. Jackson, "The Double-Barreled Burden of Child Abuse and Current Stressful Circumstances on Adult Women: The Kindling Effect of Early Traumatic Experience," *Journal of Traumatic Stress* 18, no. 5 (2005): 467, 470.

[180] Ira M. Schwartz, Jose A. Rendon, and Chang-Ming Hsieh, "Is Child Maltreatment a Leading Cause of Delinquency?" *Child Welfare League of America* 23, no. 5 (2011): 651-652.

[181] Allan V. Horwitz, Cathy Spatz Widom, Julie McLaughlin, and Helene Raskin White, "The Impact of Childhood Abuse and Neglect on Adult Mental Health: A Prospective Study," *Journal of Health and Social Behavior* 42 (2001): 184.

[182] Centers for Disease Control and Prevention, National Center for Injury Prevention and Control, *The National Intimate Partner and Sexual Violence Survey (NISVS): 2010 Summary Report*, by M.C. Black, K.C. Basile, M.J. Breiding, S.G. Smith, M.L. Walters, M.T. Merrick, J. Chen, and M.R. Stevens, 3 (Atlanta, Georgia: 2011).

[183] Centers for Disease Control and Prevention, National Center for Injury Prevention and Control, *The National Intimate Partner and Sexual Violence Survey (NISVS): 2010 Summary Report*, by M.C. Black, K.C. Basile, M.J. Breiding, S.G. Smith, M.L. Walters, M.T. Merrick, J. Chen, and M.R. Stevens, 3 (Atlanta, Georgia: 2011).

[184] Centers for Disease Control and Prevention, National Center for Injury Prevention and Control, *The National Intimate Partner and Sexual Violence Survey (NISVS): 2010 Summary Report*, by M.C. Black, K.C. Basile, M.J. Breiding, S.G. Smith, M.L. Walters, M.T. Merrick, J. Chen, and M.R. Stevens, 24 (Atlanta, Georgia: 2011).

[185] Centers for Disease Control and Prevention, National Center for Injury Prevention and Control, *The National Intimate Partner and Sexual Violence Survey (NISVS): 2010 Summary Report*, by M.C. Black, K.C. Basile, M.J. Breiding, S.G. Smith, M.L. Walters, M.T. Merrick, J. Chen, and M.R. Stevens, 3 (Atlanta, Georgia: 2011).

[186] Centers for Disease Control and Prevention, National Center for Injury Prevention and Control, *The National Intimate Partner and Sexual Violence Survey (NISVS): 2010 Summary Report*, by M.C. Black, K.C. Basile, M.J. Breiding, S.G. Smith, M.L. Walters, M.T. Merrick, J. Chen, and M.R. Stevens, 24 (Atlanta, Georgia: 2011).

[187] Michelle A. Fortier, David DiLillo, Terri L. Messman-Moore, James Peugh, Kathleen A. DeNardi, and Kathryn J.Gaffey, "Severity of Child Sexual Abuse and Re-

victimization: The Mediating Role of Coping and Trauma Symptoms," *Psychology of Women Quarterly* 33 (2009): 314.

[188] Jane M. Ussher and Christopher Dewberry, "The Nature and Long-Term Effects of Childhood Sexual Abuse: A Survey of Adult Women Survivors in Britain," *British Journal of Clinical Psychology* 34 (1995): 177, 181, as cited in Robin Fretwell Wilson, "Children at Risk: The Sexual Exploitation of Female Children after Divorce," *Cornell Law Review* 86 (2000): 274-275.

[189] Rebecca M. Bolen, "Predicting Risk to Be Sexually Abused: A Comparison of Logistic Regression to Event History Analysis," *Child Maltreatment* 3 (1998): 157, 164, 167, as cited in Robin Fretwell Wilson, "Children at Risk: The Sexual Exploitation of Female Children after Divorce," *Cornell Law Review* 86 (2000): 255.

[190] Jane M. Ussher and Christopher Dewberry, "The Nature and Long-Term Effects of Childhood Sexual Abuse: A Survey of Adult Women Survivors in Britain," *British Journal of Clinical Psychology* 34 (1995): 180-181; W.D. Erickson, N.H. Walbek, and R.K. Seely, "Behavior Patterns of Child Molesters," *Archives of Sexual Behavior* 17 (1988): 77, 84; Diana E.H. Russell, *The Secret Trauma: Incest in the Lives of Girls and Women* (1986): 226 table 15-9, all as cited in Robin Fretwell Wilson, "Children at Risk: The Sexual Exploitation of Female Children after Divorce," *Cornell Law Review* 86 (2000): 275.

[191] Ferol E. Mennen and Diane Meadow, "The Relationship of Abuse Characteristics to Symptoms in Sexually Abused Girls," *Journal of Interpersonal Violence* 10 (1995): 259-274, as cited in Kimberly A. Tyler, "Social and Emotional Outcomes of Childhood Sexual Abuse: A Review of Recent Research," *Aggression and Violent Behavior* 7, no. 6 (2002): 575.

[192] Diana E.H., *The Secret Trauma: Incest in the Lives of Girls and Women* (1986): 232; Joseph H. Beitchman, Kenneth J. Zucker, Jane E. Hood, Granville A. DaCosta, Donna Akman, and Erika Cassavia, "A Review of the Long-Term Effects of Child Sexual Abuse," *Child Abuse and Neglect* 16 (1992): 112; David Finkelhor, *Sexually Victimized Children* (1979), 104, all as cited in Robin Fretwell Wilson, "Children at Risk: The Sexual Exploitation of Female Children after Divorce," *Cornell Law Review* 86 (2000): 276.

[193] Centers for Disease Control and Prevention, National Center for Injury Prevention and Control, *The National Intimate Partner and Sexual Violence Survey (NISVS): 2010 Summary Report*, by M.C. Black, K.C. Basile, M.J. Breiding, S.G. Smith, M.L. Walters, M.T. Merrick, J. Chen, and M.R. Stevens, 2-3 (Atlanta, Georgia: 2011).

[194] Centers for Disease Control and Prevention, National Center for Injury Prevention and Control, *The National Intimate Partner and Sexual Violence Survey (NISVS): 2010 Summary Report*, by M.C. Black, K.C. Basile, M.J. Breiding, S.G. Smith, M.L. Walters, M.T. Merrick, J. Chen, and M.R. Stevens, 3 (Atlanta, Georgia: 2011).

[195] Centers for Disease Control and Prevention, National Center for Injury Prevention and Control, *The National Intimate Partner and Sexual Violence Survey (NISVS): 2010 Summary Report*, by M.C. Black, K.C. Basile, M.J. Breiding, S.G. Smith, M.L. Walters, M.T. Merrick, J. Chen, and M.R. Stevens, 1-3 (Atlanta, Georgia: 2011).

[196] Centers for Disease Control and Prevention, National Center for Injury Prevention and Control, *The National Intimate Partner and Sexual Violence Survey (NISVS): 2010 Summary Report*, by M.C. Black, K.C. Basile, M.J. Breiding, S.G. Smith, M.L. Walters, M.T. Merrick, J. Chen, and M.R. Stevens, 20-21 (Atlanta, Georgia: 2011).

[197] Laurie E. Powers, Mary Ann Curry, Elizabeth McNeff, Marsha Saxton, Jennifer L. Powers, Mary Oschwald, "End the Silence: A Survey of Abuse Against Men With Disabilities," *Journal of Rehabilitation* 74, no. 4 (2008): 46.

[198] Craig S. Rosen, Paige C. Ouimette, Javaid I. Sheikh, Jennifer A. Gregg, Rudolf H. Moos, "Physical and Sexual Abuse History and Addiction Treatment Outcomes," *Journal of Studies on Alcohol and Drugs* 63 (2002): 683, 686.

[199] Debra Boyer and David Fine, "Sexual Abuse as a Factor in Adolescent Pregnancy and Child Maltreatment," *Family Planning Perspectives* 24 (1992): 4-11, as cited in Kimberly A. Tyler, "Social and Emotional Outcomes of Childhood Sexual Abuse: A Review of Recent Research," *Aggression and Violent Behavior* 7, no. 6 (2002): 571.

[200] Heidi R. Riggio, "Parental Marital Conflict and Divorce, Parent-Child Relationships, Social Support, and Relationship Anxiety in Young Adulthood," *Personal Relationships* 11 (2004): 106.

[201] Anne Koci and Ora Strickland, "Marginality and Physical and Sexual Abuse in Women," *Health Care for Women International* 30 (2009): 86.

[202] Bradley D. Stein, Lisa H. Jaycox, Sheryl Kataoka, Hilary J. Rhodes, Katherine D. Vestal, "Prevalence of Child and Adolescent Exposure to Community Violence," *Clinical Child and Family Psychology Review* 6, no. 4 (2003): 261.

[203] Said Pournaghash-Tehrani and Zahra Feizabadi, "Predictability of Physical and Psychological Violence by Early Adverse Childhood Experiences," *Journal of Family Violence* 24 (2009): 417, 419.

[204] Margaret W. Baker, Andrea Z. LaCroix, Chunyuan Wu, Barbara B. Cochrane, Robert Wallace, and Nancy F. Woods, "Mortality Risk Associated with Physical and Verbal Abuse in Women Aged 50 to 79," *The American Geriatrics Society* 57, no. 10 (2009): 1799.

[205] Jane Leserman, "Sexual Abuse History: Prevalence, Health Effects, Mediators, and Psychological Treatment," *Psychosomatic Medicine* 67 (2005): 906, 911.

[206] Gillian Mezey, Loraine Bacchus, Susan Bewley, Sarah White, "Domestic Violence, Lifetime Trauma, and Psychological Health of Childbearing Women," *BJOG: An International Journal of Obstetrics and Gynecology* 112 (2005): 197.

Dilemma by Design: Child Welfare Policy and Ethical Problems at the Frontline

By Ruth A. White

As the U.S. Children's Bureau reaches its 100th anniversary, there is widespread acknowledgement that America's child welfare system is broken in a number of ways (U.S. Department of Health and Human Services (HHS), 2005; *Improving Child Welfare*, 2005a; *Improving Child Welfare*, 2005b; Pew Commission on Children in Foster Care, 2004). Indeed, according to Ronald Hughes and Judith of the Institute for Human Services, "The child welfare profession faces mounting moral and political pressures to improve its effectiveness and accountability and to demonstrate its public value" (Rycus & Hughes, 1998, p. 112). In 2000, the federal monitoring system was re-designed to measure states' ability to create positive outcomes for youth involved in the child welfare system on the core goals of safety, permanency, and well-being. Since that time, the highest performing state met only nine of the 14 performance measures. The average score was six (U.S. Department of Health and Human Services [HHS], 2012).

This article will focus on the one factor contributing to the poor performance of America's child welfare system, the federal financing system designed to fund it. The current funding structure under Title IV-

215

E provides little flexibility to address the kinds of problems that are most likely to place children at risk of abuse and neglect.

The problems most closely associated with child maltreatment, particularly the most common form of maltreatment, child neglect, are poverty and unemployment (Pelton, 1989; Sedlak & Broadhurst, 1996; Drake & Pandy, 1996; Lindsey, 1994). One might expect, then, that federal funding for child welfare services would be designed to address or reduce poverty and other economic conditions. This is not the case. Instead, more than 90 per cent of federal child welfare funding is tied to out-of-home placement for at-risk children (Geen, 2001; HHS, 2005; Wulczyn, Barth, Yuan, Harden, & Landsverk, 2005). Additionally, according to Blome (1996), the open ended entitlement to foster care for poor children (Title IV-E) is remarkably durable, yet efforts to gain a similar entitlement for federal funding to reunify and preserve families or expand Title IV-B (the section of the Social Security Act of 1935 aimed at keeping families together and safe) fail, consistently. The most recent legislative attempt to address the failure of the current funding structure, *Child and Family Services Improvement and Innovations Act of 2011,* has not yet been implemented. This law will allow up to thirty states over three years to apply for waivers from the federal finance system to some degree, but will not create wholesale change. As this law has not been implemented, it will not be addressed at length in this article.

In the absence of an appropriate match between resources and the presenting problems of families, frontline child welfare workers are placed in the unenviable position of making choices between undesirable service options or leaving children in dangerous situations (Gonzalez, Faller, Ortega & Tropman, 2009; HHS, 1997; Courtney, McMurtry, & Zinn, 2004; Shdaima, 2009). According to Dolgoff, Loewenberg, & Harrington (2005) such a situation amounts to an ethical dilemma in social work practice. When such a dilemma occurs, it is the individual social worker, not the policymaker, who must share the news with a mother that, for example, her children will be placed into a foster home because appropriate alternatives are not available.

The phenomenon of frontline workers negotiating ethical dilemmas borne out of poorly designed public policy was first identified in 1980 by a professor Michael Lipsky of the Massachusetts Institute of Technology. In *Street-Level Bureaucracy: Dilemmas of the Individual in Public Services*, Lipsky explained that when bureaucracies generate public policies, these policies are not self-implementing. Instead, policies must be activated and carried out by "public services agents who interact directly with the public in their jobs and have considerable discretion in the execution of their work" (1980, p. 3). Coining a new phrase, Lipsky labeled these individuals "street-level bureaucrats." Child welfare workers are included in this group along with teachers, police officers, public housing workers, and others working under similar conditions.

This article will employ Lipsky's street-level bureaucrat concept to understand the conditions imposed upon street-level bureaucrats in the child welfare system as they attempt to reconcile conflicting federal child welfare policy, professional standards, the ecological systems theory base of social work, and the family-centered practice expectations of child welfare work. This article makes suggestions for further study regarding the extent to which the frustration visited upon workers in this environment ultimately drives many professional social workers to flee the field of child welfare. Finally, this article offers recommendations for minimizing these dilemmas in the short and long term.

Conceptual Framework

Work at the frontlines of social work is remarkably complex. This is a function of the residual model of child welfare that essentially requires that a family be at the point of breakdown before they can be assisted (Kadushin & Martin, 1988). Additionally, child welfare operates as a system of last resort for troubled families for whom many safety nets have failed. Unlike virtually any other bureaucracy serving families, foster care maintains an entitlement to funding under Title IV-E of the Social Security Act of 1935. When families have exhausted all other resources, child welfare cannot turn them away. Given the current political and economic climate, suitable alternatives such as employment, affordable housing, adequate child care arrangements, and TANF are more difficult to come by and thus more families are driven to child welfare.

It is increasingly the responsibility of caseworkers to "engage with clients whose lives have been laid bare under the backdrop of ticking time clocks and strict work requirements" (Watkins-Hayes, 2009, p. 32). Front-line child welfare workers are dealt a very difficult hand as street-level bureaucrats go. Lipsky's conceptual framework is an excellent fit to organize the exploration of the experiences of these individuals.

Lipsky hypothesized that the following commonalities characterize the working conditions of street-level bureaucrats: 1) Resources are chronically inadequate relative to the tasks workers are asked to perform; 2) Goal expectations for the agencies in which they work tend to be ambiguous, vague or conflicting; and 3) Performance oriented toward goal achievement tends to be difficult if not impossible to measure (1980, p. 27-28).

This article will explore evidence of these experiences in the field of child welfare. Additionally, drawing on elements of Watkins-Hayes's (2009) concept of the "catch-all bureaucracy," this paper will assert that the ethical dilemmas experienced by child welfare workers are unique and arguably among the most challenging facing street-level bureaucrats today.

The Ethical Dilemmas of Child Welfare

According to Dolgoff, Loewenberg, & Harrington (2005) an ethical dilemma occurs in "situations in which the social worker must choose between two or more relevant, but contradictory ethical directives, or when every alternative results in an undesirable outcome for one or more persons" (2005, p. 6). Generally, this ethical dilemma is child welfare is framed in terms of family preservation versus child protection (Maluccio, Fein, and Davis, 1994; Barth, 1999). For example, in the absence of resources to remediate the economic challenges of the family (homelessness, lack of access to medical care, lack of access to child care, etc.), if concrete services are not available, the worker must decide between two clear choices: 1) leaving the child to live with their parents under dangerous conditions or 2) placing the child into foster care, thereby guaranteeing, at least to some degree, the child's safety.

This ethical dilemma reviewed in this article can be framed as the choice to provide economic supports to vulnerable families in order to protect children versus separating children from these vulnerable families to protect the children temporarily until the families can acquire the necessary resources to regain custody and protect the children themselves. Therefore, this article will consider how the ethical dilemma presented by resource allocation at the federal level plays out in the casework of the street-level child welfare bureaucrat. It will view this ethical dilemma from this perspective.

Applying Lipsky's Concept of the "Street-Level Bureaucrat" to Child Welfare Resources and Tasks in Child Welfare

Federal Funding and Policy Issues

Child welfare workers are confronted with a well-documented and persistent mismatch between the resources they have available and the tasks at hand. Attempts to address this mismatch between resources and presenting problems at the policy level have failed. For example, when introduced, both the Senate and House versions of the Adoption and Safe Families Act (ASFA) of 1997 (P.L. 105-89) contained proposals that would have introduced considerable flexibility to the child welfare funding stream, capturing both preservation and reunification services within the federal entitlement.

When passed, ASFA continued a long-standing policy of encouraging child welfare agencies to incorporate family preservation programs into their service models. However, proposals for funding flexibility were dropped. Consequently, ASFA provides no associated funding or concrete or material aid to support the family-centered work promoted in the legislation (Pelton, 2008; Barbell & Freundlich, 2001).

Similarly, the Fostering Connections to Success and Increasing Adoptions Act of 2008 (P.L. 110-351) promotes practices that keep families together and safe but provides no associated increase in concrete resources to facilitate such efforts. The precursor to this P.L. 110-351, the "Invest in Kids' Instruction, Development, and Support Act" (H.R. 5466) included a provision that allowed states to include in their state plan a child and family services program to prevent children from needlessly entering foster care.

When merged with the Senate bill, this funding flexibility proposal was dropped. Again, a piece of landmark child welfare legislation affirms a set of expectations for frontline child welfare workers but leaves them without the appropriate tools with which to meet such standards.

As a result, according to the federal department overseeing child welfare, the U.S. Department of Health and Human Services (HHS), "the current funding structure is inflexible, emphasizing foster care. Title IV-E funds foster care on an unlimited basis without providing for services that would either prevent the child's removal from the home or speed permanency" (2005, p. 4). As one might expect, this poorly designed federal resource allocation mechanism finds its way into the professional work of street-level bureaucrats in numerous ways, not the least of which is the persistent inability to appropriately match services to need.

Services Matching Problems

Several studies have found evidence that these funding problems have a profound impact upon the work of professionals in the frontlines. Researchers have operationalized this concept by studying service matching (Hess, Folaron, & Jefferson, 1992; HHS, 1997; Ryan & Schuerman, 2004; Rodenborg, 2004). Service matching studies measure the extent to which a client's presenting problem is matched with an appropriate service (HHS, 1997; HHS, 2005).

In 1992, Hess, Golaron, & Jefferson applied the Professional Review Action Group model to 62 cases in several Indiana counties. Using a case study method, these authors from the Professional Review Action Group at Indiana University reviewed 62 case files from a public child welfare agency to better understand the impact of services upon family reunification rates and the recurrence of maltreatment. The most common problem contributing to reentry of children into foster care (affecting 79 percent of the families) was inappropriate or inadequate service allocation to problems.

Through a secondary analysis of data from HHS (1997) study Rodenborg (2004) confirmed major services matching problem within child welfare. What is more, the Rodenborg study revealed that when resources are made available, race is the best indicator of whether or not a family will be provided with these resources. For example, Rodenborg reports that when families present a housing problem to child welfare, they are unlikely to receive a matched housing service. However, when they do, race is the best predictor of whether that need will be met. The opposite is true for parenting classes. Black families are twice as likely as white families to receive parenting classes when child welfare identifies a family of being in need of such services.

Research by Courtney, McMurtry, & Zinn (2004) in Milwaukee documented a mismatch between the expressed needs of parents for housing assistance and the caseworker's perceptions and actions. By way of explanation, the authors offer that this phenomenon may result from workers' tendency to ignore existing problems "rather than deal with the cognitive dissonance caused by the fact that they cannot help their clients with this important need" (p. 417).

Chambers & Potter (2008) studied the need-services matching in an effort to better understand the child welfare workers' ability to meet needs. They found that a particularly low rate of match—indeed, the lowest—capacity to match services to need was among the mental health/economic need/domestic violence group. In this group, more than half of the needs reported are unmatched (Chambers & Potter, 2008).

Finally, annual the Child and Family Service Review process carried out by HHS consistently reveals that states struggle to match services to the needs of families and youth in the child welfare system (Children's Bureau, 2004). For example, the 2004 CFSR found problems of services matching to be "most pervasive." A total of 43 states needed improvement in providing accessible services to children and families; 27 failed to meet the standard for the responsiveness of services to children and families; and 22 states did not meet criterion on tailoring services to the unique needs of children and families (Children's Bureau, 2004).

Working in an atmosphere where opportunities for proper services matching are so rare and ethical dilemmas so common it must be particularly difficult for workers who are held to both the ethical and theoretical standards that undergird the field of child welfare. Indeed, it is important to underscore the considerable conflict between these standards and the reality that child welfare workers face daily. Consequently, like other street-level bureaucrats, child welfare workers face conflicting goal expectations.

Goal Expectations in Child Welfare Are Ambiguous, Vague, and Conflicting

Professional Ethical Standards Conflict with Reality on the Ground

Child welfare is largely the domain of the social work profession. According to Folaron & Hostetter (2007), child welfare is a specialized field within social work. This relationship between child welfare and the social work profession is sanctioned by the federal government (Folaron & Hostetter, 2007). Approximately 28% of child welfare cases in the U.S. are handled by professional social workers (Lieberman, Hornby, & Russell, 1988). Further, according to Mulroy & Lauber (2004) "social workers are in positions of responsibility for the development, administration, and evaluation of program initiatives that implement new federal and state social policies intended to reform public welfare, child welfare, and public housing" (p. 574). Given this relationship between the field of child welfare and the social work profession, child welfare workers are often held to the ethical code of the social work profession and practice models tend to be derived from the academic and theory base of social work.

Sound ethical decision-making is an important tenant of the social work profession and therefore, child welfare. In fact, Reamer (1994) claims that the ethical base defines the profession. "To state that values and ethics have been central to social work since its inception understates the profound. Social work *is* its values" (Reamer, 1994, p. 4). According to Rycus & Hughes, social work "more than any other secular profession, has as its professional end, the systematic application of fundamental ethical values" (1998, p. 4).

Given the pervasive services mismatch in the child welfare field, street-level bureaucrats appear to be in constant jeopardy of violating that the National Association of Social Workers (NASW) Professional Code of Ethics that governs their work.

Additionally, the NASW Professional Code of Ethics and the Child Welfare League of America Professional Standards appear to go hand in hand. These NASW Child Welfare Standards call social workers in the field to "demonstrate a commitment to the values and ethics of the social work profession, emphasizing client empowerment and self-determination, and shall use the NASW Code of Ethics (1999) as a guide to ethical decision-making standards" (p. 21). On the other hand, the Child Welfare League of America Standards for Services for Abused and Neglected Children and Their Families (2003) states, "services should be provided to the family...based on the needs and risks within the family, not the availability of the service" (p. 50). This particular standard acknowledges that resources might not actually be available, but still offers the expectation that works need to match services to needs.

Street-level bureaucrats are not only expected to match the presenting needs of families, but to conduct sophisticated assessment to reveal needs on multiple levels that could potentially place children and families at risk. Most assessment tools employed in the field of child welfare are based on the ecological/transactional model (Scannapieco & Connell-Carrick, 2005; Ryan, Wiles, Cash, & Seibert, 2005) and as such are intentionally comprehensive in nature.

The Theory Base of Child Welfare—Ecological/Transactional Theory—Raises Expectations that Are Not Supported by Resource Allocation

Currently, the most comprehensive and rigorous explanatory theoretical model of child maltreatment is the ecological/transactional model (Scannapieco & Connell-Carrick, 2005). This is derived from the work of Urie Bronfenbrenner (1979). The ecological/transactional model contains both the multi-level structure of the ecological model and the associated impact on child development derived from the transactional model.

This approach to family assessment takes into account issues in the parents' childhood that might impact their parenting behaviors (ontogenic), within family factors (microsystem), the family's place in their community including socio-economic status (exosystem), and finally, how the family and their community fit into the larger context of American society (macrosystem). This model requires that a child's developmental functioning is influenced by the interplay of factors from all of these levels (Scannapieco & Connell-Carrick, 2005).

The expectation that child welfare workers interact with families and assess their wellbeing from an ecological/transactional model is in accordance with social work values (NASW, 2005). However, given the restrictive nature of federal programs, child welfare workers seldom have the resources necessary to respond to the needs revealed through this type of global assessment. Gambrill (2008) questions the merit of dispatching workers into families' homes with assessment tools based on the ecological systems theory. She asserts that the multiple tools and methods that child welfare workers use to determine safety and judge ongoing family stability are of no real consequence to the task at hand, given the current structure of child welfare policy and funding. The author poses the following question at the end of her work, "Why train staff in effective assessment skills if they have neither the time nor the tools needed to use them?" (Gambrill, 2008, p. 190). This simply places workers in the position of assessing the maximum and addressing the minimum.

These tools are not just encouraged by the social work profession, but the comprehensive nature of these tools is written into federal regulations. The four federally-defined domains of family functioning assessments are derived from the ecological/transactional theory (Schene, 2003). Such regulations are influenced to some degree by experience in the field, but like the work of other street-level bureaucrats, regulations are influenced and pressed into place by factors outside the field.

Politicians and Outside Experts Offer Ever-Changing and Conflicting Goals to the Field

Despite the well-documented fact that appropriate resources are insufficient to support workers in their efforts, practice standards and experts outside public agencies impose the expectation upon workers that they preserve and reunify families. Pressure from above is common among street-level bureaucrats. According to Lipsky (1980): "The social service industry of managers, management consultants, public administrators, foundation officials, and academics whose business is to tinker with social service improvement insures that public perception of street-level bureaucracies is one of constant alterations in the structure of social services delivery" (p. 187).

Generally, the cast of experts offering advice, data, and best practice models, coupled with substantial oversight of the system, makes for a child welfare system that while never really reformed, is in a constant state of flux. Britner & Mossler (2002) reviewed the factors that influence the work of frontline workers and concluded that "legal and theoretical definitions of what constitute grounds for removal vary greatly" (p. 321), and that "decision-making involving out-of-home placements is often a difficult and confusing process" (p. 328). As Alvin Schorr says, "Child welfare is variously influenced by elected officials, academics, foundations such as the Annie E. Casey Foundation and its related operating foundations, the courts, the media, etc. Consequently, the child welfare system has faced confusion about its purposes and methods, declining professionalism, and progressive disorganization" (quoted in Stoetz, 2008).

So, is difficult for street-level bureaucrats to know what is expected of them and as such, front line workers struggle to understand if their work is effectively helping families and children for the better.

Performance Oriented toward Goal Achievement in Child Welfare is Difficult to Determine

Accountability tends to be tied to policy and practice standards, not resources. This holds constant, despite evidence and agreement that the system is designed so that resources seldom match the rhetoric of policy and practice. This creates an environment where performance is difficult to measure and goals are assigned, even though meeting them is not possible. Goal achievement, then, is often unrelated to skill or training— but rather dependent upon resource availability both within and outside the child welfare system. In her study of the impact on child welfare of the phrase "reasonable efforts," Blome (1996) raises a compelling example of a worker caught between expectations and reality:

> Ordering a social worker to find housing for a welfare mother who receives $350 per month in an area where rents average over $800 and the public housing waiting list is over four years does not make it happen. Barring extreme incompetency, the worker knew housing was needed and, had it been available, would have acquired it (p. 144)

More than a third of the children currently living in foster care are there because their parents lack decent housing (Doerre & Mihaly, 1996), so this example raised by Blome is a common dilemma faced by child welfare workers. Housing, like so many other economic challenges, tends to be a common problem that does not lend itself well to creativity by a savvy caseworker. With little control over resource allocation, economic challenges present a daily sense of frustration for these street-level bureaucrats in child welfare (Shdaimah, 2009; Ellett, 2000).

Frustration at the Frontlines

The continued inability of the child welfare system to provide frontline workers with tools that adequately reflect the reality faced by families in the child welfare system may be a missing element in the current debate about workforce retention among child welfare administrators. Decisions about resource allocation at the federal level serve to complicate and constrain the practice decisions of public child welfare workers in numerous ways, not the least of which is by impeding their efforts to make sound practice decisions that reflect the true needs of families (Lipsky, 1980). This must be extraordinarily frustrating.

Gonzalez, Faller, Ortega & Tropman (2009) interviewed former child welfare workers about why they left the field and what it would have taken to keep them in the child welfare workforce. Workers expressed that the frustration related to a mismatch between resources and needs was a common reason for leaving. One of the interviewees shared this response as to what it would have taken to keep her in a public child welfare organization:

> I guess if I'd felt like I had more flexibility to make decisions and
> less of a feeling of being held accountable for everything. I felt like
> we weren't doing social work anymore, we were just trying to cover
> our butts all the time. It was hard work with families when the agency
> had an agenda, I guess (Gonzalez, et al., 2009, p. 54).

Coupled with the finding by Courtney, et al. (2004) regarding workers who experience cognitive dissonance it becomes clear that workers are left to cope with working conditions that present situations that are all too often an exercise in futility.

Further complicating the child welfare work is the residual model of the child welfare system that results in workers facing a grab bag of problems that other social service agencies have failed to meet. As such, child welfare is a "catch-all bureaucracy."

Child Welfare Workers as Catch-All Bureaucrats

Watkins-Hayes (2009) suggests, "it is a mistake to lump all street-level bureaucrats together—harboring the inaccurate assumption that they contain similar levels of social meaning and subsequently face similar organizational dilemmas" (p. 30). Instead, those individuals who work in the catch-all bureaucracies are expected to respond to any problem that arrives at the agency door. Given the current political and economic climate, suitable alternatives such as employment, affordable housing, adequate child care arrangements, and TANF are more difficult to come by and thus more families are driven to child welfare. It is increasingly the responsibility of caseworkers to "engage with clients whose lives have been laid bare under the backdrop of ticking time clocks and strict work requirements" (Watkins-Hayes, 2009, p. 32).

Too Few Alternatives to Foster Care—and Foster Care is at Best an Unclear Technology

Workers are often left without an alternative to foster care. In this regard, they would be judged at least partially as having met the mandate to keep the child safe. However, workers are likely to know that foster care is not always a means by which to keep children safe, which may lead them to further question their efficacy. There is little empirical evidence that supports foster care placement as a desirable option for family preservation—even when services cannot be provided to remediate neglect. A recent study by an economist from MIT calls into question the wisdom of removing child a to protect that child from neglect. In comparing the outcomes of children from families of equally neglectful circumstances, Doyle (2007) found that children who were removed from their families versus children who were left with their families had significantly poorer outcomes.

Further, the act of separation itself can have a profound negative impact upon the child and can create intense attachment and trauma issues, therefore "that effect must always be a principal consideration in decision-making" (CWLA, 2003, p. 47). Indeed, placement in out of home care can seriously affect the child-parent bond (Fantuzzo, Stevenson, Abdul Kabir, & Perry, 2007).

Given these conditions, one can imagine why individuals—particularly social workers—might suffer from an underlying sense that they are not providing optimal or effective services. Indeed, Lipsky asserts that "some jobs just cannot be done properly given the ambiguity and the technology of particular social service" (1980, p. 31).

Discussion

This article highlights the important disharmony between the ethical, practical, and theory-based expectations of street-level bureaucrats in the child welfare system. Coupling services matching data with the work of Gonzalez et al. (2009) and Courtney et al. (2004) provides great insight into the constant frustration and cognitive dissonance brought to bear on workers as they confront these ever-present ethical dilemmas. Indeed, over time these conditions could potentially affect not only work satisfaction among these individuals, but their mental health. Rein (1971) discovered "significant correlations between relatively poor mental health and three indicators of street-level bureaucrats: resource inadequacy, overload, and role ambiguity (as quoted in Lipsky, 1980, p. 32)."

It plausible that this mismatch would affect licensed social workers because they, more than their peers, are beholden to the NASW ethical and practice standards. Indeed, Smith (2005) reports that public child welfare workers, especially MSW workers who were more motivated by the intrinsic value of their work, were not more likely to remain in their positions than workers motivated by external rewards. The information compiled in the article suggests that future research must focus on the extent to which workers motivated by the intrinsic value of their work are *more likely* to leave because of the value conflicts inherent in child welfare work.

Based on the material compiled in this article, a natural question that might emerge is this: *With so much agreement that the system is broken, why does this resource allocation problem persist?* This article does not purport to provide a comprehensive answer to this question; however, some answers can be found in the larger context of American social policy.

Policymakers and the Entitlement to Foster Care Funding

Dolgoff, Loewenberg, and Harrington (2005) point out that priority-setting on the national level is deeply-rooted in the first-order societal value of equity which calls for each American to have "an equal right to obtain social benefits and an equal duty to carry social burdens" (p. 124). This, in turn, leads to the expectation that social workers are obligated to "distribute available resources on an equal basis to all clients" (p. 124). Notice that the operative word here is "available" resources. Further, Rycus & Hughes (1998) use the term "naturally occurring resources." When it comes to economic, community, and other non-foster care services, in the absence of federal entitlement status, this obligation applies only insofar as the resources are available.

Why might federal policymakers choose to add entitlement status to foster care placement but not economic interventions? Social work historian Phyllis Day suggests that these choices are endemic in American social policy and play out in the social work profession in this way, "Social work ethics reflect Judaeo-Christian values, but social practice owes more to other, more individualistic values, society's goals for social welfare are more accurately based on more individualistic values" (Day, 2005, p. 5).

Russell (2006) studied this phenomenon identified by Day and found that indeed that was an explanation and justification for this choice throughout American history. Russell observed that America only "begrudgingly" developed social policies to support the poor. He postulated that the capitalist economic and social policy system that the colonists brought to America from Europe took on a decidedly Calvinist approach in comparison to the more Augustinian approach adopted by the Europeans. The Catholic tradition as interpreted by St. Augustine viewed the poor as a part of the larger society who were entitled to assistance from more fortunate members of the community. Calvinists, on the other hand, generally took the position that the poor were pre-destined to live in poverty as a consequence of their fate as preordained by God. Russell points out that American policymakers converted this into a secular form, "viewing the poor as undeserving of charity or state aid because their plight was evidence, not of God's disfavor, but of their not having the unchallenged work ethic or other necessary moral qualities" (p. 48).

As a result of these divergent approaches, European policymakers were expected to adopt social welfare policies that guaranteed a certain standard of living for all citizens, but the Americans were expected to be good stewards of tax dollars by providing assistance only to those who were unable to survive alone in the market system. Children fit into this category of deserving poor. Parents, do not. Hence, America maintains an entitlement to foster care but not to family services.

Child welfare funding policy seems to have evolved in a way that supports Russell's assertion about resource distribution in the U.S. Getting resources directly to parents to enable them to care adequately for their own children has been an ongoing struggle since at least 1935 with the enactment of Title IV of the Social Security Act (McGowan, 2005). However, attempts to aim resources directly to the families have historically been assailed by more conservative lawmakers and have been scaled in favor of foster care.

The Child Abuse Prevention and Treatment Act (CAPTA) is a good illustration of how child welfare dollars are allocated in accordance with this tradition. While the name implies a program that would provide treatment and preventative services to keep children safe, the provisions of the original and revised legislation are more focused on reporting requirements. Indeed, the program is chronically underfunded and funding is provided to states to enforce mandatory reporting systems. Funding was not provided for the titles of the bill aimed at "child abuse prevention or treatment." In this way, the federal government takes measures to ensure child safety that do not include supporting vulnerable families—even though this seemed to be the original intent of the legislation (Mallon & Hess, 2005).

Recommendations

Without adequate tools, workers feel that their ability to do social work is compromised and as a result, they leave the field (Ellett, 2000). If the child welfare system could expand the toolbox for workers, it would not only enable them to act in a more ethical manner, but would increase their self-efficacy—and perhaps their retention rates. This finding could go a long way to convince the child welfare policy-makers to expand access to resources for workers and, as a result, the families who need them.

Suggestions for Future Research

In light of recent research suggesting that low self-efficacy scores among child welfare workers are correlated with high intent to leave the workforce (Ellett, 2000; Schene, 2003), Bandura's work on self-efficacy enables us to better understand the extent of this mismatch upon frontline workers and particularly social workers.

Bandura's theory of self-efficacy, in which he postulates that individuals gravitate toward situations about which they feel competent and avoid those about which they do not (1997) might provide an appropriate framework to understand how the lack of appropriate tools affects the desire to remain in child welfare. These findings coupled with research by Ellett (2000), demonstrating that low self-efficacy scores among child welfare workers indicate high intentions to leave the workforce, raise concerns about the potential impact of this kind of resource deficit on child welfare workforce retention.

Conclusion

It is not and should not be the responsibility of the child welfare system to solve all of the problems of vulnerable families. However, because there is abundant evidence that the child welfare system is indeed a catch-all bureaucracy, resources must more closely match the pressing needs of families. Gambrill (2008) recommends that the best way to improve decisionmaking and overall clinical practice in child welfare is to emphasize exposing the gaps between what is done and what is needed in child welfare.

In order to raise awareness of this mismatch, Gambrill suggests a "State-of-the-Gap" report be issued annually by clients, staff, and others and be widely disseminated. Regrettably, this article is not Gambrill's State-of-the-Gap Report. Instead, it attempts to illuminate the mismatch between needs and services, offer an explanation for the existence of this gap, and demonstrate how the persistent inability of child welfare policymakers to match resources to needs deals constant ethical dilemmas to frontline workers.

Absent serious and sustained efforts to erase the mismatch between resource allocation at the federal level and family problems that place children at risk, child welfare we must admit defeat and lower the expectations of what it can reasonably do. This, of course, is not an attractive option—not to policy makers, street-level bureaucrats, or the American public. Americans must find a means by which to create a smarter, more ethical child welfare system or the foster care crisis will surely persist. Otherwise street-level bureaucrats will continue to function in a system that is rife with dilemmas by design.

References

Bandura, A. (1997). *Self-efficacy: the exercise of control.* New York: W.H. Freeman.

Barbell, K. & Freundlich, M. (2001). *Foster care today.* Washington, DC: Casey Family Programs.

Barth, R.P. (1999). Risks and rates of disruption. In Pierce, W. & Marshner. C. *Adoption factbook III.* Washington, DC: National Committee for Adoption, 381-392.

Blome, W. (1996). Reasonable efforts, unreasonable effects: A retrospective analysis of the "reasonable efforts" clause in the Adoption Assistance and Child Welfare Act of 1980. *Journal of Sociology and Social Welfare, XXIII* (3), 133-150.

Britner, P.A. & Mossler, D.G. (2002). Professionals' decision-making about out-of-home placements following instances of child abuse. *Child Abuse and Neglect, 26,* 317-332.

Bronfenbrenner, U. (1979). *The ecology of human development: experiments by nature and design.* Cambridge, Mass.: Harvard University Press.

Chambers, R.M. & Potter, C.C. (2008). The match between family needs and services in high-needs neglecting families. *Journal of Public Child Welfare, 2* (2), 229-253.

Child Abuse and Treatment Act of 1990, Title III, "Certain Preventive Services Regarding Children of Homeless Families or Families at Risk of Homelessness" as amended by the Stewart B. McKinney Homeless Assistance Act Amendments of 1990 (P.L. 101-645, 11/29/90) (repealed by the Child Abuse Prevention and Treatment Act Amendments of 1996 [P.L. 104-235, 10/3/96]).

Child Welfare League of America. (2003). Recommended Caseload Standards. Retrieved March 15, 2008: http://www.cwla.org/newsevents/news030304cwlacaseload.htm.

Children's Bureau. (2004). Reports and results from the Child and Family Services Reviews. Retrieved August 13, 2009, from http://basis.caliber.com/cwig/ws/cwmd/docs/cb_web/SearchForm.

Courtney, M.E., McMurtry, S.L., & Zinn, A. (2004). Housing experiences of recipients of child welfare services. *Child Welfare, 83* (5), 393-422.

Day, P. (2000). Values in social welfare. In P. Day (ed.), *A new history of social welfare.* 3rd ed. (1-29). Boston: Allyn and Bacon.

DePanfilis, D. (2000). How do I determine if a child has been neglected? In H. Dubowitz & D. DePanfilis (Eds.), *Handbook for child protection practice* (121-126). Thousand Oaks, CA: Sage.

Doerre, Y.A. & Mihaly, L.K. (1996). *Home sweet home.* Washington, DC: CWLA Press.

Dolgoff, R., Loewenberg, F.M., & Harrington, D. (2005). *Ethical decisions for social work practice.* 7th ed. Belmont, CA: Brooks/Cole.

Doueck, H., English, D.J., DePanfilis, D., & Moote, G.T. (1993). Decision-making in child protective services: A comparison of selected risk-assessment systems. *Child Welfare, LXXII* (5), 441-452.

Drake, B., & Pandy, S. (1996). Understanding the relationship between neighborhood poverty and specific types of child maltreatment. *Child Abuse and Neglect, 20* (11), 1003-1018.

Doyle, J. (2007). Child protection and child outcomes: Measuring the effects of foster care. *American Economic Review, 97* (5), 1583-1610.

Ellett, A. J. (2000). *Human caring, self-efficacy beliefs, and professional organizational culture: correlates of employee retention in child welfare.* Baton Rouge, LA: Louisiana State University and Agricultural and Mechanical College.

Fantuzzo, J., Stevenson, H., Abdul Kabir, S., & Perry, M. (2007). An investigation of a community-based intervention for socially isolated parents with a history of child maltreatment. *Journal of Family Violence, 22,* 81-89.

Folaron, G. & Hostetter, C. (2007). Is social work the best educational degree for child welfare practitioners? *Journal of Public Child Welfare, 1* (1), 65-83.

Gambrill, E. (2008). Decision making in child welfare: Constraints and potentials. In D. Lindsey & A. Shlonsky (Eds.), *Child welfare research: advances for practice and policy* (175-193). New York: Oxford.

Geen, R. (2001). *Child welfare finance.* Washington D C: Urban Institute.

Gonzalez, R.P., Faller, K.C., Ortega, R.M., & Tropman, J. (2009) Exit interviews with departed child welfare workers: Preliminary findings. *Journal of Public Child Welfare, 3* (1), 40-63.

Hess, P.M., Folaron, G. & Jefferson, A.B. (1992). Effectiveness of family reunification services: An innovative evaluative model. *Social Work, 37* (4), 304-311.

Improving Child Welfare: Hearings before the Subcommittee on Income Security and Family Support of the Ways and Means Committee, 110th Cong. (2005a) (testimony of Lupe Tovar).

Improving Child Welfare: Hearings before the Subcommittee on Income Security and Family Support of the Ways and Means Committee, 110th Cong. (2005b) (testimony of Jim Purcell).

Kadushin, Alfred & Martin, Judith A. (1988). *Child welfare services* (4th ed.). New York Macmillan, 1988.

Kinney, J. M., Madsen, B., Fleming, T., & Haapala, D. A. (1977). Homebuilders: Keeping families together. *Journal of Consulting and Clinical Psychology, 45,* 667-673.

Lieberman, A.A., Hornby, H., & Russell, M. (1988). Analyzing the educational backgrounds and work experiences of child welfare personnel: A national study. *Social Work, 33,* 485-489.

Lindsey, D. (1994). *The welfare of children.* New York: Oxford University Press.

Lipsky, M. (1980). *Street-level bureaucracy: dilemmas of the individual in public services.* New York: Russell-Sage Foundation.

Mallon, G. & Hess, P. (Eds.). (2005). *Child welfare for the 21st century: a handbook of practices, policies, and programs.* New York: Columbia University Press.

Maluccio, A. N., Fein, E., & Davis, I.P. (1994). Family reunification: research findings, issues, and directions. *Child Welfare, LXXIII* (5), 489-504.

McDermott, J. (2008). Opening Statement Before the Subcommittee on Income Security and Family Support of the House Committee on Ways and Means U.S. House of Representatives, February 27, 2008. Retrieved: http://waysandmeans.house.gov/hearings.asp?formmode=view&id=6789.

McGowan, B.G. (2005). Historical evolution of child welfare services. In *Child welfare for the twentieth-first century: a handbook of practices, policies, and programs.* G. Mallon & P. Hess. (Eds.) (10-46). New York: Columbia University Press.

Mulroy, E.A. & Lauber, H. (2004). A user-friendly approach to program evaluation and effective community interventions for families at risk of homelessness. *Social Work 49* (4), 573-586.

National Association of Social Workers. (2005). *NASW Standards for Social Work Practice in Child Welfare.* Retrieved March 11, 2008: http://www.socialworkers.org/practice/standards/NASWChildWelfareStandards0905.pdf.

National Association of Social Workers. (1999). *Code of Ethics.* Washington, DC: Author.

Pelton, L. (2008). Informing child welfare: The promise and limits of empirical research. In D. Lindsey and A. Shlonsky (Eds.), *Child welfare research: Advances for practice and policy* (pp. 25-48). New York: Oxford University Press.

Pelton, L. (1989) *For reasons of poverty: a critical analysis of the public child welfare system in the United States.* New York: Praeger.

Pew Commission on Children in Foster Care (2004), *Time for reform: executive summary.* Retrieved: http://pewfostercare.org/research/docs/journey.pdf.

Reamer, F. (1994). *The philosophical foundations of social work.* New York: Columbia University Press.

Rein, M. (1971). "Welfare and Housing," Joint Center Working Series Number 4, Spring Issue. Cambridge, MA: Joint Center for Urban Studies.

Rodenborg, N.A. (2004). Services to African American children in poverty: Institutional discrimination in child welfare. *Journal of Poverty, 8* (3), 109-130.

Russell, J. (2006). *Double standard: social policy in Europe and the United States.* Lanham, MD: Rowman & Littlefield.

Ryan, J. & Schuerman, J. (2004). Matching family problems with specific family preservation services: A study of service effectiveness. *Children and Youth Services Review 26,* 347-372.

Ryan, T., Wiles, D., Cash, S., & Siebert, C. (2005). Rick assessments: Empirically supported or values driven? *Children and Youth Services Review, 27* (2), 213-225.

Rycus, J. & Hughes, R. (1998). *Field guide to child welfare: foundation of child protective services, volume I.* Washington, DC: Child Welfare League of America Press.

Schene, P. & Associates. (March 2003). *Analysis of models of assessment: first interim report for statewide assessment approach project.*

Scannapieco, M. & Connell-Carrick, K. (2005). *Understanding child maltreatment: an ecological and developmental perspective.* New York: Oxford University Press.

Sedlak, A. J., & Broadhurst, D. D. (1996). *Third national incidence study of child abuse and neglect (NIS-3).* Washington, DC: U.S. Department of Health and Human Services, National Center on Child Abuse and Neglect.

Shdaimah, C. (2009). Rescuing children and punishing poor families: Housing related decisions. *Journal of Sociology & Social Welfare, XXXVI* (3), 33-57.

Smith, B. D. (2005). Job retention in child welfare: Efforts of perceived organizational support, supervisor support, and intrinsic job value. *Children and Youth Services Review, 27*, 153–169.

Stoetz, D. 2008. Heeding Horton: Transcending the child welfare paradigm. In D. Lindsey and A. Shlonsky (Eds.), *Child welfare research: advances for practice and policy* (pp. 25-48). New York: Oxford University Press.

U.S. Department of Health and Human Services (2005). *Federal Foster Care Financing: How and Why the Current Financing System Fails to Meet the Needs of the Child Welfare System.*

U.S. Department of Health and Human Services (1997). *National Study of Protective, Preventive, and Reunification Services Delivered to Children and their Families.* Washington, DC: U.S. Government Printing Office.

U.S. Department of Health and Human Services, Children's Bureau. (2003). *The AFCARS Report #8.* Retrieved April 29, 2008: www.acf.dhhs.gov/programs/cb/publications/afcars/report8.htm.

U.S. Department of Health and Human Services (2012). *Child Maltreatment 2011.* Washington, D.C.: U.S. Government Printing Office.

Watkins-Hayes, C. (2009). *America's new welfare bureaucrats.* Chicago: University of Chicago Press.

Wulczyn, F. Barth, R.P., Yuan, Y.T., Harden, B.J., & Landsverk (2005). *Beyond common sense: child welfare, child wellbeing, and the evidence for policy reform.* Chicago: Chapin Hall Center for Children.

Appendix 1
Amicus Curiae Brief of the Society of Catholic Social Scientists in *Troxel v. Granville*

No. 99-138

♦

In The
Supreme Court of the United States

JENIFER TROXEL, et vir,

Petitioners,

TOMMIE GRANVILLE,

Respondent.

♦

On Writ Of Certiorari
To The Supreme Court Of Washington

♦

BRIEF *AMICUS CURIAE* OF THE
SOCIETY OF CATHOLIC SOCIAL SCIENTISTS
IN SUPPORT OF RESPONDENT

♦

Stephen M. Krason
President, Society of
   Catholic Social Scientists
Counsel of Record
Franciscan University
Franciscan Way
Steubenville, OH 43952
(740) 283-6416

Richard W. Garnett
Assistant Professor of Law
Notre Dame Law School
Notre Dame, IN 46556
(219) 631-6981

i

TABLE OF CONTENTS

Page

TABLE OF AUTHORITIES

Page

iii

TABLE OF AUTHORITIES – Continued

Page

TABLE OF AUTHORITIES – Continued

Page

TABLE OF AUTHORITIES – Continued

TABLE OF AUTHORITIES – Continued

1

INTEREST OF THE *AMICUS CURIAE*[1]

The Society of Catholic Social Scientists ("SCSS") respectfully submits this *amicus curiae* brief in support of the Respondent, Tommie Granville. We believe the question presented in this case has serious implications for American law and public policy relating to the rights of parents, the integrity of the family, the freedom of religion, and the powers of government.

SCSS is an interdisciplinary association of Catholic social scientists. Its purposes are to pursue and produce knowledge about the social order; to evaluate contemporary social-science work in light of Catholic social teachings; to apply these teachings to the challenges posed by modern society; to encourage distinctively Catholic scholarship in the social sciences; and, where appropriate, to put the tools of social science at the service of the Church's evangelizing mission. These purposes reflect and respond to Pope Pius XI's call over 50 years ago for "the building up of a true Catholic social science." Pope Pius XI, *Reconstructing the Social Order* 19-20 (1931).

The SCSS publishes the only interdisciplinary Catholic social-science journal in North America – *The Catholic Social Science Review* – as well as other research-oriented

---

[1] The parties have consented to the filing of this *amicus curiae* brief. Letters to this effect have been filed with the Clerk of the Court. Counsel for a party did not author this brief in whole or in part. No person or entity, other than the *amicus curiae*, its members, or its counsel, made a monetary contribution to the preparation and submission of this brief. *See* S. Ct. Rule 37.6.

2

publications;[2] sponsors periodic conferences and symposia; issues statements and papers on important social and political questions; recognizes and awards outstanding contributions to a distinctively Catholic approach to the social sciences; and assists students who are interested in integrating social-science careers with the faith and tradition of the Catholic Church.

SCSS is particularly interested in protecting, through research, scholarship, and advocacy, the dignity and rights of the family. This commitment reflects the Catholic Church's position that the family is "the first and vital cell of society" and that "[i]t is from the family that citizens come to birth and . . . find the first school of the social virtues that are the animating principle of the existence and development of society itself." Vatican Council II, *Decree on the Apostolate of Lay People* 11 (1965). We follow the Catholic Church – and the precedents of this Court – in believing that it is "a grave and pernicious error" to think that government "should at its option intrude into and exercise control over the family" and in holding that such intervention is justified only when "there occur grave disturbances of mutual rights." Pope Leo XIII, *The Condition of Labor* 14 (1891). It is, in other words, a fundamental principle both of Catholic social teaching and of constitutional law that "the child is not the mere creature of the state." *Pierce v. Society of Sisters*, 268 U.S. 510, 535 (1925); *see also, e.g., Catechism of the Catholic Church* Sec. 2202 (The family is "prior to any recognition by public authority").

———————◆———————

[2] *See, e.g.,* Stephen M. Krason & Paul C. Vitz, *Defending the Family: A Sourcebook* (1998).

3

SUMMARY OF THE ARGUMENT

The fundamental rights of parents to direct and control the upbringing of their children and the autonomy of the family have been recognized time and again by this Court. These rights and this autonomy are not creatures of positive law, but are grounded in the natural moral order. The family is the "building block" of civil society and has as its natural end, or *telos*, the nurturing and development of flourishing human persons and good citizens. Given this natural purpose, the rights of the family and of parents to pursue this end must be respected and protected by public authority. In particular, government must not disrupt, intervene in, or second-guess parents' decisions about child-rearing except in grave cases where it is necessary to prevent real harm.

The history of our Nation's various child-welfare, or "child saving" movements serve as a warning against excessive government intrusion into parents' decisions, even when such intrusion purports to be motivated by noble goals. There is always the danger that religious, ethnic, cultural, or class-based prejudice will color the "experts' " view of the "best interests" of the child and of parents' competence. Such prejudice clearly tainted the efforts of the early juvenile-justice reformers. In addition, the current sensationalism surrounding the problem of child neglect and the abuses of the child-neglect-reporting system during the last thirty years provide further basis for caution when it comes to second-guessing parents in the name of "child protection." Given what we know about the costs of, and harm caused by, overzealous intrusion in the family and unsubstantiated reports of abuse, this is certainly not the time for this Court to in

4

any way undermine the *fundamental* nature of parents' constitutional rights.

————————◆————————

ARGUMENT

I.

The Government Should Not Second-Guess or Interfere with the Decisions of Competent, Non-abusive Parents Concerning the Education, Upbringing, and Welfare of Their Children.

This Court has held and re-affirmed that the rights of parents to direct and control the upbringing of their children without unjustified intrusion or oversight by the State are fundamental and sit at the heart of the "liberty" protected by the Fourteenth Amendment's Due Process Clause. As this Court observed in *Wisconsin v. Yoder*, 406 U.S. 205, 232 (1972), "[t]he history and culture of Western Civilization reflect a strong tradition of parental concern for the nurture and upbringing of their children. This primary role of the parents in the upbringing of the children is now established beyond debate as an enduring American tradition." Indeed, parents' rights and family autonomy are not merely "enduring American tradition[s]," but are "essential, basic rights of man." *Stanley v. Illinois*, 405 U.S. 645, 651 (1972). It is therefore "cardinal . . . that the custody, care and nurture of the child reside first in the parents, whose primary function and freedom include preparation for obligations the state can neither supply nor hinder." *Ibid.; see generally, e.g., Meyer v. Nebraska*, 262 U.S. 390 (1923); *Pierce v. Society of*

5

Sisters, 268 U.S. 510 (1925); *Prince v. Massachusetts*, 321 U.S. 158 (1944); *Santosky v. Kramer*, 455 U.S. 745 (1982).

We believe that the constitutional pedigree of parents' rights are well established, as is the rule that any law that infringes on these rights must be narrowly tailored to serve a compelling state interest. In this *amicus curiae* brief, we hope to assist the Court by focusing on *foundational* arguments that are consonant with, and provide additional support to, the relevant constitutional principles.

A. The Foundations of Parents' Rights.

Common sense and human experience reveal that parents' responsibility for and right to direct the upbringing of their children are not merely conventions, but are grounded in the natural order of things. *See, e.g., Catechism of the Catholic Church* Sec. 2207 ("The family is the *original cell of social life.*") (emphasis in original). These objective facts supply parents with the moral right to exercise their authority – within the limits of reason and morality – free from unwarranted interference by outsiders, including government. *See id.,* at Sec. 2209 ("[L]arger communities should take care not to usurp the family's prerogatives or interfere in its life."); *see also, e.g.,* John Locke, *Two Treatises of Government* 348-49 (Peter Laslett ed., 1960) (3d ed. 1698) ("The power . . . that parents have over their children arises from that duty which is incumbent on them, to take care of their offspring during the imperfect state of childhood.").

These claims are neither novel nor sectarian. Philosophers have long recognized that the family is the fundamental "building block" of human society: "Nature has

6

instituted this small but fundamental group, first of the natural societies and the most basic unit of the state, for the purpose of reproducing the human species." Rafael T. Waters, "The Basis for the Traditional Rights and Responsibilities of Parents," *in* Stephen M. Krason & Robert J. D'Agosino, eds., *Parental Rights: The Contemporary Assault on Traditional Liberties* 20 (1988). Moreover, "the family is the necessary productive unit requiring the complementary abilities, personalities, and contributions of both parents so that the child can learn and develop habits . . . and moral virtues." *Id.*, at 22. The purpose, or *telos*, of the family imposes duties upon parents to accept and exercise responsibility for the process of producing – of *creating* – new persons and new members of civil society. *Id.*, at 22-23; *see also Smith v. Organization of Foster Families*, 431 U.S. 816, 844 (1977) (Constitution protects the integrity of the family because of "the role it plays in 'promoting a way of life' through the instruction of children"). This end toward which the family – the primary natural association – is directed is the basis for the moral rights and responsibilities of parents.[3]

Parents' natural moral duties, obligations, and responsibilities carry with them moral rights which the state is obligated to respect and protect. This is because the imposition of a moral duty on a person requires permitting that person to comply with it, and one person's enjoyment of a moral right imposes a duty on other

---

[3] On the notion that the natural *telos* or "end" of a thing is the lodestar for moral claims *about* that thing, *see, e.g.*, Aristotle, *The Nicomachean Ethics* Book VII, c.8, 1115a; St. Thomas Aquinas, *Summa Theologica* I-II, q. 90, a.1.

persons to respect that right. *See* Pope John XXIII, *Peace on Earth* 28-29 (1963); Thomas J. Higgins, *Man As Man: The Science and Art of Ethics* 226-227 (1992); *see also Parham v. J.R.*, 442 U.S. 584, 602 (1979) ("[O]ur constitutional system . . . [has] asserted that parents generally have the right, coupled with the high duty, to recognize and prepare [their children] for additional obligations.") (citations and internal quotation marks omitted). Parents' rights, then, are grounded in the fact that their natural moral obligations "cannot be met without the possession of rights with respect to other members of the community." Waters, *supra*, at 25.

Again, the natural purpose of the family, and therefore the obligation of parents, is to create, shape, and nurture new members of the human family and the civic community. Parents and families are not only morally entitled, but are *by nature* better able, to carry out these tasks than is any other entity or institution:

> The mutual love of the parents, the aid they can give to each other and the intimacies they share, are all a proper climate for the [child]. . . . The struggle for its due completion which every being seeks . . . is culminated best in family life where there exist two people who love the offspring, more than anyone else can, by a deeply ingrained attitude established in the nature of the parents. . . . His parents love him more than . . . the state possibly could love him. Therefore, they are best fitted to supervise the development of their own offspring.

Waters, *supra*, at 26-27; *see also Parham*, 442 U.S. at 602 ("[H]istorically it has been recognized that natural bonds of affection lead parents to act in the best interests of

8

their children.") (citations omitted).[4] This common-sense fact is not surprising. *See Smith*, 431 U.S. at 844 (noting the "emotional attachments that derive from the intimacy of daily association"). As Pope John Paul II has observed, "public agencies . . . are dominated more by bureaucratic ways than by concern for serving their clients. . . . It would appear that needs are best understood and satisfied by people who are closest to them." Pope John Paul II, *The Hundredth Year* 48 (1991).

It follows that the state violates a fundamental moral principle, upsets the proper ordering of civil society, and undermines the natural end of the family when it substitutes its judgment for parents', except where absolutely necessary, in special and difficult circumstances. *See Catechism of the Catholic Church* Sec. 2209 ("The family must be helped and defended by appropriate social measures. *Where families cannot fulfill their responsibilities,* other social bodies have the duty of helping them and of supporting the institution of the family."). This is the heart of the principle of *subsidiarity,* which holds that "[i]t is an injustice and at the same time a grave evil and disturbance of right order to assign to a greater and higher association what lesser and subordinate organizations can do." Pope Pius XI, *supra,* at 79; *see also* E.F. Schumacher, *Small is Beautiful: Economics as if People Mattered* 244

---

[4] These are, obviously, general principles. *Of course* it is true that *some* parents may be unable or unsuitable to raise their children, but this fact does not undermine the suitability and rights of parents, as a general matter, to direct and control the upbringing of their children.

9

(1973).[5] The subsidiarity principle applies to family-state relations as well as to relations between different levels of government: "Following the principle of subsidiarity, larger communities should take care not to usurp the family's prerogatives or interfere in its life." *Catechism of the Catholic Church* Sec. 2209.

Not only do parents enjoy a superior right to the state in raising their own children, they must enjoy such a right with respect to private third parties – even well-meaning, capable, and loving third parties. Even extended family members do not share the same natural intimacy with children that parents do. The bond between children and their extended family is, of course, real and precious and – all things being equal – this bond should be cultivated and nurtured. But this bond is simply not interchangeable, either in biology or in moral right, with that between parents and their children. The integrity of the family and the rights of parents are fundamental, objective, and natural facts, and the state should set itself against them only in cases of the gravest need.

---

[5] This principle of subsidiarity overlaps considerably with and promotes many of the same goods as does our constitutional federal system of dual sovereignty. *See, e.g.,* W. Gary Vause, "The Subsidiarity Principle in European Union Law – American Federalism Compared," 27 Case W. Res. J. Int'l L. 61 (1995); George A. Bermann, "Taking Subsidiarity Seriously: Federalism in the European Community and the United States," 94 Colum. L. Rev. 331 (1994).

B. The History and Tradition of Parents' Rights.

The philosophical arguments sketched above have been embraced in our legal tradition. It is well established that "parental rights were ardently upheld at common law." John W. Whitehead, *Parents' Rights* 85 (1985). Indeed, "the common law recognized parental rights as a key concept . . . [and viewed] the family as a basic social, economic, and political unit"; parental rights were "even more fundamental than property rights." Bruce C. Hafen, "Children's Liberation and the New Egalitarianism: Some Reservations About Abandoning Youth to Their 'Rights,' " 1976 B.Y.U. L. Rev. 605, 615. As one court proclaimed, nearly 150 years ago:

> No teacher . . . has any authority over the child, except what he derives from its parent or guardian; and that authority may be withdrawn whenever the parent, in the exercise of his discretionary power, may think proper. . . . The doctrines of the common law are in accordance with these principles. It is the duty of the parent to maintain and educate the child, and he possesses the resulting authority to control it in all things necessary to the accomplishment of the parent over the child, except that it must not be exercised in such a manner as to endanger its safety or morals.

Commonwealth v. Armstrong, 1 Pa. L.J. Rep. 393, 395-397 (1842). In our legal tradition, parents' rights have long been recognized as "inherent, natural right[s], for the protection of which, just as much as for the protection of the rights of the individual to life, liberty, and the pursuit of happiness, our government is formed." *Lacher v. Venus*, 188 N.W. 613, 617 (Wis. 1922). This longstanding

11

solicitude for parents' rights does *not*, we submit, simply reflect a notion of children-as-property,[6] but rather a commitment to the role of the family as the fundamental and autonomous unit of civil society, within which parents and their authority are protected precisely in order that they may discharge their obligations to their children *and to the greater common good*.

It is important to recognize in this regard that our tradition, while committed to preserving family autonomy, rejected the extreme position taken in more ancient legal systems – in particular, the Roman doctrine of *paterfamilias* – which gave fathers complete control over the life and death of their children. As Blackstone put it, "[t]he power of a parent, by our English laws, is much more moderate; but still sufficient to keep the child in order and obedience. He may *lawfully* correct his child, being under age, *in a reasonable manner*; for this is for the benefit of his education." 1 William Blackstone, *Commentaries on the Laws of England* 440 (Oxford Reprint 1966). That said, American courts for most of our history recognized that "[p]arental power . . . is essentially plenary. This means it should prevail over the claims of the state, other outsiders, and the children themselves 'unless there is some compelling justification for interference.' " Whitehead, *supra*, at 91-92.

---

6 *Cf.* Barbara B. Woodhouse, "Who Owns the Child: *Meyer* and *Pierce* and the Child as Property," 33 Wm. & Mary L. Rev. 995, 997 (1992) ("*Meyer* and *Pierce* constitutionalized a narrow, tradition-bound vision of the child as essentially private property.").

12

The traditional rationale and foundation for the respect accorded parents' rights in our constitutional tradition reflects not only the Framers' libertarian commitment to natural, individual rights, but also their republican recognition that the family is the basis for society and the seed-bed of civic virtue. *See* Higgins, *supra*, at 428 (The family is the "the cell of society, biologically and morally; that is, future citizens are prepared for life in society by the family . . . [T]he family is first among natural societies."). It is families, and not de-contextualized, atomistic individuals, that contribute most meaningfully to civil society, because individual citizens' identities, morality, and consciousness originate in, and are nurtured by, the family.

These claims accord not only with Catholic teaching but with Western traditions generally. Aristotle identified the importance of the family to the creation of civic virtue and political well-being over 2,300 years ago. And, as was suggested above, this ancient, foundational commitment to family integrity – grounded in the natural law – continued in our common-law and constitutional traditions. *See generally* Edward S. Corwin, "The 'Higher Law' Background of American Constitutional Law," 42 Harv. L. Rev. 149 (1928); Russell Kirk, *The Roots of American Order* (1974) (outlining roots of America's constitutional heritage in the ancient and medieval natural-law traditions).

It is, of course, not this Court's task to expound and apply the natural law. But this Court's properly limited role does not detract from the historical fact that natural-law principles and reasoning were absorbed into our Constitution's guarantees and into the claims of the Declaration of Independence. And as they were absorbed,

13

they were refined. This Court need not be concerned that, because of their natural-law basis, parents' rights are vague, subjective, or nonjusticiable. They are not. The deeply rooted, traditional protections accorded parents' rights and family integrity are well-established, and their outlines no less clear than those of the other fundamental rights protected by the Constitution.

*   *   *

We believe that the decision of the Washington Supreme Court below, which resoundingly held that the "family entity is the core element upon which modern civilization is founded" (Pet. 14a), and therefore that "the state may interfere [with the constitutional right to rear one's child and the right to family privacy] only 'if it appears that parental decisions will jeopardize the health or safety of the child, or have a potential for significant social burdens,' *Yoder*, 406 U.S. at 234" (Pet. 17a), was correct and should be affirmed. We have attempted to show that our commitment to the integrity, dignity, and autonomy of the family as the fundamental unit of civil society, charged with the solemn duty of producing well formed citizens and human persons, is one that coheres fully with and has been embraced by this Nation's legal traditions.

II.

Parents' Rights and Family Integrity Are Being Undermined by Certain Trends in Contemporary American Law and Policy and This Court Should Therefore Reaffirm That These Rights Are Fundamental.

Because parents' rights to direct the upbringing of their children are fundamental, any States' laws that limit

14

these rights must undergo strict judicial scrutiny. We agree with the Washington Supreme Court that the broad third-party visitation laws at issue here cannot survive this Court's review.[7] In what follows, we attempt to bring to this Court's attention certain social trends that make all the more crucial a clear re-affirmation of the fundamental nature of the rights this Court vindicated in *Pierce, supra,* and *Meyer, supra.*[8]

A. The *Parens Patriae* Doctrine and the "Child Savers."

The rights of parents have never been *absolute* in our tradition. *See generally,* Allan C. Carlson, *Family Questions: Reflections on the American Social Crisis* 242 (1988) ("[A]longside th[e] affirmation of parental rights, the law also recognized the power of the courts to intervene into families and take away children in order to the protect the interests of the larger community."). As the court below recognized, family integrity is subject to the state's

---

[7] We do not believe this Court needs to decide whether a more cautious and less intrusive "grandparent-visitation" law could survive strict scrutiny.

[8] Some commentators have suggested that *Pierce* and *Meyer,* and the fundamental rights they upheld, are no longer useful in today's society. *See, e.g.,* Abner S. Greene, "Why Vouchers Are Unconstitutional, and Why They're Not," 3 Notre Dame J. of Law, Ethics, and Pub. Pol'y 397 (1999); Stephen Arons, "The Separation of School and State: *Pierce* Reconsidered," 46 Harv. Educ. Rev. 76 (1976). We reject the dangerously statist implications of such claims.

15

police and *parens patriae* powers (Pet. 15a-16a).[9] These powers, when judiciously exercised in pursuit of the common good, need not undermine parents' rights. But this Court has emphasized that, precisely because of the central importance of family integrity, the state may exercise these powers only when necessary to redress or prevent real *harm* to a child. *See* Pet. 16a (citing *Yoder*, 406 U.S. at 206).

The *parens patriae* power is *not* a license for re-shaping society by second-guessing parents. We believe that certain excesses in the exercise of the *parens patriae* power today threaten parents' rights and, more broadly, the integrity, privacy, and well-being of families. These excesses – committed in the name of protecting children – have often, in fact, harmed children, not simply by exposing them to the nightmare of arbitrary government action but also by impairing their natural development, removing them from their families, and undercutting their parents' authority.

History cautions against using the *parens patriae* power to justify excessive state intervention. In the American colonial period, some local courts, following English practice, intervened in family affairs and even removed children from their parents if these courts found the

---

[9] The phrase *parens patriae* literally means "parent of the country." *See generally* Douglas R. Rendleman, "*Parens Patriae*: From Chancery to The Juvenile Court," 23 S.C. L. Rev. 205 (1970). The doctrine initially developed in medieval chancery courts. It was first used in an American court in the case of *Ex Parte Crouse*, 4 Whart. 9 (Pa. 1838), where the court used the term to justify the continued detention of a girl in a "House of Refuge" over the objections of her father.

16

parents unfit or decided that the children were not being raised in an approved manner. *See generally* Michael D. Rosenbaum, "To Break the Shell Without Scrambling the Egg: An Empirical Analysis of the Impact of Intervention Into Violent Families," 9 Stan. L. & Pol'y Rev. 409, 411 (1998) ("[L]ocal authorities had the authority to remove abused children from parental guardianship, a right to act against parents on behalf of children derived from the medieval doctrine of *parens patriae*."); Carlson, *supra*, at 242 (describing 1646 statute enacted by Virginia's House of Burgesses that authorized taking children from parents to work in flax houses). In a similar vein, the 19th Century reform-school movement promoted laws which removed delinquent or "ill-treated" children from their usually urban homes to rural reform schools. The families targeted for the "benefit" of the state's attention were typically poor immigrants. As in colonial New England, the state was viewed by some as an appropriate mechanism for re-shaping family life in the interest of a more homogenous common good. *See generally, e.g.,* Carlson, *supra*, at 243 ("The reform school movement which swept the nation during the nineteenth century represented a bonding of traditional values to coercive social engineering."); Sanford J. Fox, "Juvenile Justice Reform: A Historical Perspective," 22 Stanford L. Rev. 1187, 1206-1209 (1970); Anthony M. Platt, *The Child Savers: The Invention of Delinquency* 44-49 (1969).

The often oppressive "child saving" movement gained its strength from the *parens patriae* doctrine, which was invoked to justify removing children from their parents – with minimal procedural protections – whenever they were judged unworthy to rear their children. *See generally*, Platt, *supra*, at 3-4, 98-99; Susan R. Bell, Comment, "Ohio Gets Tough on Juvenile Crime: An Analysis Of Ohio's 1996 Amendments Concerning the Bindover Of Violent Juvenile Offenders to the Adult System and Related Legislation," 66 U. Cinn. L. Rev. 207, 208-209 (1998) ("These civic-minded 'child savers' had a two fold agenda that included 'instilling proper civic and moral values' in these children and 'mitigat[ing] the law's often harsh treatment of children.' ") (internal citations omitted). The child-saving movement spurred the development of juvenile courts, which were given the authority to remove children from their parents' care if they determined the children were "probable delinquents." Again, it was mostly children from immigrant, poor, and various minority communities who were targeted. *See* Fox, *supra*, at 1221-1228; Mason P. Thomas, Jr., "Child Abuse and Neglect Part I: Historical Overview, Legal Matrix, and Social Perspectives," 50 N.C. L. Rev. 293, 323-325 (1972).

The stated methodology of the early juvenile justice courts was therapeutic: parents and children were "clients" and the "the best interests of the child" was the guiding principle. In truth, though, the child-saving movement and its courts were coercive, and sought to reshape their "clients" along the lines of an ideal notion of the American family as determined by middle-class social workers and juvenile court judges. Later, they targeted not just minority groups, but all parents. *See* Carlson, *supra*, at 244-248. Not surprisingly, the "child saving" movement eventually came under criticism, and the juvenile justice system became known for its procedural nightmares, arbitrariness, and cruelty. Indeed, in

1870 the Illinois Supreme Court ruled that, notwithstanding the State's invocation of the *parens patriae* power, the constitutional rights of a 14-year old boy who had been committed to Chicago's reform school were violated: "The State, as *parens patriae*, has determined the imprisonment beyond recall. Such a restraint upon natural liberty is tyranny and oppression." *People ex rel. O'Connell v. Turner*, 55 Ill. 280, 287 (1870). Importantly, the Illinois court grounded its decision in the observation that "[t]he parent has the right to the care, custody, and assistance of his child[.] . . . The duty to maintain and protect it is a principle of natural law. . . . Before any abridgement of the right, gross misconduct or almost total unfitness . . . should be clearly proved." *Ibid.*

Eventually, policy-makers awakened to the danger of using coercive state power, and removing children from their parents, simply to homogenize society in accord with middle-class Protestant norms. Carlson, *supra,* at 249-250; *see* Eric K. Klein, Note, "Dennis the Menace or Billy the Kid: An Analysis of the Role of Transfer to Criminal Court in Juvenile Justice," 35 Am. Cr. L. Rev. 371, 377 (1998) ("[W]hile it was hoped that the courts would protect delinquent children and serve their best interest, because of the lack of procedural protections, children accused of crimes or even status offenses were often being arbitrarily and unfairly punished."). The abuses and injustices of this system were only halted – or at least curbed – by this Court's landmark decision, *In re Gault*, 387 U.S. 1 (1967), which condemned much of the theory and practice of the "child savers" and their courts. *Id.*, at 16. *Gault* should be read as a warning against an expansive reading of the *parens patriae* power, even when that power is being invoked by government agents, or well meaning private parties, in the service of what they assure us is a good cause.

B. Present-Day Policies Relating to Child Abuse and Neglect.

As the old, harsh juvenile justice system crumbled – or at least improved – in the wake of *In re Gault, supra,* a new avenue soon opened up for experts' "child saving" impulses. The "newly discovered" problem of child abuse, increased media attention to this issue, and the efforts of scholars, professionals, and activists led to a host of new laws relating to the reporting of and official response to child-abuse accusations. Between 1963 and 1967, every State and the District of Columbia enacted laws requiring reporting of child-abuse cases. *See* Rosenbaum, *supra,* at 412; Carlson, *supra,* at 250-251. Then, in 1974, Congress passed the Child Abuse Prevention and Treatment Act of 1974 (the "Mondale Act"), which opened the door to massive and unprecedented governmental intervention in American families. The Act's generous promises of federal grants prompted state and local governments to set up hundreds of child-protective agencies, ostensibly in response to the hitherto unremarked national epidemic of child abuse and neglect. States were encouraged by Mondale Act funds to pass sweeping statutes which, *inter alia,* required a range of professionals – and, in some States, all citizens – to report even suspicions of abuse to specialized child-protection agencies, and gave blanket immunity from prosecution or civil suit to persons making reports (even if false or exaggerated), even while making those required to report liable for failing to do so. *See generally*, Douglas J. Besharov, " 'Doing Something' About Child Abuse: The Need to Narrow the Grounds for State Intervention," 8 Harv. J. of Law and Pub. Pol'y 545 (1985). These statutes typically authorized intrusive government intervention in families and investigation of parents on the basis of vague, undefined, and persistently unclarified terms like "abuse" and "neglect." *See* Stephen M. Krason, "Child Abuse: Pseudo-Crisis, Dangerous Bureaucrats, Destroyed Families," *in* Stephen M. Krason & Robert J. D'Agostino, eds., *Parental Rights: The Contemporary Assault on Traditional Liberties* 167-173 (1988).

The Mondale Act and its progeny caused a ballooning of child-abuse and neglect reports, unprecedented state intervention into the family, and – in many high-profile cases – outright destruction of families. Indeed, it is "no coincidence that [many] spectacular child abuse cases emerged shortly after the passage of the Mondale Act, which provides huge increases in funds for child protection agencies and abuse investigators. The appearance of huge amounts of government money produced enormous increases in agencies and staff, which in turn created investigations culminating in accusations of child sex abuse on a scale never seen before." James E. Beaver, "The Myth of Repressed Memory," 86 J. Crim. L. & Criminology 596, 601 (1996) (book review); *see also* Dorothy Rabinowitz, "A Darkness in Massachusetts," Wall St. J., Jan. 30, 1995, at A20; ("That the wave of spectacular child-abuse trials emerged in the 80's was no accident. . . . With the outpouring of government money came a huge increase in agencies and staffs, which in turn begat investigations and accusations of child sex on a grand scale. An industry had been born.").

Consider these numbers: In 1963, when the first generation of (limited) abuse-reporting laws were enacted, there were 150,000 reports nationwide; by 1972, just prior to the passage of the Mondale Act, there were 610,000; in 1982 – eight years after the Act – there were 1.5 million; and by 1993, there were nearly 3 million. This is an increase of 1857% in thirty years, an increase that cannot be explained by increases in actual abuse or in a massive uncovering of secret neglect. It is now evident that many of these millions of reports were and are completely unsubstantiated. *See generally* Stephen M. Krason, "A Grave Threat to the Family: American Law and Public Policy on Child Abuse and Neglect," *in* Paul C. Vitz & Stephen M. Krason, eds., Defending the Family: A Sourcebook 235-236 (1998).

It appears, ironically, that the expansion of the government's intrusive power into the family has led to a situation even *more* dangerous for at-risk children, as the States' child-protective systems are "overburdened with cases of insubstantial or unproven risk." Besharov, *supra*, at 540; *see also* Krason, "A Grave Threat," *supra*, at 257-258. Moreover, because the post-Mondale Act statutes are often so unclear in defining "abuse" and "neglect" that estimates of the number of reports that are unfounded may *understate* the number of unfounded reports. Krason, "A Grave Threat," *supra*, at 245-250. It could well be, that is, that many perfectly acceptable

22

parental actions make up a good percentage of the "substantiated" or "founded" claims because agencies arbitrarily determined them to be abusive or neglectful. *See generally* Mary Pride, *The Child Abuse Industry* (1986); Brenda Scott, *Out of Control: Who's Watching Our Child Protection Agencies?* (1994).

The problem of false abuse reports is more than a statistical problem. Many good parents have endured legal difficulties, disruption of their family, social stigma and loss of job opportunities resulting from being placed in state child-abuse registries, loss of their children temporarily or permanently, and even imprisonment – all because of false neglect charges. These human costs are real, and provide a solid basis for caution in this area. *See generally*, Rabinowitz, *supra*; John Merline, "Who's Abusing America's Kids? All Too Often It's Those Trying to Protect Them," Investor's Bus. Daily, Sep. 5, 1995, at A1; Ruth Shalit, "Witch Hunt," The New Republic, June 19, 1995, at 14. Unfortunately, notwithstanding these costs, parents caught up in today's version of the "child saving" movement are often denied the procedural and other protections the Constitution affords criminal defendants as a matter of course and that this Court required in the juvenile courts in *In re Gault, supra. See generally* Merline, *supra*, at A1, ("In some cases, innocent parents' homes are searched without a warrant, the children are interrogated, strip searched, and temporarily removed from the home altogether – sometimes for years"); Pride, *supra*, at 168-169; Scott, *supra*, at 131-151; *cf. Santosky v. Kramer, supra*, at 755 ("When the State moves to destroy weakened familial bonds, it must provide the parents with fundamentally fair procedures.").

*　　　*　　　*

23

In sum, as a result of the Mondale Act and its progeny, and as a legacy of this Nation's earlier "child saving" movements and present-day media sensationalism, the State's *parens patriae* power has all too often been abused, and the admirable motives of child-protection laws undermined, by bureaucratic agencies and officials who have wrongly assumed a near-plenary power over parents' childrearing practices in the name of combating neglect. Such oppressive intrusion flies in the face of the American constitutional tradition and of the Fourteenth Amendment's "liberty" guarantee.

We emphasize that nothing said here should be taken as questioning the duty of the state to intervene in clear cases of *real* abuse and neglect. Parents' rights are fundamental, but they are not absolute. Still, given that these rights *are* fundamental, the conduct of government and its bureaucrats – whether well-meaning or malevolent – must be held to a demanding standard. The States' laws regarding child-abuse reporting, custody, termination of parental rights, *and third-party visitation* must be subject to *strict scrutiny*. In this case, the Washington Supreme Court correctly determined that, whatever may be said about the importance, generally speaking, of a child's relationship with his or her grandparents, the statutes at issue here are far too broad, and far too intrusive, to satisfy the Constitution's requirements. *See* RCW 26.10.160(3), RCW 26.09.240.

————————◆————————

24

CONCLUSION

For all the foregoing reasons, *amicus curiae* the Society of Catholic Social Scientists urges this Court to affirm the judgment and reasoning of the court below.

Respectfully submitted,

STEPHEN M. KRASON
Counsel of Record
President, Society of
    Catholic Social Scientists
Franciscan University
Franciscan Way
Steubenville, OH 43952
(740) 283-6416

RICHARD W. GARNETT
Of Counsel
Assistant Professor of Law
Notre Dame Law School
Notre Dame, IN 46556
(219) 631-6981

December 1999

Appendix 2
Amicus Curiae Brief of the Society of Catholic Social Scientists in *Camreta v. Greene/Alford v. Greene*

In The
Supreme Court of the United States

BOB CAMRETA,

Petitioner,

v.

SARAH GREENE, personally and as next friend
for S.G., a minor, and K.G., a minor,

Respondents.

JAMES ALFORD, Deschutes County Deputy Sheriff,

Petitioner,

v.

SARAH GREENE, personally and as next friend
for S.G., a minor, and K.G., a minor,

Respondents.

**On Writs Of Certiorari To The
United States Court Of Appeals
For The Ninth Circuit**

**BRIEF FOR THE SOCIETY OF CATHOLIC
SOCIAL SCIENTISTS AS *AMICUS CURIAE*
IN SUPPORT OF RESPONDENTS**

STEPHEN M. KRASON
Counsel of Record
President, Society of
   Catholic Social Scientists
FRANCISCAN UNIVERSITY
Steubenville, OH 43952
(740) 284-5377
catholicsocialscientists@gmail.com

i

TABLE OF CONTENTS

Page

ii

TABLE OF CONTENTS – Continued

iii

TABLE OF AUTHORITIES

Page

TABLE OF AUTHORITIES – Continued

TABLE OF AUTHORITIES – Continued

Page

TABLE OF AUTHORITIES – Continued

Page

TABLE OF AUTHORITIES – Continued

TABLE OF AUTHORITIES – Continued

1

INTEREST OF THE *AMICUS CURIAE*[1]

The Society of Catholic Social Scientists ("SCSS") respectfully submits this *amicus curiae* brief in support of the Respondents, Sarah Greene, et al. We believe that the questions presented in this case have serious implications for American law and public policy relating to the rights of parents, the integrity of the family, and the powers of government. They concern the dignity and rights of the human person and the family, which are central to Catholic social and moral teaching.

The SCSS is an interdisciplinary association of Catholic social scientists, devoted to upholding the teachings of the Church. Its purposes are to pursue and produce objective knowledge about the social order, evaluate contemporary social science work in light of Catholic social teaching, consider how this teaching might be applied to the problems of modern society, encourage distinctively Catholic scholarship in the social sciences, and (where appropriate) to put the tools of social science at the service of the Church's evangelizing mission. These purposes reflect Pope Pius XI's call eighty years ago for "the building up of a true Catholic social science." Pope Pius XI, *Reconstructing the Social Order* (1931). The SCSS carries out its programs by such means as conferences, a week-long summer institute, an

---

[1] No counsel for a party authored this brief in whole or in part, and no counsel or party made a monetary contribution intended to fund the preparation or submission of this brief. No person other than *amicus curiae*, its members, or its counsel made a monetary contribution to its preparation or submission. The parties have consented to the filing of this brief. Letters of consent are on file at the Court.

annual scholarly journal (*The Catholic Social Science Review*), a book series and other publications, and an M.Th. program in Catholic Social Thought through the Graduate Theological Foundation.

———————— ♦ ————————

SUMMARY OF THE ARGUMENT

The fundamental rights of parents to direct and control the upbringing of their children and the integrity and liberty of the family have been recognized time and again by this Court. These rights and this liberty are not mere creatures of the state or positive law, but are grounded in the natural order of things. The family has the end or purpose of developing good human persons and good citizens. Parents' rights are necessary for them to pursue this high calling and duty. As such, the state may not interfere with parental decision-making except in grave cases when it is truly necessary to prevent genuine harm.

The child protective system ("CPS"), from its inception almost forty years ago, has intervened with abandon into families across the country, often even removing children from the custody and control of their parents without justification. It has done so on the basis of vague and overbroad statutes on, and confused official notions about, child abuse and neglect. Some CPS practices, as in the present case, have been harmful to the very children it claims to be protecting. Due to legal immunity, its operatives have been largely unaccountable for their routine violations of parental rights, unwarranted intervention into the family, and readiness to accuse

3

the innocent. There is a crucial need for this Court to establish a standard that permits the abridgement of parental rights and CPS intervention into the family only when there is a compelling state interest.

————— ♦ —————

ARGUMENT

I.

Due to the Fundamental Character of Parental Rights, State Intervention Into the Family and Interference with Parental Decision-making Should Be Permitted Only When Absolutely Necessary, Pursuant to a Compelling State Interest, and then Should Be Carried Out in a Reasonable Manner.

To begin, it is worth quoting what the SCSS stated in its *amicus curiae* brief in support of the Respondent in *Troxel v. Granville,* 530 U.S. 57: "This Court has held and re-affirmed that the rights of parents to direct and control the upbringing of their children without unjustified intrusion or oversight by the State are fundamental and sit at the heart of the 'liberty' protected by the Fourteenth Amendment's due process clause." Brief, at 4. This Court has spoken about the liberty of parents and guardians to direct the upbringing and education of their children. *Pierce v. Society of Sisters,* 268 U.S. 510, 534 (1925). It has called it "cardinal...that the custody, care and nurture of the child reside first in the parents whose primary function and freedom...the state can neither supply nor hinder."

4

Stanley v. Illinois, 405 U.S. 645, 651 (1972). In *Troxel*, this Court stated that, "it cannot now be doubted that the Due Process Clause of the Fourteenth Amendment protects the fundamental right of parents to make decisions concerning the care, custody, and control of their children" and that it "is perhaps the oldest of the fundamental liberty interests recognized by this Court." *Troxel*, at 66, 65. This Court has also included parental rights among the "basic civil rights of man." *Skinner v. Oklahoma*, 316 U.S. 535, 541 (1942), and has indicated that they are "intrinsic human rights." *Smith v. Organization of Foster Families*, 431 U.S. 816, 845 (1977). This suggests awareness by this Court that parental rights, as important as they have been in American constitutional law, are not grounded exclusively or fundamentally in that but in the natural order of things—the natural law, to be sure—as this brief goes on to explain.

To be sure, this Court has never held that parental rights are absolute, that there can never be occasions when they may be abridged by the state. *See*, e.g., *Wisconsin v. Yoder*, 406 U.S. 205, 230 (1972). Indeed, there are circumstances when these rights may even be outright terminated, even though the state must meet a significant evidentiary burden to do so. *See Santosky v. Kramer*, 455 U.S. 743 (1982). In spite of such statements as the above in its opinions, some members of this Court have been reluctant to accord parental rights the same level of constitutional recognition and protection as rights specifically enumerated in the Bill of Rights because of an apparent concern about judicial arbitrariness.

5

See, e.g., *Troxel*, at 91-93 (J. Scalia dissent). These concerns are well taken, but not justified. If unenumerated rights are solidly grounded in the common law tradition—and thereby clearly identifiable—these dangers are much attenuated. Such is the case with parental rights. *See* John W. Whitehead, *Parents' Rights* 85-86 (1985). Even if one sees parental rights as ultimately grounded in natural law, as discussed below, this should not be the basis of concern that giving them strong legal protection would open the door to arbitrariness. While the debate about a natural law-based jurisprudence is an old one in this Court (*see*, e.g., *Calder v. Bull*, 3 Dall. 386 [1798], *Adamson v. California*, 332 U.S. 46 [1947]), judges relying on a sound notion of natural law are much less likely to slip into arbitrariness than those of a more positivistic bent. This is because of their understanding that judicial decisions must be grounded in sound, perennial principles transcending their mere will. *See* David F. Forte, "Natural Law and the Limits to Judicial Review," 1 *Catholic Soc. Sci. Rev.* 42-47 (1996).

Moreover, even though this Court has repeatedly recognized parental rights as fundamental, it has been hesitant to say in specific terms—at least in the absence of a corresponding claim of free exercise of religion (*see Wisconsin v. Yoder, supra*)—that a compelling state interest is required for their infringement. We believe that the fundamental nature of these rights and the crucial importance of the family to a sound political order, as discussed *infra*, require that this finally be done.

6

A. The Philosophical Foundations of Parental Rights.

As one philosopher puts it, while mutual love and mutual aid are sought in the marital state the human species also has the inclination to reproduce itself. Once conjugal rights are assumed the parents take on "an obligation which their natures and the nature of the domestic society [the family] have imposed on them: to accept full responsibility for continuing the process of producing a new man." Nature has provided the wherewithal for parents to carry out the arduous tasks associated with childrearing. "The mutual love of the parents, the aid they can give to each other...are a proper climate for the nestling," so childrearing is done "best in family life where there exist two people who love the offspring more than anyone else can." Raphael T. Waters, "The Basis for the Traditional Rights and Responsibilities of Parents," in Stephen M. Krason & Robert J. D'Agostino, eds., *Parental Rights: The Contemporary Assault on Traditional Liberties*, 21, 23, 26 (1988). To carry out the duties involved in the rearing and education of offspring requires rights. Nature would be providing very insufficiently for man if upon imposing duties or obligations on him it did not give him corresponding prerogatives—i.e., rights—to enable him to carry out those duties. By their very nature rights and duties are linked, and must be respected by other persons and the community. *See* Thomas J. Higgins, *Man As Man: The Science and Art of Ethics* (rev. ed.), 226-227 (1992); Pope John XXIII, *Peace on Earth* #28-30

7

(1963). Thus, sound philosophy recognizes the natural rights of parents. Waters, 25-26.

There is yet another ethical consideration. As is indicated *supra*, parents in the nature of things are better able to carry out tasks and decision-making within the family than are outside and distant entities such as the state. The principle of subsidiarity in social ethics is pertinent: "[I]t is an injustice and at the same time a grave evil and a disturbance of right order, to transfer to the larger and higher collectivity functions which can be performed and provided for by lesser and subordinate bodies." Pope Pius XI, *supra* #79; *see also* E.F. Schumacher, *Small Is Beautiful: Economics as if People Mattered* 244 (1973). This principle stands behind the familiar American notion of federalism, but "applies to family-state relations as well as to relations between different levels of government." SCSS A.C. Brief in *Troxel* 9.

Even apart from the matter of the natural rights of parents, the state should respect family integrity for its own benefit. Aristotle stressed the character-building role of the family. As such, it is the spawning ground of good social and political relations; it helps form good citizens. *See* Aristotle, *Politics* II, iii; II, iv.

Despite the stress on parental rights and family integrity in our ethical and legal background, including the decisions of this Court, it is clear that the state is intruding on these in a wholesale way today. This was strikingly seen in the results of an extensive study undertaken by the Institute for American Values, which showed that most American

8

parents nowadays *take for granted* that the state has absolute power to monitor their families, shape their child-rearing practices, and even remove their children from them. *See* Dana Mack, *The Assault on Parenthood*, 62 (1997). This is especially illustrated by the facts about the child protective system (CPS) *infra*, which was involved in the present case and is a major source of such interference with the family.

B. Catholic Church Teaching on Parental and Family Rights.

While the philosophical and ethical discussion *supra* makes clear that parental rights do not have their basis just in specific religious traditions, they are strongly upheld by Catholic teaching. The Church teaches that the family "is the *original cell of social life*" *Catechism of the Catholic Church* #2207 (1994) (emphasis in original). It is "the first school of the social virtues that are the animating principle of the existence and development of society itself." Pope John Paul II, *Apostolic Exhortation on the Family*, III, iii (1982). It is incumbent upon the state to "respect and foster the dignity, lawful independence, privacy, integrity, and stability of every family." Holy See, Charter of the Rights of the Family, art. 6 (1983). Attempts by the state or even private organizations "in any way to limit the freedom of couples in deciding about their children constitute a grave offense against human dignity and justice." Id., art. 3. Still, the Church agrees with this Court's precedents that parental rights and family independence are not absolute. Pope Leo XIII, who set out the modern social teaching of the Church, specified the criteria for what today would be called state intervention into the family: The state may not "at its option intrude into and exercise intimate control over the family." It may do so only when it is in "exceeding distress, utterly deprived of the counsel of friends, and without any prospect of extricating itself," or "if within the precincts of the household there occur grave disturbances of mutual rights." Pope Leo XIII, *Rerum Novarum* #14 (1891). As the discussion *infra* makes clear, the CPS routinely and sweepingly oversteps such bounds.

While it is indisputable that the possibility of sexual abuse, as in the present case, would involve such a "grave disturbance of rights" justifying state intervention, it does not follow that the state may simply disregard parental rights and conduct an investigation of the family in an unreasonable manner. Specifically, the state did not have the right to conduct a intensive, pressuring, and suggestive interrogation of the child (S.G.) in a threatening and extended manner, without the consent of her mother, the Respondent Sarah Greene—who was in no way suspected of any illegal or improper actions— or the sanction of a court order. It did not have the right to prod and "grind down" the child until she gave them an answer that its operative wanted, which S.G. says is what happened. *See Greene v. Camreta, Alford, et al.,.* No. 06-35333 (9th Cir.), at 16303. By the way, this Court should not think that such CPS practices were unique to this case or to sexual abuse allegations. There is abundant evidence that they are not uncommon for the CPS

10

around the country. *See* Brenda Scott, *Out of Control*, chap. 8 (1994); Stephen M. Krason, "A Grave Threat to the Family: American Law and Public Policy on Child Abuse and Neglect," in Krason, *The Public Order and the Sacred Order* 178 (2009). If this Court overturns the 9th Circuit and closes off the opportunity to hold the CPS accountable for its actions under federal civil rights laws—as it is, the CPS and its operatives generally are immune from tort lawsuits and typically use confidentiality requirements designed to protect families to avoid transparency (*see* id., 170-172)—it may have the effect of stimulating more such troublesome investigatory practices. Most of the latter take place pursuant to the massive number of unfounded reports of alleged abuse and neglect involving mostly innocent parents each year (*see infra*). The CPS may interpret such a decision as a kind of imprimatur from this Court for its conduct.

II.

The Decades-Long Experience with the CPS Shows its Basic Arbitrariness and Systemic Violation of Parental Rights.

The numbers of false reports of child abuse and neglect each year are staggering. Douglas Besharov of the University of Maryland, perhaps the leading scholarly authority on the CPS, writes that consistently over the years approximately two-thirds of child abuse and neglect reports nationwide are unsubstantiated or unfounded. Besharov, "Child Abuse Realities: Over-Reporting and Poverty," 8 *Va. J. of Soc. Policy and the Law* 165, 179-180 (2000). Other critical assessments of the CPS agree with this figure. *See* Stephen M. Krason, "The Critics of the Current Child Abuse Laws and the Child Protective System: A Survey of the Leading Literature," 12 *Catholic Soc. Sci. Rev.* 307, 340 (2007). In 1997—not an atypical year—that amounted to almost 1.98 million false reports involving over 2 million children. Besharov, "Child Abuse Realities," at 176, 179-180. Besharov points out, "the rate of substantiated reports has definitely declined, even while the total number of reports keeps increasing." Id., 179. Even most of the "substantiated" reports involve minor matters. Scott, 29-33. Moreover, the lack of certainty and clarity about what constitutes child abuse and neglect in state statutes—spawned by the federal Child Abuse Prevention and Treatment Act (CAPTA - the "Mondale Act") of 1974—suggests that the estimates of the number of unfounded reports may actually be understated. *See* Krason, "A Grave Threat," 245-250. While not pertinent to the facts of the present case, it is troublesome that courts have been reluctant to apply the vagueness and overbreadth analysis used in other areas of the law to the child abuse/neglect statutes (*see* id., 166) when it is apparent that perfectly normal and legal parental behaviors are what trigger most CPS investigations. The context of the present case, however, would permit this Court to firmly and clearly mandate the need for a compelling state interest before parental rights may

12

be abridged. If such a constitutional requirement were in place, the regimen of easy, unjustified CPS intervention into families would likely be attenuated.

Other factors besides the vagueness of the statutes are responsible for this problem. One is the legal immunity of CPS operatives (noted *supra*) and also of "mandatory reporters" (e.g., physicians, nurses, psychologists, counselors), who must report even "suspected" abuse and neglect (without, again, clearly defining it). Krason, "A Grave Threat" 171. Another is that the CPS operatives and mandatory reporters *are unable to agree among themselves* about what constitutes abuse and neglect. *See id.* 168-169; Richard Wexler, *Wounded Innocents* 86-87 (1990). Yet another reason is the long-term problem of insufficient qualifications of many CPS operatives. *See* Scott 57-59; Wexler 320; Mack 73.

The *unreliability and untrustworthiness* of the CPS is further suggested by other facts about how it operates. It has long exhibited the troubling perspective that parents cannot be trusted. *See* Krason, "A Grave Threat" 169. A survey of critical scholarly, legal, and journalistic writings about the CPS showed that most accused it of an anti-parent bias. Krason, "The Critics of the Current Child Abuse Laws," at 340. This is seen, by the way, in the present case in the interrogation of S.G. without her mother's, Respondent Sarah Greene's, consent and the barring of the latter from being present at the medical examination of S.G. *See Greene*, at 16306-16307. Next, contrary to a basic tenet of the Anglo-American legal tradition, once parents face a report

13

of abuse or neglect they are essentially presumed guilty, and bear the *de facto* burden of having to establish their fitness to parent their children to the satisfaction of the CPS. *See* Krason, "A Grave Threat," 160; Scott 131-134, 137. Even when cases get as far as juvenile court, parents are at a serious disadvantage when facing the CPS. Paul Chill, "Burden of Proof Begone: The Pernicious Effect of Emergency Removal in Child Protective Proceedings," 41 *Family Court Review* 457, at 460-461 (2003). Further, the CPS operates by a series of what one source calls "doctrines," which lack reasonableness, are sometimes contradictory, and often are not backed up by facts. One is that parents are to be blamed for everything concerning their children, and so the CPS is ready and even eager to find fault with them. More, it sees all parents as potential abusers. Another of its doctrines is that when a child states that a parent has been abusive— even if this comes after suggestive questioning—he is always telling the truth. By the same token, it holds that if a child later recants his allegation against a parent—as happened in the present case— the recantation is not reliable. Another doctrine, apparent in the present case, is that sexually abused children almost automatically cover up the abuse. Further, the CPS harbors the extravagant belief— ostensibly built from the beginning into CAPTA and its state statutory progeny—that it is somehow possible to identify any parent who is likely to abuse his or her child in the future, even if there has been no actual allegation of abuse. Mary Pride, *The Child Abuse Industry* 41-50 (1986). Besharov says that

14

such a claim is simply "unrealistic." Besharov, "'Doing Something' about Child Abuse: The Need to Narrow the Grounds for State Intervention," 8 *Harvard J. of Law and Pub. Policy* 539, 574-575 (1985).

Beyond its unreasonable doctrines, the CPS shows its untrustworthiness and unreliability in other ways: 1) It almost routinely assumes the veracity of almost any abuse/neglect report it receives, even those coming from anonymous hotlines. Scott 134; Krason, "A Grave Threat" 171. For the most part, no probable cause-type standard is required to launch an investigation of a parent. Stephen M. Krason, "Child Abuse and Neglect: Failed Policy and Assault on Innocent Parents," 10 *Catholic Soc. Sci. Rev.* 215, 222 (2005). 2) Prior to lower court decisions of the past several years, the CPS believed itself not subject at all to the Fourth Amendment as far as concerns its operatives entering and searching the private homes of families (see Krason, "A Grave Threat" 173-174). A different type of Fourth Amendment question, of course, is raised in the present case. 3) For a long time, the CPS embraced the highly questionable and now discredited "recovered memory" therapy, which claimed that therapists could tap suppressed memories in children of abuse even years in the past. Scott 147-148. 4) It frequently mistakes medical conditions of children for abuse. See Krason, "A Grave Threat" 162. 5) The lack of a reasonable definition of "abuse" and "neglect," epidemic of over-reporting, and the CPS's preoccupation with false allegations and insignificant matters frequently

15

diverts it from dealing with situations where children are genuinely endangered. In fact, a substantial percentage of children who die from maltreatment have had previous contact with the CPS. Besharov, "Child Abuse Realities," at 192. All this points to a system that is ineffective, counter-productive, and unaccountable, while at the same time violative of parental rights and family integrity. Moreover, it is also typically unwilling to acknowledge its failings or mistakes. *See*, e.g., Scott 38. It is often not even willing to permit the return of children once their parents have been exonerated. *See* Krason, "A Grave Theat," 160; Chill, at 460.

All of this makes it imperative that this Court decide that: 1) the CPS is not immune from federal civil rights liability, and 2) the CPS should be restrained from violating parental rights and intervening into the family unless it is able to show a compelling state interest.

III.

The Nature of the Interrogation of S.G. Violated Her Dignity as a Person, and thereby Her Fundamental Human Rights, and Also Went Against Constitutional Precedent.

The Catholic Church stresses the utter essentiality of upholding human dignity. "A just society can become a reality only when it is based on the transcendent dignity of the human person." *Compendium of the Social Doctrine of the Church*

16

#132 (2004). The Church holds, "the roots of human rights are to be found in the dignity that belongs to each human being." Id. #153. The Preamble of the UN Universal Declaration of Human Rights expresses this same belief of human rights as grounded in human dignity. *See* Univ. Decl. of H. Rts. Among the offenses that the Church teaches is against human dignity is torture, "which uses physical or moral violence to extract confessions, punish the guilty, frighten opponents, or satisfy hatred." *Catechism of the Catholic Church* #2297. Torture, of course, is condemned by the Universal Declaration (sec. 5) and is rejected by international law generally. *See* Winston P. Nagan & Lucie Atkins, "The International Law of Torture: From Universal Proscription to Effective Application and Enforcement," 14 *Harvard Hum. Rts. Jour.* 87, 95-102 (2001). Torture is defined as the infliction of physical or psychological pain and suffering "by a victimizer who dominates and controls." Id. 93. In the realm of criminal law, some writers have alleged that the use of, in effect, psychological torture by prosecutorial authorities to pressure defendants into plea bargains has become commonplace. *See* Paul Craig Robert & Lawrence M. Stratton, *The Tyranny of Good Intentions*, chap. 9 (2000); John H. Langbein, "Torture and Plea Bargaining," 46 *Univ. of Chicago L. Rev.* 4 (1978). We do not suggest that international law or standards have to be the basis for this argument. This Court has long made it clear that under the Constitution official conduct of the nature of torture violates due process and is not acceptable as a means of extracting evidence. *See*

Rochin v. California, 342 U.S. 165 (1952). While this has involved persons charged with crimes, how much more this standard must be held to apply to interrogations of innocent persons—indeed, supposed victims—and even more to children. Moreover, psychological torture is no less torture because it does not involve the direct infliction of physical pain. Often, as in the present case—where S.G. went home after the duress of the extended interrogation and vomited five times (*see* Affidavit of S.G. in District Court Case)—psychological torture has physical manifestations. Again, such CPS interrogation practices are not unique to this case.

While this episode vividly illustrates damage done to a child by CPS practices, the harm it does to children in so many other ways—when supposedly protecting them—is not always so readily observed but nevertheless is pronounced. One is the danger posed by the foster care arrangements that the CPS typically places children in when removing them from their homes. Besharov states, "Long term foster care can leave lasting psychological scars...it can do irreparable damage to the bond of affection and commitment between parent and child." Besharov, "'Doing Something,'" at 560. The rate of child maltreatment in foster care is considerably higher than in the general population. Chill, at 460; Mack, 67. Even if children are not taken from their parents, unwarranted intervention has such consequences for children as: "anxiety, diminishing trust, loosening of emotional ties, or an increasing tendency to be out of control." Joseph Goldstein, Anna Freud, & Albert Solnit, *Beyond the Best*

18

Interests of the Child 25 (1973). Psychological harm to children, parental anger toward their children, and increased family tensions can result. Id., 25, 72-74. The stresses caused sometimes lead to family break-ups. Chill, at 460. Thus, in many way the CPS assaults the dignity of the very children it claims to serve.

———————— ♦ ————————

CONCLUSION

For all the foregoing reasons, *amicus curiae* the Society of Catholic Social Scientists (SCSS) urges this Court to affirm the judgment of the 9th Circuit and also to require a compelling state interest standard for abridgement of parental rights and intervention into the family.

Respectfully submitted,

STEPHEN M. KRASON
Counsel of Record
President, Society of Catholic Social
  Scientists
Franciscan University
Steubenville, OH 43952
(740) 284-5377
catholicsocialscientists@gmail.com

January 2011

Index

abortion, 41, 52, 57, 62, 88, 89, 101
abuse:
  alcohol. *See* alcohol
  drug. *See* drugs
  emotional, 2, 14, 22, 28-30, 53, 126(n63), 156, 161, 163, 164, 165, 172, 175, 177, 178, 182, 183, 186-87, 188;
  medical symptoms of, 15-16, 21, 27, 73n139, 113-16;
  of law, 46-7;
  of parents, 169-170;
  passive, 17;
  physical, of child, 2, 11, 22-3, 29, 48, 69(n48), 71(n103), 80(n259), 88, 126(n63), 131(n89), 142, 152, 156, 162, 166, 169-70, 172, 175-76, 177, 181-82, 183, 184, 185-90, 197;
  physical, of spouse/partner, 156, 157, 159, 161-62, 163, 164, 165, 166, 169-70, 175-76, 182, 196;
  potential, 30, 31, 43, 47, 51, 63, 77(n180), 77(n187), 197;
  psychological, 14, 48-9, 54, 162, 166, 172, 186, 196;
  sexual, 2, 8, 11-14, 16, 19, 22-23, 24, 29, 31, 48, 54, 71(n101), 71(n103), 75(n163), 76(n164), 80(n159), 100, 113-15, 126(n63), 127(n67), 129(n76, 129(n78), 162, 166, 169, 172-73, 175, 177, 181, 182-85, 186-90, 195-96;
  sibling, 179-80;

  verbal, 132(n94), 184, 187, 196
  See also child abuse
Adam Walsh Child Protection and Safety Act, 7
  See also national registry of child abusers
adoption, 35-6
Adoption and Safe Families Act of 1997 (ASFA), 35, 58, 76(n191), 219
aggression:
  in children, 185;
  psychological, 159, 163, 165;
  sibling, 179-80;
  spousal, 161, 168, 182;
  towards children, 170
alcohol, 31, 41, 126(n64), 163, 185-86, 195, 196
allegations:
  of child abuse, 10, 12, 19, 58, 71, 58, 75(n163), 109, 111, 125(n59), 129(n76), 129(n78), 145;
  false, 2, 7-10, 11-14, 22, 25, 32, 33-34, 46, 53-56, 58-60, 63-66, 105, 148-49;
  of neglect/maltreatment, 110, 140, 143;
  unsubstantiated, 7-8, 59, 69(n47), 69(n60)
American Civil Liberties Union, 7
Anderson, Jack, 14
anxiety, 48, 141, 166, 168, 171, 187, 196
Aristotle, 66
Arizona, 16

child protection worker. *See* child
welfare worker
child protective agency (cpa):
cases involving, 12, 15, 18-20, 22;
damages against, 40;
definition of abuse, 29, 61;
foster-care and, 48;
Fourth Amendment restraints on, 39;
harm of children in custody of, 46,
47;
parental rights, 50;
probable cause, 40;
reports of abuse to/investigations, 8,
10, 12, 32-33, 39, 51
See also child protective system,
child protective services (CPS)
child protective system (CPS):
abuses by, 16, 21-22, 52-53, 57, 64;
coercion by, 116;
constitutional rights and, 116, 119;
ex parte warrant, 107, 116;
Fourth Amendment, 152;
investigations by, 146-47, 149-150;
medical examination by, 113;
removal of child from home by, 99,
100, 104, 108-109;
"search and seizure"/Fourth
Amendment, 37, 40, 57;
confidentiality and, 34-35;
false reporting and, 9-10, 50-51, 55;
history of, 3-6, 56;
homeschooling and, 21, 57 (*see also*
homeschooling);
human rights principles and, 87, 95;
international law and, 63-64, 84, 87-
91 (*see also* law, international);
legal proceedings and, 35, 53-54, 58-
59;
medical neglect and, 15-16 (*see also*
medical neglect);
Mondale Act, 1-3, 54;
parents and, 24, 30, 38, 48-49, 52,
53, 87, 113, 196-97;
reform of, 55, 58-62, 65-66;
reporting to, 32-33, 54, 65;
research about, 49-58;
standards of, 28-29, 51, 52, 61, 172;
See also child protective agency,
child protective system
child protective workers. *See* child
welfare worker

Child Sexual Abuse Accommodation
Syndrome, 31
child welfare bureaucracy, 18, 22
child welfare workers:
anonymous tips to, 140, 149, 150;
CAPTA and, 40;
See also Child Abuse Prevention and
Treatment Act (CAPTA)
cooperation with, 143, 144-52;
definitions of abuse, 14, 28-29, 32;
demographics of, 30, 41;
education of, 30, 41, 61;
employee retention, 217, 225-26,
227-28, 229-30;
entry into home/Fourth Amendment,
37, 39, 107-108, 140-42, 144-52;
ethical dilemmas of, 216, 219, 222,
227, 231;
ex parte orders, 116-117;
findings of
abuse/neglect/maltreatment by,
16-17, 25, 28, 48, 104-105, 118;
foster care and, 226;
homeschooling and, 139;
homosexuality among, 30;
liability of, 59, 114, 115, 116-117,
119;
mandated reporters. *See* mandated
reporter;
medical examination of children by,
113-16, 151;
meeting needs of clients, 220-21,
223-25, 227, 230;
parental discipline and, 26;
potential abusers and, 51, 99;
seizure of children by, 13-14, 37, 99,
100, 108-112;
"street-level bureaucrats," 217, 231
childrearing, 27-28, 55, 58, 63, 65;
state intervention in, 45, 62, 64
child-saving movement, 3
Chill, Paul, 35, 37, 49-50, 58
Christians, 3, 5, 15, 18, 49, 91, 228
citizen advisory board, 57
clan care, 52
Cleveland County v. Stumbo, 40, 146-
47, 148-49
Clinton, Hillary, 43, 65
cohabitation, 41, 55, 156, 161-66, 169,
171, 177, 182, 195
Coleman, Doriane, 140

About the Contributors

Stephen M. Krason, Esq., Ph.D. is Professor of Political Science and Legal Studies at Franciscan University of Steubenville and co-founder and President of the Society of Catholic Social Scientists. He is co-editor of *Parental Rights: The Contemporary Assault* on *Traditional Liberties* and *Defending the Family: A Sourcebook.*

William L. Saunders, Esq. is a human rights lawyer in Washington, D.C.

Michael E. Rosman, Esq. is the General Counsel of the Center for Individual Rights.

James R. Mason, III, Esq. is Senior Counsel at the Home School Legal Defense Association.

Patrick F. Fagan, Ph.D. is Senior Fellow and Director of the Marriage and Religion Research Institute (MARRI) at the Family Research Council, Anna Dorminey is an Associate Editor at MARRI, and Emily Hering is a MARRI intern and a student at Franciscan University of Steubenville.

Ruth A. White, M.S.S.A. is co-founder and Executive Director of the National Center for Housing and Child Welfare and former Director of Housing and Homelessness for the Child Welfare League of America.

Richard W. Garnett, Esq., who with Stephen M. Krason, drafted the SCSS's *amicus curiae* brief in *Troxel v. Granville* (Appendix 1), is Professor of Law and Concurrent Professor of Political Science at the University of Notre Dame and Associate Dean for Faculty Research at Notre Dame Law School.